SHAKESPEARE 1971

SHAKESPEARE 1971

Proceedings of the
World Shakespeare Congress
Vancouver, August 1971

❦

edited by Clifford Leech
and J.M.R. Margeson

University of Toronto Press

© University of Toronto Press 1972
Toronto and Buffalo
Printed in Canada
ISBN 0-8020-1906-4
microfiche ISBN 0-8020-0244-7
LC 72-86265

Preface

We have the privilege of introducing a volume which makes public some of the proceedings of the World Shakespeare Congress held in Vancouver, Canada, from 20 August to 29 August 1971, under the sponsorship of the University of British Columbia, Simon Fraser University, and the Canada Council. It should indeed be emphasized that only a selection of its many activities can be represented here. We have included all available papers in the plenary sessions, a very few of the 'special sessions' papers, an 'address at a banquet,' and the reports of the chairmen of the Investigative Committees (who generally look perhaps more to the future than to the present).

A full account of what happened at Vancouver would fill a volume two or three times the length of this one. Every paper in the plenary sessions was followed by contributions from panellists and from speakers from the floor (some of which will be vividly remembered by those attending) : we can include only those panellists' contributions that took the form of prepared papers, and we are grateful to Professor Fredson Bowers and Professor Herbert Berry for letting us print such contributions.

Chairmen's remarks were themselves often major contributions, but there is no space for them. In addition we had a symposium on 'Psychoanalysis and Shakespeare,' with Professor M.D. Faber in the chair, two 'Theatre Colloquia,' relating to the performance of two scenes from *Troilus and Cressida*, under the direction of Professor Rudolf Stamm, and several stage and film showings.

Among our theatre-presentations special mention should be made of the production of *Every Man in his Humour* by the Department of Drama of the University of Calgary and – our special triumph – the first showing in North America of Grigori Kozintsev's film of *King Lear*. We have the honour of printing in this volume Professor Kozintsev's lecture relating to this.

This preface cannot omit a tribute to the enthusiastic and indefatigable Director and Executive Secretary of the Congress: Professor Rudolph E. Habenicht and Professor J.A. Lavin.

It is important to record that, at the suggestion of the Investigative Committee on International Co-operation, we set up a small committee to explore the possibilities of establishing an International Shakespeare Association, which, along with other activities, might organise further world congresses. Professor John Russell Brown of the University of Sussex, England, is the chairman of this committee.

Meanwhile we offer this volume as a contribution to a knowledge of Shakespeare studies as they have been in 1971.

C.L.

J.M.R.M.

Toronto 1972

Contents

John C. Meagher
Vanity, Lear's Feather, and the Pathology of
Editorial Annotation / 244

Roy Daniells
An Address at a Banquet / 260

APPENDIXES

Contributors

Jonas Barish *University of California, Berkeley*
Bernard Beckerman *Columbia University, New York*
Herbert Berry *University of Saskatchewan*
David Bevington *University of Chicago*
Mihail Bogdan *University of Cluj, Romania*
Fredson Bowers *University of Virginia*
M.C. Bradbrook *University of Cambridge*
John Russell Brown *University of Sussex*
Wolfgang Clemen *University of Munich*
Roy Daniells *University of British Columbia*
Michel Grivelet *University of Dijon*
Elemér Hankiss *Hungarian Academy of Sciences, Budapest*
G.R. Hibbard *University of Waterloo*
Charlton Hinman *University of Kansas*
C. Walter Hodges *Sussex, England*
R.W. Ingram *University of British Columbia*
Jean Jacquot *Centre national de la recherche scientifique, Paris*
H.D.F. Kitto *University of California, Santa Barbara*
Grigori Kozintsev *State Cinema Institute, Leningrad*
Jill Levenson *Trinity College, University of Toronto*
John C. Meagher *St Michael's College, University of Toronto*
Harrison Meserole *Pennsylvania State University*
Toshikazu Oyama *Seijo University, Tokyo*
Norman Rabkin *University of California, Berkeley*
Sally Yeates Sedelow *University of Kansas*
Robert Weimann *Deutsche Akademie der Wissenschaften zu Berlin*

Committees

EXECUTIVE COMMITTEE

DIRECTOR
Rudolph E. Habenicht *Simon Fraser University*

EXECUTIVE SECRETARY
J.A. Lavin *University of British Columbia*

MEMBERS
David Galloway *University of New Brunswick*
Berners Jackson *McMaster University*
Clifford Leech *University of Toronto*
Trevor Lennam *University of Calgary*
Paul J. Marcotte *Université d'Ottawa*
Gerald Newman *Simon Fraser University*
D.F. Rowan *University of New Brunswick*

CONSULTANT
R.W. Ingram *University of British Columbia*

INTERNATIONAL ADVISORY COMMITTEE

EUROPE
Peter Alexander †
Alexander Anikst *Institute of the History of the Arts, Moscow*
Gabriele Baldini †
Wolfgang Clemen *University of Munich*
Sir John Gielgud *London, England*
Elemér Hankiss *Institute of Literary History of the Hungarian Academy of Sciences*
Stanisław Helstzynski *Neophilological Committee of the Polish Academy of Sciences*
Jean Jacquot *Centre national de la recherche scientifique, Paris*
G. Wilson Knight *Exeter, England*
John Lawlor *University of Keele*
Martin Lenhert *Humboldt University, Berlin*

SHAKESPEARE 1971

❧⟨e··⟩❧

C. Walter Hodges /
The Arguments for and against attempting a full-scale Reconstruction of an Elizabethan Playhouse, and the Uses such a Building might (or might not) have

Though the title of this paper is long it may at least be agreed that it is reasonably explicit. It has seemed to me for some time that it would be useful if a proper investigation were made into the actual practicality of the scheme, so often proposed but just as often withdrawn again, to rebuild in its original form Shakespeare's Globe theatre. I shall here try, or at least begin, to make such an investigation.

I shall proceed in three stages. First, I will attempt to justify the idea of building it at all. Next I will discuss the usefulness of such a building if it were built. And lastly I will outline – though, in the limited space of this paper, I regret incompletely – the physical form which in my opinion it should have.

First, then, the idea of building it at all: how mad, how futile, or on the other hand how sensible is it?

Let us at least agree this far, that there is no question as to the fascination of the idea in general, especially if we are to judge by its historical persistence. Ever since the first essays towards a systematic reconstruction were made, not in England (strangely enough) but by Ludwig Tieck in Germany in the 1830s, the idea has been continually reviving itself. Not a generation has passed without its reappearance, until now in our own time when it has grown to be almost an obsessive preoccupation in certain quarters. Clearly there is something about it which seizes the imagination; and not the scholarly imagination only but, if newspaper interest is any guide, the popular imagination as well. Let us say it has that quality about it which catches the fancy;

and tell me, if you can, where is this fancy bred – or in the heart or in the head? I must ask you to consider, moreover, that Fancy is not a negligible thing, but a powerful force: indeed the whole history and practice of the theatre itself is founded upon it. And this particular fancy about reconstructing the Globe theatre is one that seemingly commends itself not only to actors and artists and scholars and other such egregious and fanciful folk, but also, as I have found, to calculating business people (who are usually classed as 'hard-headed') as well. These, it seems, tend to believe that if the old Globe were actually rebuilt it would be attractive enough actually to attract money. This also is perhaps a fancy: I cannot judge. I only instance it here to support my general opinion that an idea which has been and remains so persistent in so many ways to so many different kinds of people must have what Dr Johnson once called 'a bottom of good sense' in it, somewhere.

But where? And what could be the sense or purpose of putting up such a building nowadays? For my part I can see four separate and specific purposes to justify the physical reconstruction of the Shakespearian Globe playhouse. Let me enumerate them:

1 / It should be built *as a replacement* of a lost item of the first importance in the history of the theatre. It is both remarkable and regrettable that the great world-episode of the Elizabethan and Jacobean drama is the *only* area of major importance in the history of the theatre – one might even say in the whole history of western culture – which has left behind it no single physical structural relic of its existence, neither stick nor stone. We possess now in excellent condition very many theatres and amphitheatres from the ancient world of Greece and Rome. From the Italian Renaissance we have such beautiful, well-furnished examples as the famous Teatro Olimpico at Vicenza, or the Teatro Farnese at Parma. At Almagro in the Ciudad Real province of Spain there still exists a little corral theatre from the days of Lope de Vega. In Sweden there is the famous Drottningholm theatre dating from the middle of the eighteenth century, with its unrivalled original collection of scenery; and from that date onwards an abundance of historic theatres of every kind, great and small. But of the theatre of Shakespeare, Jonson, Marlowe, Webster, Dekker, Beaumont and Fletcher, Marston and Middleton, and all the rest of them – nothing. There is a great hole, a deplorable gap. *Must* it be allowed to remain?

2 / It should be built *as a national – or even an international – monument.* I will not dwell upon this, except to say that if there is any

value at all in the theatre as a cultural influence in human affairs (and who denies it?) ; and if there is any value at all in having monuments to great persons and great occasions (and, though it may be debatable, it is generally accepted that there is) ; and if the world-wide renown and influence of William Shakespeare and his fellows is really so great and well deserved as we are given to suppose (which the mere calling-together of this Congress may testify for itself), then surely somewhere in the world we might reasonably erect a monument to commemorate the theatre which was 'the quick forge and working house' of so much genius; and if so a reconstructed Globe Playhouse would surely be a most appropriate monument to meet the case. And of course for preference it would be very suitable to have it in England, perhaps even by the river Thames on Bankside, where the original once stood.

And so I pass to my third point:

3/It should be built *as a tourist attraction*. This follows naturally from the previous point, though it may seem at first to strike a cracked note of bathos. The word 'tourist' sounds in this context unwelcome. It calls to mind the vulgarization of great or beautiful places cluttered up with gewgaw boutiques and large car-parks. But tourism, like love, is here to stay, whether we like it or not, and has been since long before the days of the Canterbury pilgrims. Besides, we should do well to remember who the tourists are. All those other people, they were all tourists, were they not, that day in Venice when you and I were visiting St Mark's? Tourists (like you and me) go to visit great and beautiful places for many different reasons, but none of them are bad reasons.

(I should here take note of a legitimate objection. Usually the great and famous places that are visited are the originals, not reconstructions. I accept the point. It would be better if we did possess the original Globe, even if only in part. Yet, since we do not, then the only alternative is a reconstructed Globe, and that in my opinion would be far, far better than no Globe at all. Only let it stand long enough and that, too, will become old, if it is age that has the virtue. Meanwhile in North America some very fine reconstructed sites have been erected, such as the 'Plimoth Plantation' in Massachussetts, with its excellent reconstruction of the ship *Mayflower* lying offshore; or the celebrated reconstruction of the township of Williamsburg in Virginia. America is the richer for having such places, not the poorer.)

So now to my fourth point:

4/It should be built *as an aesthetic and educative research tool.*

These are fine words, and I suppose I should bear in mind the old English proverb that 'fine words butter no parsnips.' It is therefore possible that extreme lovers of buttered parsnips may be tempted to abandon me at this point. But I ask with a passionate expectation of the affirmative whether it is really believed that these fine words cannot be made good. Who would deny that a rebuilt Globe – if it were fully and properly reconstructed without any misshaping compromises (a matter against which one would have to stand most carefully on one's guard) – who could possibly deny that it would provide a most stimulating, educative, and aesthetically rewarding experience? It hardly needs saying that it would have the greatest value for schools and educational services at all levels. As for the aesthetic element, I suppose that may be harder to justify, since aesthetic sensations are personal and subjective. Yet, let me ask, could anyone who is at all responsive in aesthetic matters, just ordinarily responsive to pleasant or interesting architecture, let us say; could any such person deny the pleasure there would be to stand in the mere physical presence of this structure, this rather small, rather high, galleried enclosure, with its stage and stage-objects, it ranges of carved and painted posts, the Heavens above, and the sense of expectation from the tiring house beyond? ... Well, that is visionary matter. I had best leave it, and pass to the last of my three fine words, the word research. In the company of this Congress at least I can be sure that the need for such a building as a research tool will at once be accepted. Many of us here have our different theories about the nature and stage practice of the Elizabethan theatre. I myself have advanced quite a number, and I fear it may be possible that not all of them are right. If, then, for no better reason than to put me down and shut me up, there is need for a rebuilt Elizabethan playhouse, which could and should have room for adjustments, especially at the rear areas of the stage and about the tiring-house, so that theories of every kind can at last be properly tried out, and some part at least of this important, craving gap in the history of our culture be satisfied.

I pass now to a more difficult argument. It is this: Having erected such a building, what (in the fullest sense) would be the use of it? Implicit in this question, of course, is the possibility or otherwise of commercial profit. Though it is not a matter one would wish to dodge, it is a large one by itself, and there is little space for it here. The following, however, must be said, and clearly. In nearly every case where the rebuilding of the Globe is proposed by practical men, often but not always men of the theatre, the proposal is to build and use it *as a commercially viable theatre*. Let me say at once that in my opinion such proposals are ill-judged, unpractical, financially ruinous, and doomed to failure from the start. If one should build an *historically useful* reconstruction of an Elizabethan playhouse, even supposing it were built of such strong and fire-resistant materials as would satisfy the responsible public licensing authorities (which could be done), by the time one had complied with all the other necessary regulations as are imposed by those authorities for the safe arrangement of a theatre – spacing of seats, width of aisles and corridors, disposal of exits, etc. – the audience capacity would be likely to be reduced to a level well below that which commercial theatre managements usually consider worth their while. It has also to be borne in mind that a performance of a Shakespeare play in an Elizabethan theatre, under 'true' Elizabethan circumstances and with those certain truly Elizabethan discomforts and lacks of facility which would be entailed, though it would be a truly interesting and, doubtless, rewarding experience for all the spectators there, these would, when they had had it once, have had it for good. They would like it and they would recommend it to others, but they would not themselves feel any urgent compulsion to go back. Thereafter they would go as before to more comfortable modern theatres. But if, to avoid all these commercial disadvantages, one were to increase the audience capacity, provide comfortable seats with good sight-lines, install various modern easements and facilities, and comply with normal safety regulations; and if one were then to provide the sophisticated equipment for modern play-production techniques which would enable this supposed Elizabethan theatre to be used in a flexible and commercially viable manner for modern needs, one would then have not an Elizabethan playhouse at all, or anything remotely like it (except for one single though admittedly important characteristic, the thrust-out 'apron' stage). One would have in fact what we have already, thanks to the moving spirit and imagination of the late Sir Tyrone Guthrie, an excellent modern theatre specializing in open-style productions, as at Stratford, Ontario; at Minneapolis; at Ashland, Oregon; at Chichester in Sussex; and at many other places throughout the world.

Therefore, since all this is undoubtedly the case, I ask again: if the Globe is to be rebuilt, and since, if it is to be the Globe it could not be rebuilt *as a theatre* in the modern sense, what then could or should be the use of it?

I submit that its use should be considered under two separate but equal headings: as an exhibit; and as an auditorium. The first (as an exhibit) has already been touched upon with reference to tourism and education; as to the second it should be remembered that in modern terms an auditorium is not the same thing as a theatre. Let me now carry both these points a little further.

1/As an exhibit, the Globe would have the following uses:

A As already suggested, it would be an attraction in its own right, simply as an object of unique interest to be visited. It would, after all, be a building unlike any other in the world, and a theatre that has not been seen under the sun for over three hundred years.

B As part of its attraction there could be presented in it, perhaps three or four times a day at certain seasons, short demonstration performances of, let us say, half-an-hour's duration. These performances would be given to standing audiences and would show the typical uses of the stage and its effects under Elizabethan conditions. They would show, for example, Romeo at Juliet's window; the descent of a throne in glory from the Heavens; Faustus being dragged down by devils into Hell. There would be perhaps a drum and trumpet entry to symbolise an army, and a battle of 'four or five most vile and ragged foils.' There would, of course, be Elizabethan music, and there would be a Presenter to comment and explain. It hardly needs saying that a demonstration of this kind, perhaps more extended, would be of the greatest value to school audiences.

C As a variant (or continuation) of the two uses just described, the Globe would house a theatre museum or exhibition, of which it would itself be the principal exhibit. Thus, visitors would go not only into the galleries but into the tiring-house also, where they would find the costumes, make-up, properties, promptbooks, and all the other gear of an Elizabethan player-company, laid out as if ready for a performance. (It will of course be noted that none of these three uses would be effective unless the building were in fact a reconstruction in the fullest possible sense. In a 'modernized' Elizabethan, or 'Elizabethanized' modern theatre they would have no meaning nor any interest.)

2/I come now to the Globe used as an auditorium. Here the matter becomes more controversial. I feel, though reluctantly, that certain modifications would have to be made for the sake of practicality. These modifications could be concealed, however. As an example, let us take the height of the stage, and its relation to the yard in which it stands. There is no question that it would be necessary for the yard to be seen normally clear of seats, as if for the standing audience of 'groundlings' around a high stage. But it might – indeed it very likely would – for some purposes be convenient and necessary to place seating in the yard, and for a seated audience the stage would then be too high. Therefore its height should be made adjustable. It could be made to sink mechanically to a lower level when required. Another modification very hard to disallow concerns the roofing-over of the yard. I have previously written strongly against this, and I do not wish here to upset the effect of the passionate eloquence which I then attempted, since the openness to weather and to daylight from above is perhaps the most characteristic of all the famous features of this famous playhouse. Yet even so, however reluctantly, I feel it has to be conceded by a reasonable man that to be useful nowadays in England it might indeed be preferable to keep the weather and noise out. That need not and should not mean, however, that the sky above the yard would not still be the main source of light into the theatre. This will be referred to again, a little further on. It is sufficient for now to say that with these and perhaps other *concealed* adjustments, the Globe auditorium would be convertible for many different purposes (though always easily reconvertible to its original and true appearance as an Elizabethan theatre). Possible uses would include: A/plays – an annual season of plays presented in an Elizabethan manner, for special audiences; B/concerts (especially chamber music and jazz); C/certain types of sporting events (wrestling, fencing, etc.) D/conferences; E/flower shows, auctions, wedding receptions, anything, in fact, that might take place in a small hall.

Finally I come to what may be thought the most debatable matter of all: the actual form which an Elizabethan theatre reconstruction ought to have.

I am aware that throughout the whole of this paper there has been an underlying question, if not an absolute doubt, in the minds of many of my learned hearers, who have said to themselves: 'That is all very well, but ultimately the real reason why such a reconstruction has not yet been built is simply that we do not know well enough what the original actually looked like.'

May I now say with respect that I do not agree? It is my submission that in all respects we now know enough to allow us to proceed with considerable confidence and with no sacrifice of scholarly discipline, provided arrangements are made for variabilities, especially in the arrangements for staging, as has been mentioned above. But more than this, I put it to you that in certain respects we know with a clarity approaching actual precision what ought to be done. The arguments with which I would support this bold statement are unfortunately too long for discussion here. So for the present I will content myself with making one general and comprehensive point.

It is proposed, then, that we ought to rebuild an Elizabethan playhouse, and it is agreed that the most suitable for the purpose would be a reconstruction of the Globe. Now it happens by good fortune that the Globe is the *only* such playhouse of which it can be said that we do know what it actually did look like; and we know it really and truly and as a matter of sober fact. Only it is the Second Globe, the one which began its career in 1614, which we know so well, not the First Globe of 1599. Unfortunately, by an obtuseness born perhaps of a kind of literary sentimentality, it is the First Globe, the one with the picturesque roof of thatch which so romantically caught fire in the summer of 1613, which persons like myself have all this while been trying so hard to reconstruct. The First Globe was 'Shakespeare's Globe'; the First Globe was the Globe of *Hamlet, Macbeth,* and *Othello*; the First Globe was the darling birthplace of genius; and so naturally it is the First Globe we want so much to restore. But if we are to reconstruct with authenticity we must work with authentic material, even if it is not quite the material we expected. Now the Second Globe has been authentically recorded for us in the famous etching, and the preliminary pencil sketch for it, drawn on the spot in full view of the original, by the hand of the Czech emigré artist Wenzel Hollar. Hollar was not only a good artist but, as it happens, the foremost topographical draughtsman of his day, and what he tells us about the external appearance of the Second Globe is something which, making only a small allowance for some fallibility even in an expert hand, we can certainly rely upon. But (unfortunately again) what he tells us is something we do not quite like, something we find hard to accept. His Globe is an odd, curious, rather clumsy-looking building. We do not know quite what to make of it, and perhaps simply because it is rather unattractive in itself, nobody has ever seriously tried, or at least not tried very hard, to make anything of it on its own recognisances at all. I myself briefly attempted a reconstruction a few years ago, and published a drawing which I now believe is wrong. Recently, however, I have had cause to go into the matter more deeply, with results that seem to me as rewarding as they are surprising. I now believe that the oddly shaped proportions of the building Hollar shows us provide a riddle which contains its own solution, and the solution is one which can be tested for accuracy in structural terms alone, and should thus enable us to create a very acceptable reconstruction. The details are those which as I said earlier are beyond the scope of this paper and must wait for a further occasion. Meanwhile I have three points to end with.

The first is this: Why should we not consider that the Second Globe is 'Shakespeare's Globe,' just as much as, if not even more than, the First? Are we really to suppose that when the playhouse which was the source of his prosperity burned down in 1613 he did not himself come to London to take a hand in the planning of the new building which was to replace it? It may indeed be doubted if he had nearly as much influence at the planning of the First Globe as he did of the Second, when he was a senior member of his partnership. This is, of course, only a speculation, but it is worth a passing thought.

Secondly I ask, if the hazards which beleaguer old buildings had spared us the original Globe, or even only a part of it, so that we had something, some foundation or some curve of a wall, to make a guide for our rebuilding (which, if we had indeed been left such a thing, would surely have been attempted before now), what Globe would it have been? It would of course have been the Second Globe; and that, therefore, with Hollar's help, would have had to be the one to be rebuilt.

My last point is small but practical, and it is one to which I promised to return. It concerns roofing the yard. Because of the smaller area and clear semi-circular shape of the opening over the yard at the Second Globe, and the fact that the surrounding galleries were roofed with tiles, not thatch, the structural problem of covering this opening with a glass roof should not be great, nor need it be unsightly or spoil the general feeling of an authentic reconstruction. If we must swallow a roof, this one, if not entirely palatable, would, I think, at least prove digestible.

The proposition, therefore, which I put forward, and the principle which I hope will find support, is that the Globe Playhouse ought to be reconstructed somewhere and soon in its original form; and that the form in question which it is proper and feasible to reconstruct is that of the Second Globe, as Hollar shows it.

Herbert Berry /
The Playhouse in the Boar's Head Inn, Whitechapel
III

The remark about the Boar's Head playhouse in *The Oxford Companion to the Theatre* (1967) puts succinctly what we commonly accepted five years ago. There were two Boar's Head inns used as playhouses, one outside Aldgate but inside the City, where the Privy Council directed the Lord Mayor to suppress a play in 1557, and the other 'somewhere in Middlesex ... in use between 1602 and 1608.' Our Companion has simply combined remarks in Chambers and in Harbage and Schoenbaum. Where the later playhouse was in Middlesex and under what conditions it functioned, not from 1602, but from 1598 until at least 1608, I tried to demonstrate in my first piece about the Boar's Head. I try to refine both matters in my second and to describe the stage and surrounding house.[1] As my third Boar's Head piece, I shall here try to deal with the other half of the statement in *The Oxford Companion*, that there were two theatrical inns, an early one in the City and a later one outside.[2] I shall argue that we have all been wrong: that very likely there was only one Boar's Head outside Aldgate, that, though it was in Middlesex not the City, the Lord Mayor raided it in 1557, and that some 45 years later it became the third regular, licensed playhouse. At the same time, I shall try to introduce the man who evidently owned it in 1557.

He was John Transfeild (as he spelled his name in his will). He must have been born about 1500. He became a gunner and a good one, and during the reign of Henry VIII gave 'true and faithful service ... in wars abroad.' As a consequence, in 1522 he and a John Sandford acquired one of the 30-odd gunnerships in the Tower of London, though with the awkward provision that it would lapse when one of them died. Three years later, in 1525, Transfeild acquired another gunnership, this one with John Robinson, and this one to continue until both men were dead. Each position paid 6d a day: £4.11s.3d paid at Lady Day and as much at Michaelmas.[3] At the same time, in 1525, Transfeild appears as a substantial resident of the parish of Whitechapel (where the Boar's Head was), which is near the Tower, in Middlesex but just outside the City. He does not appear in the list for Whitechapel of the first subsidy due that year, nor in the lists for earlier years. In the list for the second subsidy of 1525, however, he gave his goods as worth £6.[4] The parish was a very populous one. Many men had goods worth more, and many worth less, but most, no doubt, were not worthy to be on the lists at all. Transfeild was on his way. One of his possessions was a house outside Aldgate which he rented to a John Reynolds, clothworker (who may have been a relative), for three nobles (i.e., 20s) a year.

If he was not already, he soon became an innholder in Whitechapel, and the inn he held was probably the Boar's Head. He also made himself known in Cromwell's circles. In 1534 he was one of fifty gunners in Ireland. A man who signed himself H. Halgrave wrote from Ireland to curry favour with a Thomas Alen, brother of the recently slain Archbishop of Dublin, John Alen. Thomas lived at Rayleigh in Essex, the road to which from London lies past the Boar's Head. 'Yt was shewed me here,' Halgrave wrote, 'by yo.r olde [h]oste Rayleigh in Essex, the road to which from London lies past the Boar's In the subsidy for 1535, Transfeild gave himself as worth £20, more than three times as much as he had given eleven years before. Only five people in the parish confessed to owning more, and only eleven others to owning as much.[6]

In 1538, Transfeild was back in England, but he was needed elsewhere. A commission of Cromwell's to look into the Irish operations (including, among others, a John Alen) wrote Cromwell urging that 'necessaries' for the guns be sent 'hither w.t spede by Transfelde who hath good experience boath of this lande and for the conveying of suche things. / We haue no souche choise of men now here as we may spare any to sende thither for souche purpose.'[7] At about the same time, perhaps while he was back in Ireland, he had a wife who was dealing with Reynolds – and, it seems, raising his rent to five nobles. Apparently she died early, leaving him no children alive in 1561.

Transfeild was a reliable as well as prosperous parishioner in the summer of 1539. Two years before, an illiterate bricklayer, John Harrydaunce, had preached the gospel out of the window of his house in Whitechapel 'w^tout licence or sufficient aucthoritie.' Because the echoes of the Pilgrimage of Grace were still very much in the air, the Lord Mayor arrested the man at once, examined him and the parish priest, and notified Cromwell, who promptly had man and examinations sent over to Westminster. Now in July 1539, Harrydaunce preached again. The parish priest (a new man) questioned his parishioners about his rival. Transfeild told him darkly 'that certen off the citie reparyd to his howsse att that tyme / but for what causse he ys oncerten.' His house must have been his inn. Presumably the Lord Mayor arrested Harrydaunce again, for he and some of his aldermen examined Harrydaunce and the parish priest again, as well as one of Harrydaunce's hearers, but this time more than three weeks after the offence. The papers went off to Westminster again, but there is no evidence that Harrydaunce did too.[8]

In 1540, when he was taxed again, Transfeild gave his goods as worth £30. Now he was collector of taxes for the whole parish and listed first on the subsidy roll – a detail which may have to do with his living at the Boar's Head, near where the parish begins, rather than with his place as collector.[9] The next year Sanford died and Transfeild perforce surrendered that gunnership, recommending a James Swygar *alias* Reynolds for it who, like the other Reynolds, may have been a relative. At about the same time, he threatened to evict his tenant Reynolds, who had recently spent £4 on the place. Reynolds, of course, promptly sued him.[10] So prosperous was Transfeild by now that he contributed £4 (the lowest amount acceptable) to the royal loan sought in 1542. About 104 people in London and Middlesex contributed. In each of the six subsidies collected from 1545 to 1549, he gave his goods as worth £40. He was one of the five or so most prosperous men in the parish.[11]

Almost immediately after, however, he gave his goods as worth £34 (in a roll dated only 'Edw. vi'), and £20 in 1551. In 1555, John Assheton, the owner of the Three Nuns, an inn just along the street in the City, bequeathed him 'my gowne furred with conye and I clerelie forgive hym the xx^s that he oweth me.'[12]

Most property in Whitechapel, including the Boar's Head, was held by copyhold of the manor of Stepney. That manor had belonged to the bishops of London since before the Conquest. In 1550 Bishop Ridley passed it to the crown, and a few weeks later the crown passed it to Thomas Lord Wentworth. The Wentworths had in their entourage a family named Poley, the head of whom was squire of Badley in Suffolk. Since 1549 that had been John, who had married one of the sixteen children of Lord Wentworth. Poleys began appearing in Transfeild's affairs. Edmund and Richard Poley collected eleven of the twelve payments of Transfeild's gunnership due from Michaelmas 1552 to Lady Day 1558, possibly because Transfeild had assigned the payments to them for ready cash. Edmund collected the first eight, Richard the other three. The two men were very probably younger brothers of the squire of Badley, hence brothers-in-law to Lord Wentworth's daughter.[18]

One of Transfeild's responses to these symptoms of ill luck, if that is what they are, was to remarry. Or perhaps his second marriage was the cause (he could have had to pay a very large jointure, including the Boar's Head). The lady, in any event, was Jane Grove of White Walton in Berkshire, who must have been many years younger than Transfeild. A Thomas Grovys had been one of Transfeild's fellows at the Tower.[14] She set about bearing two daughters, Frances, who was a child in 1561, and Anne, who was born in July 1561.

Another of Transfeild's responses was to allow the players to use the Boar's Head. The auguries, however, were not propitious. In June 1557 the Privy Council ordered the Lord Mayor, 'that Where there were yesterday certaine noughtie plaies plaied in London, as the Lordes [of the Council] were here enfourmed/he is willed bothe to make s'che for the said plaiers, and having founde them to sende them to the commissioners for religion to be by them furder ordered, and also to take order that no play be made hencefurth wth in the Cittie except the same be firste sene & allowed, & the plaiers aucthorized.' At the beginning of August, moreover, the City issued a proclamation designed to expel from the City and suburbs 'all vagabondes maisterles men and other ydle persones whatsoeuer havinge no handy crafte or lawfull occupacionne to lyve by.' Such language might then include players. All freemen of the City and suburbs who owned lodging places were to throw such persons out of them. The Privy Council had urged the City to make such a proclamation three years before.[15]

Transfeild's players may have been authorized and so thought themselves secure. At a meeting on 5 September at St James's Palace, however, someone told a Privy Council increasingly alarmed at the government's slender place in the affections of the citizenry that players meant to perform that day at the Boar's Head a play with an ominous title. The Council acted at once. They ordered the Lord Mayor of London 'to gyve ordre fourthew^th that sum of his Officers do fourth^{wt} repayre to the Bores hed w^{t}out Algate Where the L*ords* [of the Council] are enfourmed a Lewde playe called a Sacke full of Newes shalbe plaied this daye/ The players whereof he is willed to app^{r}hende and to com*m*itt to salfe warde vntill he shall here further from hense/and to take thiere playe booke from them and to send the same thither.' The Lord Mayor, too, acted at once. He arrested the players that day, sent them to prison, and presumably sent their play book over to Westminster. The next day, having rifled, no doubt, the sack full of news and found it innocuous, the Council wrote the Lord Mayor again, 'willing him to set at libertie the players by him apprehended by ordre fromhence yesterdaie and to giue them and all other plaiers thorough out the Cittie in Commaundement and charge not to playe any plaies but betwene the feast of All S^{ts} [1 November] and Shrofetide [the three days before Lent] and than only suche as are seen and allowed by thordynarye.' If the players were handled gently, Transfeild apparently was not molested at all. The Exchequer continued to pay his money for the gunnership.[16]

Late in 1561 Transfeild was mortally ill. He made his will on 5 November, describing himself as innholder, leaving his affairs to his wife, and leaving £20 to each of his daughters on their marriages. He mentioned his brother-in-law, John Grove, and godson, John Borne, son of another John Borne who may have been the licensed keeper of a tippling house in Whitechapel. He signed his will with his mark – one supposes he was illiterate – and it was witnessed by, among others, Edmund Poley, who had collected his annuity five years before.[17] Transfeild died a few days later. He was buried at St Mary Matfellon (the parish church of Whitechapel) on 11 November, and his widow proved the will and took possession of the Boar's Head and other properties on the 14th. The Exchequer paid his annuity no more.[18] Exactly two months later, at the same church which had baptised her daughter the summer before and buried her husband the gunner, she married Edmund Poley.[19] Did she, like Alice of Bath, hate a mouse that had but one hole to jump into? It was as Poley's widow in 1594 that she made the lease which ordained the buiding of a new public playhouse, as distinct from an occasional playing place, in the Boar's Head.

Now, you will have noticed that I have made several leaps in my argument. I have made the gunner and the innholder the same man when nothing necessarily combines the two. However, the numerous ways in which the two coincide, especially the ending of the gunner's annuity after the innholder's death, can leave only a little doubt that the two were the same. I have also made the innholder own the Boar's

Head in Whitechapel when he could have owned some other inn there; no document necessarily connects the two. My reasons for thinking that his inn must have been the Boar's Head are first, of course, that from at least 1581 the Poleys owned it; next that after 1535 Transfeild's name appears always near the top or bottom of the lists of residents of Whitechapel in the subsidy rolls – the Boar's Head was at the western extremity of the main road in the parish; and that, when the place was leased in 1594 and then sold in 1621, Jane Poley's name was more prominent than those of wives and mothers usually were, as though the place were hers rather than her second husband's. In 1594, her name appeared first, her eldest son's second, yet that son was 24 years old when his father died (in 1587) and nearly 32 when the lease was made. In 1621, the heir repeatedly gave his title as descending from his father and mother, not just from his father. Doubt must remain, but it is very likely that Transfeild passed the Boar's Head to his second wife either as a jointure or as part of his will.[20]

Finally, how was it that the Lord Mayor suppressed a play outside the City? It was an unwillingness to believe that he could have done so which led Chambers, Harbage, and Schoenbaum, and others (including me) to believe that there were two Boar's Heads.

The nicety about jurisdiction, especially when the Privy Council directed, seems to have applied more in Elizabethan times than in earlier ones, but even in Elizabethan times the Privy Council sometimes assumed that the Lord Mayor controlled the suburbs just outside the City. The Privy Council, for example, addressed the letter which licensed the Boar's Head, in March 1602, to the Lord Mayor, though that house was manifestly outside the City.[21] In earlier times, the Privy Council often used the Lord Mayor and his brethren in cases of sedition and treason, though committed outside the City by people who lived outside the City. Harrydaunce is a spectacular case. The Lord Mayor twice arrested a resident of Middlesex for offences committed in Middlesex, and took depositions from him and from his parish priest, who presided over a parish wholly in Middlesex. The Lord Mayor often sat on juries for treason: he actually presided over the trial (held in Guildhall) of the poet, the Earl of Surrey, in 1547 for an offence committed in Norfolk by a resident of that county. The Lord Mayor probably arrested the Earl of Bath's players in 1546 for playing 'Lewd plays in the Suburbs of London.' At the Privy Council's order, he certainly released them from the Counter and bound them not to play without the Council's special licence.[22]

The Marian Privy Council increasingly used the Lord Mayor to control the suburbs as its tenure ran out. He and one of his sheriffs examined a man in May 1556 who had spoken treason near Finsbury Fields. In November of that year the Privy Council ordered the Lord Mayor 'to cause secret and diligent s^rche to be made for oone *Chris*-tofer Rawson being vehemently suspect of coyneng Who is supposed to be haunting at the Cocke in Shordiche, and to apprehende him and to comitte him to safe warde, and to s^rche in his lodging for suche coyneng yrons or other matter as he [the Lord Mayor] supposeth may s^rue to the practiseng of his lewde Doings, and to signify what he shall do herein wth speade.' In July 1557 the Privy Council ordered one of the sheriffs and the Recorder to question a man about robberies in London 'and thereaboutes.'[23] Finsbury Fields and Shoreditch bore exactly the same relation to the City as Whitechapel. All were 'suburbs' as Stow used the word – outside but adjacent to the City wards – and all were in Middlesex. The Lord Mayor interfered more often in Southwark, where the Globe, Swan, Rose, and Hope eventually were, but, though in Surrey and the diocese of Winchester, that place from 1550 was the twenty-sixth ward of the City.

The Privy Council, then, could order the Lord Mayor to act outside the City and, if he thought the Privy Council would support him, he could even do so on his own, as he did at least once in Harry-daunce's case. One reason must have been that the City appointed the sheriff of Middlesex. It had bought that right from the Crown in the twelfth century. In practice, the two sheriffs of London jointly served 'for the time being' for six hundred years as sheriff of Middlesex.[24] The Lord Mayor, therefore, must have been a handy channel through which an impatient Privy Council could use the police of that county.

There must be little reason to suppose that the Boar's Head was in the City in 1557 merely because the Lord Mayor arrested persons there at the order of the Privy Council. There must be correspondingly little reason to wonder why two innholders would have used the same sign within yards of each other on the same street. Very likely, then, there was but one Boar's Head, that which in 1581 was just outside the City Bars in Whitechapel.

NOTES

1 The first is in *The Elizabethan Theatre I* (Toronto 1969); the second is in 'The Elizabethan Theatre III,' which is in press.
2 I am indebted to the Principal's Fund of the University of Saskatchewan, Saskatoon, for a grant which made much of the work possible. Transcripts of documents in the PRO appear by permission of the Controller of HMSO.

I do not give the sources of information when they appear in my first or second part. (See note 1.)

3 c.66/641/6/m.23; c.82/566/1

4 e.179/141/116/m.7–8; he is called John Dransfeld, and his name is in the lower two thirds of the list.

5 s.p.60/2/f.61; the letter goes on, 'I wold be right glade to haue some worde of yor amendment for as nowe I haue no speciall frynde to trust vnto but you.' It is dated 8 November 1534.

6 e.179/141/122/m.2; his name is tenth of 17. The tax was only for those who had at least £20.

7 s.p.60/7/f.104–5. The letter is dated 24 August. In October 1536 a Thomas Transfeld was paid for providing carts, harness, and other necessaries: s.p.65/1/p.1.

8 s.p.1/124/f.118, 155; e.36/120/f.133–6. Even though he gave part of his sermon before the Lord Mayor and his aldermen and declared that he would give it at length before the Privy Council, Harrydaunce does not seem to have come to much grief: he gave his goods as worth £3 in the 1520s and £6 in the 1540s (e.179/141/113/m.4; /116/m.7–8; /154/m.19; /140/m.5^v).

9 e.179/141/131/m.5. Of 26 persons, omitting the 'strangers,' only one had as much as Transfeild and only one had more (£48.13s.4d). Only the amount of tax appears, but from other parishes it seems that the rate was 6d in the pound; Transfeild paid 15s.

10 c.66/704/15/m.34; c.1/1055/17 (which is only partly legible and only under ultra violet). A James Swegar alias Reynolds, who was apparently also called Mr Reynolds, had married an Alice Stansfelde and had cousins Robert and Nicholas Grove. He died a rather wealthy man in 1551. A widow of the family (Alice Stansfelde), who died in 1554, lived a few yards from the Boar's Head in Aldgate Street and owned an inn next door to where she lived. In the list for the subsidy which he collected in 1540, Transfeild's name was first written 'Stansfeld'; then someone struck out the 'S' and inserted an 'r' after the 't.' (Guildhall, m.s.9171/12/f.94–6, 81–2;/15/f.224^v–5^v, 285; m.s.9051/2/f.125–6: p.r.o., prob.11/34/36)

11 e.179/141/136 (upwards of 20 people lent £4); and /146/m.6 (Transfeild is second; nobody whose name is legible had more goods), /138/m.2^v (he is third in a list mostly illegible), /140/m.5^v (he is fifth; one man has more, £100), /160/m.11 (he is second; one man has more, £50), /154/m.19 (he is fourth; one man, a stranger, has more, £100), and e.179/142/167 (he is first; two men have more, £70 and £60).

12 e.179/142/179 (he is second from the end), /186 (he is second); Corporation of London, Husting Roll 248/114. Assheton left many men small bequests and in nearly all cases mentioned their wives. He mentioned none for Transfeild.

13 e.405/118/m.16, 35; /119/m.29, 46; /120/m.29^v, 85; /121/m.47, 99^v; /122/m.41, 107; /123/m.33^v, 96^v. The odd payment was made to Thomas Skevington, a fellow gunner at the Tower. For the relationship between John, Edmund, and Richard Poley, see the wills of Edmund Poley Sr, d 1549 (who had sons John, Edmund, Henry, Richard, and Thomas) and Jane Transfeild Poley (whose husband, Edmund, was certainly the son of Edmund Sr): p.c.c., 31 Populwell, 47 Woodhall. In April 1547 a John

Polley was servant to Lord Wentworth; he was paid 46s.8d for 'bringing of a priest out of Suff[olk] and his retorne backe': E.315/439/f.14ᵛ.

14 *Cal. of Letters and Papers, Foreign and Domestic, Hen. VIII, 1524–6,* 869–70

15 *Acts of the Privy Council, 1554–6,* 73; P.C.2/6/p.590; Corporation of London, Journal 17, f.42ᵛ, and Letter Book s, f.143. Earlier in the proclamation the undesirables are 'all manner of ydle vagabonds valyaunt beggards and maysterles men and such like havinge no occupacionne or mysterie.'

16 P.C.2/7/pp.695, 696; E.405/123/m.33ᵛ, 96ᵛ; /124/m.19ᵛ, 51ᵛ

17 The original will (part of which is perished) is Guildhall MS 9172/4; the register copy (which is complete) is MS 9171/15. After small bequests, he left 'The residue of all my goods movable and vnmovable whatsoever they be my funeralls, Debtes, and legacies fullie contented and paid ... vnto the seyd Jane Transfeild my wife whome I make my sole Executrixe of this my presente Testamente and laste will.' For Borne, see Middx. R.O., MR/LV/1/[5–5ᵛ, 17ᵛ], lists of those licensed in 1553 to keep alehouses and victualling houses in Whitechapel and Stepney. Evidently inns were neither, for no innholder appears. The records of the Innholders Company begin well into the seventeenth century: Guildhall MSS 6647–64.

18 E.405/126/m.15ᵛ, 68, payments due at Michaelmas 1560 and Lady Day 1561, after which Transfeild's name does not appear: /127, /128, /129. The roll has been lost showing payments due on Michaelmas 1561, which Transfeild would have collected, and Lady Day 1562, which he would not.

19 Poley got the license on 12 January and the wedding took place on the 14th: *Marriage Licences Issued by the Bishop of London, 1520-1610* (London 1887) 23; G.L.C., P.93/MRY 1/1/I/f.2ᵛ.

20 Either way, the transaction, like any others concerning the property, would not normally have been entered in the central courts of record nor mentioned in the will. It would have been entered on the court roll of Stepney, only fragments of which survive from before 1654. Information about the lease of 1594 survives because the lease became the subject of lawsuits. The inn was enfranchised in 1618, after which freehold transactions should have been entered in the courts of record.

21 The Privy Council, however, addressed the letters of June 1600 and December 1601 which licensed the Globe (in Southwark) and Fortune (in Middlesex) quite properly to the Lord Mayor and justices of the peace of Surrey and Middlesex. The letter licensing the Boar's Head did not mention its location, but did mention the Oxford-Worcester Company, which on other evidence was using the Whitechapel Boar's Head then.

22 See the papers in K.B.8, especially those printed in the *Third Report of the Deputy Keeper of the Public Records* (London 1843), appx II, 245–7, 255, 263, 267–8; and Add. MS 5476, f.197ᵛ.

23 *C.S.P., Dom., 1547–80,* p.83; *Acts of the Privy Council, 1556–8,* 124; P.C.2/6/pp.455, 523, 550

24 Philip E. Mather *Compendium of Sheriff and Execution Law* (London 1903) 3; S. and B. Webb *The Parish and the County* (London 1963) 288, n 1

M.C. Bradbrook /
Shakespeare and his Collaborators

My title carries the implication that any plays doubtfully Shake-spearian are likely to be collaborative. However, all drama, being an art of performance, is by nature collaborative.[1] As full member of the most famous Elizabethan guild of players, Shakespeare gained his privilege by never being merely a writer. That perhaps may have made him the kind of writer he was; participation is deeply invited by his dramatic style, whereas the lyric poet of *Venus and Adonis*, if splendid, is not incomparable.

After a brief survey of the history of our theme, I shall concentrate on one early and one late play – these being the two periods in which Shakespeare is assumed to have collaborated with other poets.

Among scholars deep wishes for some new epiphany of the Divine Shakespeare conflict with deep impulses to separate his pure essence from base accretion. This conflict can be traced in the historic outline of my subject.

The First Folio of 1623 'gathered' and 'collected' such plays as had been before unworthily printed, with 'all the rest, absolute in their numbers as he conceived them.' Seven plays, including *Pericles*, were added in the Third Folio of 1663 from the store that booksellers had found profitable to attribute to Shakespeare. The eighteenth century's growing idolatry swelled the hope for new plays, till in 1796 William Ireland gratified it with an entire tragedy, *Vortigern and Rowena*, staged at Drury Lane by Sheridan and exposed as forgery by Malone.

A counter-move from the Romantics showed Coleridge prepared to disencumber Shakespeare of every word unworthy of his genius. 'I think I could point out to half a line what is really Shakespeare's in *Love's Labour's Lost* and other not entirely genuine plays,' he modestly averred in *Table Talk*; in the Porter's speech of *Macbeth* he distinguished that Shakespeare 'with the remaining ink of a pen otherwise employed, just interpolated the words':

I'll devil-porter it no further; I had thought to let in some of all professions that go the primrose way to th'everlasting bonfire

the main speech having been 'written by some other hand, perhaps with Shakespeare's consent.'[2]

In 1841, Charles Knight cautiously added a volume of Doubtful Plays to his *Illustrated Shakespeare*. With ecclesiastical overtones, as of a General Council of the Church promulgating Holy Writ, the contents of the Folio became 'the Shakespeare Canon,' and, by analogy, any appendages 'the Apocrypha.'

The last quarter of the nineteenth century and the first quarter of the twentieth was the fashionable era of Shakespearian disintegrators – an age when Homer too was parcelled out among many poets. Greene's jibe at the 'upstart crow,' and the habits of Henslowe's literary bondslaves seemed to warrant an author who continually cobbled other men's works or his own. The age that opened with Fleay's *Metrical Tests applied to Dramatic Poetry* (1874) culminated in the work of J.M. Robertson, who finally left to the master only one play uncontaminated and unrevised – *A Midsummer Night's Dream* (he is now remembered merely as prompting T.S. Eliot's iconoclastic essay on *Hamlet*). In 1924 E.K. Chambers disposed magisterially of *The Disintegration of Shakespeare* in a British Academy Lecture; although traces of a revisionary Shakespeare, who blotted many a line and revised yet more, may be found in the first volumes of the Cambridge New Shakespeare, where all rhymed passages tend to be read as verse fossils – generally the fossilized remains of those once described as the University Half-Wits.

Bridge's notorious essay of 1907 blames the audience for 'preventing the greatest poet and dramatist in the world from being the best artist.'[3] The disintegrators created, largely in their own image, a purist tinkerer, who would have given the maximum inconvenience to the players studying their parts while offering the minimum novelty to the audience.

Meanwhile, the new school of bibliographers and paleographers added a collaborative work to the canon. First proposed as partly Shakespearian by Spedding in 1871, *The Book of Sir Thomas More* was so well established by the series of essays which Pollard collected in 1923, *Shakespeare's Hand in Sir Thomas More*, that the relevant sections have since been reprinted in several editions of the complete Works. Younger scholars carried out the vindication of Heming's and Condell's choice; yet difficulties revealed about the First Folio printing of one or two plays suggested that beyond the fringe lay other works, ephemera that yet may float among interstellar spaces with *Love's Labour's Won* and *Cardenio*. It is as hard to limit the possibility of Shakespearian collaboration as to crystallize a definitive text.[4] Within 'the Shakespeare area' all kinds of compositions may lie at greater or lesser approximation to the centre. It was sheer common sense that prompted E.K. Chambers to hazard 'I am prepared to think that Shakespeare wrote some very poor work,' and Hardin Craig in 1948 to defend 'Shakespeare's Bad Poetry.'[5] Within a decade, however, Jan Kott was writing (in 1957) '*Titus Andronicus* is already Shakespearian theatre; but a truly Shakespearian text is yet to come.' In the new theatre of the fifties, the sovereignty of the text had been replaced by the sovereignty of the sub-text: performance claimed to have supplied a check on authenticity.

The doubtful plays remained editorially very much a side-issue. Alfred Hart's vocabulary tests and Edward Armstrong's image clusters improved on the discredited verse tests of Fleay;[6] soon the computer may yield new and more objective methods of determining Canon and Apocrypha, since it has already been applied significantly (I believe) to an even more august collection, the Epistles of St Paul.

Without reaching further than a modest probability, however, evidence of a sort other than the purely stylistic or verbal might be brought to bear. It may be that, if not asking the wrong questions about the doubtful plays, we have at least ignored another set of questions that might also be asked.

In the last twenty-five years, no area has been more intensively studied than the social and physical aspects of Elizabethan performance. Indeed, in popular interest it ranks so high that the sensation of the age has been not the 'discovery' of a new play but the 'discovery' of what is claimed as a picture of the Globe interior. This news made the headlines.

The development of the modern open stage, of workshop techniques, of audience participation, has led to reinterpretation of many Elizabethan plays; minor works of Shakespeare have succeeded on the boards where till recently some of them were never seen. Unfortunately, the doubtful plays outside the Folio are not good box office.

Yet the work of Harbage, Nagler, Wickham, Jacquot, Hosley, and others suggests the question: for what kind of theatre and for what kind of audience do these doubtful plays appear to have been written? Do they appear to fit in with what is known of Shakespeare's working life? Assuming the general acceptance of *Pericles* in part and *Sir Thomas More* in part, I shall look at two which remain doubtful, *The Raigne of King Edward III* and *Two Noble Kinsmen*. My conclusions, which I will give in advance, are that the first is probably not by Shakespeare but comes from his circle; the second, as stated on the title page, is by Fletcher and Shakespeare in collaboration; that both were written for the private stage, the first perhaps for a noble household.[7]

'A Book entitled Edward III and the Blacke Prince their Warres with John of France' was entered in the Stationers' Register on 1 December 1595, and in the nineties printed twice as 'The Raigne of King Edward III, as it hath been sundry times plaid about the Citie of London.'[8] Neither author nor company is given, so it could hardly have been a notable public success. The first two acts – attributed to Shakespeare[9] – present Edward's wooing of the Countess of Salisbury, and remain entirely detachable; they could have been an addition, since the original title omits this theme. A prologue scene sets out the English rights to France – the King has rather surprisingly to be informed that his mother was the French king's daughter and heiress – and both parts are thematically joined by the 'argument' of the whole play, which turns on feudal loyalty, the nature of allegiance, and the sanctity of an oath; being rhetorically based on pleas and counterpleas. The lady repulses the king's siege of love by reminding him that the marriage oath is more venerable than the oath of allegiance, and that he is guilty of High Treason against Heaven's King if he commits adultery. Unwillingly enlisted as devil's advocate under his own oath of allegiance, her father ingeniously turns his plea into a dissuasion. The Countess, exacting a promise from the king to perform her commands if she submits, demands the murder of both their spouses. When to her horror the king agrees, she whips out her wedding knives and prepares to kill her husband, lodged within her heart, unless the king swear an oath to desist. He suffers an instant conversion and departs for France, where, however, the Black Prince rather than his father holds the stage.

Although the play celebrates Creçy and Poitiers, it in no way resembles a civic show; the battles are not presented by drum and trumpet fighting but in long descriptive orations, and one or two heraldic entries. The common soldiers are not shown or given speaking parts; not so much as a pair of single combatants appears! Such treatment of great victories would have been totally unacceptable to the common stages, and strongly suggests the play was written for private production by non-professional players or by boys.

In the second part the sanctity of an oath is upheld by the Dauphin against the King, his natural lord and father; the English Queen pleads with her lord the King against his unkingly decree to hang the burghers of Calais: both pleas succeed.

This noble theme would appeal to readers of Malory or courtly romance, but lacks the direct popular appeal of battle plays. The concept of imperial rule and the nature of sovereignty was made use of by Henry viii to free himself from papal authority; it was a live issue still in late Tudor times,[10] especially in relation to the north country, where feudal ties still held.

The first part has been compared with Edward iv's wooing of Lady Grey (*3 Henry VI* iii, 2) but, by comparison with that lively scene, it is more like a set debate, rhetorically poised. Even in the Earl of Warwick's speech to his daughter, retracting his first plea, which has been singled out as 'the best poetry in the play'[11] we have a 'field of reasons' or a catena of proverbs, among which is incongruously set one of the most powerful lines from Shakespeare's sonnets:

> The freshest summer's day doth soonest taint
> The lothed carrion that it seems to kiss,
> Deep are the blows made with a mighty axe:
> That sinne doth ten times aggravate itself
> That is committed in an holy place:
> An evil deed, done by authoritie
> Is sin and subornation; Decke an Ape
> In tissue and the beauty of the robe
> Adds but the greater scorn unto the beast.
> A spatious field of reasons could I urge
> Between his glorie, daughter, and thy shame:
> That poison shews worst in a golden cup:
> Dark night seems darker by the lightening flash;
> Lilies that fester smell far worse than weeds:
> And every glorie that inclines to sinne,
> The shame is treble by the opposite.   (ii.i.437–53)[12]

Shakespeare does not literally repeat himself like this and in Sonnet 94 the ebb and flow of feeling – what Empson called its 'interpenetrating and fluid unity'[13] – dramatically culminates in the spurt of love and loathing that associates the floral emblem of purity with corrupted flesh by the power of the concentrated metaphor 'fester':

> So shall I live, supposing thou art true,
> Like a deceived husband; so love's face
> Shall still seem love to me, though alter'd new ...   (Sonnet 93)

> For sweetest things turn sourest by their deeds.
> Lilies that fester smell far worse than weeds.   (Sonnet 94)

A totally different set of Shakespearian connections is provided in both parts by thematic likenesses to two plays which Shakespeare had not yet written – *Henry V* and *Measure for Measure*, both of which are subsequent to the publication of *Edward III*. Again, however, rhetorical persuasion of a non-dramatic kind distinguishes this work from Shakespeare's, even in the set speech of consolation to a young man facing death. The Duke's consolation to Claudio in *Measure for Measure* does not hammer at the topic as does the speech of old Audley which is intended to strengthen the Black Prince against the odds at Poitiers:

> To die is all as common as to live:
> The one inch wise, the other holds in chase;
> For from the instant we begin to live,
> We do pursue and hunt the time to die:
> First bud we, then we blow, and after seed,
> Then presently we fall; and as a shade
> Follows the bodie, so we follow death.
> If then, we hunt for death, why do we fear it?
> If we feare it, why do we follow it?
> If we do follow, how can we shun it?   (IV.iv.133–42)[14]

If the play was written for private performance, appealing to chivalric ideals rather than civic sentiment, and if it may be regarded as belonging to earlier forms of the private stage (as later, for instance, Chapman's rhetorical history plays), it could have been used at feasts within the City – for instance those of 'Prince Arthur's Knights,' the city archers; or it could have been used at a great house in compliment to a great lady. The literary references tie it close to the date of publication, i.e., in the period 1594–5. The boys' theatres shut down in 1590 and during 1592–4 the public theatres were also closed for plague. It is possible that Shakespeare, like Marlowe, took refuge with a noble patron. *Love's Labour's Lost* and *A Midsummer Night's Dream* were very possibly written for private performance. The first was regarded with especial interest by the Southampton family;[15] it has been suggested that *A Midsummer Night's Dream* was composed for the remarriage of the Dowager Countess of Southampton. If she presided over her son's fortunes during his minority, she might well be the further object of compliment in a play written for his circle, which glorified her ancestress, the Countess of Salisbury (both were Montagues, and it was through his mother that young Southampton was linked with the old nobility).

Could this play have been written by a friend during the period when all theatres were closed, but enacted by Shakespeare as part of a private group? If so he could well have had it in mind with the rest of the early repertory which has occasionally echoed even in his latest work.[16] The author would thus have quoted Shakespeare's private unpublished sonnets, and glanced at the poem addressed to Southampton, while Shakespeare in turn refashioned the material into something far more powerful when later he composed *Henry V* and *Measure for Measure* – the first as Southampton was leaving for Ireland with Essex, the second as he was released from the Tower by King James, where he had lain for three years under sentence of death for the Essex conspiracy.

The briefest comparison between *Edward III* and *Sir Thomas More* – now datable after 1590[17] – reveals that they belong to quite different types of performance. This is the jest-book style of history; a great man but one with the common people, More jests with his friends, his servants, even on the way to the scaffold, where his courageous mockery has been foreshadowed in that of the common rebel, John Lincoln, and Doll Williamson. Not only does the play depict the rioters of Ill May Day sympathetically, it hints at state matters that under the present 'fifty years' rule' would be only just released. The play appeals to the solidarity and sense of humanity among the Londoners, in the same manner as Peele's *Edward I*; but the aliens depicted in More's Shakespearian speech – his appeal to the rioters – are quite inconsistent with the swaggering thieving scoundrels of the opening scene, who try to abduct the redoubtable Doll.

Five hands collaborated in *Sir Thomas More*, mainly the work of

Munday, a city pageanter, who was used to work with a group; in the Shakespearian plea of More, the living accents of persuasion, urgent and passionate, are heard. To compare it with *Edward III* is like comparing Brutus' oration with Antony's; the one is correct according to the books, the other flows out in an appeal to imagination, sympathy, and participation:

> Grant them removed, and grant that this your noise
> Hath chid down all the majesty of England:
> Imagine that you see the wretched straingers,
> Their babies at their backs and their poor luggage,
> Plodding to th' ports and coasts for transportation,
> And that you sit as kings in your desires,
> Authority quite silenct by your brawl,
> And you in ruff of your opinions cloth'd,
> What had you got? I'll tell you: you had taught
> How insolence and strong hand should prevail,
> How order should be quell'd; and by this patterne,
> Not one of you should live an aged man,
> For other ruffians, as their fancies wrought,
> With selfsame hand, self reasons and self right
> Would shark on you, and men, like ravenous fishes,
> Would feed on one another.   (II.iv.92–107)

These two early histories have in common only a certain elasticity. Each could have been expanded or contracted; More plays a jest which is attributed to Thomas Cromwell. The story of Edward III and the Countess of Salisbury was not told as historically established, even by such a liberal embroiderer of fact as William Painter in his *Palace of Pleasure*; in relying on social assumptions, in one case chivalric and in the other civic, the plays celebrate the societies to which they were addressed.

In our own day, the need to interpret Shakespeare's histories has led to adaptations in the home of classic Shakespearian performance, the Royal Shakespeare Theatre at Stratford. In his introduction to *The Wars of the Roses*, Peter Hall observed that stage adaptation is not like 'improving' a painting, when the damage is irrevocable. Moreover, any performance involves some adaptation and selection – as does any other act of interpretation. 'But a production cannot help creating as well as criticizing, and so turning the original text into something it is not by itself.' The aim, he concluded, was to fill out what was taken to be Shakespearian thematic design. 'It is a piece of directorial interference certainly but it is not a piece of Shakespearean pastiche';[18] this text should not be used as a basis for other productions, for it was designed for one time and place, one set of actors. The emphasis on order and degree reinforced for the modern audience assumptions which would have been implicit in Shakespeare's own day.

The play which a French critic recently termed 'le chante de cygne de Shakespeare'[19] can safely be assigned to the King's Men, the Blackfriars, and the year 1613; it is difficult to resist also the claims of the title page of 1634 that it was 'written by the memorable Worthies of their time: Mr John Fletcher and Mr William Shakespeare, Gentm.' The Jacobean audience would have hastened to see what most readers look on as its chief weakness – the Jailor's mad daughter, a parody of Ophelia, in her unrequited love for Palamon. In a wood near Athens, this She-Fool entertains the bridals of Theseus and Hippolita with a Morris Dance of Country People, which had been presented at Court in the Masque of the Inner Temple and Gray's Inn to celebrate the nuptials of Princess Elizabeth and the Elector Palatine, married on St Valentine's Day 1613. The Masque, by Francis Beaumont, was introduced by its antimasque, in which all characters, instead of being of the same species, and dressed alike, were 'a confusion or commixture of all such persons as are proper for country sports' to signify the love of the common people. 'All these persons apparell'd to the life,' the twelve 'Dancers, or rather actors, expressed every one their part so naturally and aptly' that the audience were deeply stirred and diverted, and raised 'the laughter and applause above the music.' The King himself called for an encore.[20]

A repeat performance before a select audience at Blackfriars by the King's Men would be highly profitable; but the antimasque was brief, as the professional act had been only a curtain-raiser to the main masque of young lawyers. The play was perhaps only commissioned to provide a setting for the antimasque. It is said that in performance the Jailor's daughter turns out to be the star part.[21]

Two years before, the dance of satyrs from Jonson's *Masque of Oberon* (given 1 January 1611) had been seen in *The Winter's Tale*; but mention of Oberon is sufficient to recall the conflict of national feelings which later lay behind the façade of gaiety – the 'mirth in funeral and dole in marriage.' On 6 November 1612, Henry, Prince of Wales, the Oberon of the Court, gallant, popular, and only eighteen years of age, died of typhoid fever in the beginning of his sister's wedding festivities. His funeral was celebrated in December, the postponed wedding following in February. Many of the marriage odes were bound up with elegies for the Prince; brother and sister had been devoted to each other.[22]

The hymeneal opening scene of *The Two Noble Kinsmen* keeps decorum, therefore, in being crossed by the dark pageant of three mourning queens, whose plea for their dead husbands brings funeral rites to the wedding, postponing the festivities. When Theseus has avenged them and conquered Thebes, the two young kinsmen are carried on for dead – though with hopes of revival. The ritual of the three Kings' funerals follows, with the ceremonial parting of the queens (a mimetic rendering of the Virgilian 'Mille viae mortis') :

> This world's a city full of straying streets,
> And Death's the market place, where each one meets.   (i.v.15–16)

This concludes the first act, generally thought to be Shakespearian. The story of the kinsmen follows to its conclusion, which again combines the wedding of the widowed bride Emily, to Palamon, with the funeral of his rival Arcite, follower of Mars (Henry too had been martial).

A chivalric tale, which had been staged with great success early in Elizabeth's reign, is here presented in ritualized fashion; the comparison is with the tradition of *Edward III* rather than with that of *Sir Thomas More*. War and love are still the argument, which, however, is given by spectacle rather than debate. A most percipient critic has observed that the Shakespearian scenes

are static and, though with splendour, stiff. They are slow and dense, compared with Fletcher's easy liquescense. They have a deliberate yet vague grandeur, a remote and half exhausted exaltation; they are expressed through a clotted rhetoric that is the poetry of a man that has finished with action.[23]

As Theodore Spencer goes on to say, 'Slow lines move, like figures in heavy garments' to 'an adagio rhythm, haunting, evocatory, spoken as it were behind a veil.' The lovers never exchange anything but formal words in public with the princess, the final combat occurs offstage (and of course Palamon never meets the Jailor's daughter). Theseus dismisses the shattered wreck of the victor as if his whole life had been artifice:

> His part is played, and though it were too short,
> He did it well. (v.iv.118-19)

The three altars of Venus, Diana, and Mars could have come from Lyly's stage; neither crowd scenes nor elaborate stage effects were used; the play requires none of the extravagant setting that distinguished *King Henry VIII*, staged the same year. In the Shakespearian scenes, images of rivers and fishing, of pastoral and woodlands suggest a scene 'far in a Western brookland,' culminating in the May Queen's invocation by Arcite:[24]

> O Queen Emilia,
> Fresher than May, sweeter
> Than her gold buttons on the boughs, or all
> Th'enamelled knacks o' the mead and garden ... (iii.i.4-7)

This is in 'Diana's wood'; by contrast, Auden has well noted the 'humiliating and horrid' imagery of Palamon's invocation to Venus, and 'the disgust expressed at sexual vanity.' 'To make a cripple flourish with his crutch' and bring an octogenarian to wed a girl of eighteen leads a monster into Venus's pageant, almost a death's head, to the bridal:[25]

> The aged cramp
> Had screwed his square foot round,
> The gout had knit his fingers into knots,
> Torturing convulsions from his globy eyes
> Had almost drawn their spheres, that what was life
> In him seemed torture. (v.i.116-21)[26]

The widowed queens use a beautiful but terrifying image of a beheaded dove (Venus' bird), Hippolyta can talk unmoved of cannibalism among the vanquished (i.iii.15-19), but Emily is no Amazon and responds directly to the tears of the widows:

> Pray you, say nothing, pray you.
> Who cannot feel nor see the rain, being in't,
> Knows neither wet nor dry. (i.i.130-2)

Her nullity is part of the pattern; when invited to preside over the combat for her hand ('you the only star to shine') she refuses and would rather die herself:

> I am extinct.
> There is but envy in the light which shines
> To shew the one the other.   (v.iii.26–8)

For Theodore Spencer, 'the whole thing is two dimensional and un-real, a piece of tapestry, not like the story of Troilus and Cressida, an active conflict.' But since it is meant to replace a masque and to throw into relief the rapid gaiety of the antimasque, this effect is not inappropriate. Moreover, the peculiar flatness of the characters – what Spencer terms their 'albinism' – allows the handling of a situation with both heterosexual and homosexual elements.

Palamon and Arcite, like the older pair, Theseus and Pirithous, are symbols of masculine devotion; in prison they claim that each replaces for the other wife and offspring, indeed the whole social world. Their quarrel over Emily simply replaces love by hate without weakening the bond; they fight for her as an object, a 'jewel,' and as she says, 'The misadventure of their own eyes kill 'em' (iii.vi.191). In Fletcher, fighting and insults as a form of erotic play are common enough. The two sisters discourse on the rivalry of sexual love and male friendship, and Emily describes her childhood love for a girl who died at eleven years, with whom she shared all actions and preferences.

This formality of structure, the masque-like concern with rôles rather than characters, allows the topic of homosexuality to become pervasive without being acknowledged. The relation of the kinsmen to each other lies at the centre of the action, and their theme reflects what everyone knew to be the habits of the monarch himself.

In condemning both lovers to death for fighting without the cere-mony of the lists, the chivalrous Theseus may be reflecting James' Edict against Private Combats (October 1613); but he too in the end submits to Fortune, the sovereign deity of the play, whose influence overrules Diana, Mars, and Venus.[27]

In the cosmic order which Stuart masques celebrated, the highest and most godlike states are embodied in the chief masquers, as when in Daniel's *Vision of the Twelve Goddesses*, Pallas descended in the form of Queen Anne, 'being otherwise no object for mortal eyes.'

The stately grief of the main story is contrasted with the antimasque for which it was a setting, out of which grows the story of the sub-plot. The Jailor's daughter, chief figure of the antimasque, falls in love with Palamon, and sets him free at peril of her father's life; following him to the greenwood on May Eve, she hopes that the rites of the time will be celebrated with rustic freedom. Like the Morris

Dance itself, the exchange of rush rings and a night in the greenwood belonged to that old 'Merry England' which had already passed away.[28] This is *not* Diana's wood:

> Let him do
> What he will with me, so he use me kindly,
> For use me so he shall, or I'll proclaim him,
> And to his face, no man.   (ii.vi.28–31)

Missing her tryst she grows melancholy, plaits rush rings by the water-side in a parody of the forsaken Ophelia, whilst imagining Palamon to enjoy the favours of innumerable country girls; she is cured by her humble lover, who puts on Palamon's garments and takes her virginity. At their meeting, the Jailor's daughter, now imagining herself at sea, begins to imitate another famous scene from the elder collaborator's repertory:

> DAUGHTER You are Master of a ship?
> JAILOR Yes.
> DAUGHTER ... For the tackling, let me alone.
> Come, weigh, my hearts, cheerily all! O,O,O, 'tis up!
> The wind's fair, top the bowline! Out with the mainsail!
> Where's your whistle, mariner?   (iv.i.181–91)

This bold piece of parody, a scene of intimate jesting, puts a new antimasque into the players' own domestic repertory. If 'an art which plays over the whole gamut between firm convention and complete realism'[29] is stronger than one which ranges from the sublime to the ridiculous without ever touching the realistic, this show reveals limitations in spite of great variety. The Jailor's daughter, in her tragic-grotesque vision of Hell, castigates her own early hopes, and displays that kind of 'dislocation' which Clifford Leech has distinguished as the main feature of Fletcher's art.[30] In the same way, the two Kinsmen at one point condemn the licentiousness of Thebes, at another glee-fully recall their own amorous exploits, and yet again, Palamon, at the end, primly repudiates such conduct. This is possible only in an 'olla podrida' which included parodies of theatrical art. If acted with the 'variety' that distinguished the quick-moving antimasque, the two halves of the show might cohere as theatrical collage, designed to reflect the confusion which had so pleased in the original entertainment at court. The work was perhaps too topical to be revived in the public theatres, but to condemn the whole play as 'nothing more than frivolous'[31] is to ignore its dual character – an old, native heroic setting for an avant-garde hit.

In the following year Ben Jonson parodied *Two Noble Kinsmen* in *Bartholomew Fair*. Rival suitors, whose fate is to be determined by drawing lots, chose the names of Argalus, out of *Arcadia*, and Palamon 'out of the play'; 'Palamon' wins the lady (iv.iii.67–8). The puppeteer shows two faithful friends Damon and Pythias falling out for love of Hero, and abusing each other till the puppet master intervenes and is himself abused – whereat he retorts 'I say, between you, you have but one drab.'[32] *Bartholomew Fair*, with its puppets leaning out of the booth, must visually have evoked the two prisoners leaning out of their prison window; it testifies to the earlier show's success; for Jonson would not waste his satire on a failure.

The case for Shakespeare's part-authorship is so strong that, as Kenneth Muir says, the onus of proof really rests on the sceptics; yet few would follow Paul Bertram[33] in assigning to Shakespeare the whole play. The reasons for collaboration may have been, first, speed; secondly, to emphasize variety by engaging the two best authors of the King's Company. If the whole town were talking of the antimasque, it would be profitable to put it on quickly, and Shakespeare had rushed out a play on at least one previous occasion. He wrote the slow stately opening and closing acts, Fletcher added to the piquancy of the jests and jibes by recalling his new partner's successes, while shaping the work of his former partner Beaumont who had composed the original antimasque, the speediest merriest part of the show.

Jacobeans loved variety; two famous names on the playbill would be an asset. Yet, since the main design was Fletcher's and hardly amounted to a drama, it remained outside the collection made a decade later in Shakespeare's memory. Piety and curiosity will always search for fragments of his work which may throw light on his greater achievement; but the First Folio may well represent what the writer himself would have wished to be remembered by.

NOTES

1 'All art is a collaboration': Synge, preface to *Playboy of the Western World*.
2 T.M. Raysor *Coleridge's Shakespearean Criticism* (1930) i, 75
3 Robert Bridges *Collected Essays* (1927) i, 29
4 See E.A. Honigmann *The Stability of Shakespeare's Text* (London 1965)
5 In *Shakespeare Survey* i (1948)
6 Alfred Hart *Shakespeare and the Homilies* (1934); Edward Armstrong *Shakespeare's Imagination* (1946). The image clusters – a group of sub-

consciously associated words – are much used by Kenneth Muir in what is the best study of the doubtful plays, *Shakespeare as Collaborator* (London 1960).

7 There is, I would think, no case to be made for any of the other doubtful plays attributed to Shakespeare; a number of them are dealt with in Baldwin Maxwell's *Studies in the Shakespeare Apocrypha* (New York 1956). C.F. Tucker Brooke's collection (London 1908) remains the best edition of these plays.

8 The printer also published good quartos of *Love's Labour's Lost* (1598) and *Romeo and Juliet* (1599).

9 Capell was the first to do so.

10 See F.H. Hinsley *Sovereignty* (London 1966) 118–19.

11 Muir *Shakespeare as Collaborator* 44

12 Quotations from *Edward III* and *The Two Noble Kinsmen* are from C.F. Tucker Brooke, ed *The Shakespeare Apocrypha* (Cambridge 1907).

13 William Empson *Some Versions of Pastoral* (London 1935) chapter 3

14 In line 42, 'follow' is my emendation for 'fear.'

15 It was given before Anne of Denmark as entertainment by this family (see E.K. Chambers *William Shakespeare* [1930] II, 332).

16 The old plays of *The Rare Triumphs of Love and Fortune* and *Clyamon and Clamydes* are recalled in *Cymbeline*. As an actor Shakespeare must have learned many plays by heart.

17 See I.A. Shapiro, 'The Significance of a Date' *Shakespeare Survey* 8 (1955) 104–5.

18 Peter Hall, in introduction to *The Wars of the Roses* (London 1970) viii, xxv

19 Pierre Leyris, 'Le chante de cygne de Shakespeare' *Nouvelle revue française* (1 November 1970) number 215

20 Beaumont's masque is reprinted in *A Book of Masques in Honour of Allardyce Nicoll* (Cambridge 1967).

21 See the Signet Classics Shakespeare Edition, ed Clifford Leech, page xxxvi.

22 See Elkin C. Wilson *Prince Henry in English Literature* (New York 1946).

23 Theodore Spencer in *Modern Philology* 26 (1928) 255–76; reprinted in Clifford Leech's edition of *The Two Noble Kinsmen* (New York 1966)

24 See Marco Mincoff *English Studies* (1952) 97–115, for a study of the imagery.

25 A mask of death's heads at a bridal occurred at the wedding of Alexander III of Scotland; see I.S. Ekeblad, 'The Impure Art of John Webster' *Review of English Studies* n.s. 9 (1958), reprinted in G.K. Hunter's *John Webster* (Penguin Books 1969). For Auden's views see his introduction to William Burto's Signet Classics edition of the *Sonnets* (1964).

26 M. Leyris ascribes the mood to Shakespeare and quotes Yeats on his old age: *The Spur*.

27 See i.i.64–5, iii.i.15–16, iii.vi.16, v.iv.16–17, iii.ii, and for Fate, i.ii.102, i.iii.41.

28 Stubbes, in *The Anatomy of Abuses* (1583), wrote a well-known rebuke to the traditional rites of May. The Morris Dance was a May Day celebration.

29 I.S. Ekeblad, 'The Impure Art of John Webster.' The comparison of the 'charivari' scenes from *The Duchess of Malfi* with the mad scenes of the

Jailor's daughter is enlightening: both belonged to the King's Men and were staged in 1613.

30 *The John Fletcher Plays* (London 1962) 32

31 Norman Rabkin *Shakespeare and the Common Understanding* (New York 1967) 230

32 This jest was flung at Beaumont and Fletcher – see Aubrey's *Brief Lives* (A. Clark, ed, 1898) 1, 96.

33 Muir *Shakespeare as Collaborator* 110; Paul Bertram *Shakespeare and 'The Two Noble Kinsmen'* (New Brunswick 1965). His case, which is mainly linguistic, has been strongly challenged by Cyrus Hoy in *Modern Philology* 67, 1 (1969).

Charlton Hinman /
Shakespearian Textual Studies:
Seven More Years

This paper will first notice some of the principal accomplishments of textual study during the past seven years, will then mention a particular problem that seems much in need of further study, and finally will urge a change in editorial practice that to some may seem rather shocking.

The accomplishments of the last seven years only, because the many retrospective studies called forth by Shakespeare's four hundredth birthday included some that surveyed textual study from the beginnings to 1964 – and indeed, shifting from history to prophecy, even beyond. This I know because my own paper for the Shakespeare Conference held in Stratford-upon-Avon in 1964 was entitled 'Shakespeare's Text – Then, Now and Tomorrow.' Accordingly I then said a few words about Shakespearian textual scholarship between 1623 and the beginning of the twentieth century, and I proceeded (with the invaluable aid of the late F.P. Wilson's splendid essay called 'Shakespeare and the New Bibliography') to a somewhat fuller account of the great period in the earlier part of the century in which Pollard, McKerrow, and Greg – to mention the giants only – so revolutionized the investigation of Elizabethan dramatic documents and so clearly redefined the editorial problem in Shakespeare. I also suggested that what might be called the New*er* Bibliography was ushered in by the publication of Dr Alice Walker's *Textual Problems in the First Folio* in 1953, and I tried to describe the differences in emphasis that seemed to distinguish the New*er* from the merely New, differences that became increasingly apparent in the decade just prior to 1964 – above all an interest in how Shakespeare's text was treated by its first printers. Finally, having thus done my duty as historian, I felt free to consider the present and the future, which I proceeded happily to do – happily, though as Professor McKenzie has since pointed out,[1] perhaps less wisely than I might have.

Delivered earlier in 1964 than my own was a lecture similarly titled but otherwise very different, and by a far more authoritative voice. I mean Professor Bowers' paper entitled 'Today's Shakespeare Texts, and Tomorrow's,'[2] in which are set forth both the editorial accomplishments of the past and what Shakespearian textual scholarship needs to provide in the future.

So there seems ample warrant for taking the quatercentenary year as my point of departure today. And perhaps I can most easily proceed from ante to post 1964 by mentioning four publications which, though of recent date, are intended not merely to keep alive the memory but to make once again accessible some of the works of such worthy friends and fellows as were our great predecessors. Let me notice first, because representing the hero of the New Bibliography, as F.P. Wilson rightly called him, *The Collected Papers of Sir Walter Greg* edited by Professor J.C. Maxwell and published by the Clarendon Press in 1966. Then in 1967 the Cambridge Press reissued as a single volume both A.W. Pollard's *Shakespeare's Fight with the Pirates* (1920) and the collection of important essays which Pollard edited as *Shakespeare's Hand in the Play of Sir Thomas More* (1923). Next, reprinted in 1969 after being out of print for over twenty years, was McKerrow's *Prolegomena for the Oxford Shakespeare* – for an old-spelling Shakespeare, that is, and thus what Professor Bowers considers one of our most urgent future needs. And finally came F.P. Wilson's tribute to these same men; for only last year the Clarendon Press published, in a separate little volume, *Shakespeare and the New Bibliography*, revised and updated by the expert hand of Dame Helen Gardner.

Very soon after the quatercentenary appeared two entirely new works which may be described as Shakespearian textual studies, though one of them is by no means exclusively so. I am referring to E.A.J. Honigmann's book, *The Stability of Shakespeare's Text* and J.M. Nosworthy's *Shakespeare's Occasional Plays*, both published in 1965. Both deal to some extent with textual alterations, and with alterations for which Shakespeare is supposed responsible, but they are otherwise very different indeed. Mr Nosworthy is concerned with a considerable variety of problems, including important textual ones, connected with four plays – *Macbeth, Troilus, The Merry Wives*, and *Hamlet* – plays which are held to be exceptional in that originally they were 'designed for presentation before particular audiences on particular occasions' – and three of them subsequently revised, by Shakespeare, the better to suit the needs of the popular theatre. Professor Honigmann, although he also has a good deal to say about *Troilus*, and about other individual plays, is mainly concerned with them as illustrations of a general principle – and with Shakespearian revision of another kind altogether. Let me explain.

It came to be one of the tenets of the New Bibliography as exemplified by Greg that the authoritative early editions of the plays were based upon either 1 / the author's 'foul papers' – i.e., his last draft of the play in question, and in the main 'foul' only from a prompter's point of view, because of irregularities in stage directions and speech prefixes; or 2 / the scribal transcript of these papers, after they had been so edited as to suit the prompter's purposes, which served in the theatre as the 'book' by which performances were governed; or 3 / a transcript of foul papers or book, or a printed text that had been corrected by one or the other (as for instance Folio *Hamlet* is supposed based upon a copy of Q2 as corrected by the prompt book). Greg was not happy with any view which postulated, as he wrote in 1955, 'a class of manuscripts for whose existence we have no external evidence whatever.' Hence he rejected Dr Walker's 1953 suggestion, since subscribed to by Bowers and others, that the peculiarities exhibited by certain texts, such as the Quarto and Folio versions of *2 Henry IV*, can best be accounted for by supposing a scribal transcript intermediate between foul papers and prompt book. Nor could he believe that Shakespeare – save perhaps, on rare occasions – himself made fair copies of his foul papers. But this is precisely what Professor Honigmann proposes as perhaps at least tolerably common: not just one holograph, the foul papers, our best authority for the text as Shakespeare was content to leave it, but sometimes dual 'arch-texts'; for what 'I envisage,' writes Professor Honigmann, is 'two copies of a play, each in the author's hand, disagreeing in both substantive and indifferent readings' (p.2). 'Rejecting the notion of a finalized text' in the foul papers, he pictures 'an author so unconceited with himself and so fluent that little verbal changes, not necessarily for the better, ran quite freely from his pen when the process of copying refired his mind' (p.3). After adducing various arguments in support of his position, including an analysis of some of the Quarto/Folio variants in *Troilus, Othello*, and *King Lear*, Professor Honigmann comes in due course to a consideration of the editorial policy – an eclectic one – which he believes we should adopt 'when dealing with plays probably resting on two arch-texts' (p.170). What he has especially in mind, of course, is that handful of plays – *Richard III* and *Hamlet* as well as the three just named – for which we have Q and F versions of at least roughly equal authority, and about which there continues to be much disagreement.

Of these two 1965 books Mr Nosworthy's may seem to many readers the better organized, the more expert in marshalling and presenting evidence, and generally the more attractively written – a thoroughly competent performance even if some or all of its conclusions are found unacceptable save as interesting speculations. To be sure it may be said that Professor Honigmann's conclusions are also speculative, that the changes he invites us to regard as Shakespeare's are often of just the kind that either a scribe or a compositor might also make. But what I wish above all to notice now is that *The Stability of Shakespeare's Text* not only deals with a big and most troubling textual problem but does so in a pretty revolutionary way, for it calls into question some of the most fundamental tenets of the Shakespearian textual study of the past forty years. It asks for a radical modification of, if not a downright revolt against, the New Bibliography as represented by Greg with respect to the nature of the copy behind the substantive editions of a number of Shakespeare's greatest plays; and it also voices a strong protest against the Newer Bibliography, especially as represented by Dr Alice Walker, with her emphasis on compositorial error as a significant factor in textual transmission – about which I shall have something more to say presently. Moreover, since he argues that Shakespeare's practices are likely to be analogous to those of certain later poets – for instance Burns and Shelley and Keats – of whose works both rough drafts and variant fair copies survive, Professor Honigmann may be described as in some measure a deductive reasoner. Which brings us to Professor McKenzie.

For Shakespearian textual bibliographers the most important work of recent years is unquestionably, in my opinion, Professor D.F. McKenzie's critical survey of the conclusions which those bibliographers have lately been reaching, in the absence of such printing-house records as the eighteenth century provides, by inductive means. His long essay, 'Printers of the Mind: Some Notes on Bibliographical Theories and Printing-House Practices,' is both a lively appreciation of useful work done and a devastating attack on the generalizations this work has prompted us to make or to accept. It is based largely upon his own monumental study, *The Cambridge University Press, 1696–1712*, published by Cambridge in two volumes in 1966, or rather upon this and upon some supporting documents from later in the eighteenth century. Those of us to whom his strictures apply may be tempted to take up a defensive posture and insist that McKenzie's evidence comes from a time some century and more later than ours, and that much of it applies rather to an academic establishment concerned with the careful reproduction of works of scholarship than to the commercial presses of London which printed such merely popular literature as Shakespeare's plays. And perhaps there is something in this – something: not much, but a little, and above all in just those areas of discourse which are of greatest interest to Shakespearians. For questions of edition size and of composition and presswork speeds, matters to which 'Printers of the Mind' gives a good deal of attention, are not ordinarily of much immediate importance to editors of the plays; but whether the substantive print of a given play was set seriatim or by formes is, and so is the question of how much real care the printers of the First Folio and of the substantive quartos took to insure the accuracy of Elizabethan play texts (and hence to what extent we are indeed dependent upon compositors for such reliability as these texts may have). Let me therefore make the two following observations. First, I was certainly wrong if, in the final paragraph of my introductory chapter for *The Printing and Proof-Reading of the First Folio* – trying, I suppose, to puff the importance of what was to come – I encouraged the inference that the methods that produced the Folio are likely to have been followed in producing all, or even many, other books. Yet I think it has now been shown beyond the possibility of reasonable doubt, as I believe Professor McKenzie allows, that at any rate the First Folio was set throughout by formes; and that, for whatever reason this method of working may have been adopted, it rendered Shakespeare's text liable to certain specific kinds of error. Second, I wonder if deductive reasoning really obliges us to think that the texts in the First Folio – or indeed that Elizabethan play texts generally – were normally subjected to what Professor McKenzie describes as the three (at least) traditional stages of proof-correction, and that the press variants now known represent but the last and least important stage? McKerrow pointed out in 1931 that printed texts of Elizabethan plays characteristically show many more errors than most other texts of the time. Is this *only* because some of them were set from foul papers? Or were plays perhaps simply not proofed with such care as books of heraldry, say? There is at least some room for doubt, I should think – even though we acknowledge, as I believe we must, that it is quite wrong to suggest that the proof-correction methods described by Moxon in the 1680s have no relevance whatever for the 1620s.

We must acknowledge, in short, that in at least most of what he says in 'Printers of the Mind' McKenzie is absolutely right. It simply will not do to shrug off his criticism as based on evidence from a different time and from a different kind of printing-house. He is well aware of these differences; and he is also well versed in the bibliographical scholarship of our Elizabethan period, and above all – for these are his principal targets – with the generalizations we have been promulgating during the last fifteen years or so. And we have indeed been guilty of unwarranted statements about what normal Elizabethan practice was. Moreover, and making this plain seems to me one of the greatest values of the corrective we have so fortunately been given, some of us have been much less demanding about what we accept as probative evidence – of setting by formes in quarto printing, for instance – than we should have been. To be more rigorous is certainly one of our future needs, then; and, for the present, although of course I cannot speak for Professor Bowers or for Professor Todd (also taken to task in 'Printers of the Mind'), I am myself only too happy to subscribe to the principle of concurrent printing as *normal* procedure in the Elizabethan period as later, and, in fact, gratefully to kiss the rod which Professor McKenzie has been willing not to spare – even though, before I have fiinished, it may seem that I have not yet taken my lesson sufficiently to heart. For I now come to the second part of this report, where I hope, after speaking of certain other accomplishments of the last seven years, to say something about another future need – and the need, if you please, to emend Shakespeare.

We have so far been considering theory rather than practice; yet the final product of textual scholarship is not the treatise on printing but the edited text. When in 1964 Professor Bowers spoke of 'Today's Shakespeare Texts, and Tomorrow's' he began with remarks about the Old Cambridge editors and their Globe text of 1864 which 'in substance,' he declared, 'has remained the only complete text worth mentioning formed from a systematic re-examination of the textual situation, save in a limited sense for the New Cambridge [i.e., the Dover Wilson] edition ... the final volumes of which are only now appearing with the assistance of other editors.'[3] Later, to be sure, Bowers singled out a number of recent editions that are not altogether without merit, though none of these is wholly satisfactory either, not even what he calls 'in some respects the best' of the complete editions, that of the late Peter Alexander, published in 1951. He also recognized the exceptional merits of Dover Wilson's *Hamlet*, but he pointed out that the best of the other multi-volume editions (probably the Pelican) is uneven, because executed by persons of widely different qualifications. This is especially true of the New Arden, though it is acknowledged to have 'a few examples of the very best in modern editing' (p.49). Editing, that is, which produces, like the Globe and practically all the rest, whether in one volume or many, a modernized text. For most of the latter part of the Bowers lecture is devoted to our need for old-spelling editions – for a kind of interim or 'transition' one now, or at any rate as soon tomorrow as practicable, and then a 'definitive' one – 'in the twenty-first century.'

With much of what is said here, and especially with what is said to the prejudice of modernized texts, I feel bound to disagree. Perhaps it is true that old spelling, whether Shakespeare's or merely a compositor's, 'will reveal fresh nuances, associations [etc.]' that modern-spelling editions must inevitably destroy. Perhaps. And possibly the punctuation found in the substantive authorities really has, for any properly trained reader of today, all the virtues claimed for it. Perhaps. But doubts arise – particularly when Professor Bowers himself tells us that 'no one is so foolish any more as to argue that punctuation – now demonstrated to be mainly compositorial – is Shakespeare's own or that it represents in any way the authority of the playhouse' (p.65). Of course I do not mean that there should be no editions of Shakespeare except modernized ones; however, with all the respect I owe and feel toward my teacher and my much-admired friend Mr Bowers, let me say that an old-spelling edition will not *ipso facto* be good, nor a modernized one necessarily bad: unscholarly, without apparatus to inform the realer about choices the editor has made, and perhaps even those he might have but did not. I do not believe that we edit Shakespeare for the benefit of the 'linguist and lexicographer' mentioned by Professor Bowers (p.55), who, I should think, will wish to work rather from the primary documents, or from good facsimiles of them, than from edited texts anyhow. I am very sceptical of the 'new and definitive norm' which, we are told, an old-spelling edition might establish and on which all merely popular modernized editions might thenceforth be based (p.57). Nor am I sure that we are likely, even in the twenty-first century, to be provided with what the twenty-second will be content to regard as a truly *definitive* edition, 'the final and authoritative form of Shakespeare's text, that need never be changed except in minor detail' (p.65).

But perhaps I digress. I cited the Bowers lecture in the first instance because it gives me an opportunity to observe, and still under the heading of what has recently been accomplished, that although the New Arden Shakespeare is still in progress, Dover Wilson and Professor Maxwell completed the New [Cambridge] edition in 1966, the multi-volume Pelican was finished in 1967, and in 1969 the revised Pelican texts, still under the General Editorship of Professor Harbage, were published in a single volume. This is the first one-volume Shakespeare we have had in a long time, and I believe it is being well received; but Houghton-Mifflin is soon to publish another, for which G. Blakemore Evans prepared the text – a modernized text but certain to be a scholarly one none the less – and one hears that still others are a-making. Meanwhile a new multi-volume paperback series, the New Penguin Shakespeare, with Professor T.J.B. Spencer as General Editor, is in progress. This is a kind of British analogue to Professor Harbage's Pelicans; but it is also like the New Ardens, for the notes and the textual apparatus are generally – as for instance in Professor Honigmann's New Pelican *Richard III* – more extensive than in most of the American Pelicans. Finally, it can be reported that the New Variorum Shakespeare has recently taken a new lease on life. The principles according to which plays are now being edited are set forth in detail in a *Shakespeare Variorum Handbook/A Manual of Editorial Practice*,[4] completed only this summer. And nearly ready for publication are not only several plays that have never hitherto appeared in the New Variorum series but also thoroughgoing revisions of a number of others. All will perhaps qualify as members of such a transitional old-spelling edition as Professor Bowers has envisaged for 'tomorrow.' Not definitive, however; for nothing of this kind can be hoped, as the Bowers lecture makes plain, until we have a great deal of information we yet lack, including above all information about individual Elizabethan compositors. Since on this subject I am in complete and enthusiastic agreement with Professor Bowers, let me offer a few particulars about it and so, as Bottom says – 'and so grow to a point.'

Already in print for ten years in 1964 was Dr Walker's study of the relative accuracy of Jaggard's Compositors A and B as shown by the substantive changes each made when setting the Folio version of *1 Henry IV* from the 1613 quarto of that play.[5] What was brought out was that Compositor A's stint of eleven pages showed twelve corrections of Q mistakes (probably right though only guesses) and eighteen new errors, an average of one in approximately 80 lines. Compositor B's fourteen and a half page stint, on the other hand, showed not only some twenty-two corrections but 113 new errors, an average of one every fifteen or sixteen lines set – five times as many as A's. At this rate, if B had set the whole play he would have introduced about 200 substantive errors – errors that affect meaning – into its text.

Significant as these facts must have been thought, relatively few like studies appear to have been made. But some have, and here are the results of two of them. First (a little amplifying of what I reported in 1964), the compositor who set the whole of Q1 of *1 Henry IV* made but a single error in resetting the 296 lines of Q0 that have survived. At this rate he would have made only about ten, as against Jaggard B's 200, in the whole play; whereas Simmes A, the compositor who set the 'good' 1600 quarto of *2 Henry IV*, made nine substantive errors in resetting about 165 lines of this play. This is one error in approximately eighteen lines, a total of about 180 if his work for the whole play was similarly inaccurate; and we find that in resetting all 2796 lines of the second quarto of *Richard II* (1598) from the first (1597), he made 155 substantive errors – or, once more, precisely as in the smaller sample from *2 Henry IV*, one such error in each eighteen lines set. Of these 155 errors, to be sure, only a handful are immediately recognizable as errors, for Simmes A (who also set the whole of the 'good' first quarto of *Much Ado* and most or all of a number of other play texts of great importance to editors) seldom made mistakes of this kind; yet he evidently had a very poor ear, since his errors often produced metrical irregularity even though not obviously misrepresenting the sense of his copy.[6]

My second offering is only a tidbit, but one of the two workmen it concerns is Jaggard C, about whose quality we should certainly welcome fuller information. Just under twelve pages of Folio *King John* were set by the notorious Compositor B, and they show at least twenty readings that may be regarded as obvious compositorial mistakes; but the rest of the play, just under ten Folio pages, which were set by C, show about the same number of such mistakes and hence a slightly higher incidence of error than B's more numerous pages. Now it is only conjectural, as far as I am aware, whether an Elizabethan compositor was likely to make fewer or more numerous errors when setting from manuscript than from printed copy – except that only manuscript copy can well be thought to produce graphic errors, misreadings. No doubt much depended upon the difficulty of the manuscript, or on how much if at all the printed copy had been edited; and no doubt different compositors showed widely different degrees of accuracy, even when setting from the same manuscript. Yet it seems reasonable to suppose, until we know better, that Jaggard's compositors were not greatly *more* accurate in setting from Shakespeare's foul papers for *King John*, say, than from printed Q5 of *1 Henry IV*; and also to suppose that the man who made x errors when setting one of these plays probably made something like the same number when setting the other, appropriate allowances having been made for the differences of the two plays in length. On the basis of these suppositions, then, Compositor B's stint for *King John* probably contained roughly 90 errors (though only about a quarter of them manifestly errors) and Compositor C's stint about as many more – a total of approximately 180 for the play.

These facts, I suggest, are striking partly because they show such wide differences in reliability between various compositors but above all because they show so high an incidence of error in the work done by men who had large shares in setting the authoritative texts of Shakespeare's plays. Simmes A set the whole of two of the 'good' quartos upon which all editors now base their texts. About Jaggard C we still know practically nothing, not even how large a share he had in setting the First Folio (though A.S. Cairncross has recently presented evidence that he had a much larger share than hitherto recognized) ;[7] but B set more of the Folio than all Jaggard's other compositors put together; more than half the volume represents his work.

However much or little trouble the Jaggards and other Elizabethan printers in fact took to insure the accuracy of play texts, however much or little these texts were proof-corrected, they yet do show the multitudes of compositorial errors we have been noticing. Or at least most of the reprints, of those that can be tested, do; and who can suppose that most of those set from manuscript copy were very much more carefully produced and far more accurate? How can it reasonably be doubted that compositors played an important part in the transmission of Shakespeare's text? An important part, even though we cannot yet say precisely how important. For it is abundantly plain that we need to know a great deal more than we now know about the various individuals who put the substantive editions of Shakespeare into type. We must first identify as precisely as possible (probably with computer aid) what each of them set, then learn everything we can about the quality of their work. These are not goals we are likely to reach overnight, perhaps not even before the twenty-first century. So what should editors do meanwhile? Texts of Shakespeare will continue to be in demand, and new editions will continue to appear. But editors ought not any longer, it seems to me, to proceed as if compositors, all alike, were almost always faithful to their copy, and as if presuming to correct compositorial errors were the most heinous of the deadly sins. I am calling, in short, for more emendations. I am suggesting that one of our present and future needs is for editorial practice which makes use – albeit tasteful and judicious use – of what we have been finding out during the past fifteen years or so about the treatment Shakespeare's text received in the Elizabethan printing house.

Please do not misunderstand. I am certainly not recommending irresponsible emendation. I too was brought up on the doctrine that the primary task of the editor of the twentieth century is to repair the damage done by the all-too-freely emending editors of the eighteenth. I too have been taught and still believe that the emendation of Shakespeare must observe certain rules. There should be good reason for thinking that the reading to be emended is indeed corrupt; the emender should be able to explain – not always, perhaps, but usually – how the corruption came about; and the emendation should be, as Greg put it long ago (in 'Principles of Emendation in Shakespeare,' the British Academy Shakespeare Lecture for 1928), 'one that strikes a trained intelligence as supplying exactly the sense required by the context.' These conditions, if rigorously applied, are not easy to satisfy. But in my opinion they can be satisfied far more often than they have been by most recent editors – and mainly, I think, because these editors do not sufficiently take into account the numbers and kinds of errors to which certain individual compositors were demonstrably prone. For example:

1/In Folio *King John* 269 (Globe i.i.256) Lady Faulconbridge, addressing her bastard son, confesses that she was false to wedlock when he was conceived and exclaims:

Heaven lay not my transgression to my charge

– in which the second 'my' makes very poor sense at best:

Heaven lay not my transgression to *my* charge.

The hope that her son will not suffer from her offence seems what the context requires, and the presence of 'my' in the preceding line, also earlier in this same line, and also in each of the next two lines of the speech might well have been responsible for its appearance in place of 'thy' here. Compositor B set this passage, and he makes many such errors. Surely we should read

Heaven lay not my transgression to *thy* charge

as Dover Wilson does, but as neither the New Arden nor the Pelican does – nor apparently (to judge by the new Spevack Concordance which is based on it) does the forthcoming Houghton-Mifflin text either.

2/In the *Much Ado* 'good' quarto of 1600, at line 1072 (II.iii.259) Beatrice responds to a 'thank you' from Benedick by remarking that 'I took no more pains for those thanks than you take pains to thank me.' She leaves almost at once and Benedick in lines 1080-2 (II.iii. 268-9) musingly repeats what she has said: 'Ha! ... "I took no more pains for those thanks than you *took* pains to thank me." ' As Benedick is here quoting Beatrice he should have ended as she did, '... than you *take* pains to thank me.' In short, the context actually vouches for the proposed emendation, and that the speech begins 'I *took* no more pains' seems a sufficient explanation of the appearance of 'took' again, instead of 'take' at the end; for Simmes A, who set this quarto, was much given to just such small verbal errors. But again no one emends.

3/In the 'good' 1597 quarto of *Richard II*, at line 2385 (v.ii.18) we find:

Whilst he from the one side to the other turning

– an irregular line in one of the most regular of plays. But again it was set by Simmes A, who frequently produced irregularity, though not nonsense, by just such a monosyllabic interpolation as the first of the line's two 'the's here seems to represent. Nor is it hard to understand, since the 'the' before 'one' both anticipates and balances the 'the' before 'other': '*the* one to *the* other.' In this instance, it is true, one cannot declare that the quarto line is certainly corrupt, hence that any change is really required, though anyone familiar with the work of Simmes A can be pardoned for thinking that he is far more likely than Shakespeare to be responsible for the metrical peculiarity of the line in question; and the future editor who omitted the first 'the' and read:

Whilst he from one side to the other turning

could hardly, with justice, be too severely condemned. For it is not the function of an editor of Shakespeare simply to retain every reading in his copy text which can conceivably be regarded as acceptable – and so to preserve as Shakespeare's all but the most obvious and egregious errors of compositors (and sometimes of scribes and perhaps others as well). Neither of course is it his function to emend wantonly, without good cause. But it is his duty to give appropriate consideration to everything that is known about his copy text, including what is known of the peculiarities of the individual workmen who set it into type. And whenever the best knowledge and taste and judgment he can bring to his task tell him that the text before him is corrupt, and that the compositor who set it is one who often corrupts his copy in the same way, and when he also believes that he can restore what Shakespeare actually wrote, then it is his positive responsibility to do so – to emend – though in all but a few instances he will in fact only be taking into his own text an emendation made long ago by someone else. In any event, however, and whether he is presenting a modernized or an old-spelling text, he will record fully what he has done. Thus both the emendations he originates and those he merely accepts will be available for scrutiny – and for the twenty-first century, in its computer-generated wisdom, to accept or reject as it will.

NOTES

1 'Printers of the Mind' *Studies in Bibliography* 22 (1969) 1–75, to be considered in some detail later in this paper.
2 *Studies in Bibliography* 19 (1966) 39–65
3 Ibid 39
4 (New York 1971)
5 *Studies in Bibliography* 6 (1954) 45–59
6 For this information about Simmes A's performance in setting Q2 of *Richard II* I am indebted both to the unpublished University of Kansas dissertation of Dr Alan Craven and to the typescript of an article by him, forthcoming in *Studies in Bibliography*.
7 A.S. Cairncross *Papers of the Bibliographical Society of America* 65 (1971) 41–52

Fredson Bowers /
Seven or More Years?

In the course of his paper Professor Hinman has started a number of hares, not all of which will give the hounds an equally good run. The hares appear in the first, or survey part. Later, when he puts his emphasis on the need for more compositorial identifications and analyses before we can progress to the New Emendation Era he proposes, I can only give a hearty View Halloo – Lay on Macduff! It is always agreeable to have one's own prejudices confirmed. In this appendix to his paper I shall give only the most summary comment on the hares, speaking in a practical vein from the point of view of a hound. I must grossly oversimplify because space is short though art is long, and because I am deliberately talking in very practical doggy terms.

What, I ask, is the practical effect for the short as well as the long term of the recent trend in textual studies that Professor Hinman has sketched, when we consider it on the narrow and concrete basis of how it will improve future editions of Shakespeare's texts? Not on how it will increase the total sum of human knowledge, with a few spin-offs that will benefit the manufacture of editions in the home. But on how the next editions of Shakespeare will directly benefit in comparison with their predecessors: I might almost say, how will the textual editors of the proposed South Carolina old-spelling edition become bigger and better boys (and girls) in terms of their expertise? To me, the answer is slightly discouraging. The hare with the shortest run is my colleague Don McKenzie but through no fault of his own spryness. That Professor Hinman should even have mentioned his article 'Printers of the Mind' in any direct relation to Shakespeare textual investigations is only one more indication of how much the thrust of this brilliantly controversial article has been misunderstood. Indeed, for our limited purposes here, Professor Hinman has put his finger on the only point that matters. Professor McKenzie's philosophical arguments about the virtues of internal versus external evidence, or the rights and wrongs of inductive versus deductive reasoning, have nothing whatever to do with such established facts as that the printing of the First Folio was by formes – with all that this means for a textual editor. Professor Hinman might have added that they have nothing to do with the solid and demonstrable kind of evidence in commercial quarto printing (as in folio) that buttresses spelling evidence for the identification of a compositor by typographical means, the following of a workman's operations through a book from positively determined type-pieces in his cases and from demonstrably individual typographical peculiarities in the manner of his setting, in the manner of Gerritsen and Howard-Hill, so that we know what parts of a book he set, both when and where. Professor McKenzie usefully warns us against too imaginative extrapolation and interpretation of certain kinds of technical evidence in the arsenal of analytical bibliography. But, if I understand him right, as an historian of printing he does not attack the linchpin of textual criticism, the established methods for compositorial identification and analysis. If at times he might seem to have verged on this perilous act, it was only as a by-blow; when tempted to be a trifle naughty in using the guilt-by-association form of argument, he may have allowed an unwary reader to take it that his examples of faulty scholarship in the employment of certain techniques were intended to reflect upon analytical methods in general, or certain of them – a quite different matter. As Professor Hinman properly points out, the major contribution of modern textual scholarship to the problems of editing is the emphasis upon the identification of compositors and the practical application of what can be determined about their characteristics to the solution of specific textual cruxes, minor as well as major.

Both Professors Honigmann and Nosworthy, whom Hinman has singled out for special mention, are concerned with the copy behind the printed Shakespearian texts, what may be called the pre-printing transmission of these texts. This has always been and will continue to be a highly conjectural form of investigation, as the unprincipled examples of Fleay and of Robertson suggest. Nonetheless, in my opinion it is a matter of considerable and – on special occasions – of crucial importance. Thus I do not wish to be misunderstood when I remark as a practical editor, who is yet no novice in the art of such conjectural reconstruction, that in many cases I am tempted to draw an analogy with Greg's comment on Sisson's paleographical surmises. They were chiefly useful, he said, to support conclusions already arrived at by other means. I speak again as a practical editor who, like Professor Hinman, is concerned with the problem of identifying and then of emending if possible the specific verbal corruptions in a text. It is a hard fact that the standard situation in Shakespeare, and even more in the other Elizabethan play-texts, is the one in which we have but a single substantive text. In this situation, I take it, an editor must chiefly proceed on the accordion principle, the postulate of simplicity, which collapses all intermediaries between the lost holograph and the printed text into one agent. That is, the only concrete evidence we have is the single printed text. All else is speculative and not usually susceptible of specific application to the precise solution of textual cruxes. For example, the compositor may be thought to have set directly from the author's holograph, in which case there is one known intermediary as the source of variation. A compositor may be thought to have set from a scribal transcript of the holograph, in which case there is one known and one unknown intermediary. Any extension only repeats the same situation by adding more and more possible corrupting agents who cannot be identified or evaluated with any precision or confidence. To be severely practical, let us take as an example a problem in the opening lines of *Julius Caesar*. The Cobbler is being quizzed by Marullus. When he comes to his private joke about being a mender of bad soles, it is Flavius in the Folio who suddenly interjects 'What trade, thou knave? Thou naughty knave, what trade?' So far no problem, for Flavius may be presumed to have reached a boiling point about the Cobbler's equivocations and it is a sound dramatic device not to have him standing mute for too long. Nevertheless, when the Cobbler answers what would be Flavius' demand in the Folio with 'Nay I beseech you sir, be not out with me; yet if you be out, sir, I can mend you,' it is, oddly, Marullus who takes the speech as directed to himself and who replies, 'What meanest thou by that? Mend me, thou saucy fellow?' Editors have split pretty evenly on the speech assignment of 'What trade, thou knave?' There is the concrete evidence of the speech-prefix in the Folio that Flavius intervened; yet to this intervention the Cobbler, on the evidence of Marullus' answer, speaks directly to Marullus as if it were he who had made the angry question, not Flavius. In his recent old-spelling edition of the play for the Shakespeare Workshop (London 1970), Peter Thomson retains the Folio assignment on the argument that it is a perfectly viable piece of theatrical byplay. But the theatrical argument is double-edged, for something can be said for the superior authority given Flavius when he later does enter the dialogue – and which continues – if it were indeed Marullus who addressed the Cobbler. The precise question is, whether the Folio is correct and Marullus' reply an anomaly that must be rationalized, or whether an error has somehow occurred in the speech assignment and Flavius should delay his first address to the Cobbler until Marullus has reached a dead end. An editor cannot palter. He must follow the Folio, or on his own responsibility assign the question to Marullus. Now obviously it would be useful to have some evidence as to how the error occurred if an editor – as I do at the moment – proposes to emend. If the Folio had been set from holograph foul papers or authorial fair copy (we could scarcely distinguish in any useful manner), Compositor B would be to blame. If the copy derived from the promptbook (as is commonly believed) or from some intermediate pre-promptbook scribal transcript (as I take it to be), another agent could have been the villain, someone (whether or not associated with the company) who thought it would be a good idea not to let Flavius be silent too long. Nevertheless, even if the scribal copy had read *Marullus*, Compositor B could still have thought this to be an error and set *Flavius* instead. As an editor concerned with what reading I must print, I confess I am so uncertain about the source of the error that it makes no real difference to me in this instance whether the play was set from holograph or from scribal copy. If I vouched the promptbook or scribal transcript theory as an explanation, I should be deceiving my reader by tendering him a plausible reason that actually had nothing behind it that could properly be called evidence, only speculation that is readily susceptible of quite a different answer. It seems to me that without a whole complex of other evidence from the text that I am not sure is there, or that is applicable to the specific case of assignment, we are back at the postulate of simplicity. Otherwise one's only recourse is not to appeal to theories of copy but instead to follow Professor Hinman's hard-nosed recommendations and make a special study of Compositor B's practices in relation to the assignment of speeches. This might or might not offer some evidence that could carry any weight in sorting out the responsibility. But is there time for each emendation to be made the occasion for a special compositorial study by the editor himself, or should we recognize that in the distant future such information will have been digested for editorial benefit in what we hope will be the final established text, one that will not only offer convincing emendations but make them more convincing by the presentation of evidence that tends, at least, to a more precise explanation for the occurrence of each error than is now possible (a state of beatitude that I fear will never come to pass). Indeed, would anyone who was editing this play, in the present state of our knowledge, allow what had been found about Compositor B to influence him for or against the emendation? In this particular case would we not, *teste* Greg, be merely rationalizing an editorial decision already taken on what is assumed to be the sense? I particularly ask – regardless of the evidence that may or may not be available about Compositor B – whether any editor would allow the hypothesis about theatrical copy to sway him in a decisive manner to make this emendation if he would not make it if the copy were supposed to have been foul papers? I know I am arguing *ad hominem* and there are several holes in my reasoning; but do not let this simplification affect an estimate of my point that questions of copy are often not the prime consideration affecting a specific emendation. There are too many intangibles. If one must make a choice I should unhesitatingly plump for compositorial evidence as a conjectural reason I hoped would sway men's minds. Yet even so, we should be far outside the field of demonstration. In fact, in most cases of emendation no demonstration in the true sense of the word is possible. The only appeal is to the consensus of enlightened opinion. That this may shift does not disturb me. I am, of course, in part attacking the false confidence that so-called 'explanations' of error can give us, although focussing it in this particular case on hypotheses of copy as the basis for editorial decision. Speculative theories of copy as the immediate justification for emendations can rapidly fall into glib rationalization, a confidence game, as on a few, rare, occasions some of Dover Wilson's rationalizations have shown us when the rigour of what may properly be called evidence was relaxed and fancy substituted.

When we deal with a text as a whole and not with an editor struggling with one specific reading, I am far from suggesting that it is not generally useful to come to some conclusions about the copy of single-text plays. It is quite true that if a text were set from holograph, the errors are more likely to be naïve and to be the results of misreading combined with misinterpretation of the sense. The degree of sophistication should be less than if the departures from copy of one or more scribes must be added to those of the compositor. I do not underestimate what I call the climate of opinion within which an editor approaches the details of his text: this 'feeling' certainly has some influence on the semi-instinctive boldness or caution with which he engages himself to emendation. But when the chips are down, an edited text is only a series of coherent individual and specific decisions. If corruption is present, the source is usually undeterminable by any standards of rigorous evidence, and the explanation is correspondingly a rationalization. Does an error appear to be a misreading of handwriting? After all, a scribe can misread a hand as readily as a compositor, and memorial errors often resemble misreadings. Theoretically, questions of copy might enter in a single-text play when corruptions of a kind not usually associated with the compositor start popping up – that is, if one knows enough about the compositor to be able to isolate such variants – a tricky business indeed. We keep coming back to our knowledge of the compositor, and, if we are wise, not only to the incidence of error to be expected from him but also to the kinds of error, the qualitative standard that it is so important to apply. Statistics I have read about compositors usually obscure the true issue by failing to distinguish typos from manipulation of the sense. The real incidence of error drops markedly, on occasion, when mechanical error of little concern to an editor is removed from these statistics. The transposition of two letters in a word has nothing to do with whether that word has been set with fidelity – as the word intended.

In short, and grossly to oversimplify, we have built up this question of copy to inflated proportions for single-text plays except for the climate of opinion, which I should be the last person in the world to ignore as a powerful even though often vague and subconscious determinant on editorial decision.

On the other hand, when we have two texts of some substantive pretensions, it is obvious that no editor can move a muscle until the relation of these texts (which is to say, their copy) has been determined. Nevertheless, how common is this situation in Shakespeare? If for the moment we put aside the question of bad quartos, the answer is that it is quite uncommon. I am not a slave to the bad-quarto hypothesis and I think we have ridden this horse too hard in trying to explain all memorial texts according to the same set of conditions. Without altogether knowing why, I am prepared to admit that the cases of *Hamlet* and of *The Merry Wives* differ markedly from the cases of *King Lear* and, say, *Richard III*. But an editor must know where he stands. If he is to apply the same editorial criteria to the quarto text of *Richard III* that he does to the quarto text of *Othello*, or of *Troilus*, then I think he is in for serious trouble. In this connection I urge a clearsighted analysis of these double texts in order to divide the sheep from the goats and editorially to treat the sheep as sheep and the goats as goats, and not as some strange mythological combination like a specially invented Elizabethan satyr. I speak feelingly because I have just emerged from grappling with the problem of *Doctor Faustus*. Bad quartos have their own special difficulties which can be isolated and dealt with on the basis of their unique status and the special problems that arise therefrom, not only in themselves and their constitution but often in their physical relationship to the printed good text. An editor must face the questions of largely individual or of communal memorial reconstruction; he must come to grips with hypotheses for annotated copy when the bad influenced the good text in the printing, or of conflation in the course of typesetting in the printer's shop, as I suspect happened with the first act of *Hamlet*, perhaps with *Henry V*, and almost certainly with Marlowe's *Elegies*. Textual decision after decision involving specific authority will depend upon the over-all hypothesis of the formation and the transmission of the copy up to the point when a printed edition of the good text was put on sale. But these decisions are quite different in their nature and import from those involved with *Troilus* and with *Othello* and even with the simpler case of *2 Henry IV*. If what have generally been thought of as bad quartos are indeed good texts, then the case must be argued play by play on those grounds, and not in Shakespearian isolation but with wide reference to the body of non-Shakespearian bad quartos. Their status must be determined in a manner that will win common consent before anything but confusion can result from treating *King Lear* and *Richard III* as texts having two substantive forms like *Othello* and *Troilus*.

I am in no position to defend Greg's postulate of simplicity in respect to the copy behind the Shakespeare texts, play by play. But I do suggest that Professor Hinman is in some error when he associates Professor Honigmann's theories with Greg's methodology. As I understand it, Greg's main concern was to pin down single texts, or the single units (or plays with two substantive texts), to the simple proposition of holograph or scribal transcript. He was the enemy only of 'intermediate transcripts' in the narrow sense that he did not find external evidence for the existence of scribal copies that were made from foul papers in anticipation of the promptbook, and were not used as the promptbook itself. I believe I can come close to demonstrating such an intermediate transcript partly marked for prompt as the copy for the Folio *Julius Caesar*. This position has nothing to do with a revising author and with *Othello*. (Incidentally, Professor Hinman has what I consider to be an eccentric definition of foul papers.)

I write on vacation and away from my books, but for better or worse my memory tells me that Professor Hinman should not isolate Greg's personal theories, which are greatly involved with all his logical and sometimes narrow prejudices, and treat them as if they constitute a whole methodology or school of textual bibliography which can be usefully contrasted as different in kind from Dr Walker's simple extension by change in emphasis, important as it certainly was. Especially I should object to any suggestion of a continuum from Greg and Walker to the major shift found in Professor Honigmann's conjectural attempts to deal with the pre-printing history of certain Shakespearian texts. If I understand him, Professor Honigmann, in treating plays like *Othello* and *Troilus*, is relatively conventional in his views. Again if I understand him, it is when he begins to deodorize what have been assumed to be bad quartos that he strikes out into new areas of speculation which should be examined on that narrow basis alone before our ears are open to arguments about revisions in their pre-printing history. I grant that the possibility always exists that a bad-quarto text can represent an early state of a later revised text, and *The Merry Wives of Windsor* and certainly *Doctor Faustus* offer some grounds for such speculation. But I think we must insist that the evidence for investigating revision between the Quarto and Folio *Merry Wives* is of a very different order indeed from that available to us for *Troilus*. I am diffident about confusing the case of *King Lear* with that of *Othello* unless one is also prepared to assert that the quarto text of *Othello* may also have its memorial features – a difficult proposition to maintain.

I have had no opportunity to deal properly with many of the points raised by Professor Hinman. In closing I want to emphasize my wholehearted agreement with Professor Hinman's main argument in the second half of his paper. There are two quite distinct aspects of the question of the copy for play-texts. One that is accurately described as the pre-printing history must necessarily deal with the nature of the manuscripts, and their derivation from the author – whether in single or separate holographs – for the relatively few Shakespearian plays that have true double texts and do not consist of a bad quarto and a good text. This is a legitimate and vital field of enquiry, for no editor can deal with any specific variant in *Othello* or in *Troilus* until, to his own satisfaction, he has come to some conclusions about the compositional relationship of the two texts as a whole. But Shakespearian textual criticism cannot be concentrated exclusively on the peculiar problems of this limited class of plays, and even with them the question of the printer's copy, whether independent manuscripts or annotated quartos, is also of significance, and the traits of the compositors can never be overlooked. These are questions that are involved in the printing-stage. Thus, from the practical point of view of what seems to me to be of the most pressing importance, I come down as heavily as I can on the side of Professor Hinman in his plea for more searching compositorial analyses so that as editors we can enjoy the benefit of what they have to teach us. On some occasions such analyses can be applied to questions of copy. For example, it seems to me inconceivable, now that we know that the same two Roberts' compositors set *The Merchant of Venice* as well as Q2 *Hamlet*, that anyone could fancy both manuscripts were holograph as was generally assumed before the era of compositor analysis. But this analysis can be a working instrument on quite another plane, as Professor Hinman has pointed out. What we can determine from many more test cases than have as yet been explored – in fact scholars have been singularly deficient in taking up this new line of investigation – is in measurable manner the application to the day-by-day specific emendation of Shakespeare's texts on new evidence, both quantitative and qualitative, of the characteristics of identified compositors. Professor Hinman's proposals in emendation do not shock me so long as they are grounded on evidence, not fancy.

This is the real practical hope for the future of Shakespearian editing and it is indeed a shameful situation that we have so few tools to our hands, although the methodology has been recognized for some years. If we are to put our major emphasis on these studies, our successors will bless us when the time comes to think in really serious terms about what can properly be called the final establishment of Shakespeare's text both in modernized and in old-spelling form – because these two do differ materially in their requirements. I wish I had some time to discuss the establishment of these texts, for my views differ somewhat from those of Professor Hinman about what we should mean by that perhaps imaginative word – establishment. But for present purposes it seems to me that enough is enough. I hold my peace.

Jonas A. Barish /
Continuities and Discontinuities in
Shakespearian Prose

Thirty years ago an unassuming article by Henry W. Wells entitled
'The Continuity of Shaksperian Prose'[1] set forth some general observations on its subject which seem to me to have held up surprisingly
well. Wells was concerned with the prose style and its evolution, and
its relations to the verse. His main thesis – that Shakespeare's prose
matured early, but then changed relatively little over the course of
the career, and that such change as can be perceived consists mainly
in a widening of range, in the use of prose for increasingly serious
and powerful effects – seems nearly unarguable to me, but Wells
illustrated his thesis so perversely, with so many infelicitous terms
and so many queer examples, that one might have been mistakenly
prompted to dismiss the whole proposition. My aim in the next few
pages will be even more modest than Wells': to annotate a portion
of his argument, particularizing it, correcting it where necessary, in
order, I hope, to arrive at a somewhat sharper and more focussed
version of it.[2]

According to Wells, one can, if one is bent on charting a changing
course, roughly distinguish three phases in Shakespeare's prose style,
corresponding to the familiar division of the canon into early, middle,
and late. Wells labels the three phases the euphuistic, the poetic, and
the baroque, and with these labels we run into immediate trouble,
since they do not form a coherent set of categories. One is a literary
stylistic term, based on specific rhetorical and grammatical features,
one a vague epithet of approval that has in the past meant all things

to all men, and one a concept loosely borrowed from art history, trailing with it a good many emotional overtones (most of them pejorative in Wells' day). Wells makes nearly no attempt to define his terms, and, worse, he applies them so as to create a muddle. After illustrating them from the three epochs of the career, he proceeds to argue the more fundamental unity of the prose by pointing out that 'the euphuistic, or bookish style based on parallelisms, occasionally occurs in both Shakspere's later periods, the baroque tendency, based on subtler elaborations, in both his earlier ones, and a poetic prose sporadically in all three' (p.176). Now, to define the 'euphuistic' with such off-hand haste as 'a bookish style based on parallelisms' may possibly pass muster, but to go on, as Wells does, to illustrate it by citing Falstaff's tavern play-acting as King Henry IV, is wantonly to promote confusion, since the passage in question consciously parodies the euphuistic style. One cannot cite, as evidence of an author's habitual recourse to a certain way of writing, a moment in which he is, with deliberate exaggeration, holding that way up to ridicule. Nor can one, to exemplify 'the baroque, based on subtler elaborations,' instance such other moments of highly calculated and exceedingly *un*subtle caricature as Armado's letter to the King of Navarre, or Hamlet's derisive mimicry of Osric. If these passages fairly represented Shakespeare's use of the styles in question, one would be justified in concluding that he was rejecting them utterly, which is not Wells' point at all. Lastly, as instances of 'poetic' prose before and after the central period, Wells offers Shylock's ravings over his lost ducats and Volumnia's gloating over her little grandson's ferocious ways with butterflies, going so far as to declare Shylock's prose 'more deeply poetic' than the 'gorgeous verse-rhetoric' of the same play (p.178). But this is to blur categories unmercifully, to abandon all pretence at objective criteria, and to pitch us into a nebulous impressionism. Wells discards the only sane method of distinguishing prose from poetry – metre – and then supplies no clue as to why he has singled out some prose passages rather than others for the accolade 'poetic.' One assumes it is for their vitality and expressive energy, but these qualities they share with three-quarters of all Shakespearian prose and verse.

Still, as I have said, his main contentions seem sound, that from the start the prose shows an assurance and a competence that the verse only gradually acquires, but that it thereafter evolves very little compared to the verse. In an earlier discussion, George Rylands had suggested that Shakespearian verse reaches maturity by gradually incorporating the effects of the prose – its colloquialism, rhythmic flexibility, and 'natural' word order. In the later verse, observes Rylands, the rhythms become more and more resolved, asyndeton and anacoluthon become more frequent, until metre and syntax seem to correspond no longer to those of either prose or verse, but to a fusion of both.[3] To this one would wish to add that the verse also becomes more compressed and elliptical, metaphorically denser and more volatile. It acquires the character which made Dryden complain that the 'whole style is so pestered with figurative expressions, that it is as affected as it is obscure.' 'The fury of his fancy,' says Dryden, 'often transported him beyond the bounds of judgment.' Or, again, 'it is not that I would explode [i.e., reject] the use of metaphors from passion ... but to use 'em at every word, to say nothing without a metaphor, a simile, an image, or a description, is, I doubt, to smell a little too strongly of the buskin.'[4] Dr Johnson registered a similar complaint when he taxed Shakespeare's style with being 'ungrammatical, perplexed and obscure,'[5] and Lamb gave the same phenomenon a favourable reading when he said that Shakespeare 'mingles everything, he runs line into line, embarrasses sentences and metaphors; before one idea has burst its shell, another is hatched and clamorous for disclosure.'[6] Most of us, I think, would subscribe to this last as a true description of Shakespearian verse. What needs to be added is that it does *not* also describe the prose. The verse, as Rylands says, assimilates the effects of the prose, not so the prose those of the verse.

Let me illustrate rapidly with a few lines in which the characteristic Shakespearian texture may be agreed to be present. Hamlet speaks to Horatio: 'No, let the candied tongue lick absurd pomp,/And crook the pregnant hinges of the knee/Where thrift may follow fawning' (III.ii.57–9).[7] Here I think one finds what Dryden, Johnson, and Lamb were speaking of, the first two with annoyance, and the last admiringly. Here we have the thickness of texture, the *impasto* of metaphor, together with the kinetic quality, the leaping from figure to figure, that disturbed neoclassic critics. We have the fusing of physical and mental action, and the welding of abstractions to concretions. To borrow a term from the current school of British linguists, we have a number of strange collocations. For the candied tongue to lick absurd pomp is one of those brilliant impossibilities with which Shakespearian verse abounds. In the case of the next line, 'And crook the pregnant hinges of the knee,' its precise grammatical relation to the first line has never been satisfactorily explained. The editors of the Clarendon Press edition of 1872 supposed it to be a synecdoche –

the candied tongue was now being made to represent the whole person – and Tschischwitz construed 'crook' as a neuter imperative.[8]
But these solutions seem more like desperate terminological evasions
than convincing explanations. The general sense of the lines is plain
enough. Somewhere, on the level of deep structure, there lurks a
morality-like creature, named Flattery perhaps, who first uses his
sugary tongue to lick another creature named Pomp, and then assiduously kneels to him, all this at a time and place and in such a
manner as to lead him, Flattery, to expect that he will be materially
well rewarded for his slavishness.[9] Roughly, this is how the mind
receives the lines and why we do not, as we hear them, find them
especially perplexed or obscure. Yet on the level of surface structure
(which is what we immediately apprehend), they preserve an insta-
bility which keeps the mind off balance, keeps us groping for the
terms of connection. We are in a kind of compression chamber, where
the molecules of meaning fly at such high speed that it is all we can
do to track and record their direction; we can hardly hope to arrest
or immobilize them for analysis.

For contrast, we may look at some prose lines from the same play.
This time Hamlet is addressing Rosencrantz and Guildenstern:

I have of late – but wherefore I know not – lost all my mirth, forgone all
custom of exercises; and indeed, it goes so heavily with my disposition that
this goodly frame the earth seems to me a sterile promontory; this most
excellent canopy, the air, look you, this brave o'erhanging firmament, this
majestical roof fretted with golden fire – why, it appeareth nothing to me
but a foul and pestilent congregation of vapors. (II.ii.292–9)

This has generally been agreed to be 'poetic' prose par excellence. It
has also often been taken as part of the antic disposition, since Hamlet
is here speaking to those he knows to be his spies and enemies, whereas
the lines on the candied tongue are spoken in a moment of contem-
plative quiet to his only intimate. His moody and excitable state of
mind as he greets Rosencrantz and Guildenstern, and the lofty nature
of his ruminations, might lead us to expect to find in heightened form
all of the qualities we have identified in the verse. Instead of which,
these lines display a perfectly crystalline transparency. The apposi-
tions, stiffened with anaphora, 'all my mirth,' 'all custom of exercises,' 'this goodly frame,' 'this most excellent canopy'; the explanatory
markers, 'indeed,' 'look you,' 'why,' 'so heavily with my disposition
that'; and the series of analogies – canopy, firmament, majestical roof

– all compose a clear and coherent rhetorical sequence. Figurative expressions are not lacking, but they are laid out according to an orderly plan; they know their own limits. They are hardened similes, also, rather than molten metaphors, cast in highly overt, even didactic form. Hamlet *explains* his analogies: 'this goodly frame the earth,' 'this most excellent canopy the air'; and he places the analogies to the 'air' in an ascending sequence, from canopy, to firmament, to 'majestical roof fretted with golden fire,' bringing the entire passage to a formal climax. The feeling in the passage may be as 'poetic' as one pleases, in the sense of emotionally rich and complex, filled with resonances, etc., but the lines lack the elliptical and concentrated quality of the lines about the candied tongue, and, unlike those, they can be parsed without absurdity; all is ordered, all is syntactically firm and amenable to rational analysis.

If these examples have been properly chosen, and my account of them is correct, they exemplify the first point I wish to make about the prose, which is really only a negative one: that the kind of figurative density and syntactic elusiveness found in the lines to Horatio are standard in Shakespearian verse after a certain moment in his career, and quite foreign to the prose.

With respect to range, Wells points out that Shakespeare 'repeats effects more in this medium [the prose] than in verse' (p.179), that he never tires of introducing clowns, for example, into his plays, that the clowns tend to resemble each other, and that they all speak prose. To this we may add that even the things they say in their prose remain surprisingly constant from one end of the canon to the other. The use of false logic, or mock logic, to prove nonsensical propositions or to serve as paradigms of ordered thinking for those whose thinking is on a rudimentary level, forms a persistent topos. In *The Two Gentlemen of Verona*, we have Speed matching wits with Proteus,[10] in *All's Well* the stoical Lavatch pondering the benefits of cuckoldry,[11] in *Hamlet* the riddling gravedigger debating the nature of suicide,[12] and in *The Winter's Tale* the terrified shepherd's son syllogizing his way out of the dire punishments threatening him and his father.[13] In each instance an unschooled but not uninventive rustic uses the logic of the schools partly as a means, partly as a burlesque, and to some degree as an evasion, of disciplined thinking.

A related continuity may be noted in a brief prose scene from Shakespeare's earliest surviving tragedy, *Titus Andronicus*, which seems to crop up a decade and a half later, enriched and transfigured, in *Antony and Cleopatra*. In both plays a clown thrusts himself blunderingly into the midst of the highborn personages of the story, and bandies words with them. The first clown appears with his basket of pigeons as Titus is shooting arrows up to heaven in a mad effort to secure justice from Jupiter. Unhinged by his sufferings, Titus takes the clown for a heavenly postman who will deliver messages to Olympus:

TITUS News, news from heaven! Marcus, the post is come.
Sirrah, what tidings? Have you any letters?
Shall I have justice? what says Jupiter?
CLOWN Who? the gibbet-maker? He says that he hath taken them down again, for the man must not be hanged till the next week.
TITUS But what says Jupiter I ask thee?
CLOWN Alas, sir, I know not Jubiter; I never drank with him in all my life.
TITUS Why, villain, art not thou the carrier?
CLOWN Ay, of my pigeons, sir; nothing else.
TITUS Why, didst thou not come from heaven?
CLOWN From heaven? alas, sir, I never came there. God forbid I should be so bold to press to heaven in my young days. Why, I am going with my pigeons to the tribunal plebs, to take up a matter of brawl betwixt my uncle and one of the emperal's men.
MARCUS Why, sir, that is as fit as can be to serve for your oration; and let him deliver the pigeons to the emperor from you.
TITUS Tell me, can you deliver an oration to the emperor with a grace?
CLOWN Nay, truly, sir, I could never say grace in all my life. (IV.iii.77–99)

A moment later the poor clown is dispatched with the 'oration' and a knife, only to be hanged for his pains by the villainous emperor. The equivalent scene from *Antony and Cleopatra*, too long and too familiar to quote here, contains a number of similar elements: an ignorant rustic, carrying a basket of figs, intrudes (though by invitation this time) into the presence of the great, and exchanges words with an increasingly impatient dignitary, misunderstanding the questions put to him and occasioning much verbal confusion. In one case we have the inadvertent mistaking of 'Jupiter' for 'gibbeter' or 'gibbet-maker,' the confounding of two senses of 'grace,' and the malapropisms on 'tribunal' and 'emperal.' In the other we have the malapropisms on 'immortal' and 'falliable,' and the phallic punning on 'die' and 'lie' and 'worm.' And as in one case we are unwittingly instructed in the malignity of cosmic justice, so in the other we learn of the metaphysical triumphs locked up in the bite of the worm. These clowns both display the mixture, peculiar to Shakespearian rustics, of bumptious simplicity and earthy shrewdness; like the syllogizing clowns mentioned a moment ago, their blunders with formal meaning manage to be made with a sure instinct for the kind of truth that matters to them. Naïve and without pretensions to special knowledge, they are at the same time primed with sententious folk wisdom. Their innocent-looking baskets, filled with the fruits of the earth, are destined for a bribe in one case, designed to bring death in the other, and so serve as expressive emblems of their wise yet guileless bearers. The two bearers, finally, are felt to be a link with another world; the talk in both scenes is of a journey from the land of the living to some unearthly domain.

I do not wish to belabour these parallels, or claim excessive importance for them. Clearly the scene from *Antony* is in every way more complex and assured, more profoundly and organically integrated into the play it is in. The point is simply that the two scenes *are* comparable, and in some detail; the prose of both has a similar feel, and this could not by any racking or stretching be said of the verse of the two plays, so infinitely far has Shakespeare's handling of his metrical medium progressed during the intervening years.

We can make the same point somewhat differently by looking at four strips of prose, one early, two middle, and one late, which happen to use the same rhetorical figure as a bonding device. Three of the four, also, perhaps not altogether by chance, use it for a similar purpose, to aid in the narration of off-stage events. First, Grumio's report of the vexations endured by Katherine the shrew, on her wedding journey from Padua to Petruchio's house in the country. 'Hadst thou not crossed me,' exclaims Grumio to his fellow-servant Curtis, who has interrupted him twice,

thou shouldst have heard how her horse fell, and she under her horse; thou shouldst have heard in how miry a place; how she was bemoiled, how he left her with the horse upon her, how he beat me because her horse stumbled, how she waded through the dirt to pluck him off me; how he swore, how she prayed, that never prayed before; how I cried, how the horses ran away, how her bridle was burst; how I lost my crupper – with many things of worthy memory, which now shall die in oblivion, and thou return unexperienced to thy grave.   (IV.i.63–73)

Like other set-pieces of prose in the early plays, this tends toward a certain breathlessness and open-endedness. Grumio, in his mind, follows the events he has just experienced in his person with a kind of marvelling fascination, giving us little sense of where the cataract of detail will stop, or of what the upshot of the episode is to be. He provides an abundance of anecdote, but little rhetorical forecasting. He does, however, with the anaphora on 'how,' bring us insistently back, as with a tolling bell, to the next item in the story, imposing at least a linear order on what would otherwise be a chaotic welter, for it was as a welter that the events were first perceived, and the requirement of narrative is that they be somehow made at least minimally intelligible. Shakespeare in fact makes them exceedingly intelligible, emphasizing contrasting actions by the recurrent opposed pronouns, 'she' and 'he,' 'he' and 'she,' 'she' and 'me,' 'her bridle,' 'my crupper,' and so forth, splitting the original jumbled scene into a rapid-fire sequence of vignettes, rather as in the jerky motion of an early movie, or action seen under flickering light.

Next, Borachio, the villain's henchman in *Much Ado about Nothing*, confessing to Claudio and Don Pedro his part in the slandering of Hero:

I have deceived even your very eyes. What your wisdoms could not discover, these shallow fools have brought to light, who in the night overheard me confessing to this man [Conrade], how Don John your brother incensed me to slander the Lady Hero; how you were brought into the orchard and saw me court Margaret in Hero's garments; how you disgraced her when you should marry her. My villainy they have upon record, which I had rather seal with my death than repeat over to my shame. (v.i.220-9)

This is more compact than Grumio's speech, and coalesces more readily into the antithetic flourishes one often finds in Shakespeare's prose at this juncture in his career. Borachio is more the orator than Grumio; he uses more sophisticated syntactic manoeuvres, such as the noun clause which precedes its object ('What your wisdoms could not discover, these shallow fools have brought to light'), which lend a decisive and authoritative ring to his declaration; he supplies a more or less formal introduction ('I have deceived even your very eyes'), and a decorative swirl ('which I had rather seal with my death than repeat over to my shame'), rounding off the confession almost grandly, lending it a touch of rhetorical extravagance. But the basic strategy, which it shares with Grumio's speech, continues to be the anaphora on 'how,' which permits the facts of memory to be unfolded swiftly and efficiently.

For a third instance, the clown in *The Winter's Tale*, telling his father what he has just seen at the edge of the storm-tossed sea:

I would you did but see how it chafes, how it rages, how it takes up the shore. But that's not to the point. O, the most piteous cry of the poor souls! Sometimes to see 'em, and not to see 'em. Now the ship boring the moon with her main-mast, and anon swallowed with yest and froth, as you'ld thrust a cork into a hogshead. And then for the land-service – to see how the bear tore out his shoulder-bone, how he cried to me for help and said his name was Antigonus, a nobleman. But to make an end of the ship – to see how the sea flapdragoned it. But, first, how the poor souls roared, and the sea mocked them, and how the poor gentleman roared and the bear mocked him, both roaring louder than the sea or weather.   (III.iii.84–97)

This is richer than either of the two earlier specimens, especially in the picturesqueness and propriety of its images, drawn from the tavern – the yeast and the froth, the cork, the hogshead, and the flapdragoning; these are used with great exuberance, despite the harrowing subject. Like a good many Shakespearian narrators, very much like the untutored Grumio, and like the drunken Borachio in his initial midnight confidences, the clown here is self-conscious about his narrative style, dissatisfied with his own reportorial technique, for reasons that do him credit. He sees the problem created by the tale he has to tell: the need to rehearse sequentially events that occurred simultaneously and were perceived in a flash, as a single indivisible totality. He solves the problem exactly as Grumio does, by adopting the anaphora on 'how' as bonding agent. This not only helps explain what was happening, imposing a verbal order on what was experienced as a disorder, but also helps express wonder at its unique and virtually incommunicable character.

In our final instance, from Wells' category of 'poetic' prose, and continuing a speech already quoted in part, the anaphora on 'how' has no explanatory force at all, but expresses wonder only:

What a piece of work is a man, how noble in reason, how infinite in faculties; in form and moving how express and admirable, in action how like an angel, in apprehension how like a god: the beauty of the world, the paragon of animals! And yet to me what is this quintessence of dust?

(II.ii.300–5)

This is doubtless as 'poetic' as prose ever becomes, by most ordinary definitions, yet in its exaltation and imaginative sweep it maintains the same strict syntactic ordering as the other examples, the same disposing of parallel elements in clear ranks. If we revert to Q2 pointing, we redistribute the various faculties among the various classes of beings peopling the cosmos, but without altering the hammerstrokes of the introductory 'how,' or the strong stitching of the iterated 'in.'[14] And we can say of the sentence what we said of the sentence that immediately precedes it; impassioned though it is, both in its euphoric and despondent parts, its grammar makes it less tossed and tangled, less resistant to logical explication, than many another passage of lower emotional temperature, and possibly even of lesser imaginative pressure.

In the next set of examples, borrowed from Wells' argument for continuity, we begin, I think, to verge on discontinuity, though the lines of connection remain plainly visible. 'The princes in *Much Ado*,' says Wells, 'can be really as courtly as those in *The Winter's Tale*' (p.179). He is thinking of the following passages: first from *Much Ado*,

PEDRO Good Signior Leonato, are you come to meet your trouble? The fashion of the world is to avoid cost, and you encounter it.

LEONATO Never came trouble to my house in the likeness of your grace; for trouble being gone, comfort should remain; but when you depart from me, sorrow abides and happiness takes his leave.

PEDRO You embrace your charge too willingly.   (I.i.85–92)

And from *The Winter's Tale*, this:

ARCHIDAMUS If you shall chance, Camillo, to visit Bohemia on the like occasion whereon my services are now on foot, you shall see, as I have said, great difference betwixt our Bohemia and your Sicilia.

CAMILLO I think this coming summer the King of Sicilia means to pay Bohemia the visitation which he justly owes him.

ARCHIDAMUS Wherein our entertainment shall shame us, we will be justified in our loves; for indeed –

CAMILLO Beseech you –

ARCHIDAMUS Verily, I speak it in the freedom of my knowledge. We cannot with such magnificence – in so rare – I know not what to say. We will give you sleepy drinks, that your senses, unintelligent of our insufficiencies, may, though they cannot praise us, as little accuse us.

CAMILLO You pay a great deal too dear for what's given freely.

ARCHIDAMUS Believe me, I speak as my understanding instructs me and as mine honesty puts it to utterance.   (I.i.1–19)

Now these two extracts unquestionably resemble each other in important respects. They serve a similar expository function; they both consist of courtly exchanges between noblemen concerning hospitality; they both are filled with what the Elizabethan satirists, including the melancholy Jaques, would have scornfully dismissed as 'compliment.' Both also, the second no less than the first, make use of the mannered, antithetical patterning derived from euphuism, and both tend to view hospitality in the terms of a commercial transaction. But the feeling has changed radically. A gulf has opened, in the transition from what Wells calls 'euphuistic' to what he rather disparagingly refers to as 'baroque.' In the first passage, much of the compliment seems artificial in the bad sense, a tedious spinning out of superfluous courtesies. Leonato's 'reason' for deprecating his visitor's protest – that 'trouble being gone, comfort should remain; but when you depart from me, sorrow abides and happiness takes his leave' – dances all around the mulberry bush simply to say, 'I am always glad to see you.' The second passage is not nearly so fluent or so pat; the antitheses are loaded down with delaying parentheses; the accomplished flow of civilities is interrupted by troubled breakings-off. Both speakers betray a slight self-consciousness. They are testing their feelings, tasting their own words, finding them unexpectedly strong – bordering on exaggeration even – yet they are determined to speak their minds. There is an almost Jamesian scrupulosity in the way they search for the right ways to convey their distinguished sentiments to each other, not forgetting, all the while, that they are speaking for their royal masters even more than for their private selves. They seem full-blooded, too, these courtiers, whereas Pedro and Leonato, in the quoted exchange, seem stamped out of tin. Pedro's 'You embrace your charge too willingly' seems a mere perfunctory batting back of the ball of compliment. Taken literally, it would imply that Leonato ought to embrace his 'charge,' the honouring of his highborn guest, less generously, more grudgingly. Camillo's 'You pay a great deal too much for what's given freely,' on the other hand, amounts to an honest setting straight of the record: Sicilian hospitality has been freely extended, with no thought of obligation or repayment.

To me the later passage marks a decisive advance on the first, and suggests a valid way of salvaging Wells' claim of a growing serious-ness in Shakespeare's prose. Wells' own examples – such as that of Fluellen's language in *Henry V* – tend rather to undermine his case. Surely only on the deepest level of authorial purpose would one speak of Fluellen's prose as serious, crammed as it is with so many devices of linguistic buffoonery, some of them apparently invented for the occasion. But for true seriousness, one would need to look no farther than the nocturnal debate between king and soldiers before the battle of Agincourt, in the same play. Here we have prose that is serious in the obvious as well as in the recondite senses. King and soldiers are both in profoundest earnest, Henry trying to reason out the problem of a King's responsibility for the souls of his followers, rejecting the bitter scepticism of the men, yet unable, by virtue of his incognito, to fall back on the comfortable patriotic commonplaces of court and crown.

The argumentative intensity of his speeches at this moment, their concentrated sobriety, the awareness on the part of all participants that issues of real moment are being discussed, so that levity would be an offence – all this constitutes a fresh departure in Shakespearian prose, and perhaps represents one spill-over from the verse. We find a comparable elevation of tone on several later occasions, such as in the dialogue between Camillo and Archidamus, and also, more startlingly, in the street scenes of *Coriolanus*, where it seems to embody a newly affirmative view of the plebeian multitude. Shakespeare usually makes the populace speak prose, in his English and Roman history plays, and the prose tends to repeat the same gestures and to reflect the same attitudes. In *2 Henry VI*, as Jack Cade is installing his anarchic new order, one of his followers, a Butcher, addresses him:

BUTCHER I have a suit unto your lordship.
CADE Be it a lordship, thou shalt have it for that word.
BUTCHER Only that the laws of England may come out of your mouth.
2. REBEL [*aside*] Mass, 'twill be sore law then, for he was thrust in the mouth with a spear, and 'tis not whole yet.
WEAVER [*aside*] Nay, John, it will be stinking law, for his breath stinks with eating toasted cheese.
CADE I have thought upon it; it shall be so. Away, burn all the records of the realm! My mouth shall be the parliament of England.
2. REBEL [*aside*] Then we are like to have biting statutes, unless his teeth be pulled out.   (IV.vii.3–15)

Then, the opening scene of *Julius Caesar*; the wrathful tribunes interrogate the holiday-making tradesmen:

MARULLUS You, sir, what trade are you?
COBBLER Truly, sir, in respect of a fine workman I am but, as you would say, a cobbler.

MARULLUS But what trade art thou? Answer me directly.

COBBLER A trade, sir, that I hope I may use with a safe conscience, which is indeed, sir, a mender of bad soles.

FLAVIUS What trade, thou knave? Thou naughty knave, what trade?

COBBLER Nay, I beseech you, sir, be not out with me. Yet if you be out, sir, I can mend you.

MARULLUS What mean'st thou by that? Mend me, thou saucy fellow?

COBBLER Why, sir, cobble you.

FLAVIUS Thou art a cobbler, art thou?

COBBLER Truly, sir, all that I live by is with the awl. (I.i.9–21)

These two scenes give the commoners a common style, and so present them in a common light. The English rebels trade sardonic quips among themselves as Cade is holding court; they know very well what his laws will be like. The boisterous cobbler unleashes a stream of punning retorts against the increasingly irate tribunes. These commoners may be unlettered and illogical, but they have their mother wit as a defence against the demagoguery of their leaders. Like the clowns, they have forged a variety of verbal delaying tactics.

By contrast, the mutinous citizenry of *Coriolanus* expresses itself in very different fashion. When, in the tumultuous opening moments, one of the plebeians craves leave to address the others, crying 'One word, good citizens,' he is answered thus by the 'First' Citizen:

We are accounted poor citizens, the patricians good. What authority surfeits on would relieve us. If they would yield us but the superfluity while it were wholesome, we might guess they relieved us humanely; but they think we are too dear. The leanness that afflicts us, the object of our misery, is as an inventory to particularize their abundance; our sufferance is a gain to them. Let us revenge this with our pikes ere we become rakes; for the gods know I speak this in hunger for bread, not in thirst for revenge. (I.i.13–22)

This has some of the seriousness of Henry v's speeches at the campfire, some of the same grim purpose and argumentative energy. Though filled with biting reflections on the callousness of the patricians, its harshness embodies a firm intellectual grasp of the situation. The series of generalizations leads to a militant proposal, 'Let us revenge this with our pikes ere we become rakes,' which the citizen then precisely ascribes to motives of desperation, of survival, rather than to vindictiveness.

Later, as Coriolanus prepares to wear the mantle of humility to solicit the people's voices in the marketplace, the citizens gather again to decide how they ought to react. This time it is the Third Citizen who takes the lead. Speaking of their right to deny their support to Coriolanus, he admonishes his comrades:

We have power in ourselves to do it, but it is a power that we have no power to do; for if he show us his wounds and tell us his deeds, we are to put our tongues into those wounds and speak for them. So, if he tell us his noble deeds, we must also tell him our noble acceptance of them. Ingratitude is monstrous; and for the multitude to be ingrateful were to make a monster of the multitude; of the which we being members, should bring ourselves to be monstrous members. (II.iii.4–12)

This is more colloquial than the previous passage. Certain locutions, 'we are to' do such and such, 'we must' do such and such, have a colloquial ring, as does the slightly laborious and redundant quality of the argument, and the harping on words like 'power' and 'monstrous.' But, like the First Citizen's speech, this contains genuine thinking. It does not represent clownish sophistry or burlesque logic, and it reaches intellectually creditable conclusions. To say 'We have power in ourselves to do it, but it is a power that we have no power to do' is to make a delicate distinction, in however primitive a vocabulary. The citizen is trying to teach his companions that, although they possess a formal privilege, it would, in the circumstances, be unprecedented and unjust of them to exercise it, and he offers a valid reason: 'if he tell us his noble deeds, we must also tell him our noble acceptance of them'; that is, if Coriolanus follows custom, and rehearses his exploits, the people are bound in their turn to render him customary thanks. The 'must' here has the force of tradition rather than of law or abstract logic. The antithetical structure precisely mirrors the covenant by which the patricians and plebeians have in the past felt themselves reciprocally bound, and the worthy citizen hammers home the point soundly by invoking the individual ethical responsibility of each member of the multitude not to be guilty of the sin of ingratitude.

One could cite numerous other speeches, from the anonymous supernumeraries who people the city in this play, which resemble these citizens' speeches. We find in all of them an unforeseen texture of close argument and debate, of opinion carefully pondered and discriminatingly sifted. We find an equally striking absence of the usual frenetic punning, the compulsive flippancy, the turning of every third word into a joke, that we have come to think of as a kind of Shakespearian trademark for such scenes. There is a minimum, too, now, of obvious colloquialisms, of clipped forms, slang words, homely proverbs, and references to things like toasted cheese and cobblers' implements. Little in the language in fact betrays the proletarian status of many of these speakers. The most judicious patrician would hardly have to be ashamed of the vigorous intelligence of these ragged tradesmen, who wield their epigrammatic rhetoric with a deadly aim ('What authority surfeits on would relieve us'), and command a syntax of considerable authority and energy. Despite their failure to sustain a single course of action, the commonalty, in this play, impresses us as intellectually more active and morally more energetic than its earlier counterparts, the rabbles of Hobs and Dicks, Butchers and Weavers and Cobblers; on this occasion, moreover, singleness of action, on the showing of the tragic hero himself, no longer strikes us as so unquestionably admirable. Shakespeare seems to go out of his way to make the people worthy antagonists of their mighty opposite, Caius Marcius, no more the contemptible woollen groats he takes them for than he is the ferocious tyrant some of them think him to be.

A rapid sketch such as the foregoing must of course ignore a hundred complicating particularities and exceptions of detail. I would maintain, nevertheless, that Wells is right in seeing continuity in Shakespearian prose of a tighter and stricter sort than can be traced in the verse. The major exception would lie in the increased seriousness I have tried to identify, the abatement of slanginess and comic word-games in contexts where earlier they would have been nearly automatic: here we have something like an authentic break with the earlier manner, and an emphatic advance into new stylistic territory. Yet even here, it could be argued, the change is largely tonal: the familiar processes of logic, argument, and syntactic patterning have simply been purified of a certain perkiness, and invested with a new solemnity and gravity, while their essential character remains unaltered.

NOTES

1 *The Shakespeare Association Bulletin* 15 (1940) 175–83
2 It may be noted that, though criticism has not been idle since Wells wrote, discussions of Shakespearian prose have tended to centre on philological, usually lexical, questions – on colloquialisms in the dialogue, imitations of popular speech, experimental word formations, and so forth. The emphasis in many of these studies is not on style at all, but on the history of the

English language: Shakespearian speech is studied in order to ascertain Elizabethan usage and so lay the foundation for a historical grammar.

Critics concerned with style in its rhetorical aspects (such as, most recently, Brian Vickers *The Artistry of Shakespeare's Prose* [London 1968]), have rightly tended to stress the formality of the prose more than its colloquialism, its reliance on well-defined grammatical patterns, and its persistent habit, in almost any context, of crystallizing into set-pieces of rhetoric.

But the vocabulary for discussing the prose remains rudimentary, eclectic, and unsatisfactory. Elizabethan rhetorical terms, such as those compiled by Sister Miriam Joseph (*Shakespeare's Use of the Arts of Language* [New York 1947]), help remind us of the formal basis of a great deal of otherwise innocent-looking Elizabethan writing, but leave out of account large areas of idiom and procedure. Some of this comes into view in the categories of traditional grammar, probably still our most useful instrument, but too abstract and general to connect us closely enough with the range and particularity of the prose. So far, neither transformational grammar nor recent British structural linguistics has been very helpful. What one usually feels, in stylistic analyses with a linguistic basis, is a vast disproportion between the intricate and difficult linguistic apparatus and the tiny returns in meaningful critical comment. A rare exception would be the pilot studies of R.H. Ohmann (e.g., 'Generative Grammars and the Concept of Literary Style' *Word* 20 (1964) 424–39, and 'Literature as Sentences' *College English* 27 (1966) 261–7), but these have so far been merely indicators, with no sequel. Perhaps the most promising new approach is that of Stanley E. Fish, who views all writing as a form of continuous action, of 'doings and happenings,' capable of being analyzed from moment to moment as a manipulation of reader expectation and response; see 'Literature in the Reader: Affective Stylistics' *New Literary History* 2 (1970) 123–62.

3 George H.W. Rylands *Words and Poetry* (London 1928) 161

4 From 'The Grounds of Criticism in Tragedy' *Dramatic Poesy and Other Essays* William Henry Hudson, ed, Everyman ed. (London 1912) 126, 141–2

5 From 'Preface to Shakespeare,' Johnson *Works* VII *Johnson on Shakespeare* Arthur Sherbo and Bertrand H. Bronson, eds (New Haven 1968) 93

6 *Specimens of English Dramatic Poets Who Lived about the Time of Shakespeare* (London 1827), 356

7 Citations from Shakespeare will be to *The Complete Works* Alfred Harbage, ed, revised Pelican ed. (Baltimore 1969).

8 *Hamlet* Horace Howard Furness, ed, New Variorum Edition (15th ed, Philadelphia 1918) I, 232

9 John Dover Wilson, in the notes to his New Cambridge Edition of the play (paperback ed, Cambridge 1968) 197, refers us to Caroline Spurgeon's *Shakespeare's Iterative Imagery*, where the present passage is shown to embody an associational complex that includes dogs and sweets and fawning behaviour. 'The image is that of a spaniel at table, its tongue "candied" with sweetmeats, yet "fawning" for more.' This is plausible, but we cannot substitute speculations about authorial psychology for syntactic analysis. Even if we knew for certain that the lines contained the associational cluster identified by Miss Spurgeon, we would not have solved the

syntactic dilemma, but rather compounded it, for we would be obliged to posit a fawning dog in one line and a human agent in the next: dogs do not, after all, crook the pregnant hinges of their knees in sign of servility.

10 'The shepherd seeks the sheep, and not the sheep the shepherd; but I seek my master, and my master seeks not me. Therefore I am no sheep' (i.i.86–8). See the pioneer article of Hardin Craig, 'Shakespeare and Formal Logic,' in Kemp Malone and Martin B. Ruud, eds *Studies in English Philology* (Minneapolis 1929) 380–96.

11 'He that comforts my wife is the cherisher of my flesh and blood; he that cherishes my flesh and blood loves my flesh and blood; he that loves my flesh and blood is my friend: ergo, he that kisses my wife is my friend' (i.ii.43–7).

12 'Here lies the water – good. Here stands the man – good. If the man go to this water and drown himself, it is, will he nill he, he goes, mark you that. But if the water come to him and drown him, he drowns not himself. Argal, he that is not guilty of his own death shortens not his own life' (v.i.13–18).

13 'She being none of your flesh and blood, your flesh and blood has not offended the king, and so your flesh and blood is not to be punished by him' (iv.iv.681–3). The syllogism here, it may be noticed, uses the same ingredient as that from *All's Well* – the equivocation on 'flesh and blood,' where the different meanings of the phrase are assiduously confounded so as to produce a certain predestined result: release from the care of cuckoldry in one case, and from the fear of bloody punishment in the other.

14 'What peece of worke is a man, how noble in reason, how infinit in faculties, in forme and moouing, how expresse and admirable in action, how like an Angell in apprehension, how like a God:' *Hamlet*, 1605, sig. F2, facs. ed. (Menston, England, Scolar Press 1969).

G.R. Hibbard /
'The Forced Gait of a Shuffling Nag'

The words that provide the title for this paper, chosen on the spur of the moment, will be familiar to everyone here. Nevertheless, I should like to begin by putting them into their context, because that is germane to my argument. The context is act III scene i of *1 Henry IV*. Hotspur has proposed to have the course of the river Trent altered, but Glendower has refused to entertain any such plan, telling his prickly ally that he will say him nay. Thereupon Hotspur retorts: 'Let me not understand you then; speak it in Welsh.' Here is what follows:

> GLENDOWER I can speak English, lord, as well as you;
> For I was trained up in the English court,
> Where, being but young, I framed to the harp
> Many an English ditty lovely well,
> And gave the tongue a helpful ornament –
> A virtue that was never seen in you.
> HOTSPUR Marry, and I am glad of it with all my heart!
> I had rather be a kitten and cry mew
> Than one of these same metre ballad-mongers.
> I had rather hear a brazen canstick turned
> Or a dry wheel grate on the axle-tree,
> And that would set my teeth nothing on edge,
> Nothing so much as mincing poetry.
> 'Tis like the forced gait of a shuffling nag.   (119–33)[1]

Now, this is only one, though a particularly forceful and devastating one, of the fairly numerous expressions of either dislike for or distrust in poetry that are uttered by characters in the plays. Touchstone, attempting to seduce Audrey by syllogism, wishes that she were 'poetical,' since her profession of 'honesty' would then be mere feigning, and not a serious obstacle to the satisfaction of his desires. Viola uses the same word to describe and, I think, to mock and devalue the speech she has prepared in praise of Olivia; and Timon, with a fine irony that goes unnoticed and unappreciated by his hearers, voices his contempt for the time-serving Poet by telling him:

> And for thy fiction,
> Why, thy verse swells with stuff so fine and smooth
> That thou art even natural in thine art.[2]

To equate these disparaging remarks with Shakespeare's own attitude to poetry would be ridiculous; but there are enough of them to make it plain that this view of the medium in which he worked was by no means foreign to him. It would be strange if it were, for one of the things we are coming increasingly to realize is the duality of his vision, the extraordinary ability he had not merely for perceiving, but also for embracing, at least for dramatic purposes, the most violent contrarieties. Indeed, Hotspur's lines offer a superb example of precisely this capacity, since his dislike for poetry takes the form of a splendid piece of true dramatic poetry, of verse which not only renders the feeling with sensuous exactness but which also contrives to do several other things simultaneously with it, as great dramatic poetry must. The speech endorses that instinctive antipathy between him and Glendower which contributes to the action of the play by weakening the rebel cause; it is in perfect keeping with his rash, downright, undiplomatic nature; and it is couched in that homely idiom, replete with images drawn from everyday life, and especially from life in the country, which we have come to recognize as his ever since the moment, in i.iii, when he spoke of the courtier, whose 'chin new reaped/Showed like a stubble land at harvest home' (35), and it has to be spoken 'thick.'

I have started with these exchanges between Hotspur and Glendower for two reasons: first, because I want to speak in the rest of this paper about what I shall call 'The Making of Shakespeare's Dramatic Poetry,' meaning the process by which the art, so evident in this passage, came into being and was perfected; and, secondly, because I think Shakespeare's distrust of the 'poetical,' a distrust which only developed gradually, was an asset of great importance to him in the creation of that incredibly flexible instrument which gives life and reality not only to individual characters as diversified as Hotspur, Glendower, and Falstaff, but also to the world in which they move and to the events in which they take part.

At this point, having mentioned Falstaff, who habitually speaks prose, in connection with dramatic poetry, I must make clear the sense in which I am using this term. By 'dramatic poetry' I mean the language of plays written by poets employing all the resources of their craft to secure that compression and heightening of experience which 'the two hours' traffic' of the stage demands. Because it aims at compression, this language will tend towards the figurative, no matter whether it be in prose or verse. It will also avail itself to the full of those other forms of expression – spectacle, stage effects, and, above all, physical movement – which make dramatic poetry radically different from all other kinds of poetry. The climax of *Coriolanus* is wordless, yet the simple human gesture, called for by the stage direction *'Holds her by the hand, silent,'* is, it seems to me, dramatic poetry of the highest order, because it is impossible to conceive any other way of saying half as well what it says so perfectly. In drama there is an intimate relation between what is said and what is done. A speech is, of course, in itself a form of action, but there are some speeches which are far more active than others, while a physical action, such as that of Coriolanus, can on occasion speak better than words. The great problem that confronts the dramatic poet is that of gearing the words to those two other basic constituents of a play, the action and the characters; and, the more richly endowed as a poet the poet is, the more difficult he may find it. This, I suggest, was the chief problem that the early Shakespeare had to solve.

To explain and exemplify what I am driving at here, I now turn to a scene from *Titus Andronicus.* I am assuming that the play is very early, and that it is substantially, if not entirely, the work of Shakespeare. Happily, the particular scene I shall be concerned with, II.iv, is so close to *The Rape of Lucrece* that his authorship of it seems beyond reasonable doubt. It opens with the striking stage direction *'Enter the Empresse Sonnes, with Lavinia, her hands cut off, and her tongue cut out, and ravisht.'* The final word there suggests that there must have been some visible signs, immediately intelligible to the audience, to indicate Lavinia's unhappy state. The ten lines of dialogue that follow are indubitable dramatic poetry, arising directly out of the action that has just taken place off stage and fitting in perfectly with the characters of Chiron and Demetrius. In clever mannered verse, full of parallelisms, her two ravishers mock Lavinia in alternate speeches, skilfully working their way up to the final gibe which they share between them:

> CHIRON An 'twere my cause, I should go hang myself.
> DEMETRIUS If thou hadst hands to help thee knit the cord. (9–10)

It is outrageous, but it is dramatically right. The deliberate studied quality of the writing goes with the calculated brutality and callousness of the action. What is said chimes in with what is being and has been done.

The two young men then make their exit, and they are replaced by Lavinia's uncle Marcus, who comes in from hunting to see his niece running away from him. The rest of the scene, devoted to one long speech of forty-seven lines from Marcus, is the most bizarre thing that Shakespeare ever wrote. The discrepancy between what is heard – poetry of the most 'poetical' kind, full of brilliant alliteration, of picturesque adjectives, and of similes worked out in loving detail – and what is seen – the ghastly figure of Lavinia – is such that Dover Wilson, in the Introduction to his New Cambridge edition of the play, finds it impossible to take it seriously. He writes of Shakespeare 'laughing behind his hand' (p.li), and describes the entire speech as 'caricature' (p.liv). I believe that he is quite wrong to do so, because I think I know the main end that Shakespeare has in view in the first part of it. This is a discovery scene, and it seeks to outdo the greatest of discovery scenes in pre-Shakespearian drama, the opening of II.v in *The Spanish Tragedy*, where Hieronimo enters in his shirt, crying 'What out-cries pluck me from my naked bed,' finds a corpse hanging in his apple-tree, cuts it down, recognizes the clothes it is wearing, and finally discovers the body is that of his son. The process by which Hieronimo moves from the finding of the body to the realization of whose body it is occupies seven lines, as well it might, since the time is night. Shakespeare, out to better Kyd, takes no fewer than seventeen lines to cover the period that elapses from Marcus' first seeing Lavinia to his full realization of her plight, though the scene is set in broad daylight. As a result, instead of sharing Marcus' experience, we are irritated by his slowness, and almost driven to conclude that he must be either half-blind or half-witted.

As well as conveying the gradual realization all too gradually,

Marcus' speech also seeks to draw a harrowing contrast between Lavinia as she was and Lavinia as she is. This is done through an extended use of elaborate and carefully worked out similes. In a narrative poem of the Ovidian kind these figures would be right, but on the stage they are unnecessary and intrusive. The audience has seen Lavinia as she was, they are looking at her as she is. Moreover, these similes are so picturesque that they draw far too much attention to themselves, so that one soon becomes aware of an appalling incongruity between the frightful spectacle of the ravished girl, with her bleeding stumps and mouth, and the 'favour and prettiness' that Marcus is turning it all into. And, to make matters worse, Shakespeare positively directs our eyes and ears to the incongruity by emphasizing the physical reality at the same time that he decorates it with verbal arabesques, as when Marcus says:

> And, notwithstanding all this loss of blood,
> As from a conduit with three issuing spouts,
> Yet do thy cheeks look red as Titan's face
> Blushing to be encount'red with a cloud.   (29–32)

My reaction on hearing that is not the heightened sense of Lavinia's shame it is meant to produce, but rather the purely practical response: 'For God's sake, man, get her to a doctor before she bleeds to death, instead of standing there talking.' That reaction is strengthened and justified by the fact that the lines are quite out of character. In this play, where everyone else is so given over to passion as to appear near-lunatic, Marcus has stood out hitherto, and will do so again, because his behaviour is, at least by comparison, rational and practical. Here, however, it is neither. In the first ten lines of the scene the poet and the dramatist synchronize their efforts; from the moment Marcus enters they go their separate ways, or, it might be better to say, each gets in the way of the other.

The problem of how to bring the two sides of his genius into a proper and fruitful working relationship with each other was, I think, one that continued to trouble Shakespeare for several years. He sought various solutions to it, but, until the time of *Henry IV*, there was something temporary about each of them. In the three parts of *Henry VI* and in *Richard III* he seems to have submitted the poet in him to a kind of discipline, almost as though he were watching himself at work. There is a fascinating passage at the opening of II.v of *3 Henry VI*, where, to mix metaphors, one sees him catching himself out just as he is about to put a foot wrong. With the battle of Towton raging about him, Henry comes in alone and compares the state of the conflict to the contention between 'dying clouds' and 'growing light' at the dawn of day. The simile occupies four lines, and then gives way to another parallel simile, based on the meeting of a high tide flowing in one direction and a strong wind blowing in the other. It is developed with much pictorial detail through some eight lines; but, at the end of it, Shakespeare the dramatist seems to have realized that by this time an audience might well have forgotten what the original point of departure was. And so, having begun with the line 'This battle fares like to the morning's war,' he concludes by writing 'So is the equal poise of this fell war' (1–13). It is clear, I think, that he is becoming wary of the figure which acquires a life and momentum of its own that takes it right out of the gravitational field of the action.

The self-critical awareness I have just pointed to is, however, more a defensive than a positive instrument. Much more important as a means of keeping the 'saying' and the 'doing' in close connection with each other was the device of organizing a speech on a firm logical pattern, very similar, especially in its reliance on antithesis, to that of the Elizabethan sonnet. The effect of this patterning, though it begins, I think, at the level of the single speech, does not end there, for there is an intimate and reciprocal relation between what is said and how it is said. The matter affects the manner; but the reverse is also true – the manner may help to determine the matter, and particularly the shape that matter takes. We have heard much in recent years about the importance of ideas in these plays, about the way in which their evolution is dominated by the notion of God's justice, linking crime to punishment in an iron chain of cause and consequence, and thus imposing on them that formality and symmetry which become so marked in *3 Henry VI* and *Richard III*. It is not a view that I want to dispute in its entirety, but I would suggest that the formalization of action in them is, in part at least, a matter of technique. The logical structure that controls the single speech is extended to the organization of a scene, and thence to that of a whole play.

To support this contention, I should like to take a quick look now at I.iv of *3 Henry VI*, the scene that made such an impression on the mind of Robert Greene. It follows directly on from I.iii, in which Clifford kills the little Rutland. In it York is taken prisoner, set upon a molehill, and then subjected to forty-three lines of taunts and savage mockery from Queen Margaret. Beginning with a statement of York's empty pretensions, cast in the form of a series of rhetorical questions, the speech then moves on to a counter-statement, made up of variations on the *Ubi sunt* motif. Then, out of the statement and counter-statement there comes significant action, so closely bound up with what has been said that it too is a form of statement, as Margaret hands York the napkin stained with the blood of his little son Rutland. At this point her speech pauses, only to mount once more in a calculated gradation of goading imprecations that culminate in yet another action – the setting of the paper crown on York's head. Finally, after another ten lines of insults, Margaret gives the order that is the logical consequence of her indictment of York: 'Off with the crown, and with the crown his head' (107). It looks as though York's torment is about to end. But it isn't. Margaret is merely playing cat-and-mouse with her captive, while Shakespeare the dramatist is holding his audience in suspense until he completes a pattern of action which is also a rhetorical pattern. As Clifford steps forward to give York his deathblow, Margaret restrains him, so that she may enjoy the sadistic satisfaction of learning from York's retort just how much she has hurt him. York gives his reply in a speech which is, allowing for a two-line interruption that does not arrest its course, even longer than hers, that takes the same shape as hers, that makes use of the same antithetical devices, and that works up to two similar climaxes of action, employing the same stage properties, the bloody napkin and the paper crown.

The dramatic strength of the scene derives from its formalization of violence. There is no disjunction here between what is said and what is done. The taunts have the force of blows, and the actions have the eloquence of words. Margaret's mockery is balanced by York's defiance. The shape of the scene and the spectacle that it offers are both parts of its meaning. It imprints on the mind of the spectator the implacable nature of the conflict between the two houses. Moreover, the shape of the scene is the shape of the play, for it too has an antithetical structure. Act v answers act i, exactly as York answers Margaret. The battle of Wakefield, a Yorkist defeat leading to the murder of Rutland in i.iii and of York in i.iv, is counter-balanced by the battle of Tewkesbury, a Lancastrian defeat leading to the murder of Prince Edward, Margaret's son, in v.v – a murder carried out by Rutland's brothers – and the murder of Henry vi himself by York's son, Richard of Gloucester, in v.vi.

Everything I have said about *3 Henry VI* applies with even more force and cogency to *Richard III*, the most formal and symmetrical play that Shakespeare ever wrote. But, having written it, he never wrote anything like it again. Why not? The answer must be that he had become aware of the limitations of the manner and the method. To illustrate very briefly what they are, by comparison with what he was ultimately to achieve, I shall turn for a moment to another scene depicting a helpless captive being interrogated. In III.vii of *King Lear* Gloucester is brought into the presence of Regan and Cornwall. The passage from *3 Henry VI* that I have just been discussing occupies one hundred and forty-three lines; in *King Lear* sixty-seven lines only account for all that happens between Gloucester's arrival and his being thrust out, now blinded, from the gates of his own castle. Yet into those sixty-seven lines there is packed far more physical action than goes into the scene between York and Margaret, because the whole relation between what is said and what is done is so much more closely knit. But this is only a beginning. In terms of experience neither York nor Margaret gains anything. From beginning to end they remain fixed in their postures, just as the scene itself remains fixed. Gloucester, on the other hand, travels a distance that is incalculable: first he pleads, then he is outraged by Regan's plucking of his beard; he tries to be diplomatic and evasive; but ultimately he takes his stand. The plucking out of his eyes follows, brought on by his words 'But I shall see / The winged vengeance overtake such children' (65–6). Finally comes the worst experience of all: the revelation that Edmund is responsible for his plight, and that Edgar was abused.

Looking back at the scene in *3 Henry VI* from this vantage point, we see at once that the logical, antithetical structure of the speeches, the marked tendency of the lines to fall into unrhymed couplets, and the proliferation of lists are, in effect, a kind of strait jacket. They serve to order experience, to prevent it from becoming chaotic, as it does in *Titus Andronicus*, but they inhibit its growth. Admirable for purposes of demonstration, they prevent discovery. By the time he had finished *Richard III*, Shakespeare knew that there was nothing further to be achieved in its manner.

I shall jump now to v.ii of *Love's Labour's Lost*. About half way through this long scene, the men, 'dry-beaten with pure scoff,' realize at last that the game is up, and that words will no longer serve their turn. Berowne speaks for them as he tells Rosaline:

> Taffeta phrases, silken terms precise,
> Three-piled hyperboles, spruce affectations,

> Figures pedantical – these summer flies
> Have blown me full of maggot ostentation.
> I do forswear them; and I here protest
> By this white glove (how white the hand, God knows)
> Henceforth my wooing mind shall be expressed
> In russet yeas and honest kersey noes.   (407–14)

Deciding to employ plain language in future, Berowne lingers over the verbal delights he is abjuring, describing them in terms of rich materials. He is like a woman in a draper's shop, handling stuff she would dearly like to buy but can no longer afford. This farewell to figures by the master of 'painted rhetoric,' the most accomplished logic-chopper that Shakespeare ever created, is itself full to overflowing with dazzling figures. The idea of the battle of the sexes gives rise to no fewer than five metaphors in the course of three and a half lines:

> Here stand I, lady; dart thy skill at me.
> Bruise me with scorn, confound me with a flout,
> Thrust thy sharp wit quite through my ignorance,
> Cut me to pieces with thy keen conceit.   (397–400)

There is a wonderful exuberance about it all, a sense of the imagination delighting in its own creative fertility; yet, at the same time, there is also the keen critical intelligence recognizing the limitations of this kind of poetry for dramatic purposes.

What I want to suggest now is that Berowne is, in a sense, speaking for Shakespeare. It must have been in something like this position that he found himself round about 1594–5. Never had his fancy been richer. As Berowne sings the praise of love near the end of iv.iii (313–60), images drawn from daily life, from books, from sensitive observation of the natural world, and from classical mythology mingle together in 'an easy commerce of the old and the new.' But the man who wrote this speech knew, as the author of *Titus Andronicus* did not, that, to quote Berowne once more, 'Honest plain words best pierce the ear of grief' (v.ii.743). And so in this play, the most magical and moving moment takes another form altogether. The Pageant of the Nine Worthies has been played; Armado has challenged Costard to a duel; the fun is at its height; we wonder what further exhibition of folly is to come. What we get is the stage direction *'Enter a Messenger Mounsier Marcade.'* A chill falls over the scene. The dialogue between Marcade and the Princess runs thus:

MARCADE God save you, madam.
PRINCESS Welcome, Marcade;
But that thou interrupt'st our merriment.
MARCADE I am sorry, madam, for the news I bring
Is heavy in my tongue. The king your father –
PRINCESS Dead, for my life!
MARCADE Even so. My tale is told. (705–11)

Abruptly the whole movement of the verse has shifted from the major
to the minor key as the reality of death intrudes on this butterfly
world. And it has all been done by the simplest and plainest bit of
dialogue in the entire play. In those few lines Shakespeare moves
over from one form of dramatic expression to another, from a mode
in which the words are primary and carry the main burden of experience, to a mode in which the words take their colouring from the
circumstances.

But Shakespeare only reaches this point in his play after going
through a process that can be seen as a sort of catharsis, or, alternatively, as one of reconciling ends with means. I think it is both. The
assault on artificiality, affectation, and extravagance, both in speech
and manners, that he makes in this play, positively demanded that
these things be exhibited in all their fantastic variety. Here was the
perfect occasion for letting himself go; and he took it. He is still more
than half in love with the linguistic excesses that he holds up to laughter. In writing it Shakespeare had his cake as well as eating it, much
as he did in the writing of *Richard II*, by turning his love of language
and figures to a dramatic use. In both plays, it seems to me, what he
actually wrote was very much determined by the resources he had at
his command, and by his attitude to those resources, which was both
fond and critical at one and the same time. Both plays, seen in the
context of the growth of his dramatic poetry, are brilliant expedients.

This is not the case with *Romeo and Juliet*, which is, I think, one
of the great growing points. There is much in it that I should like
to discuss, but I shall restrict myself to one aspect of it, the language
and verse of Juliet's Nurse. From the first time that we see her, in
I.iii, the Nurse uses a new kind of blank verse. It is, above everything
else, accommodating verse. It has to be, in order to allow room for
the prose rhythms, the parentheses and the cluttered repetitions of
the born gossip, to breathe. We know the Nurse, from the very way
in which she speaks, as we know no character before her, except,
perhaps, Cade in *2 Henry VI*, who, very significantly, is a creature of

prose. The Nurse is what she says and how she says it. The gain in dramatic scope is enormous. Listening to her, I have the sense of fresh vistas opening up before her creator. If I may be allowed to misquote T.S. Eliot, I should say of her speech: 'Uncorsetted, her ample verse / Gives promise of prismatic range.'

Let us look at what she says as she stands by the side of Juliet's bed at the opening of IV.v, on the morning after Juliet has taken the sleeping potion. Here the audience, knowing what Juliet has done, waits in suspense for the curtains to be drawn. While it is waiting, it receives something else and something extra, for through the Nurse's words a marvellous sense is created of Juliet's life as it has been hitherto. It is one of those evocative moments in which Shakespeare gives depth and shading to the action he presents by creating a past for it. This, or something like it, has, we are made to feel, happened many a time before in Juliet's life. But we know, as the Nurse does not, that it will not happen again. And so pathos mingles with comedy as the Nurse attempts to wake her charge:

> Mistress! what, mistress! Juliet! Fast, I warrant her, she.
> Why, lamb! why, lady! Fie, you slug-abed.
> Why, love, I say! madam! sweetheart! Why, bride!
> What, not a word? You take your pennyworths now;
> Sleep for a week; for the next night, I warrant,
> The County Paris hath set up his rest
> That you shall rest but little. God forgive me!
> Marry, and amen. How sound is she asleep!
> I needs must wake her. Madam, madam, madam!
> Ay, let the County take you in your bed;
> He'll fright you up, i'faith. Will it not be?
> What, dressed, and in your clothes, and down again?
> I must needs wake you. Lady! lady! lady!
> Alas, alas! Help, help! my lady's dead!
> O weraday that ever I was born!
> Some aqua vitae, ho! My lord! my lady!   (1–16)

There is not a single adjective there; there are no figures; the entire speech is made up of exclamations and the small change of human intercourse. Yet it is superb dramatic poetry, because it enacts the whole experience, from the blitheful unconcern of the beginning to the shocked realization of the end. Moreover, it is wholly in character.

No one but the Nurse would take this long to find out what has happened. But in her case the slowness is absolutely right and justified as her mind dithers between the job in hand, her affection for Juliet, and the bawdy suggestions which the thought of marriage stimulates in her mind. And, at the end of it all, I am left with a strong suspicion that she wants the aqua vitae more for herself than for Juliet. There is a world of difference between this discovery and Marcus' discovery of Lavinia's state in *Titus Andronicus*. In its bareness and its reliance on the simple, this speech anticipates the final speech of King Lear himself.

But, while the Nurse's lines hold the promise of a prismatic range, they never achieve it, because the Nurse is limited by her very nature to one end only – the infra end, if I may so call it – of the spectrum of experience. For something like the full scope of which this new, flexible dramatic poetry is capable we have to wait for Hotspur. In his mouth it encompasses, without ever losing the distinctive quality that marks it as his, thoughts and feelings as various as his generous indignation over the King's treatment of Mortimer, his hatred for 'bare and rotten policy,' his romantic response to the prospect of honour, his bantering affection for his wife Kate, and, at the very end of his life, that pregnant reflection which comes to him as he sees all human endeavour in relation to time and eternity:

> But thoughts the slaves of life, and life time's fool,
> And time that takes survey of all the world,
> Must have a stop. (v.iv.80–2)

Hotspur's verse can modulate into this other manner, take on this deeper resonance, precisely because it is not obtrusively 'poetical,' because it draws much of its vitality and its flexibility from the infusion into it of some of the qualities that are more usually associated with prose. But Hotspur is not the only character who talks supremely well, using an idiom that is indubitably his own, in *Henry IV*. There is also Falstaff; and Falstaff, in this as in so many other respects, is the obverse of Hotspur. His prose gathers its richness from the infusion into it of the qualities that are more often associated with poetry. It is, to use his own words, 'forgetive, full of nimble, fiery, and delectable shapes' (Pt 2, iv.iii.96–7). The sources from which he draws his images range from the Bible to the belly, but the images themselves are always wonderfully apt. Here is his description of Shallow as he was in his youth:

I do remember him at Clement's Inn like a man made after supper of a cheese-paring. When 'a was naked, he was, for all the world, like a forked radish, with a head fantastically carved upon it with a knife.

(Pt 2, III.ii.287–91)

That love of figures, which Berowne regretfully thought of as something to be subdued, has re-asserted itself. But the figures are no longer 'taffeta phrases'; they are, instead, whatever material is best suited to the matter in hand. It is their suitability that counts now, not their texture. With the writing of *Henry IV*, the dramatic poetry of the great tragedies was within reach. Falstaff's description of Shallow is a comic anticipation of Lear's vision of 'unaccommodated man.'

NOTES

1 All quotations from Shakespeare are taken from *William Shakespeare: The Complete Works* Alfred Harbage, ed. (London 1969).
2 *As You Like It* III.iii.12–23; *Twelfth Night* I.v.185–7; *Timon of Athens* v.i.81–3.

Norman Rabkin /
Meaning and Shakespeare

Shakespeare criticism is in trouble. One might not guess that from the ever-increasing rate at which it is produced, or from the obvious success its practitioners have had in reaching the goals they set for themselves, or from the substantial agreement on crucial plays and problems and methods. But a good deal of our agreement is based on a tacit understanding that the object of our search is the principle of a play's unity, that that principle is the play's meaning, and that meaning is therefore the umbrella under which we properly locate discussions of character, imagery, structure, dramaturgy, language, and intellectual and theatrical history. We have learned how to do very well in such explorations, and I do not want to deny their unmistakable value. But I am going to argue that the better our criticism becomes, and the more sharply it is focussed on explaining what plays are about, the farther it gets from the actuality of our experience in responding to them, so that if we do not change our critical habits we are likely to betray Shakespeare as badly as did critics who wrote about the girlhood of his heroines.

My test case is *The Merchant of Venice*. I have chosen it, first of all, because it is an acknowledged success which has retained its popularity on and off the stage. Second, it has been a centre of as much controversy as any of the plays has aroused, and the controversy has led good critics to real and crucial problems. Third, though as I shall indicate that there are still those who argue what I take to be idiosyncratic interpretations, in recent years many of the critics have reached a consensus on the play and in so doing have produced invaluable insights. And finally, for all its virtues the best criticism leaves us with the sense that it has somehow failed to come to grips with or has even in some way denied the existence of the most essential qualities of our experience of the play.

The power of *The Merchant of Venice* has moved actors and audiences, critics and readers to interpretations opposed so diametrically that they seem to have been provoked by different plays. Most disagreements have centred on character. On stage Shylock has run a course between Macklin's savage monster and Irving's martyred gentleman;[1] critical descriptions of Shylock range from a 'malevolence ... diabolically inhuman'[2] whom Shakespeare 'clearly detested,'[3] to a 'scapegoat,' an instinctively generous man who reminds his tormentors of the wickedness which they possess in greater measure than he.[4] Inevitably Portia has aroused responses similarly at odds, seeming to many the epitome of the romantic heroine, to some virtually a saint, and to others no more than a 'callous barrister' with a trump card up her sleeve;[5] Jessica is an ideal portrait of the Christian convert and a 'dishonest and disloyal father-hating minx,'[6] Antonio a model of Christian gentleness and an underground Shylock,[7] Bassanio a romanticized lover and a heartless money-grubber. Similarly, Portia's use of the law to defeat Shylock has been seen by some as a brilliant and just device, by others as a malicious and unnecessary piece of conniving.[8]

A typical contention flourishes about the scene in which Shylock, provoked to swear vengeance by his daughter's defection and her plundering of his household, learns from Tubal that one of Antonio's ships is lost. To suggest the complexity of our responses to Shylock at this point I need only remind you that he justifies his savage commitment to revenge by claiming it as the mechanical and therefore normal human response to injury, and that the claim, thus reflecting an impoverished sensibility, is the climax of his moving appeal to universal brotherhood: 'I am a Jew. Hath not a Jew eyes? ...'[9] From moment to moment, even simultaneously, we respond to signals of Shylock's injured fatherhood, of his role as heavy father, of his light-hearted mistreatment at the hands of the negligible Salerio and Solanio, of his motiveless malignity, and we try hopelessly to reduce to a single attitude our response to his self-defining scorn for Antonio, whose combination of generosity, passivity, sensibility, and spitting hatred has already led us to mixed feelings.

SHYLOCK I thank God, I thank God! is it true, is it true?

TUBAL I spoke with some of the sailors that escaped the wrack.

SHYLOCK I thank thee good Tubal, good news, good news: ha ha! heard in Genoa!

TUBAL Your daughter spent in Genoa, as I heard, one night, fourscore ducats.

SHYLOCK Thou stick'st a dagger in me, – I shall never see my gold again. – fourscore ducats at a sitting, fourscore ducats!

TUBAL There came divers of Antonio's creditors in my company to Venice, that swear, he cannot choose but break.

SHYLOCK I am very glad of it, – I'll plague him, I'll torture him, – I am glad of it.

TUBAL One of them showed me a ring that he had of your daughter for a monkey.

SHYLOCK Out upon her! – thou torturest me Tubal, – it was my turquoise, I had it of Leah when a was a bachelor: I would not have given it for a wilderness of monkeys. (III.i.93–113)

More clearly evocative of laughter at Shylock's obsessions and his speech mannerisms than other parts of the scene, these lines nevertheless engage us in a kaleidoscopic shift of emotion and touch us at the end. Rather than acknowledge the welter of our responses, however, critic after critic insists that this scene reveals a clear and simple truth about Shylock's martyred humanity or his comic villainy.[10]

These sordid disputes, on which I shall not waste our time, testify to a fact about their subject that ought to be the point of departure for criticism. In fact, however, critics have justified their occupation by constructing strategies to evade the problem posed by divergent responses. Some blame Shakespeare, suggesting that his confusion accounts for tension in the work and its audience.[11] Others appeal to a narrow concept of cultural history which writes off our responses as unavailable to Shakespeare's contemporaries because of their attitudes toward usury or Jews or comedy.[12] Still others suggest that, since the plays are fragile confections designed to display engaging if implausible characters, exegetical criticism is misplaced.[13] Though all of these strategies attract modern practitioners, they have lost ground before the dominant evasion, the reduction of the play to a theme which, when we understand it, tells us which of our responses we must suppress. The ingenious thematic critic is licensed to stipulate that 'in terms of the structure of the play Shylock is a minor character' and can be ignored,[14] or that the action is only metaphorical and does not need to be examined as if its events literally happened,[15] or that Shylock is only a Jew, or a banker, or a usurer, or a man spiritually dead, or a commentary on London life, never a combination of these;[16] or that *The Merchant of Venice* is built on 'four levels of existence' corresponding to Dante's divisions – 'Hell (Shylock), Purgatory proper (Antonio), and the Garden of Eden (Portia-Bassanio), and Paradise';[17] or that the play is exclusively about love, or usury, or whatever, and, insofar as it doesn't fit the critic's formulation, it is flawed.[18]

My chief concern today is not with such dismal stuff but rather with a less obviously procrustean kind of criticism which, accepting the play as a whole, attempts to account for its unity without expelling characters or issues or plot. The new consensus is laconically summarized by Frank Kermode:

> *The Merchant of Venice* ... is 'about' judgment, redemption and mercy; the supersession in human history of the grim four thousand years of unalleviated justice by the era of love and mercy. It begins with usury and corrupt love; it ends with harmony and perfect love. And all the time it tells its audience that this is its subject; only by a determined effort to avoid the obvious can one mistake the theme of *The Merchant of Venice*.[19]

In this view, developed by John Russell Brown, C.L. Barber, John Palmer, and others,[20] the wealth so mechanistically prized by Shylock is set against what Brown calls 'love's wealth,' possessiveness against prodigality, giving against taking. For Barber, 'the whole play dramatizes the conflict between the mechanisms of wealth and the masterful, social use of it.'[21] Problems that stumped other critics have been resolved. The bond plot is related to the casket plot, for example, by the positing of a central theme. In Brown's words:

> Shall we say it is a play about give and take? – about conundrums such as the more you give, the more you get, or, to him that hath shall be given, and from him that hath not, shall be taken away even that which he hath? The two parts of the play are linked by these problems: Portia is the golden fleece, the merchants venture and hazard as any lover; the caskets deal all in value, the bond and the rings are pledges of possession.[22]

One of the most satisfactory accounts to date is John R. Cooper's 'Shylock's Humanity,' a 1970 article which argues that at the play's core is a theological distinction between the values of Christianity and those of a Pauline version of old testament Judaism.[23] This view, essentially shared by the group of critics I have been discussing, and carried to an extreme by the man who sees the play as a Shakespearian *Commedia*, sets the Law, a rational principle according to which men should get exactly what they deserve, against Christian mercy, which gives freely to those who hazard all they possess. Cooper notes that not all the Christians in the play act like ideal Christians – a fact on which a number of schematic interpretations founder, and argues that

the fundamental opposition in the play is not between Jew and Christian but between two sets of values. On the one hand, there is the uncalculating generosity and forgiveness, the sense of one's own unworthiness and the infinite value of others, the attitude referred to by Portia as 'mercy.' On the other hand, there is the hard-headed attitude of those who have a high estimation of their own value and rights, and who demand just payment for themselves, whether in the form of money, or revenge, or a wife.[24]

In this account as in others the opposition in the play is seen as symbolized by the inscriptions on the caskets: Morocco trusts appearances and puts his faith in gold as Shylock does; Arragon demands what he deserves, insisting like Shylock on a rational justice; both are beaten by Bassanio who gives and hazards all. The opposition is seen by some as figured in the symbolic connotations of the metals of which the caskets are made, and by most as embodied geographically in Belmont, home of music and love, and the commercial Venice.

If I suggest that these critics are wrong, I shall have misstated my argument. What they describe is there, and reflecting on our experience of the play we recognize the patterns identified. Their analysis integrates the techniques developed in the last half-century for literary study and, perhaps more important, arises from unmistakably personal experiences of the play. Thus they hear verbal nuances and know how to talk about them; they know the significance of motifs and echoes, of dramaturgic and metrical effect, of structure and symbol, character and genre. Yet even their own writing conveys a sense of uneasy tentativeness that speaks of more than simple modesty or rhetorical disclaimer. In the first passage I cited, for example, Kermode puts eloquent quotation marks around the world 'about' when he tells us what the play is 'about.' Palmer, less insistent than some critics that the theme really dominates the play, seems dubious even about as much theme as he asserts: 'Nothing is further from Shakspeare's mind than to convey a lesson. But the lesson is there, product of a perfectly balanced and sensitive mind intent upon the dramatic presentation of human realities.'[25] I quoted before Barber's capsule summary of the theme: 'The whole play dramatizes the conflict between the mechanism of wealth and the masterful, social use of it.' But listen to the reservations implied by the sentence that follows: 'The happy ending, which abstractly considered as an event is hard to credit, and the treatment of Shylock, which abstractly considered as justice is hard to justify, work as we actually watch or read the play because these events express relief and triumph in the achievement of a distinction.' And later, after his demonstration of the total efficiency with which the play communicates its complex set of interrelated judgments on character, wealth, and love so that the audience is clearly instructed by the end: 'I must add, after all this praise for the way the play makes its distinctions about the use of wealth, that *on reflection*, not when viewing or reading the play, but when thinking about it, I find the distinction, as others have, somewhat too easy.'[26] And he goes on to demonstrate how much of the play – Portia's facile generosity, Shylock's comeuppance, Antonio's fudging of the usury argument, Shylock's large place in our consciousness – fails to fit even so subtle a schematization as he has made. Brown, you will recall, presents his summary as a question: 'Shall we say it is a play about ... ?' and I suggest that his rhetorical choice reflects a tacit acknowledgment that in some sense the formulation is narrower than the play. Look at the sentences immediately preceding his question: 'So *The Merchant of Venice* dances to its conclusion, its many elements mingling together joyfully. Perhaps when the dance is in progress, it is undesirable to look too closely for a pattern. But the dance does satisfy, and it is worth while trying to find out why.'[27] Or, in a passage from another essay on the play: 'Because such judgments are not made explicit in the play, we, as an audience in the theatre, may never become consciously aware of them; we would almost certainly fail in our response if, during performance, our whole attention was given to recognizing and elucidating such judgments.'[28]

Why, if as I have claimed the criticism of these men adds up to a synthesis that comes closer than anything before it to explaining the play, is their presentation so hedged? I suggest that they recognize that they have not in fact explained the very things that provoked them to the elucidation of meaning in the first place, the questions that the play like any good play raises in order to drive us to search for answers that are not forthcoming. Each critic in his own way suggests some conflict between the thematic pattern he identifies on reflection and his actual experience of the play. If we too come on reflection to a satisfying understanding that seems to resolve the constant inner conflict in which the process of the play sets us, we do so by treating as accidental rather than substantive the doubts with which we are left by the end.

Consider some of the problems that remain unresolved in the version of the comedy we have been discussing. Present in only five scenes, Shylock speaks fewer than four hundred lines yet dominates the play, haunting our memories during the suddenly etherialized and equally suddenly trivialized final episodes as we try to reach a simple position on the fairness of his treatment, or even on the truth of his response to it, funny, deflated, proud, inscrutable: 'I pray you give me leave to go from hence, / I am not well' (IV.i.391–2). The play is about the opposition of mercy to legalism. Cooper, subtle enough to realize that the distinction must not be made by separating out Christian lambs and Jewish goats, must nonetheless belie our own experience of the play, as he admits, in order to judge the disposition of the villain: 'Though his forced conversion to Christianity seems to us to be cruel and insulting, we are meant, I think and as many critics have said, to see this as the altogether kindly conversion of Shylock to the new rule of mercy and thus his liberation from the dilemma of the old Law.'[29] Note how that 'we are meant,' derived not from Cooper's response to something he sees as 'cruel and insulting' but from a thesis about what the play means, denies to Shakespeare's intention or the play's virtue what the comedy actually does to us. For Barber too our response to Shylock is a problem, but, like some critics whose work his supplants, he suggests that in that respect the play failed because Shakespeare cared more about his villain than his purpose could afford. But Cooper has the superior technology, and his conclusion is cleaner: we must deny that we even care about Shylock's harsh dismissal and his forced conversion so that we may feel, in Brown's phrase, all the elements of the play 'mingling together joyfully.' How much more considerate both of art and of our response to it is Stanley Cavell's observation in an essay entitled 'A Matter of Meaning It':

The artist is responsible for everything that happens in his work – and not just in the sense that it is done, but in the sense that it is *meant*. It is a terrible responsibility; very few men have the gift and the patience to shoulder it. But it is all the more terrible, when it *is* shouldered, not to appreciate it, to refuse to understand something meant so well.[30]

In Belmont is a lady richly left,
And she is fair, and (fairer than that word),
Of wondrous virtues, – sometimes from her eyes
I did receive fair speechless messages:
Her name is Portia, nothing undervalu'd
To Cato's daughter, Brutus' Portia,
Nor is the wide world ignorant of her worth,
For the four winds blow in from every coast
Renowned suitors, and her sunny locks
Hang on her temples like a golden fleece,
Which makes her seat of Belmont Colchos' strond,
And many Jasons come in quest of her.
O my Antonio, had I but the means
To hold a rival place with one of them,
I have a mind presages me such thrift
That I should questionless be fortunate.   (1.i.161–76)

If Quiller-Couch and, alas, too many modern directors can dismiss
Bassanio as a mere fortune hunter, we have been instructed to a more
complex judgment: though he is indeed interested in Portia's money,
Bassanio does not, as Shylock does, let money take the place of values
that matter more, and so as a social Christian he is allowed to have it.
Shylock loves only gold, material substance, we are told, while Bassanio loves Portia as well as gold; after all, he compares her with
Brutus' Portia. Yet Bassanio's way of comparing his Portia to Brutus' is
to say that the one is 'nothing undervalu'd' to the other; he praises her
first for being rich and then for being fair; it is the ambiguous quality
of 'worth' that draws the world to her; his game is thrift and his hope
to be fortunate; and he sees himself as Jason stealing the golden fleece
– a legend later reduced to its crassest implications by Gratiano (III.ii.
237–40). And of course Morocco's crazy apostrophe to the gold casket
(II.vii.37–59) will reveal exactly the same confusion of values as
Bassanio's speech, echoing its images and language and even its word
'undervalued' – and only moments before we hear of Shylock's similar
confusion between his daughter and his ducats. How is Morocco really
guilty when Bassanio is not? Portia's true gold may be spiritual, but
Bassanio gets himself out of trouble with his creditors by her material
wealth. Furthermore, if we are to believe that his superiority consists
in his ability to tell reality from appearance, we are not allowed to
forget that Portia of the beautiful soul is also a beautiful woman, a
romantic as well as a commercial prize. She herself is delighted to be

rid of Morocco because of his looks: 'Let all of his complexion choose me so,' she says as he leaves, and insofar as the word points to temper as it does to appearance, inner as well as outer, it suggests a correspondence between looks and character that the casket plot seems to be denying.

The thematic values identified by those who see the play as a conflict between the Hebrew and Christian dispensations point to rejection of the wealth returned in abundance to the Christian company and to a demonstration of the virtue of impoverished love. That the comic resolution demands worldly success as well, a return of more than has in fact been hazarded, suggests a conflict between Christianity and comedy as deep as the one generally seen between it and tragedy. If, as Brown says, the comic point is that those already rich spiritually are materially enriched by the happy outcome, my point is that constant signals in the play imply that it isn't all so simple and that they keep us from the single-minded joy Brown sees as our final state. Everything Brown says is there, and yet by the end we are not so sure that it resolves the tensions the play has aroused in us.

Had I more space I should discuss other elements in the play that cause uneasiness in an audience and difficulties for a critic who wants to make a schematic analysis – the pointed contrast between a Belmont and a Venice not really so different from one another; the peculiar characterization of the melancholy Antonio, the link between his sadness and Portia's in their opening lines, and the fact that the play is named after him; the ring plot which, though it enables Portia to teach once again her lesson about bonds and love, reminds us of her trickery and her tendency to domineer, so inconsistent with the moving spontaneity of her emotions both as Bassanio chooses the lead casket and as she speaks of mercy. But I shall cite, and briefly, only two matters.

First, the characterizations of Lorenzo and Jessica have been disputed often enough to suggest that their ambivalence is built into the play. The judgments of the best critics reflect difficulty with them. Goddard sees their villainy as necessary to prod Shylock to revenge. Burckhardt condemns them as an inversion of the true bonded love of the play's theme, lawless and mean-spirited, 'spendthrift rather than liberal, thoughtless squanderers of stolen substance,' trading for a monkey 'the ring which ought to seal their love.'[31] Yet Brown sees them as exemplars of 'the central theme of love's wealth.' He too sees them as squanderers, but in 'joyful celebration'; he praises their *'unthrift* love' and argues that if Jessica's 'reckless prodigality is a fault, it is a generous one and an understandable excess after the restriction of her father's precept.'[32] Plainly Lorenzo and Jessica subvert any schematic reading of the play. If, for example, some signals suggest that the conversion forced on Shylock is an act of kindness, Lorenzo makes us resist that interpretation of Christian treatment of the Jew:

> she hath directed
> How I shall take her from her father's house,
> What gold and jewels she is furnish'd with,
> What page's suit she hath in readiness, –
> If e'er the Jew her father come to heaven,
> It will be for his gentle daughter's sake,
> And never dare misfortune cross her foot,
> Unless she do it under this excuse,
> That she is issue to a faithless Jew.   (ii.iv.29–37)

If, as Burckhardt thinks, Lorenzo and Jessica help silhouette Portia's genuine value, their presence in Belmont and their common cause with her against Shylock complicate the play for interpretation, as does the strange excursus on music that Lorenzo delivers in the last act.

And that takes me to my second matter, the beads of language, imagery, and ideas threaded on the string of music. It is a commonplace that music – the music of the heavenly choirs, the music that Portia has sounded as Bassanio makes his choice – accompanies the life of grace, sensibility, love, and play, the life won by those who triumph in the play, while Shylock hates 'the vile squealing of the wry-necked fife' (ii.v.29ff) and mocks those who 'cannot contain their urine' 'when the bagpipe sings i'th'nose' (iv.i.49–50). As Lorenzo puts it, the play seems to say:

> The man that hath no music in himself,
> Nor is not moved with concord of sweet sounds,
> Is fit for treasons, stratagems, and spoils,
> ...
> Let no such man be trusted.   (v.i.83–8)

But Lorenzo is a poor witness, since 'treasons, stratagems, and spoils' characterizes his exploits at least as accurately as it does those of Shylock, who has other personality problems. Furthermore, Lorenzo's dialogue with Jessica is sandwiched between the episodes of Portia's

stratagem against Bassanio, the ring plot, and helps both to undercut
the enormous emotional claim she has made on the audience in the
trial scene and to call attention to the triviality at best of the game
she plays with the ring. We might note also that the chief other entry
of music into the play is the song that Portia has sung during Bassanio's ordeal with the caskets, and interestingly that song has occasioned a still unsettled debate as to whether it is simply a pretext to
suggest 'lead' through rhymes with 'bred,' 'head,' and the like.

Once again, my point is not that critics who are demonstrably right
about so much are to be dismissed, lightly or otherwise. But one may
justifiably ask how so much brain power in the most sensitive and
highly trained critical audiences has produced so little that can't be
punctured simply by watching one's own responses to details of a
play. One may ask furthermore why critical readings of similar
methodology and equal brilliance by critics of different temperaments
so often add up to radically opposed interpretations. My guess is that
our troubles stem in good part from the value we have put on reductiveness. We have been betrayed by a bias toward what can be set out
in rational argument. Before the full impact of the new romantic
understanding of art hit the professional study of literature, that bias
reflected itself in the decision of literary scholars to concentrate on
matters now seen as less than central to the understanding of the work
itself. But, under the delayed influence of Coleridge and his contemporaries in England and Germany, literary study began to realize
how far it was from dealing with the experience of art and to come
closer to it by focussing on the interpretation of texts. To be respect-
able, however, the newer study had to produce conclusions which
were derived as logically and argued as closely as demonstrations of
source and influence had been. Attracted by the spectacular possibilities of a new technology – Empson had to number the types of
ambiguity – critics fell into an invisible trap, the fallacy of misplaced
concreteness: what can be brought by self-contained argument to a
satisfying conclusion is what is worth discussing, and responses that
don't work into the argument must be discounted. Given a romantic
inheritance, given a genuine sense of the integrity of a single poem or
play or novel, given a puritanical bias which assumes that the value
of literature is moral and familiarly expresses itself in the notion of
the professor of literature as lay preacher, given a long history of
assumption that art is valuable at least half because of what it teaches,
and given an art which is verbal, so that virtually all the patterns,
parallels, structural juxtapositions, image clusters, ironic repetitions,

variations, and generic conventions a critic can find can be translated into other words, was it not inevitable that the bias toward a criticism that would produce discrete and rational arguments should culminate in the study of meaning?

There is nothing surprising about our bias towards rationality. It is perfectly consistent with our hopes for civilization, with the exigencies of the classroom, with our hierarchically structured universities and departments of literature, with our needs, both inner- and outer-directed, to write prose that is logical, coherent, defensible, documentable. And the critical paradigm that establishes the identification of a meaning as the principle of unity in a work and our experience of it is consistent with patterns that *do* exist in the plays – otherwise I could not have distinguished among the kinds of criticism I have discussed – and that need to be explicated. But it is time to recall that all intellection is reductive, and that the closer an intellectual system comes to full internal consistency and universality of application – as with Newtonian mechanics – the more obvious become the exclusiveness of its preoccupations and the limitations of its value. What our successful criticism of meaning has made clear – and I include not only naïve reduction but also that much more sophisticated criticism which argued so cogently against the heresy of paraphrase while still being concerned with summary thematic statements[33] – is its consistent suppression of the nature of aesthetic experience.

Should it not have disturbed critics interested in hypostatizing meaning that no two critics of any play really agree with one another in their formulations, that no two performances reflect identical interpretations or produce uniform responses in their audiences, that all of us return to plays we know intimately to discover that we respond to them in entirely new ways? Is not the disagreement about works of art as significant a fact for the critic as the interpretation he favours? Might a fruitful criticism not begin and end there as validly as it now does with reduction to thematic descriptions of unity?

Confidence in our methodology has enabled us over the years to sidestep the implications of what we know about the creative act. No reputable critic would attempt to validate his analysis by claiming that the meaning he extracts was in the author's conscious intention, and even poets now accept the thesis that what the critic reveals in their work, no matter how unfamiliar to them, may have been a dominant factor in preconscious activity during composition. Now if we validly appeal to pre- or sub-conscious layers of the artist's experience, we ought to be ready to do the same for the audience, whose experience of a theme may be just as remote from consciousness. And if we do so wholeheartedly, we are likely to find little reason why an abstract idea should have been the central factor either in creation or in audience experience. It is perfectly clear that the plays we care about lend themselves so handily to thematic analysis that something in them must provoke our formulations. But we do not have to believe therefore that that something is best expressed as a meaning on which no two experiences of the work can agree, or that it dominates the artist's experience or ours. The eddying signals communicated by the play arouse a total and complex involvement of our intellect, our moral sensibility, our need to complete incomplete patterns and answer questions, our longing to judge, and that involvement is so incessantly in motion that to pin it down to a meaning is to negate its very essence. We can recognize the patterns the critics have demonstrated, but having done so we are not allowed to feel that a pattern is a play. The essence of our experience is our haunting sense of what doesn't fit the thesis we are tempted at every moment to derive; in fact, the ultimate irreducibility to a schema may be the hallmark of the work of art and the source of its power.

Like many insights that have attained widespread acceptance, Keats' definition of 'negative capability' has been allowed to lose its cutting edge.[34] If Keats speaks as rightly as I think he does for artists and for us as their audiences, then the critic must learn to defer his 'irritable reaching after fact and reason' and learn to think of 'uncertainties, mysteries, doubts' as the stuff of our experience of art. To put it another way, he must treat experience as the subject of discussions of art. That is the point of John Dewey's profound and too little heeded *Art as Experience*, which sees the creation of art and the response to it as quintessentially like life, characterized by process, tension, resistance, and an ineffable sense of integrity. Keats' insight is implicit in the criticism of Kenneth Burke, who has insisted on asking what the poem does for the poet and his readers rather than what it says, who sees a play by Shakespeare as 'a device for the arousing and fulfilling of expectations in an audience,' and who has defined 'the symbolic act' as *'the dancing of an attitude.'*[35] For Dewey and Burke the job of the critic is to analyze in the work of art a set of highly complex interrelations among its elements which the audience, experiencing those elements as they are presented, perceives as a unity. And for Dewey and Burke form and content are inseparable because the experience of the work is one – hence 'the dancing of an attitude.'

That phrase, strikingly similar to Brown's reading of *The Merchant of Venice* as a dance, tempts one to wonder how much of Burke's power derives from his having first been a music critic. René Wellek, developing a theory of literature, can, despite all his better intentions, validate the search for meaning by calling the work of art 'a system of norms of ideal *concepts* which are intersubjective.'[36] But the music critic cannot look for a conceptual content at the centre of a work's intention and power. The attraction of the word 'theme' for literary critics may be its musical implications, but its prime meaning as they use it is its older lexical meaning, the text of a sermon or the subject of a discourse. For the musicologist a theme is generally one among several, and it is never to be confused with meaning. If he wants to discuss meaning, the music critic has no choice but to study in minute particularity the ways in which at each point a composition arouses and fulfills, or fails to fulfill, an audience's expectations. A new criticism of Shakespeare might well begin with the musical analysis of Leonard B. Meyer.[37] Morally concerned with music as an art that communicates, Meyer has derived from gestalt theory instruments for the analysis of the art work's complex and significant control of its audience's responses. Interestingly he is concerned with devices very much like those that have attracted literary critics of recent generations: the use of one phrase to make us think of another, recurrence, variation, parallel, the apparent emergence of pattern out of linked details. But he is not interested in the kind of reduction that such discovery generally elicits from literary critics.

In Shakespeare criticism a new wind may already be blowing. So much is suggested by Maynard Mack's essay on 'The Jacobean Shakespeare,' which treats patterns with the imagination and respect generally accorded only to meanings (as if most critics were driven by their irritable reaching after fact and reason always to shout, like Amy Lowell, 'Christ, what are patterns for?'); and by the work of Stephen Booth, who infuriatingly refuses to find a conclusion in the turbulence he demonstrates in Shakespeare. And John Russell Brown himself has argued repeatedly for a theatrical recreation of Shakespeare that will not try to pin the plays down to interpretations that constrict the range of meanings in them.[38]

But these are only beginnings. We need to embark on a large-scale reconsideration of the phenomena that our technology has enabled us to explore, to consider the play as a dynamic interaction between artist and audience, to learn to talk about the process of our involvement rather than our considered view after the aesthetic event. We need to find concepts other than meaning to account for the end of a play, the sense of unverbalizable coherence, lucidity, and unity that makes us know that we have been through a single, significant, and shared experience. We need to learn to distinguish between the art represented in its extreme form by the murder mystery, in which the end completes the gestalt figure that tells us unequivocally how we should have responded to every detail along the way, and Shakespeare's profounder art, no less powerful in drawing us to a final vantage point from which we may look back over the whole, but ultimately irreducible to an explanatory schema.

To get down to cases, what can we do with *The Merchant of Venice*? We must acknowledge that hostile and sympathetic readings of Shylock or of Bassanio and Portia are created by ambivalent signals. We must acknowledge the deep polarities in the comedy while resisting the temptation to see them as conclusively resolved in favour of one character or group of characters, or to see them defined in terms of one issue. The play's strategy sets Shylock, anality, precise definition, possessiveness, contempt for prodigality, legalism, the Old Testament Jews, dislocated values, mechanistic ethics and psychology, a fondness for bonds, stinginess, a wronged father, a conventional comic butt, an outsider, a paradoxical honesty about intention, repressive parents, distrust of emotion and hatred of music, bad luck, and failure, against Portia but also against Antonio, Bassanio, Lorenzo, Jessica, Gratiano, freedom, metaphorical richness in language, prodigality, transcendence of the law, intense commitment to legalism, stealing, the New Testament, Christians, values that sometimes seem simple and right, sometimes complex and right, sometimes complex and wrong, love, generosity, cruelty to a father, life within a charmed circle, self-deception about motivation, youth rebelling against conventional comic repressive parenthood, love of emotion and music, supreme trickery, a fondness for bonds, good luck, success. At every point at which we want simplicity we get complexity. Some signals point to coherence – thus the conflict between the ideas of prodigality and possessiveness, or between two definitions of prodigality. But just as many create discomfort, point to centrifugality – virtually every mention of a ring and every episode involving one, the grouping of characters, the links between scenes that constantly ask us to reassess what we've just seen and interpreted in terms of what we're now seeing. In terms of moral content that we can extract, we come away with precious little: by the end we know as we knew before we began that cruelty is bad and love better, just as we know in *King Lear* that love between fathers and daughters is to be prized. If *The Merchant of Venice* or any great play by Shakespeare were to be judged by what we can claim to have learned from it, or by its ability to lead critics to clear formulations that agree with each other, society would not pay for English departments. Yet by the end we have been through a constantly turbulent experience which demands an incessant giving and taking back of allegiance, a counterpoint of ever-shifting response to phrase, speech, character, scene, action, a welter of emotions and ideas and perceptions and surprises and intuitions of underlying unity and coherence rivalled only by our experience in the real world so perplexingly suggested by the artifact to which we yield ourselves. The attempt to state the meaning of the play is not much more likely to produce an accurate account than an attempt to state the meaning of life. But to say that we cannot profitably talk about the meaning of life is not to say that life is meaningless. In the understanding of art as of life the decision no longer to be tied up in fruitless attempts to reduce significant process and teeming multiplicity to prosaic meaning is a liberating beginning, an invitation to examine the thing itself.

NOTES

1 For a useful survey of the theatrical vicissitudes of Shylock, see Toby Lelyveld *Shylock on the Stage* (London 1961).

2 Paul N. Siegel *Shakespeare in His Time and Ours* (Notre Dame 1968) 245

3 John W. Draper, 'The Theme of *The Merchant of Venice*,' *Stratford to Dogberry: Studies in Shakespeare's Earlier Plays* (Pittsburgh 1961) 128

4 Harold C. Goddard *The Meaning of Shakespeare* (1951; Chicago 1960) 1, 85. In view of the argument to be developed here and my general admiration of Goddard, it should be noted that the title of his posthumous book was assigned by the publisher.

5 H.B. Charlton *Shakespearian Comedy* (1938; London 1966) 159

6 Norman Nathan, 'Three Notes on *The Merchant of Venice*,' *Shakespeare Association Bulletin* 23 (1948) 155

7 The latter interpretation is Goddard's.

8 On legal matters in the play see John Palmer *Comic Characters of Shakespeare* (London 1946) 64–5, and George W. Keeton *Shakespeare and His Legal Problems* (London 1930) 10–21.

9 My text is John Russell Brown *The Merchant of Venice* Arden ed (1955; London 1959).

10 L. Teeter, 'Scholarship and the Art of Criticism,' *Journal of English Literary History* 5 (1938) 187, sums up the conflict in exemplary fashion: 'There is little doubt that Shakespeare, consciously at least, intended this passage to raise a laugh at the expense of Shylock. Yet to many cultured readers of today it is to a large extent a pathetic speech arousing a sympathetic pity for the mistreated father.' C.L. Barber *Shakespeare's Festive Comedy* (1959; Cleveland/New York 1963) 184, argues that at the end of this scene 'there *is* pathos; but it is being fed into the comic mill and makes the laughter all the more hilarious.'

11 Thus H.B. Charlton asserts (160): 'However one reads the play, it is certain that the intentions of the author were in many ways defeated. Shylock, Antonio, Portia and Jessica do not stand forth as they were meant to do. The parts they were called upon to play by their author's prejudices did not square with those the dramatist worked out for them. There is throughout the clash of rival schemes, the proposals of Shakespeare's deliberate will, and the disposals of his creative imagination.'

12 E.E. Stoll *Shakespeare Studies: Historical and Comparative in Method* (New York 1927) 255–366

13 See for example S.C. Sen Gupta *Shakespearian Comedy* (Oxford 1950) 132 and John Middleton Murry *Shakespeare* (London 1936) 194, 199.

14 Lawrence W. Hyman, 'The Rival Lovers in *The Merchant of Venice*,' *Shakespeare Quarterly* 21 (1970) 109; see also Peter G. Phialas *Shakespeare's Romantic Comedies: The Development of Their Form and Meaning* (Chapel Hill 1966) 135, where virtually the same statement is made.

15 Hyman, 'The Rival Lovers' 110

16 A few instances will suffice. Draper, 'The Theme of *The Merchant of Venice*,' 135: 'Shylock the Jew was merely Venetian local color; Shylock the usurer was a commentary on London life.' Bernard Grebanier *The Truth about Shylock* (New York 1962) x: 'Shylock is not only a Jew, he is also a prototype of the banker,' and Shakespeare's real interest is in attacking the impersonality of banks. Siegel *Shakespeare in His Time and Ours* 245, justifies audience hatred of Shylock on the grounds that Shakespeare was after Puritans rather than Jews. Thomas H. Fujimura, 'Mode and Structure in *The Merchant of Venice*,' *PMLA* 81 (1966) 504 writes: 'The most serious obstacle to grasping the ironic mode in which he is presented is to regard Shylock primarily as a Jew. In adapting the bond story, Shakespeare stressed his Jewish traits, no doubt for the practical reason that the associations worked to communicate the theme with the greatest economy on the Elizabethan stage. But he is hateful not because he is a Jew but because he is Shylock ... Jessica ... is ashamed not of her father's Jewishness but of his "manners," that is, his character. Shylock's Jewishness is thus, in Aristotelian terms, an "accident"; his substance is his spiritual deadness or leadenness.'

17 Fujimura, 'Mode and Structure' 501

18 A notable recent example of this sort of reductiveness is the account by Phialas cited in note 14 above, where the literal meaning of the plot is traded in for a symbolic reading which, when it cannot be demonstrated fully to dominate the play, is patronized as a relatively primitive attempt by Shakespeare (though far advanced beyond the earlier plays) to dispose of some themes the dramatist had been working out. See especially 153, 168–9.

19 Frank Kermode, 'The Mature Comedies' in John Russell Brown and Bernard Harris, eds *Early Shakespeare* (Stratford-upon-Avon Studies 3) (1961; New York 1966) 224

20 Brown, introduction to the Arden edition; 'The Realization of Shylock: a Theatrical Criticism,' *Early Shakespeare* 187–210; 'Love's Wealth and the Judgement of *The Merchant of Venice*,' *Shakespeare and His Comedies* (1957; London 1962) 45–81; Barber *Shakespeare's Festive Comedy*

162–91; Palmer *Comic Characters of Shakespeare*. Despite his eccentrically systematized reading, Fujimura reads the play similarly, as does Grebanier.

21 Barber *Shakespeare's Festive Comedy* 170

22 Brown, introduction to Arden edition, p.lviii

23 John R. Cooper, 'Shylock's Humanity' *Shakespeare Quarterly* 21 (1970) 117–24

24 Ibid 123

25 Palmer *Comic Characters of Shakespeare* 86

26 Barber *Shakespeare's Festive Comedy* 170, 189

27 Brown, introduction to Arden edition, p.lviii

28 Brown *Shakespeare and His Comedies* 74

29 Cooper, 'Shylock's Humanity' 121

30 Stanley Cavell *Must We Mean What We Say?* (New York 1969) 236–7

31 Sigurd Burckhardt *Shakespearean Meanings* (Princeton 1968) 224

32 Brown *Shakespeare and His Comedies* 70

33 Though Richards, Empson, et al, succeeded in establishing the invalidity of simple meanings consistent with one statement quoted from a literary context, and Richards in his *Philosophy of Rhetoric* argued for a 'context' theory of meaning, the fruit of their labour has been a more deft exploration of more complex and inclusive meanings which ultimately leads to paraphrase. Looked at from the vantage point of the present day, Cleanth Brooks' *The Well Wrought Urn* seems less free from an overriding concern with meaning and paraphrase than it did in 1947. Though some of his argument in 'The Heresy of Paraphrase' (*The Well Wrought Urn* [New York 1947] 176–96) would seem almost to have stated my case for me, Brooks finally absorbs much of the traditional position he is attacking in his insistence on a 'real core of meaning which constitutes the essence of the poem.' 'Structure,' which Brooks proposes as an alternative to Winters' 'rational meaning,' leads equally to hypostasis because it is not finally concerned with the interaction between signal and response, focussing rather on 'the unification of attitudes into a hierarchy subordinated to a total and governing attitude' within the poem (189).

34 Lionel Trilling ed *The Selected Letters of John Keats* (New York 1951) 92

35 Kenneth Burke *The Philosophy of Literary Form* (New York 1957) viii, 9; italics his

36 René Wellek *Theory of Literature* new ed. rev. (New York 1956) 156

37 See especially *Emotion and Meaning in Music* (Chicago 1956) and *Music, the Arts, and Ideas: Patterns and Predictions in Twentieth-Century Culture* (Chicago 1967).

38 Maynard Mack, 'The Jacobean Shakespeare: Some Observations on the Construction of the Tragedies' in John Russell Brown and Bernard Harris, eds *Jacobean Theatre* (Stratford-upon-Avon Studies 1) (London 1960); Stephen Booth, 'On the Value of *Hamlet*,' in Norman Rabkin, ed *Reinterpretations of Elizabethan Drama* (New York 1969) 137–76, and *An Essay on Shakespeare's Sonnets* (New Haven 1969); John Russell Brown, 'Theatrical Research and the Criticism of Shakespeare and His Contemporaries' *Shakespeare Quarterly* 13 (1962) 451–61, and 'The Theatrical Element of Shakespeare Criticism' in Norman Rabkin, ed *Reinterpretations of Elizabethan Drama* 177–95

David Bevington /
Shakespeare vs Jonson on Satire

Most of the presumed skirmishes of the so-called 'War of the Theatres'
or *Poetomachia* have been shown never to have taken place. At one
time, early in this century when historical criticism held uncontested
sway, this Renaissance Battle of the Poets was imagined to have
encompassed almost every author living during the years 1598 to
1602. Drayton, Chapman, and Fulke Greville were all drawn into
the fray, along with Marston, Dekker, and Jonson at the centre
of things.[1] Each of these authors was identified with one or more
dramatic characters in *Histriomastix, Jack Drum's Entertainment,
Cynthia's Revels, Satiromastix, The Poetaster,* and an ever-increasing
number of plays. Naturally Shakespeare did not escape this search
for topical identity. According to H.D. Gray, for example, Shakespeare is to be identified with the public actor Aesop in *The Poetaster*
who gives information to the magistrate Asinius Lupus, accusing
Horace (i.e., Jonson) of conspiring to overthrow the rulers of the
state.[2] Such an identification would unmistakably associate Shakespeare with those persons urging a curtailment of private theatrical
activities because of their slanderous character, and would imply
Jonson's contempt for Shakespeare as one who toadied to the establishment.

The particular identification has of course long been rejected. But
the reason for such a speculation has never been entirely explained
away. In *The Return from Parnassus, Part II*, a Cambridge University play written in 1601–2 with obvious awareness of the contempo-

rary London stage, one satirical skit involves a visit by some haplessly unemployed students to the Globe Theatre, where the young men submit to an interview in hopes of finding a job. Among other items of theatrical gossip, one of the actors (Will Kemp) alludes to the stage war going on between the public and private companies, and notes with satisfaction the triumph of Shakespeare over Jonson: 'Why, here's our fellow Shakespeare puts them all down, aye, and Ben Jonson too. O, that Ben Jonson is a pestilent fellow; he brought up Horace [in *The Poetaster*] giving the poets a pill, but our fellow Shakespeare hath given him a purge that made him bewray his credit' (IV.iii.1806ff). What was this purge? Does it allude to a play written by Shakespeare to put down Jonson, or does it mean simply that Shakespeare's company administered a mighty comeuppance (in *Satiromastix*, which they performed) and that Shakespeare as a chief writer for the company lent his moral support to Dekker's and Marston's campaign? It could be, of course, that the author of the *Parnassus* play was simply misinformed by popular rumour; but even this hypothesis would lend support to the notion that Shakespeare was widely regarded as having held views in accord with those of *Satiromastix*. The *Parnassus* plays were pro-Jonson, and the passage quoted above is itself satirical, suggesting even further that the intellectual circles of Cambridge and London were full of gossip about an open rift between Shakespeare and Jonson; the *Parnassus* author openly shares Jonson's presumed resentment at what Shakespeare has done.[3]

In this essay I shall take a detailed look at the generally held notion that Shakespeare and Jonson did indeed maintain contrasting positions as to the valid uses of satire in drama, and that (although their personal relations remained cordial) this debate was at the core of the very real divisions between public and private stages. There is of course much truth to this generalization. Jonson certainly took exception on a number of occasions to Shakespeare's history plays and popular romances, and Shakespeare in *As You Like It* permits Duke Senior to express a profound scepticism as to the moral intent of satire. Even if Shakespeare and Jonson remained on good terms, the matters at issue led to angry exchanges among other authors, so that a partly knowledgeable spectator of the theatre in 1601 might well be excused for assuming Shakespeare's active engagement in the fracas on the side of the public stage. Nevertheless, Shakespeare's position was anything but rigid. He not only stayed above the personal bitterness of the *Poetomachia*, but studied the merits of the debate in warmly sympathetic terms, allowing the theory of satire to have its fair say. Moreover, he experimented with satire in his own art. Jonson showed no comparable flexibility; but Shakespeare's fascination with satire, occasioned by the new wave of satirical writings in the late 1590s, was by no means simply negative.

Jonson's comments on Shakespeare are well known, and, despite their range from critical to laudatory, they are of a piece. In his conversations with William Drummond of Hawthornden he complains that Shakespeare 'wanted art,' and offended verisimilitude by supplying Bohemia with a seacoast. In *Timber* he rebukes Shakespeare's speed in writing and failure to cut lines: 'would he had blotted a thousand!' The Induction to *Bartholomew Fair* takes a swipe at *Titus Andronicus* as a too-popular blood tragedy in the style of *The Spanish Tragedy*, and at *The Tempest* for its drolleries, monsters, and other incredible events not found in nature. The memorial verses in the Folio, though full of warm and genuine praise, do offer the learned qualification that Shakespeare had 'small Latin and less Greek.'[4] In the prologue written for the folio version of *Every Man in His Humour*, Jonson scoffs at attempts on the public stage to present 'Yorke and Lancaster's long iarres' with 'three rustie swords And helpe of some few foot-and-halfe-foote words.'[5] Although Thomas Heywood also wrote plays for the public stage about England's fifteenth-century civil wars, clearly Shakespeare was the prime object of Jonson's attack. (And yet, ironically enough, Shakespeare had acted in the very play for which these critical remarks were later written.) In the same prologue, Jonson inveighs against Choruses wafting us overseas, creaking thrones descending 'the boyes to please,' and other features of dramatic romance with which Shakespeare's name became closely associated in *Pericles, Cymbeline*, and *The Winter's Tale* (written later than *Every Man In*, but perhaps before the prologue of the folio version).[6]

Jonson, in short, held Shakespeare's genius in extremely high regard, but considered him deficient in classical training and orientation. He believed that with better command of the ancient tongues, and hence with greater knowledge of the classical dramatists and their genres, Shakespeare might indeed have written as greatly as his talent deserved. Jonson the literary dictator asked only that Shakespeare be more like him, writing as a satirical observer of men's manners. Nowhere, however, is any personal anger or resentment revealed.[7] Even during those delicious moments in Scotland when Jonson let down his hair, confiding among various matters that he had indeed written *The Poetaster* on Marston, he made no comparable confession of an urge to humiliate Shakespeare.

Jonson's manifestos in his various comedies, and the actions of the comedies themselves, demonstrate a unified neoclassical theory of satire consistent with the critical things he had to say about Shakespearian history and romance. In the prologue to *Every Man In* Jonson undertakes to design a play such 'as other playes should be,' with 'deedes and language such as men do vse, And persons such as *Comoedie* would chuse When she would shew an Image of the times, And sport with humane follies, not with crimes.' Diction must be natural and conversational, fitted to the social stations of the speakers; lofty or quaint diction is out of place in an action designed to hold up a mirror to contemporary society. The character types must be appropriate to neoclassical conceptions of comedy: not protagonists of tragedy such as kings or military leaders, but personable young men and women and their clever servants confronting miserly fathers, jealous old wooers, fops, poetasters, and braggart soldiers. Unities of time, place, and action must of course avoid the horrendous practice of having 'a child, now swadled, to proceede Man, and then shoote vp, in one beard and weede, Past threescore yeeres.' Decorum forbids the use of vaudeville slapstick merely to please the groundlings: as Jonson promises in the prologue to *Volpone*, 'no egges are broken, Nor quaking custards with fierce teeth affrighted, Wherewith your rout are so delighted.'

Most importantly, Jonsonian satire chooses to castigate human folly and to combat it with the appropriate weapon of satirical exposure. To be sure, Jonson does transgress his own precept of avoiding human crimes in *Volpone*, perhaps responding to the pressures of conventional morality since the play was performed at the Globe in 1606 by the King's Men (for whom Jonson had written plays earlier). Volpone and Mosca involve themselves in crimes, not follies, when they undertake to seduce a virtuous wife and disinherit a blameless son. These offences demand legal punishments, even though the *avocatori* of Venice are themselves corrupt, and even though the victimized Celia and Bonario are not sufficiently convincing as characters to win our sympathy. Jonson's dissatisfaction with this ending is underscored by his rewriting of *Volpone* in *The Alchemist*. Even in *Volpone*, as Jonas Barish has observed, the sub-plot of Sir Politic Would-Be and Peregrine serves to demonstrate the perfect working out of a satiric plot dealing with follies rather than crimes, thereby counterpointing the troublesome complexities of the main plot.[8] Sir Politic is a busybody and fatuous tourist whose meddlesome plans for fumigating ships with onion-water harm nothing more serious than our sense of human dignity. His comic nemesis, Peregrine, is the perfect Jonsonian satirical persona, well-bred, amused at men's folly, a disinterested observer, always cool, clever in engineering exposures, motivated not by personal animus but by a poet's desire to reveal the hypocrisy of man. His stratagem of advising Sir Politic to hide from the Venetian authorities under a tortoise shell perfectly fits the punishment to the offence: Sir Politic must be turned over on his back and exposed, like the helpless, wiggling, slow-moving dullard that he is. No action is required other than to allow him to prepare his own trap and then to reveal him publicly for what he is. Recourse to law is not appropriate; the satirical spokesman himself is judge and executioner. Significantly, no meaningful cure is effected either: Sir Politic is pronounced un-redeemable, and is laughed off stage.

Every Man in His Humour (1598) similarly follows the precept of its own later prologue to sport with human follies, not with crimes. Structurally it features the generic plot of 'a trick to catch the old one,' to which are added the satirical exposures of various humours-types. In the familiar confrontation of Plautine comedy, Lorenzo junior (or Young Knowell, as he is called in the folio version) must find ways, assisted by the knavish servant Musco (Brainworm), to outsmart his suspicious father and elope with his lady fair, Hesperida (Mistress Bridget). This plot is thoroughly neoclassical in pattern but is only a very small part of *Every Man In*, serving almost perfunctorily as a vehicle plot in which the main order of business is the collecting of humorous specimens by the amiable wags Lorenzo jr and Prospero (Wellbred). The game they play is to gather humorous types for each other's delectation, and then to see how quickly each can identify what the humour is. As Lorenzo jr says, in presenting his latest find, Stephano the country gull, to Prospero:

sir, a kinsman of mine, one that may make our Musique the fuller, and he please; he has his humor, sir.
PROSPERO [*eagerly*] O, what ist? What ist?
LORENZO, JR Nay, Ile neyther do thy iudgement, nor his folly that wrong, as to prepare thy apprehension. Ile leaue him to the mercy of the time, if you can take him: so. (II.iii)

(The folio version changed the end of this last speech to 'I'le leaue him to the mercy o' your search, if you can take him, so.') This encounter takes place where the wits have gathered for an evening of this parlor game of 'twenty questions' or 'animal, vegetable, or mineral?' The fools, wholly unaware of their absurdity, are on show in a kind of gallery or zoo. They form no essential part of the nominally central plot by which Lorenzo jr will win Hesperida and outwit his father. The fools are there to typify pet Jonsonian hates, such as cowardly braggadocio, irrational jealousy, affectation in fencing or swearing, objecting to tobacco, resort to legal process for the settling of petty quarrels, and above all poetasting. The plot device, basically simple although enriched by multiple interwoven strands, is to pit the humorous gulls against one another by arranging fabricated quarrels and abortive rendezvous. In each case the punishment fits the crime: jealousy deserves to feed on its own imagined treacheries, blustering cowardice deserves to have its bluff called to account, and so on.

All this is manipulated by the clever servant in conjunction with the wits, but the poetic justice of the ending is administered by a figure of comic nemesis: Doctor (or Justice) Clement, nominally a representative of the law (we should remember that this play too was acted on the public stage) but in fact one who regards the law as supremely irrelevant to the follies brought before him. Like Peregrine in *Volpone* he shares the temperament of the satirical poet. He suits his medicinal correction to each case: a heart-to-heart talk with Old Lorenzo (Knowell), a warning about jealousy to Thorello (Kitely), a mocking threat of legal action against Cob for inveighing against tobacco. For the incorrigible gulls, however, Clement pronounces the maximum sentence of the satirist: ridiculing exposure, and banishment from urbane society. Matheo's verses are to be read aloud and burned, after which he is banished from the Jonsonian feast of reconcilement. Clement thus stands in for Jonson as the literary dictator whose right and obligation it is to expose and destroy pretentious idiocy in the literary arts. The power assumed is not legal or institutional power, but a power of censorship exercised in the name of civilized opinion.

This peculiarly Jonsonian formula of the exposure of various humours types, often with only a tangential connection to the nominally central neoclassical plot, will be important when we get to Shakespeare's flirtation with satirical plotting in *Twelfth Night*. Equally central to the debate between Shakespeare and Jonson over the uses of satire are Jonson's observations on the problem of libel in his writings. Jonson was frequently accused of libel, in *The Isle of Dogs*, *Sejanus*, *Eastward Ho*, and others, and just as frequently he took occasion to defend his art against what he considered a vulgar and malicious misconception. In the second prologue to *Epicoene*, for example, 'Occasion'd by some person's impertinent exception' to the play, he describes art's highest purpose as the taxing of human follies; 'So persons were not touch'd' – that is, so long as individuals are not libelled. He holds that poets 'never credit gain'd By writing truths, but things (like truths) well feign'd.'

> If any yet will, with particular sl[e]ight
> Of application, wrest what he doth write
> And that he meant or him or her will say,
> They make a libell which he made a play.

Similarly his prologue to *Bartholomew Fair* describes the play as 'Sport without perticular wrong, Or iust complaint of any priuate man.'

These statements have often been turned back on Jonson as necessary disclaimers and as a license to libel with impunity, but there can be little doubt of Jonson's sincerity. The main subject at issue between Marston-Dekker and Jonson in the *Poetomachia* is that of libel. Marston and Dekker arraign the 'Horace' of their play, *Satiromastix*, in these terms: 'your dastard wit will strike at men In corners and in riddles fold the vices Of your best friends.' Both gentlemen and honest London citizens must live in fear of having their private lives 'satired and epigrammed upon' in plays like '*Every Gentleman out on's Humour*' (IV.ii). Jonson, for his part, in *The Poetaster*, accuses his rival poets and the public companies of conspiring with a hysterical government to put down dissent by labelling it as disrespectful of highly-placed individuals. Actually, charges Jonson, the public companies are merely trying to suppress the boys' companies out of a sense of economic rivalry, whereas the government is suffering from an advanced if typical case of paranoia. Government officials like Asinius Lupus merely proclaim their own guilt by seeing a resemblance between themselves and Jonson's satirical sketches. By his eloquence, Jonson raised this question of libel in satire to one of major concern among the theatre-going public of London. Jonson was recognizably the chief spokesman of satire's defence against a charge of libelling; *The Poetaster* was his *Areopagitica*. And although this play did not appear until 1601, the issues were already current with the vogue of non-dramatic satire in the late 1590s, the public burnings of 1599, and the reopening of the boys' theatre in the same year. What was Shakespeare's attitude toward, and involvement in, this debate?

Unlike Jonson's attitudes toward satire, which are plentifully revealed in his writings and private conversations, Shakespeare's attitudes are harder to pin down. With his habitual self-effacement, with his lack of pretentiousness as a critic or literary lion, and with his preference for drama of multiple viewpoint in which each character speaks for himself, Shakespeare resists cataloguing of his own biases. Compared with many of his contemporaries, Shakespeare's writings are singularly lacking in references to contemporary events – somewhat like Chaucer, whose rare mention (for example) of the Peasants' Revolt in 1381 reinforces our impression that such allusions are both peripheral and scarce. Nevertheless, Shakespeare took up the question of satire in drama with some intensity during the years from 1598 to 1602.

Prior to then, satire as a dramatic genre seems not to have been much on his mind. Despite his indebtedness to Plautus in *The Comedy of Errors*, Shakespeare concentrates on farce of mistaken identity rather than satirical exposure of folly. In *The Taming of the Shrew*, he consciously omits Ariosto's and Gascoigne's satire of the legal profession. *Love's Labour's Lost* would be satirical if directed against Ralegh, Chapman, and the 'School of Night,' but that supposed ingroup joke has not been convincingly demonstrated. Puck in *A Midsummer Night's Dream* makes a fool of Bottom as well as of the lovers, and the rude mechanicals' play spoofs inept dramatic writing, but the gentle raillery is undercut by the realization that 'the best in this kind are but shadows,' and that Bottom's wondrous dream of being lover to the queen of fairies is a precious experience denied to rationalists like Duke Theseus. Portia devises a ruse by which Shylock falls into his own trap, but the threat is seriously tragicomic and deals not with follies but with crimes. And so it goes. Shakespeare's apprenticeship to neoclassical forms of comedy during his experimental years did not extend to satire.

After 1598, however, we sense a new awareness. Shakespeare introduces Jaques in *As You Like It* (1598–1600), Thersites in *Troilus and Cressida* (1601–3), Parolles in *All's Well That Ends Well* (c 1602–3), and Lucio in *Measure for Measure* (c 1603–4). Falstaff is subjected to a comic humiliation in *The Merry Wives of Windsor* (c 1597–1602) that is more nearly satirical in effect than the complex Gad's Hill episode of *1 Henry IV*. With uncharacteristic topicality Shakespeare uses the term 'Puritan' in relation to Malvolio, and exposes him to the punishment of a satirical plot. In another striking topical reference he alludes directly to the rivalry of juvenile and adult companies in *Hamlet*. In none of these is there a direct personal reply to Jonson or any other satirist, but cumulatively one can piece together an impression of Shakespeare's view of the satiric scene, and sense its impact on his own development.

Jaques, along with Touchstone, William, and Audrey, is one of Shakespeare's most notable additions to his sources in writing *As You Like It*. These additions serve as devices with which to probe the contemporary literary scene, especially the fads in Arcadian pastoralism, Petrarchan sonneteering, and satire. Shakespeare takes the romantic situation of Lodge's *Rosalynde*, together with its penchant for graceful lyrics and its conventionalized pastoral lovers, and deliberately subjects these materials to multiple and conflicting viewpoints, juxtaposing the unreal Silvius and Phebe with the clownish bumpkins William and Audrey or with the true lovers Orlando and Rosalind. In these comparisons the literary types are seen as stilted, frozen into conventional Petrarchan postures of self-abasing man and scornful woman. Shakespeare's use and depiction of satire proceeds in much the same wryly detached spirit, and by the same method of juxtaposition. Jaques is at once a device of viewpoint used to highlight folly in other persons, and an object of our laughter.

Jaques has long been recognized as a malcontent traveller, a crabbed and mordant critic of man's hypocrisy.[9] He identifies his absurdist view of human striving with that of Touchstone, and even expresses a desire to wear a fool's motley. No event in Arden brings such alacritous response from Jaques as the appearance of Touchstone in the forest, observing that 'from hour to hour we ripe and ripe, And then from hour to hour we rot and rot' (II.vii). Jaques' view is close to this, except for the crucial difference that he wishes to expose and thereby cure. He fancies himself as a moralist. Touchstone's cheerfully detached view of life's absurdity doesn't stop him from savouring it, even to the extent of marrying with Audrey. He is an entertainer. Of course there is wisdom in his folly, but his view does nothing to deny the real happiness and reconciliation with which the play ends.

Jaques on the other hand takes offence at man's stupidity, and covets the satirist's power of ostracism and scorn. To be sure, he seems to enjoy entertaining his companions in the forest, as when he composes his affectedly melancholic reflections on the sobbing and deserted deer at the brook-side. At first, Jaques' role is virtually that of the allowed fool in Duke Senior's retinue, since his companions expect him to moralize every spectacle into his pithy analogies. If

Jaques can suck melancholy out of a song as a weasel sucks eggs, his
companions equally derive a pleasurable benefit from his sententious-
ness. As Duke Senior observes, 'I love to cope him in these sullen fits,
For then he's full of matter' (II.i) Still, in the central debate on the
uses of satire that takes place between Jaques and Duke Senior
(II.vii), Jaques fancies himself as a much-dreaded corrector of man's
manners:

> I must have liberty
> Withal, as large a charter as the wind,
> To blow on whom I please, for so fools have.
> And they that are most gallèd with my folly,
> They most must laugh. And why, sir, must they so?
> The why is plain as way to parish church:
> He that a fool doth very wisely hit
> Doth very foolishly, although he smart
> Within, seem senseless of the bob. If not,
> The wise man's folly is anatomized
> Even by the squand'ring glances of the fool.
> Invest me in my motley, give me leave
> To speak my mind, and I will through and through
> Cleanse the foul body of th' infected world,
> If they will patiently receive my medicine.   (47–61)

Like the fool, the satirist must be free to criticize everything and
everyone. His observations are never personal. When they hit home,
it is because some individual happens to be guilty of the offence
generically described. If he is wise, this person's best course is to
appear insensible of the hit, lest he foolishly proclaim to everyone his
guilt through his sensitivity to criticism.

To Duke Senior, however, this claim of satiric impartiality is simply
a veneer for a much darker motive:

> Fie on thee! I can tell what thou wouldst do ...
> Most mischievous foul sin, in chiding sin.
> For thou thyself hast been a libertine,
> As sensual as the brutish sting itself;
> And all th' embossèd sores and headed evils
> That thou with license of free foot hast caught,
> Wouldst thou disgorge into the general world.   (62–9)

Quite apart from being a moral reformer, in Duke Senior's eyes
Jaques is a sadist, one so hardened in sin that he can find relief only
in calumniating others for the offences he knows to be in himself. By
extension, satire itself is the thwarted expression of an inner hatred.
Hence it turns to libellous and personal attacks against those whom
the satirist resents or would blame for his own failures.

Jaques naturally objects to this analysis of satire's aim, and is
generously allowed by Duke Senior (and by Shakespeare) to have the
final rebuttal in this particular debate:

> Why, who cries out on pride
> That can therein tax any private party?
> Doth it not flow as hugely as the sea
> Till that the weary very means do ebb?
> What woman in the city do I name
> When that I say the city woman bears
> The cost of princes on unworthy shoulders?
> Who can come in and say that I mean her,
> When such a one as she, such is her neighbor?
> Or what is he of basest function
> That says his bravery is not on my cost,
> Thinking that I mean him, but therein suits
> His folly to the mettle of my speech?
> There then, how then, what then? Let me see wherein
> My tongue hath wronged him. If it do him right,
> Then he hath wronged himself. If he be free,
> Why, then my taxing like a wild goose flies
> Unclaimed of any man. (70–87)

Jaques is most eager to defend himself against the implicit charge of
libelling. Must he be accused of taxing any private individual with
pride simply because he cries out against pride? Is pride not as endless
as the sea? Must we not distinguish between the type of city woman
proudly dressed and aspiring above her station, and particular individuals who happen to fit the description? If the satirist caricatures
a base sort who dresses above his station, and some fellow denies the
resemblance to himself but fits his actions to the portrait, how can the
satirist be held responsible? Either the portrait is just and the individual thereby condemns himself, or there is no resemblance and
the individual is not hit.

This debate ends amicably, for Duke Senior is fond of Jaques and considers that a satirical voice in the forest of Arden offers a valuable if limited contribution to the many-sided view of reality there presented. Nevertheless the issue of satire's value to art and to society, and the issue of the satirist's motive for what he does, have been sharply joined. Is satire cleansing or contaminating? Is it crusading and zealous, or an unclean spewing forth of cheap cynicism? Is the satirist a moral guide or an envious railer? As with so many debates in Arden, this one is left unresolved. There is a point to much of Jaques' criticism, as when he charges that Duke Senior and his followers are usurpers in the forest, or that Orlando looks foolish at first in his rôle as Petrarchan lover. (Jaques addresses Orlando as Signior Love, and is addressed in turn as Monsieur Melancholy.) Perhaps Jaques inherits in part the Renaissance image of Diogenes as a crabbed but unsparing critic whose manner is unpleasant but whose counsel is salutary because disinterested.[10] Even so, we must never read Jaques' *sententiae* out of context. The debate on the uses of satire with Duke Senior is interrupted by the appearance of Orlando, who will be saved from the pitiless forest only by the humanity of his fellow creatures; and Jaques' famous 'Seven Ages of Man' speech is delivered while Orlando goes back into the forest to rescue old Adam. Jaques' observation that 'All the world's a stage, And all the men and women merely players' is called forth by the same spectacle of human misery and compassion that prompts the Duke to say, 'Thou seest we are not all alone unhappy.' Jaques has purchased his rancorous vision at the expense of reconciliation and forgiveness, and so cannot be transformed by the miraculous ending that transforms even the villains of the story. As Rosalind gently tells him, 'I fear you have sold your own lands to see other men's. Then to have seen much and to have nothing is to have rich eyes and poor hands.' To Jaques' protestation that 'I have gained by experience,' Rosalind replies, 'And your experience makes you sad' (IV.i).

The portrait of Jaques is clearly not intended as a particular hit at Jonson – that would be an ironical touch in a discussion of the impartial character of satire! Rather, Shakespeare seems to follow the guidelines set down by Jaques himself (or by Jonson or other satirists) : Jaques is a recognizable type rather than an individual, a 'Monsieur Melancholy' (with a capital M) or 'Monsieur Traveller' as Rosalind calls him, who is expected to 'lisp and wear strange suits, disable all the benefits of your own country, be out of love with your nativity, and almost chide God for making you that countenance you are' (IV.i). He is a satiric stage type, in other words, and any resemblance to actual living dramatists merely condemns them rather than proving the author's libellous intent. Jonson, like Marston or Chapman, does partly resemble the characterization. In *Every Man Out of His Humour* (1599) Jonson's Induction proclaims 'I'll strip the ragged follies of the time Naked as at their birth – and with a whip of steel Print wounding lashes in their iron ribs.'[11] And Jaques' satiric illustrations of the city woman bearing the cost of princes on unworthy shoulders, and of her foppish male counterpart, certainly do bring to mind Jonson's venomous portraits of the city wife and the uxorious husband in *Every Man Out,* which set a fashion in côterie drama (as Alfred Harbage has pointed out) for baiting of the bourgeoisie.[12] Still, one could find similar resemblances in Marston or Chapman. Besides, the portrait of Jaques is not one-sidedly unfriendly. Shakespeare's view of satire is complex and skilfully aware of the rules required for its use, as he subsequently demonstrates in *Twelfth Night* (1600–2).

Critics have long noticed a resemblance between comic sequences in *Twelfth Night* and in Jonson's *Epicoene*: the business in which Sir Andrew and Viola (disguised as Cesario) are conned into believing that each is challenging the other to a duel, and the equivalent trick played on Daw and La Foole in *Epicoene.* Indeed, those scholars who have found convincing classical sources or analogues for the other elements of *Epicoene* – such as the marriage of a reclusive man to a supposedly silent woman who is in fact loquacious, and the marriage to a boy in disguise – have discovered no closer analogue to this particular portion of *Epicoene* than Shakespeare's *Twelfth Night.*[13] In both situations, the cowardly contestants agree to the most humiliating terms in order to be freed of the challenge. There is a crucial difference notwithstanding. Jonson's Daw and La Foole are cowardly braggarts in earnest, who must finally be exposed for their boasting of sexual triumphs with Epicoene. They are incorrigible, like Stephen, Matthew, and Bobadill of *Every Man In,* and can only be condemned and ridiculed rather than cured. In Shakespeare's use of this device, on the other hand, Viola-Cesario is excused of her seeming cowardice because she is in fact a woman, whereas Sir Andrew's cowardice is inoffensive since he never claims to be a man of parts. He genially suffers Sir Toby's stratagems as a prankish expression of the bond between them. Shakespeare's treatment here is not really satirical; it is more in the hilarious spirit of farcical mistaken identity, as in *The Comedy of Errors.* At most, the device confirms Sir Toby's role as comic manipulator.

By contrast, the plot against Malvolio displays fully the character-istics of Jonsonian satire: an exposure plot manipulated by witty per-sons against a socially ambitious hypocrite who prepares his own trap, is laughed at scornfully by the audience, and is subjected to a ridicul-ing form of punishment befitting the nature of his offence. Malvolio is, as Maria observes, a time-pleaser and an affectioned ass, 'so crammed, as he thinks, with excellencies that it is his grounds of faith that all that look on him love him; and on that vice in him will my revenge find notable cause to work' (II.iii). Malvolio's overheard solil-oquy confirms her estimate, for without provocation he fantasizes himself as Count Malvolio. Maria, the chief comic manipulator, re-peatedly uses the language of satire when she speaks of a comic 're-venge,' and when she boasts she will 'gull' Malvolio and 'make him a common recreation' (II.iii). At the commencement of the overhear-ing scene, she remarks, 'here comes the trout that must be caught with tickling' (II.v). Fabian similarly observes, as Malvolio picks up the letter, 'Now is the woodcock near the gin,' and, a moment later, 'What dish o' poison has she dressed him!' The revellers subsequently extol Maria as their 'noble gull-catcher,' and refer to her stratagem with the characteristic terminology of 'device' and 'sport' (II.v; see also IV.ii). Malvolio is an unregenerate *alazon* and so must be excluded from the happy ending. To be sure, Shakespeare is temperamentally incapable of withholding peaceful overtures: Olivia protests that Malvolio 'hath been most notoriously abused,' and Duke Orsino orders his followers to 'Pursue him and entreat him to a peace' (V.i). In view of Malvolio's vow to 'be revenged on the whole pack of you,' however, these well-intended gestures of conciliation do more to clear our consciences as partners in the satirical exposure than to effect any real rapprochement. The spirit of Malvolio's rancour will remain, as C.L. Barber observes, until it is avenged with the closing of the theatres in 1642.[14]

This is not to say that the attack on Malvolio is an attack on the Puritans, for Shakespeare carefully hedges this equation after having put us in mind of the possibility. Maria protests, 'sometimes he is a kind of Puritan,' but, when challenged to explain herself, goes on to observe that 'The devil a Puritan that he is, or anything constantly but a time-pleaser' (II.iii). Compared with Jonson's later caricatures of the Puritans in Zeal-of-the-Land Busy and Tribulation Whole-some, this portrait bears little topical resemblance to church reformers and separatists at the turn of the century. Although Malvolio may wrest texts to yield a testament of the good fortune he believes to be predestinately his,[15] his behaviour is in no sense religiously inspired and his diction lacks the telltale cant of the zealot. He is *like* a Puritan only in being a sober-sides habitually dressed in black, whose chief calling in life is to deny holiday pleasure to his fellow mortals, and whose sobriety hypocritically conceals a longing for power and pleasure. The analogy to the Puritans is valid only insofar as the Puritans may be similarly guilty of such a kill-joy spirit and hypocrisy. In other words, as a stage type, Malvolio conforms once again to satiric theory: he is the type of kill-joy, and the Puritans or any other persons merely condemn themselves when they reveal a corresponding tendency in themselves. If they are free of censoriousness, the satire does not touch them; the test of truth is in them, not in the generic satirical portrait.

In sum, Shakespeare did seriously flirt with Jonsonian satire in *Twelfth Night*, after having revealed a complex appreciation of the theory of satire in *As You Like It*. If space permitted, it would be fruitful to discuss Lucio in *Measure for Measure* (as an engaging railer, who is nonetheless roundly censured for his irresponsible libels against a virtuous prince, and who thereby teaches Vincentio that a prince must carefully preserve the appearance as well as the reality of a morally correct life), Thersites in *Troilus and Cressida* (as a snarling malcontent railer in the crabbed style of Marston and of Jonson's *Every Man Out*), and Parolles in *All's Well* (as perhaps the closest example to Malvolio, since Parolles is also a slanderer gulled into a satirical exposure appropriate to his offence). Such a brief survey suggests, in any case, that Shakespeare's contact with formal dramatic satire was occasioned seemingly by the emergence of the craze for satire both on and off the stage, and that Shakespeare maintained a characteristic distance from the Jonsonian norm but still experimented in a spirit of genuine interest and commitment. Indeed, the final impression is one of vastly greater intellectual flexibility on Shakespeare's part. Whereas Jonson lambasted all popular historical drama and romance, and thus limited himself to neoclassical forms albeit interpreted with some English latitude, Shakespeare debated the issues of satire and saw no reason why he should not try it out for himself. His art was enriched by his eagerness to experiment, even if satire proved ultimately not to be his chief vein as a comic writer.

NOTES

1 See especially E. Hermann *Shakespeare der Kämpfer* (Erlangen 1879) and *Weitere quellenmässige Beiträge zu Shakespeares literarischen Kämpfen* (Erlangen 1881), Robert Cartwright *Shakspere and Jonson: Dramatic*

versus Wit-Combats (London 1864), and Josiah H. Penniman *The War of the Theatres* (Boston 1897). A more temperate survey appeared in Roscoe A. Small *The Stage-Quarrel between Ben Jonson and the So-Called Poetasters* (Breslau 1899).

2 Henry David Gray, 'The Chamberlain's Men and the *Poetaster*,' *Modern Language Review* 42 (1947) 173–9. See also T.W. Baldwin *The Organization and Personnel of the Shakespearean Company* (Princeton 1927) 232–4.

3 J.B. Leishman, ed *The Three Parnassus Plays* (London 1949) 59–60

4 E.K. Chambers *William Shakespeare: A Study of Facts and Problems* (Oxford 1930) II, 202–11

5 Quotations from Shakespeare are from *The Complete Works* Alfred Harbage, ed (Baltimore 1969). Quotations from Jonson are from C.H. Herford and Percy and Evelyn Simpson, eds *Ben Jonson* (Oxford 1925–52). The quotations from *Every Man in His Humour* are from the 1601 quarto text except for the prologue, which first appeared in the folio of 1616. Punctuation has been modernized.

6 The date of Jonson's revision of *Every Man In* is uncertain; 1605 and 1612 have both been proposed with some cogency. The prologue itself may or may not have been written at one of these times.

7 Chambers, *William Shakespeare*, cites a passage from *Every Man out of His Humour* III.i in which, he suggests, Sogliardo may represent an unfriendly glance at Shakespeare, but the instance is highly conjectural.

8 Jonas A. Barish, 'The Double Plot in *Volpone*,' *Modern Philology* 51 (1953) 83–92. See also S.L. Goldberg, 'Folly into Crime: The Catastrophe of *Volpone*,' *Modern Language Quarterly* 20 (1959) 233–42.

9 Z.S. Fink, 'Jaques and the Malcontent Traveler' *Philological Quarterly* 14 (1935) 237–52, Oscar J. Campbell, 'Jaques' *Huntington Library Bulletin* 8 (1935) 71–102, and Campbell *Shakespeare's Satire* (London 1943) 44–64

10 John L. Lievsay, 'Some Renaissance Views of Diogenes the Cynic' in J.G. McManaway *et al*, eds *J.Q. Adams Memorial Studies* (Washington 1948) 447–55

11 See the discussion of this passage in the New Variorum text of *As You Like It* H.H. Furness, ed (reprinted New York 1963) 111

12 Alfred Harbage *Shakespeare and the Rival Traditions* (New York 1952) 274

13 Herford and Simpson *Ben Jonson* II, introduction to *Epicoene*, 73–6, and x, 38. I have consulted some research on this subject by an able graduate student at the University of Chicago, Michael Flachmann (dissertation in progress).

14 C.L. Barber *Shakespeare's Festive Comedy* (Princeton 1959) 257

15 J.L. Simmons, in an essay read at the Shakespeare group of the Modern Language Association in December 1970

Wolfgang Clemen /
Shakespeare and Marlowe

Comparisons between Shakespeare and Marlowe have been undertaken according to different methods and from various points of view.
The notion of Marlowe as Shakespeare's forerunner has been abandoned long ago. Whereas scholars used to speak of 'influence' when
they found echoes of Marlowe in Shakespeare's early plays, there is
now a tendency to speak of 'new-creation to Shakespeare's own purpose in a very different context,' as Nicholas Brooke has done.[1] Today
we emphasize less the correspondences and similarities, but rather the
great differences between the two dramatists. We see now that Shakespeare and Marlowe did not only, as Irving Ribner put it, 'represent
diametrically opposed reactions to the complex of Elizabethan life,
each in his own way forging a poetically valid vision of reality beyond
the comprehension of the other,'[2] but that they also wrote plays distinct in kind and form. But what is the essence of this form?[3] For comparisons between Marlowe and Shakespeare have up to now emphasized the difference in their ideas, their moral outlook, their basic
attitudes and concepts. One could compile a whole list of such points
of contrast from the writings of F.P. Wilson, Una Ellis-Fermor, Harry
Levin, Irving Ribner, Nicholas Brooke, Wilbur Sanders, J.B. Steane,
Clifford Leech, and others. Such comparisons help us to recognize
the individuality of each dramatist more clearly. We see that at the
beginning of the 1590s there were two distinct paths which Elizabethan drama could follow, both of great promise and significance
though only one of these paths led to the summit of perfection.

But what was often neglected in these comparisons was the study of dramatic form and technique. The structure of the two dramatists' plays, their effectiveness in the theatre, and their dramaturgy, differ from one another perhaps even more strikingly than do the ideas which they express. Of course there is an interrelation between the two levels. A dramatist selects a particular dramatic technique and structure in order to give expression to certain ideas, finding for them an equivalent on the level of form. Nevertheless we can grasp only part of the dramatist's intention if we begin with the ideas expressed in a drama, and then proceed to ask what methods the author used in order to realize these ideas in dramatic form. For the form itself reveals certain intentions which are not expressed directly at any specific point in the play.

In order to discover the different intentions which Marlowe and Shakespeare had, and to understand why their plays provoke such dissimilar reactions, we must look more closely at the dramatic technique and structure of those plays which are sufficiently similar in subject matter for a discussion to be fruitful. This applies to *Tamburlaine* and *Richard III*, but even more to *Edward II* and *Richard II*, where the similarity covers not only the main characters but also elements of the story. In each case Marlowe's play preceded Shakespeare's. All the critics agree that Shakespeare knew Marlowe's play when he wrote *Richard II*, and also that he must have had Marlowe in mind when he composed the scenes of Richard's abdication and murder.

But this is not a question of 'influence' in the usual sense of the word, rather of Shakespeare's independent response to Marlowe's play. In *Richard II* we are able to see Shakespeare taking his own stand in the face of a play which might have served him as a 'model,' but in fact provoked in him a determination to do something quite different. We can observe the new direction in which Shakespeare was turning, and which he continued to follow in later plays; whereas in *Richard III* he had experimented with a dramatic form which he then abandoned, and to which he never returned. The step from *Richard III* to *Richard II* is perhaps the most amazing move in Shakespeare's whole development as a dramatist. By comparing the dramatic form and technique of *Edward II* and *Richard II* one comes closer to an understanding of the reason why Shakespeare selected for his play a form so different, which led him so far away from Marlowe's 'model.'

The emphasis on ideas and attitudes in earlier comparisons between

Marlowe and Shakespeare may be accounted for, because Marlowe more than other pre-Shakespearian dramatists set out to explore ideas and to shape them in his plays. But although this is a legitimate approach it is one which involves dangers and limitations. For the customary procedure with critics has been to start from selected speeches or passages, and then to illustrate from them the different ideas and attitudes. In employing this method we remain on the level of explicit verbal expression. The words of the play are transposed into the words of the critic, but the investigation is restricted to just one of the play's modes of expression. Yet it is possible that other impressions conveyed by a play in performance may be so strong that isolated passages referring to a specific idea merge almost completely into the background. Our endeavour to grasp the 'meaning' of a play by extracting the prevailing ideas often leads us to neglect the effect of the play in the theatre as well as the other elements of drama such as structure and technique. Clifford Leech recently spoke a warning against our search for the ideas expressed in a play: 'When talking about the plays, we inevitably refer to the ideas that they suggest to us; but we must never forget that a dramatist, when writing, is normally concerned with such things only in the second place.'[4] Moreover, the ideas expressed in a play may be, as Leech also tells us, not at all consistent, for 'in the course of writing it will often happen, that ideas and feelings will emerge that are altogether at odds with the initial purpose.'

We must therefore overcome or at least counterbalance our preoccupation with 'the meaning of a play.' We must supplement the method of interpretation based largely on quotations by an analysis of dramatic technique and form and of the impact of the play on the audience. In order to show why two plays are so different from one another and evoke such varying responses, we must describe their 'physiognomy,' their dramatic rhythm. We must ask why the dramatist composed his play in this particular manner, and in what way he rouses the sympathy and antipathy of the audience. Such considerations which have been brought to bear on Marlowe's plays by Eugene M. Waith, Clifford Leech, Robert Fricker, David Bevington, John Russell Brown, and others,[5] lead to a different approach to the plays which would be rather in the line of what Granville-Barker, Styan, Coghill, and others have attempted to do with Shakespearian drama. I should like to mention a few things which are relevant in this connection – the timing of the action, the relation between off-stage action and events shown on the stage, the handling of dialogue and speech, the use of spectacle, pageantry, and stage business, the sequence and fre-

quency of exits and entries, the occurrence of descriptive and narrative passages, the sequence of contrasting scenes, the construction of
the play with regard to plot and subplot, the inclusion of past and
future in the consciousness of the characters, the technique of preparation. This list is incomplete and is intended only to indicate the
direction one would have to go in order to provide a description of
what I choose to call the physiognomy of the play.

It is clear that the programme I have outlined cannot be treated
adequately in a short paper. I must therefore limit myself here to a
few suggestions rather than giving the detailed analysis which would
be more to my own inclination.

To begin with, how can we describe the impact which the two plays,
Edward II and *Richard II*, make upon the audience? *Edward II*
conveys the impression of stirring action, severely condensed but always urging forward, constantly resulting in violent clashes between
the characters. The rapid sequence of entrances and exits, the brevity
of most of the scenes, the quick exchange of dialogue, the restless
movement on the stage which characterizes most scenes – all this
marks the play with a distinctive, rapid, turbulent rhythm. In the
course of the action there is scarcely a pause. Whenever it seems that
such a lull is about to occur, the counteraction breaks in with undi-
minished violence, and leads to a new conflict or outburst of emotions. There are many abrupt transitions, the action appears to
accelerate from act to act, the crowded events, especially before the
fall of the king, have a bewildering effect on us.

The dramatic rhythm of *Richard II* forms a contrast. The play
progresses slowly. Many events which belong to the story are deliberately not shown on the stage but are reported as off-stage actions
or merely implied. Often we see on the stage scenes in which progress
is arrested, and the significance of these 'still' scenes is deepened and
elaborated by speeches rich in imagery, or by symbolic gestures and
actions. This 'verbal expansion of the situation' (as Stanley Wells has
described it) again and again slows down the dramatic tempo. There
are many moments of repose in which the action seems to be suspended, as if it were to be reviewed and reflected from a distance. As
Wells has fittingly remarked, 'the play constantly approaches action
only to withdraw before it happens.'[6]

In *Edward II* the characters challenge one another in vituperative
dialogue, draw their swords, pursue each other across the stage, and

are arrested and led off, so that the 'allegro' of the action is accompanied by a 'fortissimo' of loud and vehement clashes. The mood in *Richard II* is more quiet and slow, more subdued and less impassioned. Shakespeare seems to avoid the emotional outbursts – whether of despair or anger, threatening or suffering – which frequently result from the quarrels and conflicts of *Edward II*. In *Richard II* we have no alarums, no battle scenes, and the only deed of violence, the murder of the king, happens at the very end of the play. Moreover the murder itself is very different from the corresponding scene in *Edward II*, allowing more pathos and alleviated by several touches. The dramatic rhythm of *Richard II* is naturally established to a considerable degree by the steady flow of poetic verse, with frequent rhymed and regular lines, and also by the mode of ritual and formal stylization which marks several of the scenes. The lyrical, reflective, poetic quality, which distinguishes the play as a whole, resists the outbreaks of violence and hasty movement which we witness in *Edward II*.

I should like now to go beyond the initial impact of the two plays, and take a closer look at their construction and plot, their dramatic techniques and their handling of speech and dialogue.

In contrast to the restless to and fro of *Edward II*, we find in *Richard II* a pattern in which the main action progresses in a continuous line towards its end. This is evident above all in the presentation of the king's downfall. In *Edward II* the fortunes of the king go up and down, the king is at the top and then at the bottom, conqueror and then conquered, and only in the last quarter of the play does his path lead steadily down. But the king is only one of several characters whose fortunes rise and fall. As Eugene M. Waith has put it, 'a graphic representation of the structure of *Edward II* would show the intersection of at least five lines, each corresponding to the rising and falling fortunes of a major character.'[7] In *Richard II* a graphic representation of this sort would look quite different: a line moving slowly and steadily down would represent the downfall of the king, and approximately in the middle it would intersect with the equally direct ascending curve of Bolingbroke. This line, however, does not break like that of Mortimer, to end in the depths, but points to a future, which is to be taken up in the two parts of *Henry IV*. Thus a consideration of these obvious differences in the construction of the two plays may lead us (as far as their structure is concerned) to conclusions similar to those reached by Glynne Wickham, who in a recent chapter on *Richard II* and *Edward II* argued that '*Edward II*, in spite of its shortcomings, is the true tragedy in the classical sense of the word,' whereas '*Richard II* is a prelude to a catastrophe and not a self-contained tragedy,' but rather a 'chronicle play with tragic consequences.'[8]

But the relation between king and antagonist differs in other ways too. Marlowe constantly has the king clash with Mortimer, so that their antagonism is presented to us from the very beginning as a personal rather than a political conflict charged with violent emotions. Shakespeare deliberately keeps the king and Bolingbroke at a distance from one another. Their conflict does not become actually apparent until later, and even then it does not at once lead to a personal confrontation. Even when the adversaries meet face to face, which after the first act happens only twice, they remain remote from one another, participants and spectators, but not overt enemies. Bolingbroke's function as conspirator and usurper, as one who in fact had desired the king's downfall, remains quite in the background. His actions are veiled by subtle scheming and ambiguous silence.[9] He waits for the events to take their course and, as Brents Stirling has shown, makes no decision prior to act IV and even then appears not to act himself, but leaves it to others to state the implications of his decisions.[10] The action throughout the play seems to develop through some force of its own, or by divine will. In *Edward II*, on the other hand, we are always present when the plots against the king are put into action.

The stark immediacy of the action, whereby we see everything that happens as the direct result of the characters' actions and designs, is an essential factor in distinguishing *Edward II* from *Richard II*. In *Edward II* the action has a dynamic quality and energy missing in *Richard II*, where everything seems to happen in the distance, on a remote level. In Marlowe's play we constantly see how the action springs from the will of the characters; a large proportion of the lines spoken in the play could be described as 'expressions of will.' Either the characters achieve what they want, imposing their will on others, or – and this is more frequent – they are rejected, defeated, or frustrated. Therefore the feeling we are most often conscious of in *Edward II* is, as Eugene M. Waith has shown, 'the profound emotional disturbance resulting from frustration.'[11]

We could go so far as to say that the two plays reveal different attitudes to character. While of *Edward II* it is true to say, with Waith, that 'the entire play is a protracted conflict of wills,'[12] in *Richard II* it is a question rather of a conflict of principles, which is embodied in the characters, but carries implications which go beyond them.

Public concern has replaced personal conflict. To the characters in *Edward II* one may apply the remarks formulated by William Dinsmore Briggs over fifty years ago: 'Not so much the human being as an intellectual or reasoning entity, but the human being as a centre of energetic action occupied him [Marlowe] chiefly.'[13] In *Richard II*, on the other hand, Shakespeare lays the emphasis not on human will but on contemplation, reflection, on reaction rather than on action.

   With this concept of character as 'centre of energetic action,' and with his emphasis on will as the source of all action, it was inevitable that Marlowe should meet with difficulties in the portrayal of King Edward, the first weak and passive hero he created. For, as F.P. Wilson said in his brilliant discussion of *Edward II*, 'weakness does not act but is acted upon.'[14] But Edward's weakness results from a rebellious and repeatedly frustrated will, which only gains the upper hand in isolated scenes (as for instance in act IV). Even in the weakness and wretchedness of the king we still feel his latent will-power, but it is a will-power that has been flouted and broken. The stage direction in act V, '*The king rageth*' – unthinkable in the context of *Richard II* – reveals to us a man who desperately opposes the resistance which he cannot break.

   Again these differences may be illustrated from the structure and use of speech and dialogue in the two plays. In *Edward II*, rapid unadorned dialogue, consisting largely of short speeches and sharp interchanges, is the characteristic medium for the violent clashes and retorts, while longer speeches are rare. In the quarrels of the opponents, questions and exclamations, threats, challenges, asseverations, and commands prevail. 'Every other speech of the king's is an order which is generally flouted and countermanded,'[15] as Harry Levin has rightly observed.

   But, in spite of the rapid interplay of utterances, the characters rarely communicate with one another in a genuine way. There is no real discussion, no give and take in which one partner might respond to the other, as is the case with several scenes in *Richard II*. But a clash of conflicting interests is not a true dialogue. Even if we cannot agree with Una Ellis-Fermor's assessment: 'For man's relation to man he [Marlowe] cared by nature hardly at all,'[16] we must admit that in *Edward II* relations between the characters are not convincingly portrayed and do not fill a central position. In contrast to *Edward II*, longer speeches are the characteristic medium in *Richard II*. They convey to us the values and notions so important in the play. Gaunt's, York's, Carlisle's monitory and prophetic speeches, and also the speeches of the Gardener, illustrate the fundamentally different dramatic method; here the concern for England and the nation's welfare, the notion of the divine right of kings, of order and hierarchy, find expression and extend beyond the individual characters. The long speeches of the king form the chief means of his self-portrayal, of his conscious and deliberate exploitation of a situation in which he is at once performer, passive agent, and commentator. But long speeches occur in *Richard II* also when it is a matter of delivering challenges and accusations – situations which in themselves are typical of *Edward II*. The conflict between Mowbray and Bolingbroke at the beginning of *Richard II* would certainly have been presented by Marlowe in the form of a rapid and heated exchange of words. Shakespeare uses longer speeches, because they form an instrument which may serve to recall the past, establishing the pattern of guilt and retribution which extends from the past into the present, and beyond it to the future, particularly with regard to Bolingbroke. These two dimensions, past and future, are missing in *Edward II*. By introducing them, not only in this early scene but also at many other points, Shakespeare takes a decisive step, which increases the distance between himself and Marlowe. The dimension of past and future belongs to the superstructure of the history plays, which is found already, in its earliest stages, in *Henry VI*. But Marlowe, who in turn must have been aware of the *Henry VI* plays when he wrote *Edward II*, took over nothing of what Nicholas Brooke has called the 'elaborate superstructure of Divine Order overriding historical events.' 'There is none of this in *Edward II*.'[17]

So we come finally to another particularly characteristic difference between Marlowe and Shakespeare. Marlowe presents to us, in sober speech, factual, straightforward, and direct, avoiding imaginative associations, the stark event. The scene of Edward's deposition, above all the scene of his murder, grip us through this very bareness and directness. But this mode of presentation turns out to be more powerful in the theatre than are Shakespeare's corresponding scenes, so that we may still agree with Charles Lamb's opinion that 'the death scene of Marlowe's King Edward moves pity and terror beyond any scene ancient or modern.'[18] Marlowe does not invite us to reflect on the 'problem' posed by the murder of an anointed king, but he shows the finality of the brutal horror involved in this murder and degradation, from which there is no escape. No moral question is raised here, or at any other point in the play,[19] although implicitly or indirectly we are of course made to think about the moral issues involved. Furthermore, there is no suggestion of a higher order, no prospect of a better future. We are confronted with the cruel finality of a bare event, devoid of commentary. We are horrified and can provide no answer. We realize that the bare language and the rejection of all spectacular stage action, of pathos and poetic interpretation, are the dramatic means by which Marlowe achieved this effect.

Shakespeare on the other hand wished to achieve something else, and therefore chose a different dramatic structure which he could use as a framework for the intricate and subtle structure of words and ideas so characteristic of this play. The stylized ritual of the abdication scene, with the king meditating before his reflection in the mirror, is just as far removed from Marlowe as is the speculative last soliloquy, rich in imagery and ideas, in which the king once more recalls the parts he has played. We are invited to look into the future and into the past, to ask questions, to reflect on the 'problem': many associations are evoked. Shakespeare keeps us now, as he did earlier in the play, at a certain distance from the action; he lets us see the course of an event from this side and that, with changing perspectives. Not only do the characters reflect in *Richard II* – the language itself tends towards reflection and contains 'overtones and nuances of vocabulary, syntax and imagery[20] for which we would look in vain in *Edward II*. In *Richard II* we are bound to listen to the words, whereas in *Edward II* we must watch the movements of the characters.

If I had time, I would further demonstrate the basic differences, from other aspects of the play, for instance from the technique of preparation. For while preparation in *Edward II* is always directed towards the events immediately following, and is as factual and straightforward as is the speech in most scenes, in *Richard II* we find a complex and far-reaching technique of preparation, which includes the use of premonitions, of prediction through omens and portents, imaginative anticipation, and ambivalent ironic foreboding. This aspect (which I have dealt with in more detail in a recent book)[21] might form the point of departure for a discussion of that complexity of levels in dramatic structure which distinguishes Shakespeare from Marlowe. For the complex 'multilevelled' poetic drama, with mirror scenes and unfolding patterns of correspondences and similarities, clarified by imagery and recurring keywords, with changing perspectives and ambiguity both of language and form, is in fact Shakespeare's invention. It is of particular interest that Shakespeare began to develop this new dramatic mode against the background of Marlowe's *Edward II*, and probably in deliberate opposition to it.

NOTES

1 Nicholas Brooke, 'Marlow as Provocative Agent in Shakespeare's Early Plays' *Shakespeare Survey* 14 (1961)

2 Irving Ribner, 'Marlow and Shakespeare' *Shakespeare Quarterly* 15 (1964)

3 'There is uncertainty, or at least difference of opinion, concerning the kind of drama Marlowe wrote,' Clifford Leech, introduction to his *Marlowe: A Collection of Critical Essays* (1964).

4 Clifford Leech, '*Edward II*: Power and Suffering' *Critical Quarterly* 1 (1959)

5 Eugene M. Waith, '*Edward II*: The Shadow of Action' *Tulane Drama Review* 8 (1964), Clifford Leech, '*Edward II*: Power and Suffering,' Robert Fricker, 'The Dramatic Structure of *Edward II*,' *English Studies* 34 (1953), John Russell Brown, 'Marlowe and the Actors' *Tulane Drama Review* 8 (1964)

6 Introduction to his edition of *Richard II* in the New Penguin Shakespeare

7 '*Edward II*: The Shadow of Action'

8 'Shakespeare's "King Richard II" and Marlowe's "King Edward II" ' *Shakespeare's Dramatic Heritage* (1969)

9 See R.F. Hill, 'Dramatic Techniques and Interpretation in *Richard II*,' in John Russell Brown and Bernard Harris, eds *Early Shakespeare* (Stratford-upon-Avon Studies 3) (1961).

10 Brents Stirling *Unity in Shakespearean Tragedy: The Interplay of Theme and Character* (1956)

11 Eugene M. Waith '*Edward II*: The Shadow of Action' 63

12 Ibid 64

13 In his introduction to his edition of *Edward II* (London 1914)

14 *Marlowe and the Early Shakespeare* (1954) 92

15 *The Overreacher* (1952) 95

16 Una Ellis-Fermor *Marlowe* (1927) 132

17 Nicholas Brooke, 'Marlowe the Dramatist' in *Elizabethan Theatre* (Stratford-upon-Avon Studies 9) (1961)

18 Charles Lamb *Specimens of the English Dramatic Poets* (1887) 25

19 'In *Edward II* there is no moral pattern – we are not asked to consider whether Edward deserved his fate.' Introduction to H.B. Charlton and R.D. Waller eds *Edward II* (London 1930; revised by F.N. Lees 1955)

20 Stanley Wells *Edward II*, introduction

21 'Shakespeare's Art of Preparation' in *Shakespeare's Dramatic Art* (London 1972)

H.D.F. Kitto /
Why Blame Aristotle?

I am going to compare, from a special point of view, two of Sophocles' plays, the *Trachiniae* and *Ajax*, with Shakespeare's *Coriolanus*, choosing these only for convenience of exposition. If I were writing a long article and not a short paper, I would draw upon a dozen other Greek plays and at least half a dozen more of Shakespeare's tragedies – but a dozen pages are only a dozen pages.

What these three plays have in common is that a fair number of critics, of different periods, have accused them of being badly constructed, and from the same cause: they have entirely misunderstood what the plays were about. As the name of Aristotle appears in the title that I chose for this paper – a title that was a prophecy rather than a statement (and, as the priests of Delphi knew, it is always wiser to prophesy *after* the event, if you can manage it) – let me bring him in at once, by way of illustration. You will recall that he made two serious criticisms of Euripides' *Medea*: the way in which he handled the killing of the two children was 'shocking,' μιαρόν; and the final scene was illogical. In some ways the Aristotle of the *Poetics* was almost an eighteenth-century figure; he seems hardly to have understood what his own classical tragic poets were talking about. But perhaps I should not start too many hares too soon.

Neither the *Trachiniae* nor the *Ajax* accords with what Aristotle thought the structure of a tragedy should be, though as it happens he mentions neither of them. It was an ancient scholiast of unknown date who first (so far as *we* know) explained what is wrong with the *Ajax*:

'Wishing to prolong his play beyond its proper conclusion, Sophocles dissipates the tragic tension and becomes tedious.' Evidently, the 'proper conclusion' would have been the suicide of the hero; but Sophocles was foolish enough to put that near the middle of the play, and to finish with three scenes of dispute as to whether Ajax's body shall be buried, or thrown out and eaten by animals. I could produce some half-dozen modern explanations of this, differing only in their degree of banality and of unfaithfulness to the text – though I admit to having a soft spot for what was said by that lively critic, the late A.J.P. Waldock: these Greek dramatists used up their dramatic material at so furious a rate that they often had to inject more in order to keep the play going – more or less the same explanation that Sir Thomas Hanmer found, quite a long time ago, for Hamlet's failure to run a sword through Claudius at the beginning of act II.

Let us leave the *Ajax* for the moment in order to look at the *Trachiniae*. That play has caused even more consternation than the *Ajax*; for if Sophocles intended Deianeira to be the heroine – and certainly her personal tragedy is one of the most affecting that even he ever conceived – why did he put *her* suicide near the middle of the play, and thereafter scarcely mention her? But, if he intended Heracles to be the hero, it is very clumsy that the hero makes his first appearance so late in the play, when his wife is already dead and very nearly forgotten. At least, Sophocles might have confronted Heracles, and us, with her dead body.

As it happens, Sophocles wrote a rather impressive ode for his chorus to sing when they first enter. They have come to console and encourage Deianeira, who is racked with anxiety over her long-absent husband. It goes like this:

Sparkling Night always gives birth to blazing Day, who, as he dies, brings on Night. So too in the life of man: joy is always succeeded by sorrow, and sorrow by joy – even as the Great Bear wheels for ever around the Pole. You, Deianeira, have known nothing but sorrow; therefore now you may look for joy, in the safe return of Heracles. Neither does sparkling Night nor grief nor wealth remain fixed; joy follows the one, poverty the other. Besides, Heracles is the son of Zeus – and who has ever seen Zeus regardless of his offspring?

Such is the astronomically splendid song which Sophocles makes his simple maidens of Trachis deliver. Obviously they ought to have been gently enquiring into the state of Deianeira's health and spirits, not spreading before us a cosmic pattern or rhythm, of which Zeus is a personification. We, having listened, may do one of two things. Either we may murmur to ourselves: 'That was fine, and typically Sophoclean. Now let's get on with the play' – in which case we shall find that the play almost comes apart in the middle: as Jebb remarked, the tragedy of Deianeira is greatly moving, but that of the remote, legendary Heracles can leave one comparatively cold. Or we may understand that the ode, far from being an impressive though transient lyrical decoration, is in fact the background against which Sophocles intended his audience to contemplate the whole action. In the natural order of things, Deianeira and Heracles should now enjoy peace; why, in this instance, does that natural rhythm break down in what I may solemnly call a God-almighty crash?

I am not the first to remark that Sophocles was pretty good at tragic irony. 'Who ever has seen Zeus regardless of his offspring?' said the Chorus. In a short time we are being told why Heracles has been absent for so long: in a rage he had flung a man to his death from a high place, and for that Zeus condemned him to a year's enslavement. Zeus was not regardless of *that*! What we hear next is that for the sake of getting a young princess as mistress, over the head of his loyal wife, Heracles has sacked her city, killed all the men, and enslaved all the women, some of whom, forlorn and hopeless captives – the princess Iole being one – stand before us, and before Deianeira, in the orchestra. Will Zeus be regardless of this?

This it is that drives Deianeira into her desperate courses; and we should at least notice that what activates the venom in the robe that she innocently sends him is the heat from the sacrifical fire on which Heracles is making a thank-offering to Zeus for his frightful destruction of the city. Zeus is mentioned some twenty-four times in the play – the last time in the last verse: 'Nothing has happened here apart from Zeus.' This human universe of ours has indeed its all-embracing order – and if someone throws a spanner of this size into its works, a grinding crash is what we must expect.

Once we see the play against the background provided by Sophacles, instead of erecting a smaller and more familiar one of our own, we have no more trouble with the unity of the *Trachiniae* – nor with the ending of the *Medea*, nor with the unity of the *Ajax*. But space is limited, so I shall leave the *Ajax* to look after itself, and pass at once to *Coriolanus*.

I do not claim to have read everything that has been written about Shakespeare in, say, the last hundred and fifty years, but I have read a little, and what I have read about *Coriolanus* gives me the impression that usually it is not ranked very high among Shakespeare's tragedies: β?+, as it were. One critic complains that it lacks the cosmic reverberations that we find in *Macbeth* or *Lear*: it is 'claustrophobic,' closing rather than opening vistas; another, that the character-drawing is 'external,' that we do not see into the mind of Caius Marcius as we do into Hamlet's; another, that when he joins Rome's enemies merely to satisfy a personal pique we can no longer believe in the fundamental nobility of the hero, so that the last part of the play fails to hold our interest. (For that matter, I myself have never found it easy to believe in the fundamental nobility of Medea; nor, apparently, did Aristotle; possibly, not even Euripides.) Several critics, including Granville-Barker, speak of a decline in Shakespeare's energy of imagination; yet Barker (who always deserves attention) also says, about the poetic style of the play, that it rarely soars, but that 'words are crammed into the lines like fuel to stoke a furnace' – a just and splendid remark that I find difficult to reconcile with a decline in imaginative energy. From a quite recent article on the play published in a very reputable journal I quote the following:

When Shakespeare got to the last two acts he forgot what his subject had begun to be and who his hero was. He was for some reason unable or unwilling to complete the potentially great play that was blossoming out in Act III ... In a sense, both the hero and the play have slumped back here ... The reader who feels that something has gone badly wrong in the last two acts may reflect that here ... there is a reduction of imaginative power ...

Myself, I would rather say, with all the modesty at my command – and that is not much – that the reader who feels this probably agrees with what George Saintsbury said about the play, that it is, *par excellence*, 'a one-man play': every detail in the play centres upon the hero, Caius Marcius Coriolanus.

All this gives me a strange feeling of déjà vu: poor Shakespeare! poor old Sophocles! The best of us, it seems, have our off-days.

They have this in common, these two fallible dramatists: as Sophocles writes, very early in the *Trachiniae*, that ode which I have just tried to describe; as he begins his *Ajax* with Athene, and several times in the play brings emphatically to our attention that same conception of a cosmic rhythm or pattern, so does Shakespeare begin *Coriolanus* with the ancient and medieval parable of the Belly and the Rebellious Members: the body physical, symbolic of the Body Politic, which in its turn is symbolic of the divine order of the universe.

I now suggest that in more respects than one Sophocles' ode on the universal rhythm or pattern and the parable on which Menenius spends so much time resemble each other closely.

The ode and the parable: each is designed to bring to the minds of the audience a conception quite familiar to them, though not to later critics; in each case that conception is intended to be what I have already called the background to the action: as it were, the co-ordinates against which to apprehend its significance; in each case *we* are disposed to treat it casually because our attention is reserved for the Tragic Hero, with the inevitable result that in each case the play, for us, more or less falls to pieces.

In support of this I rely on two proofs: I think they can fairly be called 'proofs.' The first is that if we accept that the parable *was* designed by Shakespeare to give his audience its bearings, as it were, then all that talk of flagging imagination, change of direction, comparative failure in acts IV and V, vanishes into thin air – very thin air indeed. For me – and I speak as a fanatical Hellenist – the tragedy *Coriolanus*, in every respect, can stand up to *anything*; not β?+ but α+. This may or may not rank as a proof, but there is another, which I will take first.

It would be an eminently scholarly enterprise, worth while or not, to compare the play with its unique source: North's translation of Plutarch's *Life of Coriolanus*. Everybody says, rightly, that Shakespeare followed his source closely, and often verbally. But he *did* make some structural alterations, and those *may* deserve our distinguished attention. I cannot spare time for all, but all tend in the same direction.

In Plutarch, Volumnia is a dignified figure who remains in the background: the Mother, whom Caius Marcius so notably reveres, to the general applause; it is Shakespeare who brings her into the foreground, fills her with contempt for the plebs, and makes her say things like:

> Anger's my meat! I'll sup upon myself
> And so shall starve with feeding.

In Plutarch, we do not meet Aufidius until Coriolanus is in Antium; Shakespeare brings him too before us in act I, and never lets us lose sight of the insensate hatred that the two men bear each other, and Aufidius' consuming envy of Coriolanus. Is it entirely irrelevant, I wonder, to remark that Anger and Envy were among those Seven Deadly Sins, now, happily, things of the past? In Plutarch, the plebs

act in a sensible and restrained way; Shakespeare makes them violent
and stupid; in terms of his parable, they are the arms and legs who
can act only at random unless guided by the head. In Plutarch, the
Tribunes are responsible, though factious, leaders; it is Shakespeare
that makes them envious, malicious, and inept. So one could continue. The question therefore arises: when Shakespeare was, in
general, following Plutarch so closely, why did he choose to make so
many structural alterations?

The answer is surely obvious. Plutarch really *was* writing – to use
Saintsbury's phrase – 'a one-man drama.' His Caius Marcius is the
perfectly Aristotelian hero whose tragic fall is Plutarch's whole subject; therefore the other characters in his moral tale – Volumnia, the
plebs, and the rest – can be, so to speak, what they like. But Shakespeare was doing something quite different, as the Parable has already
told us. Certainly his Caius Marcius is magnificently the centrepiece,
but, just as certainly, he is not the sole focus of the play. Shakespeare
is thinking of the Body and its Rebellious Members; therefore each
character (with the obvious exceptions) must make his own contribution to the rage, contempt, anger, envy, violence, which, between
them, are the total negation of the natural harmony.

The second of the two proofs I shall only indicate, not work out in
any detail: it is that from this point of view every detail in the play
leaps into significance: not Caius Marcius only, but each of the
characters I have mentioned, suffers, or is near suffering, the nemesis
of his own defiance of the natural order. The plebs resorted to violence; Menenius told them:

> For the dearth,
> The gods, not the patricians, made it, and
> Your knees to them, not arms, must help. Alack,
> You are transported by calamity
> Thither where worse attends you.

So it happens, for later they are in terror lest the Coriolanus whom
they hooted out of Rome return to burn their roofs over their heads.
The proud and malicious Tribunes are told that, unless the Ladies
bring back peace, 'they'll give you death by inches.'

All this reaches its unsurpassable climax in the great scene in act v.
Comparisons, I know, can be foolish, but for a scene of comparable
tragic power I don't know where I would turn, except to the last book
of the *Iliad*, to the scene of Priam with Achilles. That Volumnia and

Coriolanus are in conflict with each other is true but secondary: the great fact is that each is, or has been, in conflict with something vastly stronger than either, and the abundant imagery from Nature, with one or two deeply ironic echoes, makes that powerfully clear. Volumnia had said: 'I mock at death with as big heart as thou'; no doubt she could – but she cannot mock at the destruction of Rome. Earlier, Coriolanus in his glory had gone down on his knees to his mother; now *she* has to kneel on 'no softer cushion than the flints' to him – and you will recall *his* comment: 'Olympus to a molehill nods ... At this unnatural scene the gods do laugh.' He, for his part, has refused even to speak to the Consul; Menenius, who had been as a father to him, he has coldly humiliated. He says, not in the words but in the very spirit of Sophocles' Ajax:

> I'll ne'er be such
> A gosling to obey instinct, but stand
> As if a man were author to himself
> And had no other kin.

But man is not author to himself, and Coriolanus cannot stand. It is surely one of the most profoundly moving moments in all dramatic literature when at last he sees this – too late, like Ajax in *his* great speech about Night and Day, Summer and Winter; sees this, breaks his long, obstinate silence, crosses the stage, and takes his mother's hand:

> O mother, mother, what have you done? ...
> But for your son, believe it, O believe it –
> Most dangerously you have with him prevailed,
> If not most mortal to him.

And at the end we may – I think *should* – hear another tragic echo. Earlier in the play Volumnia had her ecstatic vision of her son triumphing over the Volsces:

> He'll pluck Aufidius by the beard and thrust
> His head below his knee:

if we recall *that*, at the very end, when Aufidius plants his foot on Coriolanus' dead body, it will only be another of those imaginatively conceived correspondences that makes this one of the most taut and powerful tragedies that even Shakespeare ever conceived: 'Fuel to

stoke a furnace' indeed. And you will recall how Shakespeare begins
that last speech, written for Aufidius – a concluding speech at least as
memorable as that which brings *Hamlet* to its close: 'My rage is gone,
and I am struck with sorrow ...'

What is happening here is more than the worthy recognition, in his
death, of a hero's heroism. Earlier in the play Coriolanus had said:

> But then
> The fell Aufidius came within my view,
> And wrath o'erwhelmed my pity.

Now, at the end, when rage, envy, malice, pride have done their
worst, as they always will, it is pity that succeeds to rage. The moment
of truth has come.

The close of the *Iliad* provides a parallel. That poem is sometimes
called 'the tragedy of Achilles' – with some reason, but not quite
enough. It too, like the *Ajax* and *Coriolanus*, ends with a funeral –
but the funeral of Hector, not of Achilles. What has gone before?

In each case a defiance of the laws of Nature or of the gods
(between which I see no distinction worth making), and in each case
the inevitable collapse of that defiance. Achilles, in his inhuman
wrath, day by day perpetrated on Hector's body horrors which, night
by night, the gods obliterated in silent reproof. What purged Achilles
of his fury was Priam's appeal to some of the simplest facts in human
existence – an appeal strikingly similar to Volumnia's appeal that
broke the rage and arrogance of Coriolanus. So also, when Ajax's
defiance of human limitations led him straight to suicide, and then,
when the two kings, in *their* lack of comprehension – parallel to
Creon's in the *Antigone* – would have outraged all human dignity
and decency by leaving the body to be devoured by animals, it is
Odysseus' wider understanding of the human condition that averts
such an outrage. In all these cases it is a secondary matter, whether
or not the burial is the final tribute to the hero's heroism: in the
Antigone, the burial of Polynices certainly is not; what it really does
is, through pity and understanding, to reassert and commemorate
those laws of human existence that we can defy only to our bitter cost
– laws which are adumbrated, in *Coriolanus*, by the opening parable.

Plays or poems like these we find puzzling or defective only because
– for whatever reason – we no longer instinctively grasp their amplitude. We look for the Tragic Hero and his Aristotelian *hamartia*: the
classical tragic poets, Greek and English, give us something bigger.

And what, pray, has all this to do with not blaming Aristotle? Well, why should we blame Aristotle for doing what we, of the modern world, are so apt to do ourselves?

We should reflect that Aristotle was writing the *Poetics* about a hundred years after the production of, say, the *Antigone*, and a hundred years then were just as long as a hundred years nowadays. I say nothing about his general theory of literature, which is splendid, but not a few of his special theories of tragedy are of the fourth century BC and have little relation to his own classical tragedy of the fifth century – to the plays of those whom he calls 'the old poets.' This could be shown in detail; I must confine myself to two or three points only.

Twice, once in chapter xiii and again in chapter xiv, Aristotle uses the adjective μιαρόν 'repugnant,' 'shocking,' and therefore 'inadmissible.' In chapter xiii what is inadmissible is that a blameless character should fall from 'happiness' into misery or ruin; hence the doctrine of *hamartia*. But the fifth-century tragic poets, like Shakespeare, did not find it inadmissible. We have only to think of the King in Aeschylus' *Suppliants*, of Orestes, of Antigone, of Hecuba. What had *they* done wrong, that they should suffer as they do? In this passage Aristotle insists that the dramatist should respect what he calls the *philanthropon*, and the difference between the *philanthropon* and the eighteenth-century Natural Justice is hardly visible to the naked eye.

In the next chapter, what is μιαρόν is something which, as he says, 'the old poets' were accustomed to do: the deliberate killing of a kinsman. His chosen example is Medea's murder of her children. Aristotle disapproves of this, and shows that such a situation can be handled in a much more civilized way, as it is for instance in the *Iphigeneia in Tauris* – an excellent play, but not what *we* mean by 'tragedy.'

Now, what we can learn about fourth-century tragedy is not very much, but is enough to assure us that the best of it was in harmony with Aristotle's doctrines. It was evidently very different in spirit, and therefore in form, from what we think of as classical Greek tragedy. What was the difference, and to what cause can we attribute it?

We have seen that Aristotle drew the line at what he found μιαρόν, at what contravened Natural Justice. (So too did Dr Johnson: see his comments on the death of Cordelia, and his warm approval of what Nahum Tate had done to the play.) It may seem that in the fourth century there was a failure of nerve: certain uncomfortable facts in human experience were no longer suitable material for drama

– except for merely horrific drama, which Aristotle, being a gentleman, naturally despised. But we can go further than this.

It is noticeable that in all our surviving plays, except a few which, like the *Iphigeneia*, are not really tragedies, an important and sometimes dominant role is played by the gods; and of them we may say, for the sake of brevity, that they represent one or more of the unalterable realities that underline and control human experience. In such plays, they serve as what I have called co-ordinates. In the *Poetics* they are mentioned once and once only: 'Since we allow that the gods are omniscient, they can report facts past or future which no one else in the play can know.' In short, they have become no more than a useful dramatic device. No longer is tragedy an affair of Man and the gods; it is an affair only of men – and Natural Justice. (Aristotle's own god, of course, was the Prime Unmoved Mover – a god not very useful to the dramatist.) It is as if the dramatic horizon was closing in.

Why? The closing decades of the fifth century saw the beginning of Enlightenment, of an Age of Reason; of an intense, and of course very fruitful, intellectual activity. So too did the seventeenth century, perhaps with similar results. The new intellectual pursuit of truth made out of date the old apprehensive approach to truth. It was no longer enough to state: you had to *prove*, if you were to be listened to. Poetry cannot *prove*: therefore poetry had to draw in its horns. In all that was important, philosophy took over: poetry had to be content with what was left. The old amplitude was lost to drama, and soon became almost unintelligible. Hence Aristotle's objection to the end of the *Medea*: it does not follow logically from what has gone before.

Aristotle has no term corresponding to our 'tragic hero,' but he does regard a single character as the sole focus of a play, and what befalls him must be logical – with some degree of tolerance. The co-ordinates, now, are those of Natural Justice. The dramatist's universe should be the universe as *we* think it right to be. Those old poets took the universe as it *is*, gods and all. That is the reason why they included in their plays so much that the more civilized fourth century found μιαρόν.

The seventeenth century too ushered in an Age of Enlightenment, which has continued unabated – perhaps with similar results. Perhaps that is the reason why so much modern criticism has been baffled by plays like the *Ajax* and *Trachiniae*, and (if I am right) by *Coriolanus*. A tragedy is essentially a one-man show, with supporting cast. As such, these plays don't work very well. Therefore, the dramatist lost his way somewhere: as Caius Marcius said: 'Forgot! My memory is tired. – Have we no wine here?'

Once more, the horizon has closed in. This, perhaps, is the reason why *Hamlet* has become no more than the tragic story of the enigmatic Prince, and why, nowadays, we turn so avidly to articles on that play which explore the signs of a mother-fixation in the Second Gravedigger.

Michel Grivelet /
Racine's 'Dream of Passion'

'The French object to Shakespeare for his breach of the Unities, and hold up Racine as a model of classical propriety, who makes a Greek hero address a Grecian heroine as *Madame*.' So Hazlitt says in *The Plain Speaker*. 'And yet,' as Professor Eccles observes, 'he had certainly read Shakespeare, and was familiar with Sir Diomed and Lady Cressid.'[1]

The Greeks in Racine seem to have been an object of enduring interest for English critics. Dryden had already blamed the author of *Phèdre* for having sent a rough young man 'to travel from Athens to Paris, taught him to make love, and transformed the Hippolytus of Euripides into *Monsieur* Hippolyte.'[2] Voltaire, at the end of his life, took malicious pleasure in quoting the Scottish judge who had found fault with the description, in *Iphigénie*, of Agamemnon's army overwhelmed by sleep: 'Mais tout dort, et l'armée, et les vents, et Neptune' (I.i.9).[3] 'An officer,' the Scotsman had said, 'should not speak like that.'[4] Dealing with the great classical episode as treated by Shakespeare and by Racine, Macaulay concedes that 'Racine ... would have shuddered at the thought of making a warrior at the siege of Troy quote Aristotle.'[5] 'But,' he goes on, 'of what use is it to avoid a single anachronism when the whole play is an anachronism, the sentiments and phrases of Versailles in the camp of Aulis?'

To this we may imagine that Racine would have answered in much the same terms as those he uses in his preface to the play: 'I have recognized with pleasure, by virtue of the effect which all that I have imitated from either Homer or Euripides has had on our stage, that reason and good sense are the same in all centuries. Parisian taste showed itself to be in accord with that of Athens.' This is indeed a bold assertion. But those who take exception to him on this point assume no less. He feels confident that Achilles or Agamemnon were essentially French, while critics brought up on Shakespeare, and Shakespeare himself, have little doubt that they were very English.

To pursue an argument conducted in that disconcerting spirit of 'Entente cordiale' would now be rather pointless. The view that 'reason and good sense are the same in all centuries' is no longer fashionable and 'the glory that was Greece' has ceased therefore to be the symbol and test of their universal validity. Yet the Greeks, as part of the human heritage that both poets had in common, remain significant. To modern minds they may even appear all the more significant because they are now removed from the obsolete ideal of reason. This is why I have chosen them as the starting-point of an approach, I hope less antiquated than it seems, to the time-honoured subject of Racine and Shakespeare.

The Greeks of classical antiquity do not bulk large in Shakespeare's work. The Athens of Timon is hardly more essential to the play than that of Theseus and Hippolyta in *A Midsummer Night's Dream*. There are Greek names in other works and a visit to the Oracle at Delphos in *The Winter's Tale*. But they all belong to the nowhere of a world of romance. Only *Troilus and Cressida*, then, remains and the relation of this single play to the entire canon would seem to illustrate the comparative unimportance of the Greek element in Shakespeare. But a small proportion may be decisive. It may, like the mere 'dram of eale' o'erleaven 'all the noble substance,' as the Prince of Denmark says. *Hamlet* indeed, a crucial play, in many ways the epitome of Shakespeare's dramatic art, is one in which the vision of figures from the heroic past of Greece, brief and puzzling as it is, or rather because it is brief and puzzling, raises the problem of its function in modern tragedy.

The Player's speech on the sack of Troy is some fifty lines long. But, though it has often been dismissed as, at best, a chance allusion, a purely technical display, if not a caricature, it is hardly possible, after Professor Harry Levin's essay on the subject,[6] to ignore the close relation of the passage to the main texture and argument of the play. Three main figures stand out against the background of a city's tragedy. Priam, Hecuba, Pyrrhus are brought together in a moment of violence which is not without bearing upon the fatal relationship between Claudius, Gertrude, and the Prince. Though no blood tie exists between the Trojan king and his Greek foe, Priam, the 'old grandsire,' the 'unnerved father,' is too much the typical, almost mythical, parent not to place Pyrrhus as a son whose wild passion both condemns and quenches itself in his savagery to the father-figure. And in the frantic sorrow of the 'mobled queen,' Hamlet, we may feel, already enjoys the bitterness of his dimly imagined cruelty to his own mother. For the son of Achilles, like the Prince of Denmark, has a dead father to revenge. Pyrrhus is another Hamlet among 'strange images of death,' to borrow a phrase for which the author of *Macbeth* is also indebted to book II of *The Aeneid*.[7]

We should not be surprised to see the destruction of Troy thus cast its shadow upon the rottenness at Elsinore. In many plays and other works of the period, as Professor Harry Levin reminds us, the same power, we might say the same fascination, of the ancient disaster exerts itself. It is one of the great themes of European culture, a basic assumption of our consciousness since the nations of the western world deduced their origin from the relics of the old city. At an early stage in his poetic career, Shakespeare had dwelt at length upon the ruin of Troy as the background most appropriate to tragic unhappiness. The tapestry described in *The Rape of Lucrece* is not, in fact, a mere background, for under the heroine's gaze of deep distress the 'well-painted piece' comes to life again. When Lucrece raises her voice, it is to speak not her own grief but Hecuba's:

> 'Poor instrument,' quoth she, 'without a sound,
> I'll tune thy woes with my lamenting tongue,
> And drop sweet balm in Priam's painted wound,
> And rail on Pyrrhus that has done him wrong,
> And with my tears quench Troy that burns so long.'   (1464–8)

'Troy that burns so long' ... What the tapestry expresses visibly is the conviction that Ilion, the ideal city, has never ceased to suffer. Every modern tragedy is but the old sorrow endured again.

There is, however, some cause for surprise in Racine's use of the same theme. By the time that he began to write for the theatre, the matter of Troy had lost much of its traditional appeal to European minds. Whether in France or in England, poets could no longer be moved by the spirit which had animated Ronsard's *Franciade* in 1572 or Heywood's somewhat belated *Troia Britannica* in 1609. Racine's first great play dates, not insignificantly, from the very year when

Milton published his great poem, an epic for which he had thought fit to abandon his original subject of British legendary history from the landing of Brute to the times of Arthur. Yet *Andromaque* is still under the cloud of the great conflagration.

Against her confidante, Céphise, that is against that part of herself which is all for yielding to Pyrrhus, the widow of Hector argues that she may not forget. Or rather she is hesitant enough to ask whether she ought to forget: forget her husband left without burial, forget Priam lying at her feet and smearing the altar with his blood. Let Céphise remember the cruel night, a night without end for a whole people, let her imagine Pyrrhus, with glaring eyes, stepping forward in the blaze of burning palaces:

> Songe, songe, Céphise, à cette Nuit cruelle,
> Qui fut pour tout un peuple une Nuit éternelle,
> Figure-toy Pyrrhus, les yeux étincelans,
> Entrant à la lueur de nos Palais brûlans ...   (III.viii)

But while Andromaque thus pleads with herself, her very vision of the conqueror, fierce and bloody, betrays how much she pines for her own defeat:

> Songe aux cris des Vainqueurs, songe aux cris des Mourans
> Dans la flamme étouffez, sous le fer expirans.
> Peins-toy dans ces horreurs Andromaque éperduë
> Voila comme Pyrrhus vint s'offrir à ma Veuë ...   (ibid)

There is clearly much in this that resembles what the Player in *Hamlet* says of the 'rugged Pyrrhus ... horribly tricked/With blood ... With eyes like carbuncles ...' Both poets are here, of course, indebted to Vergil. But the common debt does not conceal their differences.

In Shakespeare's play, the Troy episode is not only diminutive in comparison with the whole text, it is also distant from the actual drama, though undeniably relevant to it. While contriving to give considerable impact to the grief of Hecuba, the author has been careful to stress the remoteness of Ilion from Elsinore. The Player's speech is but 'Aeneas' talk to Dido,' a narrative explicitly in the manner of the Vergilian epic. Though the woeful scene may seem to be pathetically revived, the urgency of dialogue does not force itself upon us. The tale of sorrow unspeakable is told at leisure, with a certain sense of tranquillity. It recalls in distant Carthage the tragic fate of Troy.

But the distancing effect inherent in this style of recitation is made still more perceptible by the technique of the play within a play which is here used by Shakespeare. Some emphasis is even laid on the fact that the dramatic piece from which the speech is taken was not of the kind one can feel easily enthusiastic about: it 'pleased not the million, 'twas caviary to the general.' The absence of every supporting element of dress, context, atmosphere, reinforces the strangeness of the utterance. No one can at any moment forget that this is a wholly theatrical performance, a mere rehearsal. The Danish court feels safely insulated from the contagion if not from the terror and pity of the Trojan tragedy.

The paradox is, of course, especially conspicuous in the Player himself. Adept as he is in 'forcing his soul ... to his own conceit' so that the fictitious idea takes hold of him and controls 'his whole function' as if the emotion were really heartfelt, he remains a professional, of Denmark or perhaps London, who acts a part. The very skill and energy he puts into pretending keeps him immune from the grief he revives. What indeed is 'Hecuba to him, or he to Hecuba / That he should weep for her?'

Thus, while that 'Troy that burns so long' seems to fascinate Hamlet as if it were about to engulf him in its own doom, the Prince is, in fact, doing his utmost to keep off the disaster. The playing of even a brief fragment of the archetypal tragedy has stimulated his intense meditation. It has taught him first of all that it is not by yielding to genuine emotion that an actor best masters his art. And moreover, as a Prince, he is not one to content himself with 'actions that a man might play.' He may for some time, like another Shakespeare, appear to be wholly engaged in the production of *The Murder of Gonzago*, but, as he very well knows, the act he has to perform is only too real. If then, 'in the very torrent, tempest, and ... whirlwind of his passion' the competent actor 'must acquire and beget a temperance,' a Prince born to 'set ... right' things 'out of joint' must, with still stronger reason, strive to do just that.

It is therefore clear enough that the classical element in Shakespeare's work is mainly used as a foil. Neither the fatal omen inherent in its subject nor the exemplary virtue as tragically represented is ignored. But the play does its utmost to move away from the threat and example of tragedy. Its verbal atmosphere shifts from one of brooding in which the past is predominant to one in which the present and even the future dedicate themselves not perhaps to expectation but to readiness. The hero's energies are bent upon a seriousness of action whose aim is not only to elude the deception of mere playing, the fallacy of 'a dream of passion,' but also, eventually, to ward off from Elsinore the fate of Priam's city. We are in a universe where God has left something to the human will. Even though 'there is a divinity that shapes our ends,' it is for us to 'rough-hew them.' The sadness, of course, and in the end the pity is that we do it so badly. Shakespearian tragedy, it seems to me, illustrates most of all the Aristotelian principle of *peripeteia*: what was intended to produce an ardently desired result is suddenly seen to have brought about the opposite. The curse of human action is that it somehow always falls 'on the inventors' heads.' We may all be 'hoist with our own petar.'

The dramatic use to which the sack of Troy is turned in Racine's *Andromaque* is obviously very different, though one easily overlooks how much is common to both plays on this point. In both we have to do with a narrative, a recitation of events. In both we are made to feel the impact of the past upon the present. In both our attention is drawn to the workings of remembrance. But what Hamlet remembers is an aesthetic experience, the feelings of a theatre-goer, a memory, we may say, of the imagination. The Pyrrhus of *Andromaque*, on the contrary, is not safely embalmed in a play. He is the ardent suitor she daily tries to avoid, deceiving herself with the thought that she hates the son of her husband's murderer: an ardent suitor, Céphise insists, who disclaims his past exploits and those of his father, Achilles. In answer to which Andromaque feels bound to ask whether she must forget simply because he does not remember:

> Dois-je les oublier, s'il ne s'en souvient plus?
> Dois-je oublier Hector privé de funérailles,
> Et traisné sans honneur autour de nos murailles?   (III.viii)

'Must I forget?' This is, in Racine, the great question, the great interrogation of the soul debating with itself. And the most fatal. Here, only too obviously, while Andromaque searches past wrongs and past sufferings for motives to resist Pyrrhus, she feeds her deep desire to yield to conquering strength. Much in the same way Phèdre, in spite of herself, betrays her love to Hippolyte while pretending to be lost in the memory of her passion for her husband. I burn for Thésée, she says. But, a moment after : he had your mien, your eyes, your language:

> Ouy, Prince, je languis, je brûle pour Thésée ...
> Il avoist vostre port, vos yeux, vostre langage,
> Cette noble pudeur coloroit son visage ...   (II.v)

And again she soon wanders further. In her delirious memory, Hippolyte supersedes Thésée entirely. She loves him, lavishes infinite care on his charming head. Another Ariadne, she goes down with this pseudo-Theseus into the Labyrinth, hoping with him to find her way out, or much rather to lose herself for ever:

> Que de soins m'eust cousté cette Teste charmante!
> Un fil n'eust point assez rassuré vostre Amante.
> Compagne du péril qu'il vous falloit chercher,
> Moy-mesme devant vous j'aurais voulu marcher,
> Et Phèdre au Labyrinthe avec vous descenduë,
> Se seroit avec vous retrouvée, ou perduë.   (ibid)

What Phèdre imagines is doubly unattainable: unattainable because Thésée can never be Hippolyte, or rather Hippolyte Thésée, and because it is years ago that she first met Thésée and became his wife. The most inaccessible, the unnameable, is of course for her to be the wife of her husband's son. The impossibility of the forbidden bliss cannot even be entertained as a thought. It can only be disguised into what is merely circumstantial: the fact, both reassuring and painful in the extreme, that the possibility has long been gone. The past thus becomes a substitute: not a mere tense but a mode, the mode of what is all the more urgent and immediate as it is beyond one's reach.

Georges Poulet, in his *Studies in Human Time*,[8] has written admirably on this all-powerful prestige of the past in Racine. Even when Racinian tragedy stretches forward into the future – and it often does as, for instance, in *Iphigénie* which stages a sort of prelude to the great events of the *Iliad*, or in *Britannicus* over which the crimes of Néron, the monster to be, loom so large – even then the hero, as it were, 'foresees' himself in the past. Like Bajazet, knowing in advance what is to be expected, his only hope is in despair. Foresight does not here differ from memory.

But it is of course in plays orientated towards historical or even, as in *Phèdre*, mythical antecedents that the fascination of the past is most compelling. *Andromaque* is about what happens when the *Iliad* is ended, and in the character of Pyrrhus we have, as Poulet puts it, 'the living proof that it is impossible to escape from the *representation* of [the] past in the present.' When Hermione is told that he has chosen her after all, her exultant joy expresses itself in the conviction that he is his former self again, the hero of countless exploits:

> Pyrrhus revient à nous. Hé bien, chère Cleone,
> Conçois-tu les transports de l'heureuse Hermione?
> Sçais-tu quel est Pyrrhus? T'es-tu fait raconter
> Le nombre des exploits ... (iii.iii)

Andromaque also, as we have seen, is haunted by the memory of these exploits. She thinks herself still possessed by her dead husband. She loves him in her son Astyanax. At least she says so, especially when her words may hurt Pyrrhus, as he, in his anger and despite, complains:

> C'est Hector (disoit-elle en l'embrassant toujours)
> Voila ses yeux, sa bouche, et déja son audace ... (ii.v)

But, speaking thus, she proclaims not so much her attachment to Hector as her own subjection to a sense of submerged emotion for which she longs against all reason and in spite of herself. Let Pyrrhus be what he was on that 'Nuit cruelle' and she will yield to him. She does eventually consent to marry him since he is ready to sacrifice Astyanax. But this marriage which she meant to crown with her own suicide sees Pyrrhus die the victim of Hermione's jealousy. For all his efforts to be his own present self and to live, he had no chance to escape the doom embodied in two women so madly given over to their desire of fulfilment in the past.

This strange deportment of the typically Racinian heroine may be true to feminine psychology. It expresses above all the poet's acute knowledge of the sheerness of passion. He has been called in turns tender and cruel, 'le tendre, le cruel Racine.' And indeed he seems to show a woman's sense of the ineffable brutality of love. 'Infandum regina, jubes renovare dolorem' (*Aeneid* ii, l. 3), the extreme joy is an exquisite pain. Its fierceness, its urgency must remain unspoken, unthought of. They may never emerge to the full light of clear consciousness. All they can be allowed is their exile to a world of scarcely distinct shadows too desirable not to be the object of invincible dread.

The open sesame to this dim universe is a word of admirable subtlety, a magic word in Racine, a word which seems to express the operation of speculative thought and, at the same time but more seductively, the fascination of a dream, a 'songe.' 'Songe, songe, Céphise, à cette Nuit cruelle,' says Andromaque. The word also comes and somehow dies on Hermione's lips when she thinks she has won her hero:

> Intrépide et par tout suivi de la victoire,
> Charmant, fidelle, enfin rien ne manque à sa gloire,
> Songe ...   (III.iii)

And when nothing is left to her but the thought of revenge, it is again the word she uses to express her determination: 'Que je me perde ou non, je songe à me venger' (IV.iv). Thus, in a trance, is conceived a murder she will disown when done and blame on Oreste with frantic but thoroughly sincere inconsequence.

'A dream of passion' (*Hamlet*, II.ii.578) : no term, it seems to me, could more exactly define the prevailing mode of Racinian poetry than this Shakespearian phrase. A dream, as I have tried to show, because the dark absolute of passion can neither belong with the lucidity of consciousness nor entirely escape its notice. It is therefore only remembered as the terrors and hidden joys of the night picture themselves dimly on the waking mind. The whole desperate effort of Racine, the magic of his verse, aims at fixing the unenduring vision for ever. Hence what might be called his weakness for *Bérénice*.

At the end of the play, Titus, Bérénice and Antiochus know that the time has come for them to be irrevocably separated. The cruelty of such a thought is too much to bear, as the heroine complains to the emperor. For ever! think, my lord, how dreadful the cruel word may be when one loves? In a month, in a year, how will we suffer?

> Pour jamais! Ah Seigneur, songez-vous en vous-même
> Combien ce mot cruel est affreux quand on aime?
> Dans un mois, dans un an comment souffrirons-nous ...   (IV.v)

But the suffering they must now fully explore was already there from the very beginning, embodied in the unhappy Antiochus. It was already there in his memory of the days when, left alone in the desolate east, he had wandered aimlessly in Caesarea, a city sweet to him because it was the place where he had once adored the queen:

> Dans l'Orient désert quel devint mon ennui!
> Je demeuray long-temps errant dans Césarée,
> Lieux charmans où mon cœur vous avait adorée. (i.iv)

Such is the hypnotic quality of the remembrance that, to the forsaken Antiochus, the populous cities of the east are both empty and, at the same time, like Caesarea, entrancing places. This 'Orient désert,' so unreal and yet so lucid, has all the awful motionlessness, the paralysed clarity, of dreams. Nightmare or illusion of happiness, it is the land of Racine's secret fears and secret wishes, a land where tragic grief somehow eases itself in its apprehension of permanence.

If I may risk a simplification, I would say then that, for both Racine and Shakespeare, Greece is the dwelling-place not so much of reason and good sense as of much darker powers of the mind. But while Shakespeare seems always to yearn for 'good things of Day' and especially so when, as in *Macbeth*, they 'begin to droop and drowse,' Racine is apparently in constant need of a refuge from the glare of daylight. In his poetic universe, as Roland Barthes observes, the daily apparition of the sun is a wound inflicted on the natural milieu of night.[9] Night in *Andromaque* is cruel because it is illumined by so many merciless fires. But even when it is not night itself but, for instance, the forest shade ('Dieux, que ne suis-je assise à l'ombre des forêts!'), darkness is always tender, happy, maternal, a powerful appeal for a boy who had always known himself as an orphan.

Why the trend of Racine's work should be so contrary to that of Shakespeare's remains a subject of major interest to the student of drama. The reasons are partly of an individual, idiosyncratic nature. Much is due, as I have just suggested, to the fact that the French boy was, from infancy, left fatherless, motherless, then brought up by the strict masters of Port-Royal, a 'child of the desert,' to quote the title of Charles Baudouin's penetrating book.[10] Psychoanalytic study or psycho-criticism, as Charles Mauron, another modern master of Racinian studies, would put it, has been, in this case, certainly rewarding.[11] It has not, I submit, yielded as much as might be expected in the case of Shakespeare.

There is also the fact that it must have been a very different thing to live in Elizabethan or Jacobean England than under 'le Roi Soleil.' Racine's relation to his master was one of extreme devotion, but with all the love-hate ambivalence that such attachments often imply. This royal sun was for Racine vital and deadly. The impact of the absolute monarchy on the great dramatic work has been, in recent years, the occasion for significant sociological interpretation, as in Lucien Goldman's *Le Dieu caché*,[12] or in the less known, more poetic, and to my mind more enlightening little book of Fernand Lion, *Les Rêves de Racine*.[13]

The history of the theatre must also be taken into account. The plays of Racine are in intimate accordance with the Italian picture stage. Personally I would have no less regard for the fact that Shakespeare could find it possible to be both a poet and an actor while Racine could not. Raymond Picard makes much of this in his study of Racine's career.[14] And indeed, even if the author of *A Midsummer Night's Dream* could make his Theseus say of players that 'the best in this kind are but shadows,' as an actor himself he was bound to feel that his mental, moral, and physical energies were wholly engaged in what he was doing. Action, however deceptive, could not but have a meaning for him. But Racine could only teach others to perform what he wanted to do. His son Louis tells us what great pains he took with la Champmeslé.[15] We picture him endeavouring, with anxious passion, to fashion the speech, the gestures, and attitudes of the actress who was also his mistress, trying to embody, in this inconstant, elusive, captivating woman, his dream of Bérénice.

I am not, of course, trying to argue that Shakespeare is all rectitude and moral certainty because he seems always to be saying 'Give me some light!' while Racine, as a young man, writing from the south of France, was already praising the beauty of night over that of day: 'Et nous avons des Nuits plus belles que vos Jours!'

For Shakespeare, or Hamlet, having decided to act, finds tragedy on his way to reasonable action. 'Our thoughts are ours, their ends none of our own.' The world is a 'great snare' and passion lurks even under our most considerate efforts. It is not the 'woman coloured ill' who, for the poet of the *Sonnets*, is the real challenge and the greatest scandal, but the 'man right fair.'

With no less honesty, Racine sees beyond the seduction of his dream. And this is why *Phèdre* is not only his masterpiece but a work poetically and personally decisive, his last play for the public theatre. In the view of Phèdre, though inseparable, reason and passion, night and day, are opposed in a conflict which must be fought to the death. When she first appears, she has been in the dark so long that her eyes are dazzled. She no sooner sees the light of day than she hates it. She knows herself to be descended from the Sun, the author of her family according to the myth, and her most dreaded Judge. She has come to see it for the last time: 'Soleil, je te viens voir pour la dernière fois'

(1.iii). And, of course, like every Racinian heroine, she is tempted to seek refuge in a dream, a dream of Hippolyte, a dream of passion concealed from the glaring eye of reason. 'Oh Gods! That I were seated in the forest shade': 'Dieux! que ne suis-je assise à l'ombre des forêts!' (ibid). But in the end she pays the price of choosing utter darkness, so that Death, robbing her eyes of light, may restore all its purity to the day those eyes had soiled:

> Déja je ne voy plus qu'à travers un nuage ...
> Et la Mort à mes yeux dérobant la clarté
> Rend au jour, qu'il souilloient, toute sa pureté. (v.vii)

NOTES

1 F.Y. Eccles *Racine in England* (The Taylorian Lecture, 1921) (Oxford 1922)
2 Dryden, preface to *All for Love*
3 All quotations from Racine are from the edition by Pierre Mélèse, *Le Théâtre de Racine* (Collection nationale des classiques français) (Paris 1951).
4 See *Voltaire on Shakespeare* Theodore Besterman, ed (Geneva 1967) 87.
5 Macaulay, 'Moore's Life of Lord Byron' in his *Critical and Historical Essays contributed to the Edinburgh Review*
6 Harry Levin, 'An Explication of the Player's Speech' in *The Question of Hamlet* (Oxford 1959)
7 *The Aeneid* II.369: see Kenneth Muir, ed *Macbeth* Arden edition, note to 1.iii.97.
8 Georges Poulet *Etudes sur le temps humain* (Paris 1949), translated by Elliott Coleman as *Studies in Human Time* (Edinburgh)
9 Roland Barthes *Sur Racine* (Paris 1965)
10 Charles Baudouin *Jean Racine, l'enfant du désert* (Paris 1963)
11 There are several books by Mauron on the subject; of special interest perhaps is *L'Inconscient dans l'œuvre et la vie de Jean Racine* (Annales de la Faculté des lettres d'Aix-Marseille) (Gap 1957).
12 Lucien Goldmann *Le Dieu caché* (Paris 1955)
13 Fernand Lion *Les Rêves de Racine* (Paris 1948)
14 Raymond Picard *La Carrière de Jean Racine* (Paris 1956)
15 Louis Racine, 'Mémoires sur la vie de Jean Racine' in Paul Mesnard, ed *Œuvres de Jean Racine* (Paris 1885) 1, 265

Jean Jacquot /
The Last Plays and the Masque

Though a basic distinction must be maintained between drama and court entertainment, it is well known that, during the Renaissance, there was a constant exchange of influence between both spheres. Plays were performed at the Tudor court during the traditional periods of festivity. The Gentlemen and the Children of the Chapel and the King's players were all active in the preparation of interludes and disguisings. The feat of arms and the dance were the courtier's achievements, the war games and the masquerades the chief forms of entertainment. But the display of strength or elegance was enhanced, and gave more refined pleasure, when it was transposed into a world of romance, and became the central piece of an adventure. Thus a semi-dramatic framework was provided to set off the game or the dance. And, by an inverse process, elements of pageantry or masque came to be incorporated into plays, as intermedes, or as part of the plot.

This is not the place for an historical survey, however sketchy, but the process just described acquired its full significance in the latter part of the sixteenth century, when full-fledged tragedy and comedy, or complex hybrids, succeeded the interlude. The contamination of plays by entertainment is clearly illustrated by the comedies of the children's companies: Lyly, in particular, took full advantage of the gifts of the boy actor, singer, dancer, and musician in his mythological pastorals, with their nymphs and fairies, temples and oracles, and Ovidian metamorphoses.

The Inns of Court were also influential in this respect. They had their festive traditions and their Lords of Misrule, and, besides, they were pioneers in the field of Senecan tragedy, which they adorned with elaborate dumb-shows, rich with visual and musical symbolism. Their influence can also be discerned in the revival of the so-called private theatres at the turn of the century. In the space of a few years, the playwrights for the new children's companies did much to extend the use of musical, choreographic, or processional effects to a great variety of moods and situations. Marston, in particular, had an unusual gift for tone colour, and experimented in a type of drama which relied on sensorial and emotional impact and contrasts of atmosphere rather than coherence of plot.[1]

Yet the dramatic use of voices and instruments, dances and shows, was by no means limited to the little theatres and their more sophisticated audience. The leading adult companies had a wider appeal; they had to please the common playgoer as well as higher social groups and, since they were frequently asked to perform at court, their audience ranged from the groundling to the sovereign. And courtly entertainments, as well as the more popular sorts, were introduced into their plays for various purposes. They could be used as a diversion after prolonged dramatic tension, or as a device to bring about the catastrophe in a revenge tragedy or the final reconciliation in a comedy. Examples from Shakespeare come readily to the mind. Masked lovers were mocked and rustic worthies laughed out of countenance at the court of Navarre. Sport, revelry, and nuptial rites came together in the forest of Arden. Masked visitors appeared at the feast of the Capulets, a masque of Cupid and the Amazons at the house of the prosperous Timon.

I have chosen to discuss the last group of plays because they are contemporary with a change which was to have a far-reaching effect on theatrical life and aesthetics: I mean the introduction of the Italian type of scenery by way of the masque. The period under consideration extends from 1608, when *Pericles* was first played, to 1613, when 'the shooting of certain chambers in way of triumph' during a performance of *Henry VIII* set the Globe on fire.

These were years of transition in more than one sense. With the advent of James I the Lord Chamberlain's players became the King's Men and, a few years later, succeeded the Children of the Queen's Revels at the Blackfriars. This was part of a general process which tended to place the main companies under the patronage of the royal family and the control of the court, and to move the centre of theatrical life from the Bankside to more fashionable districts. This process was eventually to lead to the decline of the theatre as a popular entertainment. But by 1609 it was still at an early stage. The King's Men were undoubtedly conscious of the advantage of an indoor theatre for the winter season. But that they still valued the Globe and its public appears clearly from their concern to have it rebuilt on the same site and with a similar structure after the fire.

Shakespeare may have had particularly in mind the audience of the Blackfriars, or the resources of its stage, when he wrote the romance plays, though there is little evidence to support this. *Pericles* was played at the Globe before the King's Men took possession of the Blackfriars, and Simon Forman saw *The Winter's Tale* at the Globe on 15 May 1611 and *Cymbeline* in the spring or summer of the same year. For Blackfriars we have only the mention by Dryden that *The Tempest* was performed there.[2] But it is reasonable to suppose that successful plays were presented in both theatres. We must remember too that *The Winter's Tale* and *The Tempest* were both played at Whitehall in November 1611, and were among the plays performed at court in the winter 1612–13 during the period of festivities which marked the marriage of Princess Elizabeth and the Elector Palatine. The fact is interesting on account of the importance, in both plays, of the nuptial theme, and the presentation, during the same festive season, of three sumptuous masques in honour of the princely couple.

It is most likely that Shakespeare, when he wrote the last plays, had in view three kinds of audiences and staging conditions: open air theatre, indoor theatre, hall at court. The deep reason for his giving up tragedy for romance will remain unknown, but we may be sure that it did not involve a narrowing of his scope: he wrote, as before, for people of different status and degrees of culture, keeping in mind the need for diversity of appeal, and flexibility of performance.

Let us now consider the Jacobean masque. In what sense was it a new departure? Little progress seems to have been achieved, through the sixteenth century, in that type of entertainment. There was the semi-impromptu variety: a group of masquers, with their spokesman, torchbearers, and musicians, pretended to come from a strange land, did a formal dance, and then offered to dance with the ladies. This was to remain the core of the Jacobean masque, with its distinction between the stately measures and the revels. But there also existed a more elaborate type of disguising, which implied the unfolding of a story through narration, dialogue, procession, and song before the culminating point of the dance was reached. The disguisings for the marriage of Prince Arthur and Katherine of Aragon, in the first year of the century, are characteristic examples, making full use of the musical resources of the Chapel Royal and requiring complex decorative units on wheels.

If we compare these disguisings with the masque of Proteus at Gray's Inn (1595), which was one of the most sumptuous of its kind in the reign of Queen Elizabeth I, we observe little sign of evolution in the treatment of the conceit leading to the climax of the dance, or in the staging technique.[3]

That Queen Anne took pleasure in court entertainments, and that James I was prepared to spend far more on them than his predecessors, accounts for the ambitious and lavish character of the Jacobean masque. But its success as an art form depended on the collaboration of various talents. Besides the poet there were several composers and choreographers and, last but not least, there was the architect-scenographer. The music which has been preserved is usually fragmentary, and reduced to the skeleton form of treble and bass, or, at best, voice part and lute accompaniment. But we know from the libretti that several consorts were used, with different functions, that subtle effects were produced by the contrast, or the blending, of tone colour. In the anti-masque, which relied largely for its effects on the professional actor, facetious dialogue was interspersed with song and dance. But in the masque proper, symphony, vocal numbers, and stately dance followed in close succession, with a more or less prolonged break for the revels, when the masquers would dance to more familiar and brisk tunes with members of the audience. The autograph manuscript of William Lawes for three Caroline specimens of the genre confirms the impression that the more solemn part of the masque tended to be conceived musically as an organic whole.[4] Singers and instrumentalists, mainly from the Chapel Royal and the King's music, were employed in large numbers. Some of them appeared on stage as allegorical figures or priests. They unfolded in solo or choral song the meaning of the scenic changes and of the evolutions of the masquers, and on some occasions accompanied them in procession from the stage or dancing area to the state at the upper end of the hall.

The introduction by Inigo Jones of a type of scenery and machinery highly developed in Italy but still little known in England was an innovation of far-reaching consequences. Decorative units such as mountain, temple, or bower had been in use for a long time. But in Daniel's *Vision of Twelve Goddesses*, which immediately precedes

Jones' experiments, they were still dispersed in different parts of the hall. The decisive factor was the use of perspective to unify stage space and all its decorative elements. Equally important was the possibility of achieving a rapid change of scenery. We need not discuss here the technical aspects of Jones' art. But it is certain that, given the opportunity, he was ready to display his virtuosity, and to undertake more and more ambitious feats. Multiple changes of sets, and the use of complex machinery, led him to use a proscenium frame which enclosed the stage. Yet we must not conceive the masque stage as containing a world of illusion entirely separated from the spectator. It was still an open stage because it had to fulfil a social function which required a communion of the lord and lady masquers with other members of the aristocratic audience. We must bear in mind, when we attempt to visualise the masque, the polarity of stage and royal state, at opposite ends of the hall, and the correspondence established, by the masque poets, between the deities of an Olympus of wood and painted canvas, and a sovereign supremely conscious of his divine right. Jones' settings and machines enhanced the illusion of a mythical and heroic world from whence masquers issued forth, descending into the hall to perform their dance and, on some occasions, march with a cortège of musicians up to the state to pay homage to the royal family.

The success of the masque as an art form depended on the unity of invention. The inevitable entry of the masquers had to be prepared in such a way that the spectators' curiosity was roused, and the discovery of the masquers came as a surprise. To take a classic example, this is achieved simply and effectively in Jonson's *Oberon*. The anti-masque of satyrs serves as a foil to the main piece, but also helps to increase the expectation as these unruly creatures, for all their pranks and antics, are full of respect and wonder for the Fairy Prince. This twofold effect of the anti-masque is beautifully combined with that of the change of scenery and the discovery, first of the façade of an illuminated palace, and then of the inside with the Prince and knights, musicians and torchbearers of the nation of Fays.

Elsewhere an element of conflict is introduced before the main masque can take place. In Campion's masque for the wedding of Lord Hayes, the Night and Flora both claim the bride, the one in the name of chastity, the other in the name of Hymen, and the Evening Star appears as a messenger from the gods to achieve conciliation. Appeasement of strife could be combined, as in this case, with the familiar device of deliverance from captivity and the returning of metamorphosed knights to their pristine form. But the task of the inventor (or inventors) was not merely to provide a story but to achieve a satisfactory balance between poetry, music, dance, and the visual arts. Jonson was never at odds with the musicians but his quarrels with Jones are well known. It was not merely the conflict of strong personalities: aesthetic principles were at stake. Jonson was ready to supply opportunities for new stage effects, but these were to remain subordinate to the poet's invention. He found justification for his attitude in a platonic distinction between soul and body which implied a hierarchy, poetry which conveyed spiritual meaning having precedence over things which flattered the senses. To him Jones was not an artist but a mere craftsman. Hence the sarcasms against the successful scenographer who stole the show: that painting and carpentry could be the soul of the masque was the extreme of absurdity.

We cannot fully agree with Jonson because we treat Jones' costumes and stage designs as works of art, as they deserve. But to consider stagecraft as an art was, in England, totally without precedent. Jonson's ambition as a humanist poet was to mix instruction with pleasure, and use fable, figure, and attribute as the outward expression of a hidden meaning. Jonson leaned, not only upon classical sources, but on the standard works of the mythologists and iconologists where all the relations between symbol and appearance were codified. So he must have felt capable of supplying all the information to the stage decorator and costume designer, and inclined to consider the latter's work as one of mere transposition, not creation. And judging from his 'Expostulation with Inigo Jones,' he may not have been very sensitive to purely visual beauty resulting from the relation of colour and form or from its faithfulness to life.

In opposition to Jonson, Daniel was resigned to admit that 'in these things wherein the only life consists in show, the art and invention of the architect gives the greatest grace, and is of the most importance.'[5] But still a different view is expressed in Campion's Lords' Masque (14 February 1614), which is entirely conceived in order to extol the co-operation, on equal terms, of the poet, musician, and architect-scenographer. The three arts are here represented by the heroic figures of Orpheus, Entheus the poetic enthusiast, and Prometheus, who combine their powers 'to solemnize These royal nuptials.' This was a double masque for the marriage of Princess Elizabeth, and the masquers first appeared as stars moving in orderly dance, before descending to earth and appearing in human form, and the lady masquers were the creatures of Prometheus once changed into statues and now returned to life. Campion, the poet-musician, was perhaps carried too far in his praise of artistic creation. Prometheus, after all, was a rebel whom Jupiter had punished. But here he appears, like his two associates, as a priestlike, almost divine figure, and Jupiter is quite prepared to grant what they seek to obtain by songs of invocation.

This ceremonious, semi-religious atmosphere is fairly constant in the serious part of the masque. The anti-masque provided quaint or grotesque entertainment (which King James seems to have enjoyed most). But it could also be a way of opposing the vulgar and the noble, the ugly and the beautiful, the profane and the sacred. Once the baser sort had been dismissed, monarchy and nobility were left to commune with the gods. Singers and musicians costumed like priests played an important part in these 'rites,' and in the incantations, or magic operations, which they required. The solemn part of the masque must have made a beautiful and impressive show. Yet its ethics were of dubious value, being based on adulation, self-glorification, and the all too easy conciliation of pleasure and virtue, or riches and honour. A greater depth of meaning was to be found in nuptial masques. Bridegrooms like the favourites of James I (to say nothing of a bride like Frances Howard) may have been persons of doubtful merit. But the celebration of Hymen was something the Renaissance artist could do supremely well. The masque poets were up to the occasion, and sang of chaste vows, of the sanctity of the marriage bond, and, with outspoken sensuality, of the expectation of the wedding night.

We have noted that Shakespeare's last plays were contemporary with a rapid development of the spectacular elements of the masque, and that, considered as a group, they had to meet the requirements of three types of stages, the Globe, the Blackfriars, and Whitehall. It seems that, from the scholarly work which has been done on the structure of both theatres, conditions of performance at the Globe and the Blackfriars did not vary considerably, though the indoor theatre may have provided greater intimacy, better acoustics, and required artificial light. The principles remained the same, dramatic illusion was based primarily on speech, gesture, and costume, location was defined by dialogue, entrances, and exits. The stage façade, whether it was bare or ornamented, was there to remind the spectator that he was in a theatre. The actor played against a background which was neutral and functional. Doors, or discovery space, or 'tarras' may have been temporarily associated with a given place. And decorative units may have been brought to denote such a place. But there was obviously no attempt to integrate, by using the rules of perspective, the elements of location into a unified space that would be the place of the action.

And yet the same plays were performed at Court during periods of festivities when masques were presented which relied entirely for their effects on perspective and change of scenery. This juxtaposition is highly significant, especially when we think that the type of theatrical illusion introduced by Inigo Jones was in course of time to modify entirely, and for centuries, the principles of Shakespearian production. Whether such principles were already employed for early performances of our plays at Court is uncertain. Inigo Jones, whose work was usually well publicized, is not known to have staged plays, except pastorals for Queen Henrietta Maria. Little is known of the Florentine Servi who did the settings of a masque for the marriage of Somerset in Jones' absence. There may have been other artists with an experience of the Italian stage, but no trace of their work seems to be extant.

The alternative might have been some transitional form. Huge decorative units were already in use at Court in the preceding reigns, and perhaps a few 'mansions' with specific location, combined with a neutral acting area in the front part of the stage, might have made it possible to act any of the romance plays, even if it required a constant shift from country to country as in *Pericles*. But this is mere speculation, since apparently no documents have survived of the staging of such plays at Court. But what is evident in the plays themselves is the reliance on word-painting and the appeal to the mind's eye. What the spectator sees, and what he must imagine, are clearly distinguished. '*Cleon shows Pericles the tomb*' (IV. iv dumb show); 'At Ephesus the temple see Our king and all his company' (v. ii. 18–19).[6] But 'In your imagination hold This stage the ship' (III. Chorus, 58–9) and again 'think this his bark' (v. Chorus, 22). In this case the 'banners sable, trimm'd with rich expense' of the prince of Tyre may have been visible on the stage. And editors, since Malone, have accepted the presence, for this scene, of 'a pavilion on deck, with a curtain before it.' But whatever the means by which it was represented, inner stage or temporary structure, this was common practice on the Elizabethan stage. And it did not exclude the appeal to imagination which rings again and again in the choric part of Gower (cf. IV. Chorus, 1; IV.iv.3).

If we consider now the opening of *The Tempest* we may observe that the shipwreck is described in three different ways. First it is represented by means of sound and motion: a tempestuous noise – orders and exhortations of master and boatswain – mariners tackling the sails – entrances and exits – conflicting movements of sailors and courtiers – confused noises and cries off-stage. Then it is described by Miranda as seen from the shore. And again by Ariel, this time by means of frightening light- and fire-imagery. Thus the dramatic event is seen from different angles, and a vivid picture emerges from the poet's word and the actor's gesture. At the time Shakespeare was writing, all the motions of a huge ship in a billowy sea had been already reproduced on the Italian court stage, and the shipwreck scene came to be materialized in course of time, in the operatic version of *The Tempest*. Yet when we read the text, it makes such a scenic feat appear superfluous. The only location which required some sort of physical representation (inner stage or decorative structure) was the cell. It is repeatedly pointed at, and serves for a discovery. I agree it is a bare minimum, and we may suppose that when this play was given at Court parts of the island in the vicinity of the cell were represented by some decorative device. Yet again this is mere guess work.

Let us now examine the affinities between the last plays and the masque.[7] With the obvious exception of *Henry VIII* they are situated in a world outside history, and three of them in a semi-legendary pagan past to which Christian values have been transferred. Episodes reminiscent of the pastoral or the romance of chivalry abound in these plays. Recourse to the supernatural, and the happy ending after unbelievable adventures, make them appear further removed from reality than the tragedies – or many of the comedies. Invocation to the powers above and magical operations accomplished with the aid of music, a frequent feature of the masque, are also characteristic of the plays. The magician Prospero comes to mind. But Cerimon is also a sage whose music is an auxiliary of his science. Pericles and Marina are also accomplished musicians and their gift is in harmony with the purity of their life. Priest-like figures of the masque have their counterpart in Thaisa, who appears with a group of nuns, as a priestess of Diana. The theophany, which occurs frequently in the masque, is an essential moment in the spiritual experience of Pericles and Posthumus, as is the angelic apparition to Queen Katherine. The theme of conciliation and renewal is present in all the romance plays and in two of them it is achieved through the union of the young. The floral rites of the pastoral in *The Winter's Tale* and the betrothal in *The Tempest*, which illustrate this theme, made both plays eminently suitable for presentation at Court at the time of a princely wedding.

Yet in spite of the analogies there is a fundamental difference between the plays and the court masques. Reconciliation and reunion are obtained, in the former, after long and patient suffering on the part of a virtuous man like Pericles, or the trial and repentance of men who have sinned, as in the case of Posthumus and Leontes. The force of evil has first to exhaust itself before the pristine happiness can be restored. A number of masques, it is true, imply a reversal of condition, the breaking of a spell and the freeing of captives. But in the plays the events leading to a happier state and a brighter vision are set in a much broader perspective, and even if we incline to interpret them as allegories their subject matter is human experience and suffering. This applies even to *The Tempest* where past events are known through Prospero's narrative, and possibilities of dramatic development are limited since no one can resist the power of his magic. Though this play has been considered to be the one most closely related to the masque, ironic detachment and undertones of bitter comedy are more easily perceptible in its final scene than in the other romance plays.

I cannot here enter into much detail but would like to examine briefly the use of music and shows and their relation to the theme of the romance plays.[8] *Pericles* was presented at Whitehall, in 1619, before a French ambassador, and we are told of an interval after the second act for refreshments. No doubt the play was selected on account of the importance of its shows. Act ii, scenes ii and iii, contains all the elements of a court 'triumph' with display of arms, tilts, banquet, knights' formal dance, and revels. Details missing in the 1609 quarto can be filled in from George Wilkins' narrative partly based on the play, and the spectacular episodes may have received further elaboration at Court, which would account for the break after the second act. The dumbshows in the play have no symbolic value; their main purpose is to break up Gower's narrative, but with their entrances and exits of princes and their trains they add to the solemnity and please the eye. The last, before Marina's monument, may be set apart as a simple and effective way of showing Pericles' extremity of grief.

Shakespeare's use of music is not to be judged by its quantitative importance, frequency, number, and variety of instruments and voices, but in relation to situation, mood, and theme. Think of what the merry tunes of Amiens achieve, or Desdemona's willow song. Occasions for music are usually few, yet it acts as a unifying factor in the play, and musical images are rarely without relevance to an important theme. In *Pericles* music is heard in the very first scene: it serves to introduce the riddle of Antiochus. And one remembers the Prince's aside, thinking of the King's incestuous daughter:

> You are a fair viol, and your sense the strings,
> Who, finger'd to make man his lawful music,
> Would draw heaven down and all the gods to hearken;
> But being play'd upon before your time,
> Hell only danceth at so harsh a chime.   (I.i.82–5)

Considering the serious treatment, throughout the play, of the theme of chastity, the comparison is carefully chosen. And it is elaborated with reference to a tradition which associates music with harmony and order in the cosmos, the body politic, and the little world of man, special emphasis being laid here on the sanctity of lawful marriage.

A solo performance by Pericles may have been part of the festive music of act II, at the court of Simonides.[9] Music is also associated with goodness in the character of Cerimon, and becomes an auxiliary of his science in the scene where Thaisa is revived. Later, Marina sings to the distracted Pericles before she attempts to speak to him, and though her music, at first, is not well received, it sets something astir, during this scene where the extremity of joy succeeds to the extremity of grief, which leads to the final rapture, the music of the spheres, and the vision of Diana.

The first music to be mentioned in *Cymbeline* is the morning song. It follows the scene where Iachimo hides in Imogen's bedchamber, and Cloten appears as another enemy of her honour and happiness. Music and verse are both attuned to Imogen's personality. And Iachimo's last words 'Though this is a heavenly angel, hell is here' still ring in the spectator's ear as he hears of the lark 'singing at heaven's gate.' Cloten's obscene remarks still sharpen the contrast, and the irony is that he complains that Imogen is insensitive to music, while it is *he* who is 'the man who has no music in himself.' Later, solemn music will serve to introduce the scene where Imogen is thought dead, and the funeral rites and song that ensue. Solemn music is sounded again when the ghosts of Posthumus' parents and brothers appear in his sleep. Then follows Shakespeare's most elaborate masque-like effect with the exception of those in *The Tempest*. The ghosts are led in procession by two groups of musicians and move in a circle (or form a circle). Their invocation to Jupiter is recited, not sung (part at least would have been sung in the case of a masque). Their allusion to Jove's amorous affairs ('with Juno chide, That thy adulteries Rates and revenges') has a frivolity which is more in keeping with the masque than with the tone of their complaint about man's unjust suffering. So is perhaps Jupiter's contemptuous rebuke ('No more, you petty spirits of region low, Offend our hearing'), since his speech is related to the Christian themes of patient suffering and Providence. Yet this scene relies on the sensational effect of the descent and the thunderbolt, and a nice balance had to be struck between the *deus ex machina* and the Christian allegory. Technically there was nothing in the scene that the traditional machinery of the Globe could not achieve. We may wonder, however, whether some lines have the mere value of poetical ornament, or draw attention to a special effect: 'Peep through thy marble mansion,' before the descent; 'Mount, eagle, to my palace crystalline,' before the ascent; and immediately after: 'The marble pavement closes, he is enter'd His radiant roof.' Jupiter may have descended from a cloud of glory which first appeared above the stage and then opened; but this must remain a supposition. Soon after, in the final scene, Jupiter's oracle will prove true and a last reference will be made to music: 'The fingers of the powers above do tune The harmony of this peace.'

If we except the final scene of the statue coming to life, all the music of *The Winter's Tale* is concentrated in the earlier part of act IV, during the various episodes of the sheep-shearing feast. This has the value of an interlude between the tragic events of the first acts and those which will lead to the final atonement and conciliation. But these festive scenes achieve much more: they set the love intrigue moving, and build up, with the antagonism of father and son, a new dramatic tension which will eventually find release in Sicilia. A comic subplot is also introduced with the roguery of Autolycus. The song and dance elements are integrated into these patterns and genuine rural entertainment is deftly combined with pastoral convention, just as nature with art in Perdita's 'streak'd gillivors.' The celebration of this country festival has been recognized as a symbol of the healing of old wrongs and the renewal of life through the love of the young. But I would like to note some analogies with the masque. Florizel sees Perdita in her 'unusual weeds' as Flora, and compares himself to the gods 'humbling their deities to love.' Ovidian mythology also abounds in Perdita's memorable evocation of spring flowers. The Prince in his vows and Perdita in her floral games praise with equal felicity the state of virginity, the temperate fires of chaste love, and nuptial joys.

Such themes are also expressed with sustained poetry in Campion's masque of Lord Hayes where Diana and Hymen are both given their due after Night and Flora have pleaded for their respective rights:

> Virginitie is a voluntary powre,
> Free from constraint, even like an untoucht flower
> Meete to be gather'd when tis throughly blowne.[10]

When the masque begins, Flora and Zephyrus can be seen gathering flowers, 'the ceremonious ornament of maiden marriage,' and strewing them about to consecrate the place while a song is sung:

> And as a rose new pluckt from Venus thorne,
> So doth a bride her bride-groomes bed adorne.[11]

Venus is praised in this masque as a goddess of nature, bringing 'into the naked world the greene-leav'd spring,' and welcome to a marriage celebration. We remember this is not the case in Prospero's masque, where more temperate deities blame her wantonness. The masque in *The Tempest* occupies the same key position in act IV as the sheep-shearing in *The Winter's Tale*. The latter may be preferred, with its whiff of country air, its variety of mood and incident, to this vanity of Prospero's art, where spirits enact his fancies while the lovers remain passive. Yet its importance is twofold, as preliminary to the marriage ceremony, and as a magical operation which requires music, and silence on the part of the beholders. Purity and self-control were needed on both occasions. If the lovers' union was not sealed with 'full and holy rite,' the heavens would not grant their blessing, and discord would ensue. And on the contemplated union depended the restoration of right and order, and the concord of two states. Yet this masque is deliberately interrupted with a discord, 'a strange, hollow and confused noise,' which is the sign that Prospero's mind is disturbed, whatever the reason, and has not yet reached the serenity that will enable him to accomplish the final reconciliation.

Music in the play must be considered, not only as harmony, but as power. It is used throughout as a symbol of Prospero's magical power, as a beautiful and theatrically efficient way of showing this power at work through the agency of Ariel. But music itself is also, according to an ancient tradition which was familiar to the Elizabethans and which is fully expressed and illustrated in John Case's

Praise of Music (1586), a power capable of stirring or calming the passions, driving people out of their wits or restoring their mental health. On the whole it had a beneficent influence, provided those who made use of it had sufficient experience and purity of mind.

In *The Tempest*, music's unifying function is carried further than in any of the other plays. If we consider the first scene, with its tempestuous noise, as an overture, music is present in all the scenes, with the one exception of III. i (Ferdinand and Miranda, with Prospero unseen). It is associated with Ariel's handling of each strand of the plot, and with the ordeals inflicted on the usurper and the rebels. Leading or driving by means of music or frightening sound is a prominent part of the physical action, and all the meandering paths eventually lead to the magician's cell.

The classical structure of the play has been frequently observed, but music is also an essential element of its organization. Besides acting as a compelling force, it relates all the themes, and provides a carefully worked-out series of contrasts. First the mysterious sea music of Ariel leading Ferdinand (I. ii). Then the solemn music which sends Alonzo to sleep, and the warning sung in Gonzalo's ear which interrupts the murder plot (II. i). Then the drunken revelry of Caliban and the jesters (II. ii) which is resumed in III. ii, and interrupted by the mocking tune of the invisible Ariel. Caliban's lines on the noises of the isle are among Shakespeare's finest poetical statements on music. They help to create an atmosphere saturated with magical sound. And they almost immediately precede the banquet scene, with its solemn and strange music, its deceiving and frightening apparitions. Dramatic tension reaches a climax with Ariel's speech and the impotent gesture of the men of sin drawing their swords. It is spoken, not sung, but it is as solemn and awe-inspiring as the Commendatore's aria in *Don Giovanni* or the scenes of trial and initiation in *The Magic Flute*. Some relaxation is introduced with the soft music and the mocking dance of the spirits, before we hear Prospero confirm the solemnity of Ariel's words. These have not been distinctly heard by the distracted men. What the least tainted of the sinners has heard is the voice of Nature proclaiming his guilt:

> Methought the billows spoke, and told me of it;
> The winds did sing it to me; and the thunder,
> That deep and dreadful organ-pipe, pronounc'd
> The name of Prosper: it did bass my trespass. (III.iii.96–9)

Here again it is the musical image relating the instrument to the cosmic order which conveys the meaning.

If we followed the critics who think of the masque as an inter-polation, we should find that something important is lacking in the structure of the play, which does not depend on plot alone but also on music and show. Besides the function we have already mentioned, the masque provides a period of dignified, quiet, and pleasant enter-tainment, closely related to the main themes, during which the urgency of time seems suspended. Prospero's distemper, and wistful comment on the insubstantiality of his show, change the mood again. After a last recourse to frightening noises and shapes to dispose of Caliban's conspiracy, solemn music is required for the last time to heal the sick brains of the men now at Prospero's mercy. The occasion is also solemn because he abjures his rough magic. And the very last music is, fittingly, a song of Ariel about to recover his freedom.

The Tempest is, potentially, a music drama, but, though music is inherent in its structure, it still has only an ancillary function and the play would be better described as a poetic drama with music and shows. It is idle to ask why England did not produce a Monteverdi, though madrigal and lute-song composers were capable of expressing a wide range of moods and emotions. One valid reason might be that spoken drama was so much alive. But whatever the cause, neither spoken drama nor the masque evolved into opera, though masque experiments like *Lovers Made Men* (1617) and *Cupid and Death* (1653) pointed that way. The masque lost its social function of direct communication with the audience and provided models for the enter-tainment within the play of the commercial theatre. In the latter part of the century John Blow and Purcell were given only one opportunity, during their career, of setting to music an entire dramatic work. And neither *Venus and Adonis* nor *Dido and Æneas* was meant for the public stage.

Matthew Locke, in the preface to his music for *Psyche* and *The Tempest*, was to say that it was vain to emulate Italy, and that music 'mixed with interlocutions' was 'more proper to our genius.'[12] *The Tempest*, during the Restoration, fared comparatively better than other plays. Purcell's music for *The Fairy Queen* is undoubtedly beautiful, but it is composed for masque-like intermedes, bearing little relation to *A Midsummer Night's Dream*. *The Tempest* certainly suffered from alterations of style and plot in the hands of Davenant, Dryden, and others. The elements of music and show were modified and expanded, but at least they retained a certain relation to the story and themes. The lavish production by the Duke's Company (1674), which further developed these elements, made full use of changes of scenes and complex machinery. The entertainment of infernal spirits which had been introduced in act II was amplified, and the play ended with an elaborate masque of sea gods. The Restoration *Tempest*, as it was revived at the Old Vic in 1959, with the best music of the successive versions (including Purcell's), was convincing enough, but one had first to forget the atmosphere of the original play.

The operatic *Tempest* can still be appreciated, not merely as an historical curiosity, but as a work of art in its own right. But if we consider now Shakespeare's *Tempest* and his other plays, we feel that the main concern of the scholar and the theatre practician should be to preserve the verbal poetry, and with it the smoothness of tempo, the flexibility of action which the Elizabethan stage had made possible. For a rediscovery of the authentic Shakespeare to take place in our century, it was not enough to reclaim the true text from fraudulent or 'improved' versions: the performance had to be freed from the hypertrophy of décor and changes of scenes. If the locations still indicated in most modern editions were followed, six different settings and seven changes would be necessary for staging *The Tempest*, where unity of place is as strictly observed as in few other plays of the canon. Fortunately it is usually performed nowadays in a single setting combining realism and fancy to suggest an atmosphere of sea adventure, magic, and wild nature.

There is no sense in laying all the blame on the Italian stage. And Inigo Jones' designs show that the new scenography could create a certain order of beauty. But having in mind the Victorian monstrosities which were still in use in the earlier part of this century we may rightly think that Jonson's warning was prophetic: the spirit was in danger of being smothered by painting and carpentry. Yet, we have seen, Jonson's attitude towards the new type of scenery was not one of rejection, but of subordination. And however strongly we may feel about the importance of the poet's word, there is a thing we must not overlook. It is the impulse, characteristic of the Renaissance, though it was partly inherited from an earlier age, to make the world of romance and mythology come to life, and unfold itself in space. You find it in Vasari's drawings for a procession of the Genealogy of the gods in the streets of Florence, or Antoine Caron's paintings of triumphs in the park of Fontainebleau. It is present also, in a more naïve form, in the engraving of Queen Elizabeth's entertainment at Elvetham,[13] or in a detail of Sir Henry Unton's portrait, with the pretty lady masquers led by Mercury and Diana.[14]

I have cited Campion as an example of a poet who was ready to co-operate unreservedly with the scenographer. Shakespeare sang of Orpheus' power over nature, and made Lorenzo speak of the heavenly spheres. But Campion, with the assistance of Jones, actually made the spheres and the trees dance on the masque stage. Between both attitudes there was a difference of degree, not of nature. Shakespeare and Campion shared the same musical culture, and were steeped in the same tradition. And we find Shakespeare himself, in the last plays, experimenting with machinery: first in a rather crude way, with the descent of Jupiter in *Cymbeline*. But in *The Tempest* he seems fascinated by the possibility of new, more subtle effects, both visual (strange shapes, vanishing figures) and acoustic (burthen dispersedly, hollow noises, twangling instruments). The feeling of impermanence, which was to haunt the baroque theatre in the midst of its spectacular excesses, is already present. He seems to look beyond the masque and explore a new form of drama. This was a form where virtuosity of stage-technique could easily defeat the poet's end. But in *The Tempest*, though the proportion of music and visual effect had increased, the function and relation of each component remained unchanged, and the play retained its nature of poetic drama.

NOTES

1 Cf R.W. Ingram, 'The Use of Music in the Plays of Marston' *Music and Letters* 37 (1956) 154–64; Michael Shapiro, 'Music and Song in Plays acted by Children's Companies during the English Renaissance' *Current Musicology* 7 (1968) 97–110; J. Jacquot, 'Le répertoire des compagnies d'enfants à Londres (1600–1610)' in *Dramaturgie et Société au siezième siècle et au dix-septième* (Paris 1968) 749ff

2 Dryden, preface to his adaptation of *The Tempest* (1674): 'The Play ... had formerly been acted with success in the Black-Fryers ...' (quoted by Kermode, Arden edition)

3 *Proteus and the Rock Adamantine*, 3 March 1595, described in *Gesta Grayorum*, W.W. Greg ed, Malone Society reprints (1914)

4 Cf *Trois masques à la cour de Charles Ier d'Angleterre* Murray Lefkowitz, ed (Paris 1968).

5 Quoted by G.E. Bentley in the general introduction to *A Book of Masques in Honour of Allardyce Nicoll* (Cambridge 1967)

6 Quotations are from *Pericles* F.D. Hoeniger ed, Arden edition

7 The relation of *The Two Noble Kinsmen* to the masque is discussed in M.C. Bradbrook's paper, see above, 29–33.

8 On the use of music in these plays, cf F.W. Sternfeld *Music in Shakespearean Tragedy* (London 1963) and R.W. Ingram, 'Musical Pauses and the Vision Scenes in Shakespeare's Last Plays' *Pacific Coast Studies in Shakespeare* (Portland, Oregon 1966).

9 Cf II.v.25–6, and F.D. Hoeniger's note to II.iii.115, S.D., in his edition of the play (the Arden Shakespeare).

10 *The Works of Thomas Campion* Walter R. Davis, ed (London 1969) 217–18

11 Ibid 215

12 *The English opera or the vocal musick in Psyche ... to which is adjoyned the instrumental musick in the Tempest* (London 1675)

13 Elvetham (1591). Cf John Nichols *The Progresses of Queen Elizabeth* (London 1823) III, 101.

14 Cf E.K. Chambers *The Elizabethan Stage*, I, *Frontispiece*.

R.W. Ingram /
Music as Structural Element in
Shakespeare

My texts are taken from Thomas Heywood and Hereward T. Price. In his *An Apology for Actors* (1612), Heywood wrote that 'a description is only a shadow received by the ear but not perceived by the eye; so lively portraiture is merely a form seen by the eye, but can neither show action, passion, motion, or any other gesture, to move the spirits of the beholder to admiration.' A soldier may be described, he may be painted, but only an actor can let an audience 'see a soldier shaped like a soldier, walk, speak, act like a soldier' (B3ᵛ). The art of the theatre appeals to the eye and the ear at the same time; the dramatist demands to be seen and heard. In plays, one thing at a time is not the rule, certainly not one thing in one way at a time. Music is but one element in the compound dramatic experience which is presented on the stage. It is an element, however, whose particular contribution is more likely to be overlooked than most outside the theatre.

After Richard II has surrendered to Bolingbroke at Flint Castle, he observes:

> For do we must what force will have us do.
> Set on towards London. Cousin, is it so?
> BOLINGBROKE Yea, my good lord.
> RICHARD Then I must not say no.   (*Flourish. Exeunt.*)
>
> (III.iii.207–9)[1]

For the reader the scene is over, his eyes skim over the stage-direction:

'*Flourish.Exeunt*' and take up 'the play' again in the Duke of York's
garden where the Queen and her ladies wonder what sport may be
devised 'to drive away the heavy thought of care.' In his study the
stage is too likely to be cleared by the period at the end of Richard's
last speech. In the theatre they order this matter better. There the
conventional but splendid sound of the flourish of trumpets proper to
a king rings out with ironic impartiality for both Richard and his
cousin as they lead their parties out: for the actual king and for the
real ruler who knew 'the strong'st and surest way to get.' They were
last seen together in act I when Richard sat in royal judgment over
Bolingbroke and Mowbray in the lists at Coventry. There the sonorous
ritual of pageantry and trumpets had been concluded by Richard
throwing his warder down and ordering 'let the trumpets sound'
which they did in a '*long flourish*' after which he gave his ruling. Now
the positions are reversed. The flourish at Flint Castle is part of that
pageantry which Richard knew as his prerogative, and relished so
much at Coventry, turned sour: now the decision has been rendered
against Richard and the flourish marks the end of his effective rule.
In the theatre it indicates the sway of power, the glory as well as the
danger and uncertainty of royal authority: not with obtrusive blazon
but with far more effectiveness than the casual eye taking in the
expected punctuation of '*Flourish.Exeunt*' might at first allow.

Kings, noblemen, and armies are leaving a crowded stage and such
music is proper to the occasion according to social custom; it is also
theatrically useful in adding a strong decorative sound to an impressive visual moment. All of this is ordinary; what is not is the thought
that has gone to add something extra to the ordinary. 'The point that
I want to make' (in the company of Hereward T. Price, whose words,
from his invaluable essay on 'Construction in Shakespeare,' I quote)
'is that Shakespeare had an eminently constructive mind. He was
disciplined; he was neither wild nor lazy nor sloppy ... He interrelates
part to part, as well as every part to the whole. His inner idea is mani-
fested in an action, with which it is intimately fused, so that the crises
in the action which move us most deeply reveal at the same time
most clearly the inner core of Shakespeare's thought' (pp.16–17).[2]
He wrote of *Hamlet*: 'It just will not do to tear a motif – the feigned
madness – out of the play and consider it all along by itself. We must
see its connection with the whole play as one of several repeated
elements, different but all alike in being linked to the central idea'
(p.16). On this occasion I want to substitute 'music' for 'feigned
madness' and consider music's connection with the whole play as one

of several repeated elements linked to a central idea. My illustrations are taken from *I Henry VI*, *Richard III*, *Richard II*, and *Troilus and Cressida*, plays dealing with war, politics, and public events and using such 'conventional' music (most of it drum and trumpet) that they could hardly be thought of as among Shakespeare's most musical plays.

The world of these plays is chiefly that of court and battlefield and its incidental music conventional and seemingly unimaginative and limited. The term 'incidental music' lends itself to misinterpretation. It is not an indication of music introduced automatically and casually. The facile playwright is, of course, known by his dull acceptance of and numbing reliance upon convention so that his music is very likely to be incidental in the pejorative sense. Shakespeare naturally accepted conventions, but as useful aids not necessary crutches. This being understood, it should nevertheless be noted that good incidental music is often just that, good and necessary but something heard rather than listened to in the same way that there are actions seen on the stage as well as actions that are watched. None of them should be carelessly treated. If they seem not always to be noted when present, they are at once missed when absent. At such rare times the careful playwright provides explanations. When Heywood wrote *The English Traveller*, for instance, his prologue warned that:

> A strange play you are like to have, for know
> We use no drum, nor trumpet, nor dumb show;
> No combat, marriage, not so much to-day,
> As song, dance, masque, to bombast out a play;
> Yet these all good, and still in frequent use.[3]

The point being, Heywood continued, that he wanted to see 'if once bare lines will bear it.' More recently Ingmar Bergman dispensed with background music in his film *The Silence* and the curious unease of the audience was remarkable and very noticeable. Much incidental music gains its purpose and strength from being expected and accepted. However, it is the expected and accepted that lend themselves especially well to those slight displacements of expectation that often lead to uneasy incursions of the odd (as Alfred Hitchcock has continually reminded us). This is especially true of the music of court and battlefield.

When Shakespeare deals with domestic and foreign wars drums and trumpets inevitably are heard. Since Morgann the very words have been a stick to beat the plays with: 'that Drum and trumpet Thing' as he called *1 Henry VI*.[4] The noise will help entertain those poor devils, the groundlings, who attend the theatre, at no slight cost to their slender purses, to snatch a quarter of an hour or so of entertainment by way of noise, smut, and vulgarity from the two hours' traffic passing before them. This military music is too easily, and too frequently, relegated to cheapness, an empty blare and rattle to please the ignorant. Of course it can be brash and vulgar when it is abused by excess, as Shakespeare is well aware. Ajax can too pompously vaunt his challenging trumpets:

> Now crack thy lungs, and split thy brazen pipe.
> Blow, villain, till thy sphered bias cheek
> Outswell the colic of puffed Aquilon.
> Come, stretch thy chest, and let thy eyes spout blood. (IV.v.7–10)

Richard II can stretch the rhetoric in the fashion of a man overplaying a role when he talks of 'the boist'rous untuned drums, with harsh-resounding trumpets' dreadful bray' (I.iii.134–5). And in the courtly round Hamlet can comment disdainfully on Claudius' crassly overwhelming use of flourishing noise. But usually the tone is that of the saner challenge, the proper spirit of confidence, as is Richmond's before Bosworth:

> Sound drums and trumpets boldly and cheerfully:
> God and Saint George! Richmond and victory! (v.iii.270–1)

Some of the disesteem felt for this typical histories' music is due to a certain unease displayed about what, loosely, I will call patriotic plays. During time of war and national stress more of such noise and boisterousness, even vulgarity in the sense of serving the vulgar – the great crowd – is called for and is supplied in public entertainments. The film industry supplied it in the 1940s and at times during his career Shakespeare helped to supply it in order to satisfy needs roused by the strain of war, the threat of invasion, the danger of dissension at home, conditions prevalent during much of his working life. Thus, in *Henry V*, the earnest critical search that descries the man as an inhumane politician, an international villain, or a cynical warmonger, should not completely shroud the fact of his plainer and simpler appeal to patriotic English feelings. Patriotism is not necessarily the last resort of a dramatist.

Shakespeare was as sensitive of the horror as he was of the heroism of war and his plays are far from being conventionally patriotic. The drums and trumpets heralded the parade of cannon-fodder as well as the 'culled and choice drawn cavaliers,' of those who went 'like horse leeches the very blood to suck' as well as those in whose breasts 'reigns solely honour's thought.' At times it is the impartiality of the battle's music that helps to underline these crucial distinctions and comparisons. The wry-necked fife is Othello's instrument, it is Alcibiades', yet it is also Falstaff's. That cold dealer, John of Lancaster, can chide the Archbishop of York for 'Cheering a rout of rebels with your drum' and, minutes later, give the order: 'Strike up our drums, pursue the scattered stray' of those rebels just sent marching home happily cheering and shouting (2 *Henry IV*, iv.ii.9, 120). The two aspects are telescoped even more dramatically in the first part of *Henry IV* when Hotspur, with infectious heroism before his last battle, rallies his friends in their treacherous cause:

> Sound all the lofty instruments of war,
> And by that music let us all embrace;
> For, heaven to earth, some of us never shall
> A second time do such a courtesy.
> (*Here they embrace, the trumpets sound.*)   (v.ii.97–100)

Here drum and trumpet connect with the whole play as one of several repeated elements linked to a central idea. Shakespeare does not always turn convention to such imaginative use; he is often unexceptional (though never unintelligent) in his handling of them. His histories contain much military and court music which is necessary and useful but serves no subtler dramatic purpose. These unexceptional soundings of music, however, gain, not only from the customary care with which they are nonetheless used, but from those other soundings which do inform on more than the informational level.

The early *Henry VI*, for instance, swells almost joyously with a young man's sense of power, a flexing of dramatic muscles that even this early are apt to answer any calls made on them very confidently. In *1 Henry VI* Shakespeare tries out several musical effects and goes far beyond mere drum and trumpet stuffing of a bombastic warplay. The structure of the play, forcefully expounded by Hereward T. Price and admirably supported by Cairncross in his Arden edition (pp. lii–liii),[5] is strengthened by music. The three interrupted ceremonies at the beginnings of the first, third, and fourth acts – the funeral of Henry v, the proceedings in the Parliament House, and the coronation of Henry vi, all have their pageantry partially evoked by music. They are all spectacular but each has its own manner and mood. As the Dead March of the funeral contrasts with the flourishes accompanying the parliamentary scene and the coronation, so all three stand in excellent contrast to the sharper exchanges of sounds heard on the battlefields.

The action is boldly accentuated by loud music. In the first two acts, for instance, the contrasts between domestic quarrels and foreign warfare are as much musical as anything else. The scuffle between Gloucester's and Winchester's men in London is more disturbing for being a battle without music sandwiched between clangorous battles before Orleans. Shakespeare freely adds thunder, lightning, and peals of ordnance at times but even then he exploits his devices dramatically rather than abuses them for cheap theatrical ends.

Shakespeare's handling of some of the music in this play initiates a series of experiments to extend the range and power of musical conventions that continue throughout his career. He is well aware, for instance, that the impact of significant visual moments – pageantry, processions, tableaux – can be strengthened by the sound of music. This theatrical effect is raised to the dramatic, however, by his alert recognition of the fact that the strains and discords that ritual and ceremony tend to cover over may be pointed up by the suggestive sound of music, especially if it is deliberately augmented. Such a moment occurs at the end of the first scene of act iii. After turbulent skirmishes Winchester and Gloucester make a grudging peace and the civil dissension is falsely subdued in the feigned amity surrounding Henry's creation of Richard 'princely Duke of York.' The 'Sennet. Flourish' rings out too brazenly for an empty accord as King and court leave the Parliament House, leaving only the distrustful Exeter behind to comment on what such 'base and envious discord' will breed. Harbingers of more far-reaching explorations can be found in the opening and closing passages of the play.

All Shakespeare's histories open arrestingly, and the three very different beginnings he devised for the three parts of *Henry VI* finely illustrate the variety and energy he could command in them. More significant in the development of his dramaturgy, however, is the way in which the black-hung funeral with muffled drums beating, the traditional conclusion of tragedy and tragic history, is used in *1 Henry VI* to begin a play. This bold reversal of device heralds later manipulations with traditional conclusions, as in the tragic ambiguity of the marches at the end of *Troilus and Cressida*. More notably in the dying falls of *Love's Labour's Lost, Twelfth Night,* and *A Midsummer Night's Dream,* where the traditional joyful harmonies – symbolic and literal – of the marriage ceremony are not the last exultant sound heard. These variations pave the way for the vision scenes of the last plays which bring promise of love and forgiveness, and of a fulfilment perhaps richer than that of the simple hopes of young lovers to live happily ever after, but which still, at the last, in the revels called up by Prospero, celebrate, on one level, a betrothal. In the vision scenes the experiments made with a traditional concluding device coalesce with another series of experiments in musical structuring involving what I have elsewhere called 'the musical pause.'[6] The musical pause comes usually towards the end of the fourth act and brings a lull in the visible action, a lessening of excitement, a momentary easing of tension, after which the final catastrophe follows more forcefully. Its purposes are better fulfilled in tragedy than comedy, but in the histories too with their often strong demands upon emotional response they may be found. In *1 Henry VI* this device appears in crude archetype as less a pause than a change in tone and pace. In the third scene of the fifth act amid wild alarums and excursions, and to the accompaniment of thunder, various fiends appear to Joan La Pucelle. This is undoubtedly rough magic but it worked on in Shakespeare's imagination. As a distinct change of pace before the final action it was moved about in later plays until it evolved into the musical pause: examples are found in *Julius Caesar* when Lucius plays a 'sleepy tune' to Brutus (iv.iii), and in *2 Henry IV* when a 'dull and favorable hand' is asked to 'whisper music' to Henry's 'weary spirit' and he is lulled into that sleep which Hal mistakes for death (iv.v). The intrusion of the mysterious and the supernatural into the everyday world, especially in the latter part of the play, was yet another device which Shakespeare was to develop further, notably in *Macbeth* (iv.i) and in *Antony and Cleopatra* (iv.iii). In the last plays it also contributes importantly to the vision scenes. Closer in time to *1 Henry VI*, Shakespeare tried other versions of this ending in the abrupt change of mood in the last scenes of *Richard II* and the double dream-visions offered to Richard iii and Richmond on the night before Bosworth. I do not want to read too much into one early history play, merely to suggest the significance that music has in it. The design of the play, says Cairncross, 'follows precise patterns of contrast; repetition of theme, often with increment; rise, climax, and fall' (p. lii). The music, sometimes a little unsophisticatedly, contributes importantly to this design. The musical part of a play's design is itself a theme that Shakespeare develops with increment of subtlety and power in sequent plays.

In *Richard III* the divorce between the musical ceremony of power and the King's person is explored. A loud flourish announces the first entry of Edward IV (II.i) but, instead of the resplendent figure suggested by the music, a dying man is borne in. The aural symbol is contradicted by the visual fact. In a broad sense the discrepancy between reality and illusion is marked by disease and rancour contrasted with stability and grandeur evoked by the musical pageantry. Thus the royal flourishes which welcome Prince Edward are misleading: as Frances Shirley notes, 'the doomed prince, powerless in the hands of his uncle Richard, goes to the Tower with a sennet ringing in his ears.'[7] Later Richard enters '*in pomp*' with a similar elaborate sennet and mounts the throne to renewed trumpet-calls in a moment of grandiose show that anticipates Claudius' over-practice of regal noise. Richard's words at this time underline the clash of symbol and fact:

> Thus high, by thy advice
> And thy assistance, is King Richard seated:
> But shall we wear these glories for a day?
> Or shall they last, and we rejoice in them?   (IV.ii.3–6)

The theme of Richard's loud misuse of music is brilliantly varied when he meets the curses of the three queens. He enters with '*his Train marching, with Drums and Trumpets.*' To bully them down he commands angrily:

> A flourish, trumpets! Strike alarum, drums!
> Let not the heavens hear these telltale women
> Rail on the Lord's anointed. Strike, I say!   (IV.iv.149–51)

The music is his prerogative as ruler and general, but he stretches claims too far when he so insists upon his right, the more so as his vaunt that he is the Lord's anointed only reminds his hearers strongly that he is not. On another level he is reduced in stature in having to use the 'clamorous report of war' to 'drown the exclamations' of women. The propriety of the music and its regular meaning thus sub-

verted are made the core of an intensely dramatic moment and a part
of Richard's general perversion of custom and ritual. At the opening
of the play Richard scathingly denounced the fact that

> Our stern alarums [are] changed to merry meetings,
> Our dreadful marches to delightful measures.   (I.i.7–8)

The changes he makes are as bad. The dramatic possibilities of directly acting upon these words uttered by Richard are, however, reserved by Shakespeare for their richest development later, markedly
in *Troilus and Cressida*, where, also, it will be Pandarus who 'capers
nimbly in a lady's chamber / To the lascivious pleasings of a lute'
(I.i.12–13).

In *Richard II* the movement is from Richard's splendid pomp and
circumstance as public monarch to his miserable death as a lonely
private man. The musical progression is from the deliberately rich
regal flourishes of Richard's court and the lists to the quiet intimate
music which he overhears from prison at the end; from trumpets to
strings, from public music to private, from bold straightforward
rhythms to the more intricate and sophisticated ones at Pomfret.[8] At
the glorious beginning Richard had no call to muse on the symbolic
meaning of music or the deeper meanings of the art. It is Mowbray,
after being banished for life, who expands a musical figure:

> The language I have learnt these forty years,
> My native English, now I must forgo;
> And now my tongue's use is to me no more
> Than an unstringed viol or a harp,
> Or like a cunning instrument cased up
> Or, being open, put into his hands
> That knows no touch to tune the harmony.   (I.iii.159–65)

The dying Gaunt talks of 'tongues of dying men' enforcing 'attention
like deep harmony,' and of 'harmony at the close' (II.i.5–6, 12). It is
only when Richard himself is banished to Pomfret at the close of his
life and, like his uncle, must breathe his words in pain, that he too
comes to the theme of 'the music in men's lives':

> How sour sweet music is
> When time is broke and no proportion kept!
> So is it in the music of men's lives.

And here have I the daintiness of ear
To check time broke in a disordered string;
But, for the concord of my state and time,
Had not an ear to hear my true time broke. (v.v.42–8)

Verbal image and music heard work thus together throughout the play. The musical contrast is not ended with Richard's speech, however, for as Exton heaves the dead Richard off at one door there enters at the other, with customary royal flourish, Bolingbroke as King.

We may look forward from *Richard II* and the consideration of the place music has in its over-all design to later plays where music and sound are matched to the progress of the action in other ways. The structure of *Julius Caesar* has always been difficult to appraise, but musically it moves from the cheerful flourishes and shouts of approval for Caesar as king, through the fiercely ominous roar of the thunderstorm only briefly interrupted, as it were, by the flourish that brings Caesar to the Senate House, to the renewed shouts of the crowd as they move from approval of Brutus to a howling for blood under the incitement of Mark Antony. This pattern of ceremonial sound and crowd voices and thunder is concluded by the resolution on the battlefield amid the military marches and alarums. The musical respite in this clamorous sequence comes in the quiet, even poignant, song of Lucius in Brutus' tent. In *Coriolanus*, with its emphasis on military prowess and the importance of people's voices, the mingled shouts, cries, and tremendous outbursts of drums and trumpets in battle, doubly redoubled in the hugely triumphant welcome to the conquering Coriolanus in Rome, fall away to the dreadful hooting that sends Coriolanus into exile. Then there is relative quiet (broken only by the offstage convivial banquet music at Aufidius' palace which is the musical pause in the action and effective, as Lucius' song was, partly for being the only private music heard amid louder public music), which gives way at the end to the repetition of the earlier clamour as '*drum and trumpets sound*' and, '*with great shouts of the people*,' Coriolanus enters Corioli again, now into a city of friends yet there to be treacherously slain. A bolder musical pattern that extends the movement in *Richard II* from pageant to private music can be found in *Timon of Athens* and *The Winter's Tale*. In these plays music helps to emphasize the two-part structure of the plays. The first part of *Timon of Athens* is loud with music. Timon's own entry is heralded by trumpets as though he were a king, and it may be that their sounding is meant to underscore both his state and his presumption. His first feast is accompanied by '*hautboys playing loud music*' and garnished by an exotic '*Masque of Ladies as Amazons with lutes in their hands, dancing and playing*' and led by Cupid (i.ii).[9] The second banquet is more loudly graced by trumpets: 'Feast your ears with the music awhile, if they will fare so harshly o' the trumpets sound' (iii.vi.32–4). It may be recalled that Queen Elizabeth was fond of having the hall resound with her trumpets for a while before dining.[10] In the latter part of the play, during Timon's exile and until his death, only the uncompromising music of Alcibiades' army is heard. The aural contrast is explicit and sharp. In *The Winter's Tale* the division is marked in an opposite manner: it is the second part of the play that is musical in a rich variety of ways.

Troilus and Cressida uses music as a structural element rather differently. It is the most imaginative drum and trumpet thing. The dissonances engendered by the conflict between bifold authority of the heart's credence and th'attest of the eyes and ears, the untuned discord of an anarchic world, are not easily resolvable into a pleasing cadence. That the play offers no such resolution is both its problem and its attraction. During its action music is continually used to mark the abrasive clash between appearance and reality, between the opposing poles of that greater struggle that encompasses the lesser one of Greek against Trojan.

Pandarus' song for Helen exemplifies the play's musical pattern. It is a parody love-song in a parody romantic scene. Paris, 'besotted' on 'sweet delights,' and his 'sweet queen' are unattractive lovers; Pandarus' attentions further degrade them. He is, in fact, a pander, and his song, all compact of depressing innuendo far removed from the direct appeal of 'O mistress mine' or 'Sigh no more ladies,' is very much a brothel song, of that love which, as Helen says, 'will undo us all' (iii.i.102).[11]

Throughout the play the clash between the chivalric pretence and the political reality is brilliantly marked by the clear interjections of the trumpet. A motto for these sounds might be found in Troilus' assertion that 'the busy day, Waked by the lark, hath roused the ribald crows' (iv.ii.8–9). The play's musical imagery draws on the theme of harmony and well-tuned notes while the world about is all too visibly at discord. Even the most ordinary image is coloured by this. 'Stop my mouth,' says Cressida. 'And shall, albeit sweet music issues thence' replies Troilus (iii.ii.126–7). Stage clichés for lovers, but not quite so here. It is not so for an audience that brings to the play its own preformed opinion of Cressida as the type of faithless lover. Whether she is, even within those limits, presented as an innocent or weak girl overborne by circumstance or, more corrosively, as an amoral plea-sure-seeker, there are overtones of more than a simple romantic ex-change. In the one case there is something that is 'out of tune,' in the other something that more harshly urges the thought that when she opes her jaws there will be heard music that differs in degree rather than in kind from that which Thersites' mastic jaws make.

In the opening scene the abrupt sound of an alarum interrupts Troilus' passionate but somewhat immature ardours with a rude reminder of war. It is a sound that Troilus dismisses unheroically: 'Peace, you ungracious clamors! Peace, rude sounds!' (i.i.85). At the end of the play he will last be seen as the warrior on the battlefield calling for the drums to strike a march. My reading of the play is more satirical than tragic, my assessment of Troilus' character less favour-able than some, especially in the early passages of the play. Nonethe-less, if Troilus' romantic passion is taken at a more serious value and its heroic rather than its immature ardour stressed, there still remains the intrusive quality of the battlefield alarum. Such calls are continu-ally to be heard sounding thus awkwardly across the more secluded rooms and orchards where love's battles range. Troilus returns to his romantic theme, and twice more alarums interrupt him. The contrast is maintained in the next scene. The favourite comedy routine of the young girl reviewing a parade of suitors is presented by Cressida and Pandarus as they watch, too gaily, the return of the Trojans from the field. A retreat is sounded and the fighters enter, but from a real battlefield, not a place of ornate ritual combat: 'Look you what hacks are on his helmet ... There's no jesting; there's laying on ... Look you how his sword is bloodied' (i.ii.193–5, 220–1).[12] The frivolity as well as the seriousness of love must contend as best it may in this sterner world of bloody warfare. After Pandarus has sung his song the sound of the retreat again signals a return from the field and finely cuts across the sensuous and corrupt atmosphere evoked in Paris' apart-ments. The talk slides easily, if not glibly, to war as if it were some amusing game, the uneasy juxtaposition excellently caught in the image of Helen's white fingers working the stubborn buckles of Hector's armour. The climactic scene of Troilus' and Cressida's night meeting and all its evocation of uneasy romantic love is followed at once by the flourish announcing the entry of the Greek leaders to talk with Calchas. As lovers exit, politicians enter: the oaths of love are set off against the sounds of the political world and its promises.

The most sustained motif is Hector's challenge, and its music relentlessly reverberates the central ideas of the play. It is introduced with much pomp of trumpets and flowery language into the debate of the Greek High Command on dissension within their ranks. Ulysses has dominated the proceedings, but, before anything resembling a plan of action to be taken can be introduced, a tucket interrupts and Aeneas enters to play his ornate and ironic little comedy of being uncertain which noble man is Agamemnon. Then, with a vigorous trumpet-call as preface, he delivers Hector's challenge. It is a challenge in the vein of knights' jousting for the honour of their ladies:

> He hath a lady wiser, fairer, truer,
> Than ever Greek did compass in his arms.   (i.iii.275–6)

It is an odd claim to advance before this company during this war. It sorts oddly with the debate that went before as well as with the hard political discussion of how best to handle it that follows between Ulysses and Nestor. Its music is next heard in the fourth act. Cressida has been handed over to the Greek envoys after an anguished farewell from Troilus. His ardent praise of her to Diomedes echoes the terms of Hector's challenge and catches closely its mode:

> I tell thee, lord of Greece,
> She is as far high-soaring o'er thy praises
> As thou unworthy to be called her servant.
> I charge thee use her well, even for my charge.   (iv.iv.122–5)

As Troilus, Cressida, and Diomedes walk aside, Hector's trumpet proclaims his challenge. It reminds the Trojans they are late and they hasten away, Aeneas with a singularly inapt figure – 'Yea, with a bridegroom's fresh alacrity' (144) – urging speed and a reliance upon Hector's 'fair worth and single chivalry' (147). His worth and chivalry is fact and stands out on the tarnished battlefield, but to rely on their power in physical struggle will prove wrong. He asserts an idealism that is, in his challenge, a little strained, and in the whole context of the war fatal. The contradictions it contains are pointed up by the way in which the Greek trumpets answer Hector's; Ajax giving the order in hollow Marlovian ranting vein, coarsely egged on by Agamemnon. This vulgar clamour of words and trumpet cheapens the design of the challenge. There is a dramatic pause after the Greek trumpet sounds, broken by Ulysses saying: 'No trumpet answers'

(IV.v.11). Then comes the cynically inappropriate and unlooked-for answer: Diomedes, rising on the toe in sprightly fashion, brings in Cressida. The futility of the romantic ethos of the challenge is underscored by the tawdry kissing game of the generals that follows. Ulysses savagely sums up this sour picture of fair worth:

> ... set them down
> For sluttish spoils of opportunity
> And daughters of the game.   (IV.v.61–3)

At this instant comes the Trojan answer to Ajax' 'brazen pipe.' *'Enter all of Troy, Hector, Paris, Aeneas, Helenus, Troilus, and Attendants,'* with an actual and symbolic flourish, superb and rich on the heels of the cheap comedy just played. The panoply of chivalry comes to defend the claims of lovely woman, with Cressida onstage and Paris to remind us of Helen. Seltzer notes in his Signet edition that the reaction line to the flourish announcing the Trojans: 'The Troyans' trumpet' becomes a pun in the theatre: 'The Troyan strumpet' (p. 143). It is an apt reminder of the play in performance and nicely marks the interpretation of this sequence of events as I have set it out. Here, and elsewhere in the play, the music keeps sounding to sharpen the point of the conflicts so relentlessly probed by Shakespeare. Thus the joust between Hector and Ajax, when finally it takes place, is brief and inconclusive, yet it is decorated with trumpet calls beyond its actual significance. In the same proud vein is the great bold exit of both sides from it, as though from some meaningful arbitration and settlement. Agamemnon commands:

> Beat loud the tabourines, let the trumpets blow,
> That this great soldier may his welcome know.   (IV.v.274–5)

Hector's welcome from them at the hands of Achilles' myrmidons is foreknown, and, were it not, the exultant exit of the glorious Hector would be a visual and aural moment easily recalled a little later when he is meanly slain and dragged out.

The last battle is relatively brief, sharply punctuated with conventional signals: ominously, both sides simultaneously beat for retreat as Hector is killed and both armies, at the end, march away, the Greeks 'patiently along' though the victors (v.ix.6), the Trojans under Troilus' command:

> Strike a free march to Troy. With comfort go;
> Hope of revenge, shall hide our inward woe. (v.x.30-1)

A triumphal march by the losers to cover their woe and replace the funeral march expected for Hector: the musical conclusion is ambivalent.

The straightforward sounds of the music in the play are continually heard for such reasons and in such situations that the audience is always aware of something 'out o' tune thus.' In *Troilus and Cressida* one can hear – and see – in the sounds of the drum and trumpet (and lute), in the presented vision of the splendour and the dirtiness of war, 'action, passion and motion to move the spirits' as Heywood sought, and witness an example of that interrelatedness of 'part to part, as well as every part to the whole' that Price rightly averred was the key to Shakespeare's sense of dramatic structure.

NOTES

1 All quotations and line references are to *William Shakespeare, The Complete Works* Alfred Harbage, general editor (Baltimore, Maryland 1969).

2 Hereward T. Price, 'Construction in Shakespeare' *University of Michigan Contributions in Modern Philology* 17 (Ann Arbor 1951)

3 *The English Traveller* J. Symonds and A.W. Verity, eds, Mermaid Edition (London 1888)

4 'An Essay on the Dramatic Character of Sir John Falstaff' in *Eighteenth Century Essays on Shakespeare* D. Nichol Smith, ed (2nd ed Oxford 1963), 226

5 *The First Part of King Henry VI* Andrew S. Cairncross, ed, Arden Edition (London 1962)

6 R.W. Ingram, 'Musical Pauses and the Vision Scenes In Shakespeare's Last Plays' in *Pacific Coast Studies in Shakespeare*, Waldo F. McNeir and Thelma N. Greenfield, eds (Eugene, Oregon 1966) 234-47

7 *Shakespeare's Use of Off-Stage Sounds* (Lincoln, Nebraska 1963) 73

8 In my interpretation of this scene Richard overhears consort music which is being played nearby in the castle. Its quieter timbre and subtler rhythms would contrast strongly with the louder sound and simpler, stronger rhythms of the conventional flourishes. This scene is commonly staged with Richard in rags in a comfortless prison cell: in this case the contrast between the setting and the sound adds to the over-all effect. However, I can see no reason why the scene should not be set with Richard comfortably dressed and housed in surroundings proper to his rank, in which case the contrast of setting and music would add an extra poignancy to the situation. In the disconcerting comfort of his prison – he is after all imprisoned – he overhears social chamber music that signifies ordinary social life elsewhere in the castle, life from which he is now cut off. In discussions following the paper at the Congress two comments were made on this

scene. John H. Long (Greensboro College), a panel-member, argued for the likelihood of the music being supplied, offstage, by a single unsophisticated player, possibly by a lutenist but probably using some simpler instrument such as a gittern. This player, it transpires, is the Groom of the Stable who has offered the music as part of what small solace he can for Richard. Michel Podolski (Belgium), from the floor, on the other hand, allowed that some sort of consort music might have been intended, or lute music, but argued that it is Richard's mind that is out of time and that, therefore, the overheard music, instead of being syncopated and marked by subtle rhythmic effects, would be in the plainest duple or triple time so that its even metre would contrast with the disturbed musings of Richard. Whichever interpretation of the musical part of the scene is accepted, the overriding contrast would still be that between the quieter, intimate music and the louder public music, between music for Richard as king, and for Richard as lonely private man.

9 M.C. Bradbook remarks of this music in *Shakespeare the Craftsman* (London 1969) that: 'The first hint that Timon is being devoured by his friends echoes through the Banquet of Sense which follows, and the Masque to feast the eyes. It is a triumph of the element Air; the music of the lutes contrasted with the more gloomy hautboys; airy dances, airy promises – celestial but childish like blind Cupid, the presiding God' (p.149).

10 Paul Hentzner *A Journey into England in the Year M.D.XC.VIII* (Printed at Strawberry Hill, 1757) 53

11 F.W. Sternfeld, 'Troilus and Cressida: Music for the Play' in *English Institute Essays, 1952* Alan S. Downer, ed (New York 1954) 107–37. This informative essay deals at some length with Pandarus' song, its function and its music, as part of a general survey of the way music stresses the corruption of life in the play. There is a good deal of valuable musicological lore in this article also.

12 The first two examples chosen by Heywood to illustrate his argument about the actor being able to walk, speak, and act like a soldier (quoted at the start of this essay) indicate how the first audiences of *Troilus and Cressida* took Pandarus' comments here, as well as suggesting the natural sympathy they had for the Trojans: 'to see a Hector all besmeared in blood, trampling upon the bulks of kings. A Troilus returning from the field in the fight of his father Priam as if man and horse even from the steed's rough fetlocks to the plume in the champion's helmet had been together plunged into a purple ocean' (B3^v–B4^r).

Grigori Kozintsev /
'Hamlet' and 'King Lear':
Stage and Film

As a theme in itself, that of making films of Shakespeare's plays is an extremely wide-ranging one. I don't think it is possible to doubt the value of having a permanent record, on film, of theatrical performances. Just imagine the possibility of being able to see now the performances of an Edmund Kean, a Henry Irving, or a Pavel Mochalov. It is only to be regretted that film was invented too late. However, the cinema doesn't interest me so much simply as a means of reproducing something. I should like to consider its possibilities as an art form, and in a less narrow sense than usual. I am interested least of all in the so-called 'cinematographic' quality of Shakespeare films, by which I mean those of the 'costumed-epic' genre. Cuts are inevitable in making a screen version of the Shakespearian text, but the gaps can't be filled by constructing huge sets and importing crowds of extras. Such means don't belong to the cinema and, in any case, Charles Kean as well as the Saxe-Meiningen troupe had already demonstrated them on the stages of Europe a century ago.

'Historical Naturalism' destroyed poetic unity. By pursuing these means we move backwards to the productions of the latter half of the nineteenth century, rather than forwards to a fuller understanding of Shakespeare.

The absence of a decorative setting in the Elizabethan theatre was the result, less of the poverty of technical means, than of the richness of the verse. The scene was distilled from the word and was not built from planks and paint. But the cinema demands a different visual technique. A different kind of convention is necessary.

While preparing to shoot *Hamlet*, I went and looked at some medieval castles. They didn't seem to me at all like locations for a tragic action. In my view Warwick Castle, for example, or the Tower of London, are less in themselves than the tragic metaphors of *Richard the Third*. If I were offered the opportunity of shooting *Hamlet* at Elsinore itself, I wouldn't take it. Historical and geographical authenticity are not the authenticity of poetry. They are often contradictory. What one sees in the mind cannot easily be translated into visual terms.

But if unavoidable cuts destroy the poetry and showing 'real' scenery doesn't make up for this lack, does this mean that screen versions of Shakespeare are pointless? No. I don't believe so. But in making a Shakespeare film it is important not to fall between the two stools of theatre and cinema. The result is likely to be either a bad production, on the one hand, or a lifeless film on the other.

The cinema is first and foremost a visual art. A screen version entails a decisive alteration of the play's structure. It shifts the stress from the aural to the visual. The problem is not one of finding means to speak the verse in front of the camera, in realistic circumstances ranging from long-shot to close-up. The aural has to be made visual. The poetic texture has itself to be transformed into a visual poetry, into the dynamic organisation of film imagery. What I have in mind is the possibility of conveying both a sense of human fate and the atmosphere of a philosophical poem – of finding the inner connections between People, Nature, and History itself.

To take an example:

It didn't seem to me to be very expressive to show Ophelia actually gathering flowers in the field. We simply imagined them. She collects a bouquet of dirty, dried kindlewood. Also the fact that the mad scene takes place during Laertes' revolt seemed to me to be important. In our film Ophelia walks about a palace that is paralyzed by alarm. Groups of servants gather, whispering among themselves, soldiers hurry in answer to battle trumpets. Gunsmoke lingers in the air and corpses lie about, waiting to be carted away. The sounds of battle, fear, hatred, reign everywhere. And in the general confusion there is only a single happy person – Ophelia. To be out of one's mind here is to be happy.

I am speaking, not only of the juxtaposition of ideas, but also of rhythm, movement, and the relation between sound and image: gentleness alongside coarseness and evil. Here, it seems to me, was where Ophelia's poetry existed – a fragile flower, bred within the iron chambers of Elsinore.

The theatre sometimes takes too literally the words 'Denmark is a prison,' and proceeds to construct a set reminiscent of a dungeon. The tragedy is in something else. Court life is comfortable. The external trappings are beautiful. But for a person of ideas and feelings this can constitute a prison. The better appointed the place, the worse it is for Hamlet. What is interesting is not the style of architecture but rather the way of life – the state with its diplomatic relations, its official holidays, the ramifications of its spy-network, and its hired guards.

Surely the loneliness of the hero is not conveyed in a soliloquy spoken against a bare background? I tried to show the reverse. The first soliloquy occurs in the bustle of a crowd with its bumps and jolts. It's the start of a new reign. It's also the beginning of someone's career. The nearer the throne the better. In the middle of this purposeful throng, but in a contrasting rhythm, walks Hamlet. Loneliness in a crowd seemed to me to be more tragic.

A similar mise-en-scène would be impossible in the theatre. A lot of important text would simply get lost. But the camera can go to the heart of the crowd, to the whirling epicentre of its life, can come close to a person and look him directly in the face. The sound track can combine the quiet inner monologue with the commotion of voices and the noise of celebration.

The process of tracing the spiritual life of Shakespeare's plays cannot be separated from the tracing of the historical process.

The essence of the art of film-making, it seems to me, consists in the linking of these two viewpoints. The close shot catches the barely perceptible spiritual movement, while the general view shows the movement of historical time. This isn't just a question of the technical possibilities of montage, but is a means of depicting the fate of human beings which differs from the means employed in the theatre.

It is not a question of the advantages of the cinema over those of the theatre. The latter has its own in the shape of a complete text. I am not speaking of competition, but of the possibility which film has of showing certain aspects which the theatre cannot manage.

In thinking about the means of expression, I tried to find forms which were alien to both Naturalism and Conventionalism, both of which seem false or generally imitative on film.

The Russian poet Samuel Marshak once said: 'Everyone of us lives in the universe, but each of us has a home address.' Isn't this the formula of a Shakespearian film – a conjunction between the specifically personal and the immensity of the general? Each nation has its own Shakespeare. The one I try to show on the screen is connected with the Russian Shakespearian tradition. I use Boris Pasternak's translations. Our literary experts have diverging opinions about the various translations. Those of Michail Lozinsky are closest to the original. He manages a positively virtuoso-like equation between the number of lines, together with a suggestion of the subtleties contained in the original. Lozinsky translates the more archaic passages by using a language which is pre-Pushkin in flavour. Pasternak set himself a different task – that of a free translation. Only a truly great poet is capable of doing this. A poet feels more closely the peculiar qualities of another poet. Pasternak wrote of the living relevance of Shakespeare and of how his realism was born in an untidy room of an inn early in the morning, 'infused,' as he put it, 'with the explosive essence of life.'

I should like to underline a distinction. The essence of life is either diluted, like water, or is highly charged with the stuff of life itself, like gunpowder. The sense of approaching catastrophe is not only seen in the darkness of clouds moving over the land, but is perceptible in the accumulation of life's numberless trivia, rendering that life senseless and draining it of its spiritual meaning.

One of the most complicated problems of making films is the question of location. The Shakespearian world can't be found either geographically or historically. It can't be fabricated. Yet bits of it can be pieced together from assorted lines of text – just as in detective stories the crime is recreated from the evidence. One has to seek out and decipher the poetic signs, the code. It's in the lines and, as always happens with poetry, it's between the lines as well.

What is the dramatic function in *King Lear*, of those lines which are assigned to Edgar/Poor Tom? To assist his impersonation of a madman in order to hide from his pursuers? If that's the case, then there's too much text. Or is it a sign of inner disorder brought on by his humiliation and resulting in a loss of human identity? Yes, this is important. But of equal importance is that these are not just the words of a character but the voice of our world. The apparently senseless words are full of profound meaning. They are a guidebook to

Lear's kingdom. Here, the world of the tragedy is unfolded for us
to see. It howls out peasant songs, laments with the voices of madmen,
groans its pleas for alms. From snatches of phrases and rhythms there
arises movement. Beggars pass by on the road – the dispossessed. Here
we see, not only the 'bare, forked animal,' but also an image of the
country itself – laid bare. There is nothing to eat and no shelter. Here,
in the specific concreteness of life, lies the source of tragedy.

The spatial world which is *King Lear* is not just the location for
the action but is the root and cause of the action itself, just as much as
are the answers which the daughters give their father, the king.

I should like to consider for a moment the part played by *place* in
the novels of Dostoievsky. The thoughts and feelings of Rodion
Raskolnikov are inseparable from the fact that the heat in St Peters-
burg that summer was unbearable, from the fact that he was nearly
suffocating in his filthy room, which was shaped like a coffin. If he
went out into the street the very air was infected with the stench.
Beggary and poverty were rife everywhere. The blind alleys and street
crossings of the novel are not naturalistic places of action, but a
materialization of the idea of the novel itself, its inner workings.

However, at the same time, these are real places. Not long ago,
Dostoievsky's grandson proved that every courtyard, each step on
every stairway in *Crime and Punishment* is described with faithful
accuracy to an existing original. But, simultaneously, this is the landscape of a tragedy. The tension of feelings, the inner connections
between the life of the streets and that of the human soul, between
thoughts and the world of objects, are fused together, filling the
commonplace with the spiritual meaning of tragic poetry.

I want least of all to suggest similarities between Shakespeare and
Dostoievsky. But the 'fantastic realism' of which Dostoievsky often
wrote helps us to glimpse a few features of the Shakespearian universe
as well.

Space is inseparable from time. A landscape where nothing has
been built by man is still an historic one. In *King Lear*, a sense of
chronological time is not felt but, through the texture of the tragedy,
glints of an epoch are perceptible like flashes of summer lightning.
These are also poetic ideas, neither static nor well-defined situations,
but signs which first appear, then disappear. The family, the tribe,
the clan – all these concepts are inseparable from the figurative associations they arouse. We, as makers of the film, tried to suggest this
in the images. Instead of placing Lear on a throne, we sat him on a
bench by the fire. His daughters approach him. This is the spectator's

focal point – the fire, the hearth – the family hearth: the ancient glow of the patriarchal fire. The clan gathers at the fire. The fire gives off light. It gives off warmth – the natural relationships between old and young – respect, love.

In the museum in Hiroshima I was surprised by the beginning of the exhibition. I expected to see terrible exhibits, but the first room simply showed pictures. They depicted how our ancestors learned to use fire. This was the beginning of progress. Man's life became warmer, lighter. But then, in subsequent rooms, there followed the history of the monstrous catastrophe. In the last room where, behind glass, is displayed what little was found in the ashes, I noticed a group of Japanese schoolchildren. They were enjoying themselves, laughing and not paying any attention to the exhibits. For them this was already ancient history, perhaps even a fairy tale.

Shakespearian tragedy is neither ancient history nor fairy tale. Perhaps to express this is the most important thing. In which period does the action of the play take place? It is in that past which can become the future.

The director's approach is, in many ways, determined by his choice of material. One can search in the past for the beautiful and the curious, the decorative details of ancient costumes, both celebratory and ceremonial. I most certainly didn't use any of this in my film of *King Lear*. I refused to shoot the film in colour, as I didn't want to draw unnecessary attention to the environment. I looked in the past for those external signs which are not usually noticed. Rags and suffering – which century is it? A mother feeds her child – which epoch is that? In ancient chronicles one finds highly coloured descriptions of knightly tournaments. But one can also read how, during a siege, cholera-infected corpses were thrown over the walls into the city. Does this differ greatly from bacteriological warfare? The screen seems to me to be a means of bringing something closer, of telescoping the past. I am speaking of problems, the answers to which people are still looking for.

When I am asked to formulate the 'theme' or the 'main idea' of a production, I find this difficult to do. Shakespeare begins where the logic of so-called interpretation ends. His themes are innumerable. Speaking of literature, Tolstoy called this phenomenon 'an endless labyrinth of connecting parts.' Every artist, every epoch, finds a new approach, discovers the logical order of some of these connections so that further connections, beyond these, can be made in the future.

I should like to concentrate for a moment on a aspect of the film version of *King Lear*. Lear is often shown as a titan. His image is associated with that of the lonely heroes of mythology. But is this really so? If we speak of the range of his intellect or his strength of character, then these are sooner apparent in those scenes of his misery, when he has become nothing. His suffering makes him one with the many. He achieves greatness through his understanding of this fact. When he thought himself greater than most, he was then most ordinary. The whims of tyrants are not rare in the history of nations. There has never yet been a despot in the history of the world who has been able to admit the absurdity of his own deification.

I tried to find striking visual motifs for the upper social strata and the lower strata of the muddy earth – in the difference between Lear, seen first as raised above the kneeling crowd and then seen as an old man from 'the lower depths' of life, among the beggars from whose number he is barely distinguishable.

Why couldn't Cordelia's soldiers find him – a helpless old man? He couldn't possibly have run away from them. It was because he was difficult to seek out – his particular condition had become like that of the general and indistinguishable from theirs.

The question is not one of literal representation but of movement, of the growth of poetic ideas, of contrasting changes of state – luxury and poverty, the powerful and the dispossessed, strength and defence-lessness. In attempting to embody the poetry in the figurativeness of film imagery I looked for it in the fluidity, the changeability, the conflicts of a landscape – the way out of enclosed places into the wide space of Nature. Man is surrounded by a crowd and is alone in the limitless void.

The tragedy unfolds in movements – on the roads between castles, on the road to Dover, in a military advance, in the act of running. *King Lear* is shot through with the rhythms of walking, marching, running. Everything is shaken from its place. Everything is in movement – the wandering beggars, the king's baggage train, the soldiers. Bands of people move over the land – then only three people: the King, Kent, and the Fool. Then Lear is left alone. Then the king walks among beggars. Human suffering walks the earth.

This relation between numbers is full of profound poetic significance.

Lear's hundred knights and squires occupy an important place in the play but have very few lines to speak. A few phrases serve to create the complete character of Cornwall's servant or the character of the officer who murders Cordelia. There's nothing at all which characterizes the gentlemen of Lear's entourage. I tried to break down the group into its component parts, to find for each actor some identifying, individual characteristic. Only then did I realize that one must not do this. Shakespeare hasn't given them text to speak because these are not people, but a representation of a way of life. The number one hundred isn't a quantity, but a specific quality. *King Lear* has its own magic number. One hundred isn't a hundred times one. In this case the number one, as a single unit, doesn't exist. In Gordon Craig's production of *Hamlet* at the Moscow Art Theatre, he wanted the set for act I scene ii to be replaced by a golden cloak, extending from Claudius' shoulders to cover the entire width of the stage. There were to be holes in it through which emerged the heads of the members of the court – a sea of gold with heads poking out of it.

In the *Lear* film the king's mantle and train become the fantastic string of carts following an old man. What are all these servants, trunks, hunting dogs, and falcons in aid of? They are there so that, subsequently, he can be shown alone in the desolation of life, so that a sense is obtained of just how much one person is ... and then two persons – father and daughter. Two people who have found each other.

These situations weren't just abstract ones as far as I was concerned. They determined the composition of a shot – the relation between people and the surrounding space.

Fortunately, the days are long past of the touring tragedians who cut everything in the play except the main part. But still the gallery of Shakespearian types has not yet been brought out into full relief. In the theatre, it is often difficult to make out the distinction between the separate levels of life. In this tragedy there are many such levels. Lear's knights aren't like Goneril's servants. The military world is quite different from the world of the court – and poverty occupies a special place of its own.

It's as if these levels were different planets, each with its own inhabitants, its own landscape, its own distinctive type of person.

There are characters who don't have much of importance to say, although in the metaphorical world their significance is important. In the contemporary theatre the element of cruelty in this tragedy is often intensified. It is most certainly there, and on a vast scale. But *King Lear* is not only 'Theatre of Cruelty' but also 'Theatre of Mercy.' The play's foreground is occupied by the figures of Cordelia, Edgar, and the Fool. On the stage it is difficult to project the thoughts and feelings of either the Duke of Albany or the King of France. Not only are these principal characters important in themselves but so, also, are the poetic concepts with which they are associated.

When thinking about *King Lear*, I remember the words of Victor Hugo: 'The world is sick with hatred. Hatred against Hatred.' I tried to strengthen the voice of Good, even in those instances when it has no words to speak. Silence, an exchange of glances, are cinematically expressive. I wanted to show both how Cordelia spoke and the manner in which she listened to the words of her sisters.

Symbols change. The Fool's cap and bells have long since gone out of fashion. Perhaps the Fool's foolery isn't quite what it used to be either? I imagined a paradoxical situation. The Fool is laughed at, not because he is foolish, but because he speaks the truth. He is the one who shams idiocy – no longer a court comedian but an urchin taken from among the most humble. The least significant tells the most mighty that he's a fool because he doesn't know the nature of his own daughters. Everyone laughs – but it is the truth.

For these people nothing is funnier than the truth. They roar with laughter at the truth, kick it like a dog, hold it on a leash and make a laughing stock of it – like art under a tyrannical régime. I am reminded of stories about how, in a Nazi concentration camp, an orchestra of prisoners was got together. They were forced to play outside in the compound. They were beaten so that they would play better. This was the origin of the Fool-musician – a boy taken from an orchestra composed of men condemned to death.

This was the origin of the particular tone of the film, its voice. In *King Lear*, the voice of human suffering is accorded more significance than the roar of thunder. Working on the score with Dmitri Shostakovitch, I dismissed the idea of dignified fanfares and the roll of drums. We were carried away by ideas of a completely different kind of instrumentation – the sound of a wooden pipe, which the Fool has made for himself. I'd asked for the film titles to be written on coarse, torn sacking. This linkage of ideas acted as a kind of key. Rags, and the soft sound of the pipe – the still voice of suffering. Then, during the battle scenes, a requiem breaks out, then falls silent. And once again the pipe can be heard. Life – a none too easy one – goes on. Its voice in *King Lear* is a very quiet one, but its sad, human quality sounds distinctly in Shakespeare's work.

Why is Edmund beaten in single combat? Is the result purely a consequence of Edgar's greater prowess as a fighter? I think the answer has to be looked for in Lear's fearlessness, after having found

Cordelia. Edmund sees their faces – neither of them looks defeated. Spiritual strength is capable of overcoming the physical. Tragedy is not a fairy tale, and such victories are fleeting. Death must take its course. Nevertheless, I tried in this screen version to make precisely this moment – the triumph of spiritual strength – the most important of all.

Of course, the idea of what is most, or least, important in Shakespeare's art, is relative. In *Hamlet*, for example, I wanted to bring to the fore the main character's speech where he compares himself to a musical pipe – a defence of human dignity. In *Lear*, on the other hand, one of the most important places seemed to me to be the scene between Lear and Cordelia in captivity – goodness encircled by iron, weapons of murder – people gripped by a mania for destruction, by hatred. And these same soldiers, having seen these two defenceless people – an old man and a young woman – having heard their voices, fall silent. The prisoners, with bound hands, walk past the ranks of men armed to the teeth, wicked men – like conquerors. This is the beginning of Edmund's defeat.

Must a man be that which the time he lives in dictates, or must he obey the dictates of his own conscience, his sense of human dignity?

The war in *King Lear* isn't shown as a series of battle scenes. Rather, it is a burning flame. Its origin smoulders in the play's opening words. The suppressed conflict of concealed passions – envy, hatred, jealousy – bursts out with enormous force. Acting on Edmund's orders, soldiers set light to the countryside. A town burns. The kingdom is burning. Lear and Cordelia, together with a group of refugees, escape from the fire. Goneril and Regan hunt for their lover in the flames of war. The screen is in flames. But on the sound track a requiem drowns the noise of battle. We wanted to make audible, not only the voices of the main characters, but also the voice of the author himself. Sometimes it sounds like the chorus of ancient tragedy. Shostakovitch composed a choral requiem – like a lament – the eternal, inconsolable lament of human kind.

The screen version seems to me to be closer to a tragic poem than a play.

What I have tried to relate makes no claim to be any kind of 'proper' way of making screen-versions of Shakespeare. This is only the result of my personal experience. Our general aim was to reveal the Shakespearian world as fully as possible and in the greatest possible depth – and to do that which every age seeks to do: to read Shakespeare in the light of the present day.

Bernard Beckerman /
The Flowers of Fancy, the Jerks of Invention, or, Directorial Approaches to Shakespeare

Holofernes the pedant advises us that, in literary art, 'Imitari is nothing.' Any creature can imitate another, 'so doth the hound his master, the ape his keeper.' But it requires a master like Ovidius Naso, divine Ovid, to smell out 'the odoriferous flowers of fancy, the jerks of invention.' However much we may regard Holofernes as an object of ridicule, we must admit that twentieth-century art seems to have heeded his advice, none more so than the contemporary theatre, which is strewn with flowers of fancy and shaken by jerks of invention. I shall discuss the Shakespearian producers of these delights.

When one speaks of Shakespearian stage history of the nineteenth century, one speaks of actors. To speak of twentieth-century Shakespearian stage history, one must speak about directors. This has long been recognized and, with increasing fervour, lamented. Muriel St Clare Byrne dates the dominance of the producer – or, in the American parlance that I shall use, the stage director – to the nineteen thirties.[1] Where once a constellation of star performers dazzled the public and filled the playhouses, only single luminaries of the magnetism of Laurence Olivier can still attract an audience to a Shakespearian play. In place of a Salvini Othello or a Booth Hamlet, we now have a Zeffirelli *Romeo and Juliet* and a Peter Brook *Midsummer Nights' Dream.*

Shakespearian scholars and critics are not exactly happy with this state of affairs. In the 1970 issue of *Shakespeare Survey* Gareth Lloyd Evans compares the interpretation-making tendencies of directors unfavourably to the experience-giving qualities of actors.[2] A few years earlier John Russell Brown warned that the recruitment of directors from men who have not been actors is bound to affect production adversely.[3] These particular criticisms represent a much more widespread suspicion that the contemporary director sacrifices Shakespeare to his own thirst for novel and bizarre interpretation.

The pursuit of novelty, while certainly a mark of contemporary Shakespearian staging, is not solely a product of the director's egotism or ambition, however. In translating Shakespeare from page to stage, the director encounters genuine sociological and aesthetic problems. In fact, his rise to power has crystallized a dilemma that has always beset the revival of classics. Gareth Lloyd Evans, as we have seen, saw the dilemma as a conflict between experience, which is supposedly reflective of Shakespeare's original intent, and interpretation, which is a projection of the director's inclinations. In a critique of Jan Kott, Patrick Cruttwell differentiates between allegiance to people, namely, Shakespeare's characters, and allegiance to ideas imposed upon Shakepeare by Kott and directors who follow him.[4] One of the more extended and astute examinations of this dilemma was recently undertaken by Robert Weimann. He sees the contradiction to lie in 'the tension between Renaissance values and modern valuation' and the director's task to reconcile the expressed content of plot and character with 'the changing impact of this on the *affect* of the contemporary spectator.'[5] His belief in the possibility of reconciling 'the expressive and affective aspects' of a Shakespearian play is not seconded by Alfred Harbage. In his British Academy lecture of 1969, Harbage seems to favour the untutored reading of Shakespeare's words as the *only* means of preserving Shakespeare's sense. Taking note of the director's claim that a Shakespearian play cannot be staged as a museum piece, he observes, rather dolefully, that if indeed it is true that a play must be interpreted in order to seem relevant to our times, then the result 'is not the play, but the producer's commentary upon it, and we cannot tell whether audiences are enjoying the play or the commentary.'[6] All these writers, however differently they may perceive the dilemma, are confronting the same issue. Can one preserve Shakespeare's text as embodiment of the unique thought, passion, and expression of his art and at the same time communicate that text in an immediate way to a living audience?

Whether this dilemma can ever be resolved to the satisfaction of scholars, critics, and directors alike is doubtful. But *how* one goes about resolving it conditions one's attitude toward theatre in general and the production of Shakespeare in particular. Naturally, in this effort at resolution, scholars and directors do not see eye to eye. Each reflects the source of his primary allegiance. The scholar's primary allegiance is to Shakespeare's words. We are all familiar with the value he attaches to an authentic text as a vehicle, first, of Shakespeare's ideas, and next, of Shakespeare's understanding of human nature. We may be less familiar with the director's values. His first allegiance is to the stage or rather to the kind of life that the stage can generate. He measures his accomplishment by his ability to stimulate an immediate response in an audience. Peter Brook speaks of levels of intensity. In directing Shakespeare, he says, the director discovers 'an essential area where meanings between actors and an audience can be shared ... This form of intensity makes all questions of the play's relations to the past unimportant. It's happening *now*.'⁷ Without that immediacy the work has no value for the director. To achieve such a level of intensity as Brooks speaks of, the director utilizes all facets of presentational technique. Whereas for the scholar Shakespeare's medium is primarily verbal, for the director, as he works in the contemporary theatre, it is comprehensive: gesture having as much validity and force as speech, both being expressive manifestations of that elusive phenomenon known as 'action.' Thus, while the scholar's activity in regard to Shakespeare is essentially *protective*, the director's activity is *explorative*. Starting from these fundamentally conflicting premises, it is no wonder that these two lovers of Shakespeare frequently disagree, that an uneasy truce exists between them, and that the claims of each remain unreconciled.

Oddly enough, the aims of the director are probably not too dissimilar from the aims of Shakespeare in his own day. After all, there is very little evidence that preserving the integrity of a text was particularly respected in the Elizabethan theatre. Any play that came to hand was fair game for alteration or imitation. Popular pieces such as *The Spanish Tragedy* and *Doctor Faustus* were no more immune from repeated tinkering than the merest hack-work. Actually, the practice of short run and brief revival made it likely that, the more popular a play was, the sooner it would be revised by someone other than the original author. In such a professional climate achieving immediacy and swinging with fashion were more persuasive pressures than preserving a text which, in all likelihood, existed only in a playhouse copy. I hasten to add at this point that my argument is not intended to justify collaboration or revision as ideal dramatic practice, but merely to illustrate the kind of conditions in which theatrical art can flourish.

At its most superficial the theatre is a house of transitory pleasure where the excitation of eye and ear induces kinetic response. At its most profound the theatre captures glimpses of general truth through the fleeting but concrete activity of the moment. In its very essence theatre is paradoxical, for no enduring idea or vision is communicable to an audience except through specific gestures and inflections made by a human being at one particular time and place.

But how to give particularity in order to communicate a larger abstraction is the artistic problem of the theatre. In its original state, the particular expression of a Shakespearian play flowed from the mainstream of the theatre out of which it appeared. Along with literary sources, Shakespeare had a repertoire of gesture, device, ceremony, inflection, dress, and stage from which to draw. They were the given components, part of the natural order of theatrical presentation in which the concrete activity and the imaginative intent fused. Because his audience could take his conventions of production for granted, it could concentrate on the unique way in which he unfolded events and revealed sensibilities.

Successive periods since then have provided alternate modes of presentation for Shakespeare's plays. For two and a half centuries, adapting Shakespeare to contemporary stage practice and values was common. The text was fitted to the prevailing fashion, a fashion that changed slowly and, when it did, moved toward greater and greater environmental and psychological realism. At the end of the nineteenth century, however, theatre, as other arts, underwent radical fragmentation. Theatrical modes proliferated, swamping the remnants of earlier traditions and destroying any common pattern of stage gesture and inflection. As a result, one of the most tantalizing problems a director faces in rehearsing and presenting Shakespeare is to find an appropriate context for the actor's physical expression, one that is capable of arousing a complex of responses commensurate with the possibilities Shakespeare offers. Please allow me to reiterate this statement. Creating immediacy and intensity is a *sine qua non* of theatre. An audience must be stirred, titillated, enraptured. The director knows that the unforgivable sin is dullness. Unfortunately, the pursuit of this end may so dominate his thinking that he sometimes sacrifices other vital aspects of a play to achieve an immediate effect. What is exceptionally difficult is to achieve the immediate effect in such a way as to activate a complex of responses commensurate with the immense opportunities that Shakespeare offers.

Since such a complex of responses can arise only from concrete acts of the performer, the rationale for selecting these acts is crucial to the depth as well as the liveliness of a theatrical presentation. What is the nature of this rationale? Here I need to discriminate between two different functions of the director. Much of what a director does falls under the heading of coaching. He guides and advises the actor in making choices. He suggests, 'try phrasing the line differently,' or 'on this word, raise your hand as if to ward off a blow.' In short, he helps the actor shape his performance. This, however, is quite a different function from conceiving and developing a context within which these choices are made. Through devising such a context, the director provides the actors with a suitable background so that they appear to be both convincing in themselves and yet part of a larger order of existence. Moreover, since the theatre is a highly compressed art, the director must schematize the features of this context, that is, select potent aspects of environment and behaviour and then relate them to each other in some meaningful way. This schematization in effect acts as a *frame* for the play. It embraces not only the geographical dimensions of setting and costume, but also – and more significantly – the imaginative dimension or world-view within which the action unfolds.

Devising a frame for a Shakespearian production is no new thing. Charles Kean and the Duke of Saxe-Meiningen made stage history by modifying the then customary frames of presentation. But not until the advent of the independent stage director has the choice of frame become one of the most, if not the most, creative act he performs. In line with the current tendency to break all traditional restraints in staging, the director of a Shakespearian play often feels compelled – within the limits of his means – to invent a stage and style from scratch.

Throughout the nineteenth century, the prevailing frame was antiquarian and spectacular. Settings depicted the Rome of Caesar or the Verona of the Renaissance. Sequence was altered so that scenes occurring in the same or similar locales could be run together, thus permitting scenic elaboration. Illustrative stage business lent a pseudo-naturalistic accuracy to life on the Rialto or in the streets of Windsor. Early in this century Robert Mantell was proud that he copied his costume for Macbeth from the thane's portrait in Holyrood Castle. Archaeological and historical authenticity was the ideal, even when the reality was spectacle and romantic indulgence. A manager, or more likely an actor-manager, showed his ingenuity by the verifiable details he could weave into the tapestry of his production.

During the last sixty or seventy years this type of historicity has gradually lost importance without entirely disappearing. No single style has replaced it. Instead we find a spectrum of frames devised for Shakespearian productions. On the basis of these frames some new styles have emerged, but in no case has any single style prevailed. Thus, the director has a grab bag from which to choose or the licence with which to invent. For this reason an understanding of alternate frames provides an insight into directorial options. In citing examples, I shall confine myself to productions of the English-speaking theatre, not because of any belief in the superiority of these productions but merely because of my need to cite only those examples with which I am quite familiar. We can catalogue these various frames under three broad headings: 1/the historical, 2/the decorative, and 3/ the symbolic or abstract.

Among the historical frames that have been influential are two of special importance. One focussed its gaze on Elizabethan England, the other on contemporary Europe and America. The frame that William Poel devised found its source in Elizabethan practice. Instead of using the customs of history, he used its manner. Poel was a director's director, and his influence has been exerted less through the accomplishments of his own productions and more through the principles they exemplified. He stressed Elizabethan scene-sequence, a more open stage, and rapidity of delivery in order to free Shakespeare's texts from the cloying romanticism of the nineteenth century and to restore the distinctive dash of the original. That he was not doctrinaire is apparent from his last Shakespearian production in 1930, when he thoroughly rearranged *Coriolanus*. In this regard he attempted to do what every director does, that is, to find a treatment of text and a pattern of playing that will not only enhance the play but unlock its most penetrating energies.

The other form of historicity, peculiar to the twentieth century, is the modern-dress production. Like the antiquarian frame, the modern-dress frame depicts a specific time and place though that time and place are the immediately recognizable present. Where the rationale for other historical frames is inherent in the subject matter of a play, the modern-dress production proceeds from an implicit or explicit analogy that the director sees between the events of a particular play and the temper of a period. I include within the definition of modern-dress production those which utilize the recent past to convey a modern image to an audience. Thus *Much Ado About Nothing* set in Spanish Texas or *Love's Labour's Lost* set in Edwardian England rely upon familiarity of context for their effect.

Although there have been a number of successful modern-dress productions since Sir Barry Jackson's *Hamlet* in 1925, there is and has been considerable critical and scholarly disapproval of this approach. Perhaps because it lends itself to gimmickry, it is often regarded with distrust. 'Modernized Shakespeare is no more acceptable than the museum version,' Robert Weimann writes.[8] If he encompasses modern-dress versions in this stricture, as I think he intends, then he is too absolute. No element of production can be treated in isolation. Every element is part of a context of presentation, and the effectiveness of a modernized treatment depends upon the way the frame does or does not integrate all facets of the action. Setting *As You Like It* in a defeated southland after the American Civil War, as was done by Edward Payson Call at the Tyrone Guthrie Theatre several years ago, only calls attention to the oddity and irrelevance of the shifted historical perspective, especially when Jaques is bearded and garbed like Robert E. Lee. But it is quite a different matter when a director's choice throws the action into fresh and rich relief. In Tyrone Guthrie's own production of *Troilus and Cressida* in 1953, Thersites was portrayed as a foreign correspondent. Clutching camera and tripod, he dashed about the battlefield, heaping scatology and abuse on friend and foe alike. This image provided a convincing basis for Thersites' blend of independence and servility and rationalized his primary action of vituperative attack. By this stroke of invention, Guthrie endowed Thersites with an inner logic for a contemporary audience.

The efficacy of modernization, as I see it, is proportionate to the director's ability to forego facile analogies of subject matter in order to tap the more fundamental analogies of action. The director has to be certain that his modernized frame satisfies pressing questions in the action itself, as, for example, in the case of Thersites, what kind of man would rail at Greek and Trojan, friend and foe alike? Or, in the case of *Measure for Measure*, how can a woman's sacrifice of her brother for her chastity be made acceptable today? The resultant frame must answer the question not merely on a level of apprehension, but on a far more profound level of credibility. It must accord with what a contemporary audience will impulsively accept as logical. In this process, modernization reverts to the ancient treatment of history as a mirror for the present rather than as an objectification of the past.

The second significant type of frame is the decorative one. It may well trace its lineage from the fancies of the court masque and seventeenth-century opera. In the twentieth century this type of frame often manifests itself in painterly terms. *Love's Labour's Lost* in the manner of Watteau – a Peter Brook production of 1946 – had just such a decorative basis. Frequently, however, the decorative frame relies upon a more generalized use of artistic sources. Plays are produced in medieval, Renaissance, and baroque fashion, using as points of reference no single painter or engraver but the artistic 'style' of the period as a whole. Allied to this use of graphic sources is a parallel use of mores, architecture, and dress. Even where the source is historical, the rationale is aesthetic. In 1966 the American Shakespeare Festival at Stratford, Connecticut, produced a *Twelfth Night* for which the frame was an Ottomanized Illyria. But neither Turkish nor Balkan history had any organic connection with the handling of incidents in the production, and so the oriental setting and costumes merely served a visual and therefore arty purpose.

Perhaps more than any other frame, the decorative has been the workhorse of twentieth-century Shakespearian production. Yet it symptomizes all that is shallow in contemporary staging. In utilizing the decorative frame, the director is usually guided by superficial considerations of appearance. Aside from personal taste, there is no larger relationship to life that shapes the style. Coupled with a skilful designer, the director may succeed in creating a striking background for a play, but too often the decorative frame plays no part in the unfolding action and may even make the action seem trivial.

The frame of a production should obviously stimulate theatrical excitement. It must have sufficient sensory appeal to stir an audience viscerally. But if that is all it does, it misses half its function. It should also be the archway into the deeper recesses of an audience's imagination. Either by its form or its content, it should induce a ready exchange between the audience and the play. We can more easily see how this occurs by noting a contemporary example. In *The Jungle of the Cities* Brecht employed a mythologized Chicago for his tale of men united by the violence they do each other. But his Chicago was a city that he and Europeans in general had distilled from films and news stories. Without being completely factual he had fantasized an essential truth that accorded with popular notions. Just so, the choice of any frame by a director is stimulating to the extent that it affords entrance into the imagination and sensibility of an audience. Toward that end, the director's choice is never and can never be solely decorative.

One word needs to be said about the connection of frame to style. The frame is one of the active components of a production. Other components are the various kinds of activities that the players present within the frame. The distinctive structure that emerges from the interplay of activities and frame is the style.

Perhaps two oversimplified examples will illustrate my point. In Kabuki theatre, setting and ceremony are highly conventionalized. Ceremony, in particular, is formal and prescribed, reflecting the rigidity of class and sex relationships. On the other hand, the characters often reveal a wild and unrestrained passion, the explosiveness of which is heightened all the more by the rigidity of the frame. An analogous dialectic can be found in Greek drama, most readily in the *Ajax* cited by Professor Kitto in this volume. The debates between Menelaus and Teucer first, and then between Agamemnon and Teucer, are also examples of a conventional frame setting off intense passion. In this latter instance the frame embodies the rationality of the Attic law courts and not the strict mores of Japanese feudal society. In both cases the style is a product of the interplay between frame and action.

The third type of framing I labelled symbolic or abstract. It embraces a wide variety of interrelated approaches that overlap psychological exploration, emotive evocation, mythic imitation, and universal ideation. Its beginning can be found in a new kind of framing that Appia and Craig devised at the end of the nineteenth century. A-historical, it sought to evoke timeless sensations of light and space. Not without symbolic intention, Appia's and Craig's work principally externalized mental and emotional states. Traces of their influence can be found in all sorts of productions through the last fifty years, but in the English-speaking theatre their kind of framing found its fullest expression in the designs of Robert Edmond Jones and Norman Bel Geddes. Jones' associate Kenneth MacGowan reports that, in his production of *Macbeth* in 1921, Jones 'attempted through significant form to create an abstract background expressing spiritual relationships of the play.'[9] Witches' masks hung over the stage as a projection of Macbeth's mind, and their triangular form was re-echoed in the arches that composed the scenery. Yet contributory though the psychological approach has been, it has never dominated Shakespearian staging. Perhaps the vibrant psychological life that Shakespearian imagery conveys rendered a wholly psychological frame redundant. In fact, the most effective application of psychological interpretation came in productions using historical or decorative frames, as in Gielgud's portrayal of Hamlet in 1934.

But, although the purely psychological frame has had limited influence, it has affected the more abstract productions which have gained currency in recent years. These productions are essentially anti-historical. They proceed from the premise that, underlying all specific manifestations of experience, there is a stream of life that transcends history. They often employ bare stages and neutral costumes; their milieu is frequently a void. They suggest a kind of existential allegory by throwing emphasis upon action devoid of locale as well as upon universal rather than particular cases. Trevor Nunn's production of *Lear* at Stratford in 1969 exhibited some of these features as, in part, did Brook's own version in the early sixties. Both productions, by seeming to forego the associational properties of a frame, required the acting to carry the full burden. At first this concentration upon the performer would seem to satisfy those who wish the word to be given full attention. In practice, however, this neutrality of background encourages simplification of ideas and grossness of effect. *Lear*, for example, moves from the courtly opulence of act I to the nakedness of act IV. In the two productions of *Lear* that I cited, as well as in the Fletcher production at Stratford, Connecticut, with Morris Carnovsky, the opening scenes were staged in what I'm moved to call a pseudo-mythic fashion: abstract regalism, primitive costumes, portentous gesture. By placing the actor in an arbitrary context, kept as bare as possible, the directors lost one of the tools for creating dramatic tension and nuance. Personally I suspect that action devoid of social or personal history has limited promise for Shakespearian staging.

These, then, are three of the principal types of frame, as I read our recent stage history. Yet I seem to have omitted one approach, in fact, *the* approach that is only now going out of fashion, namely, the vogue for relevance. One of the reservations about Peter Hall's reign at the Royal Shakespeare Company was that he too insistently pursued the cult of the contemporary. The reverse of the coin is not, however, as some critics would have it, loyalty to universals. A director has no choice of whether he will or will not be relevant. If he succeeds in inducing a genuine imaginative exchange between actor and audience, he will have achieved 'relevance,' that is, immediacy.

In current theatrical usage, however, relevance has another connotation. The word is applied to a limited range of ideas and experiences, usually melancholy, self-questioning, disillusioning, and over-physical in character. From earlier naturalism the new kind of 'relevant' production continues an interest in bodily and sexual functions. Concurrently, aristocrats are debunked and workers humanized. Pessimism is the mood of this relevance and political soul-searching its primary action. In this limited application, then, 'relevance' is not a structural feature of drama, like the frame, but a specific interpretation of the action.

In considering the matter of contemporaneity, however, we face aesthetic questions concerning the nature of a classic's relationship to an audience. In élite theatre there always exists a sizable number of spectators who prefer to see the classics produced in a familiar and fixed style. In that way they can attend to their favourite scenes or speeches or performers. Opera and ballet are graced by thousands who seek this specialized and constricted expectation. They substitute connoisseurship of the part for the impact of the whole. For them the contemporary is an intrusion since it demands a spontaneous and total response.

Fortunately, current directors of Shakespeare are trying to encourage and maintain a mass audience. They disregard the specialist for the public at large, and therefore they are, and must be concerned with, giving the impression that a Shakespearian play is a work of the present. One means of creating that impression, as I have shown, is by depicting familiar subject matter. This means some form of modernization, an admirable example of which is the Guthrie *Troilus and Cressida* already mentioned.

But creating an effect of immediacy need not rely upon the allusions and analogies of modernized dress. It can stem from multiple sensations sparked by the frame. To some degree the frame can be ambivalent. This was one of the dazzling features of Franco Zeffirelli's stage production of *Romeo and Juliet* in 1960. Without diluting the image of Renaissance Verona, Zeffirelli imparted a modern aura to the visual and oral elements of the production. This was evident, and noted at the time, in the sexual vigour of the young lovers. To frame their action Zeffirelli chose what seemed to be a conventional, almost operatic, setting. But his treatment of this kind of setting was not conventional. His opening scene, for instance, revealed a piazzetta at the junction of two diagonal streets. The scene could pass for Renaissance Verona; it could also pass for the old part of contemporary Verona which so many of us have visited. The design and detail of the setting allowed either assumption. And the players, while occasionally garbed in robes of another age, more often wore clothes the silhouette of which was not so different from our own. Scene, dress, and behaviour were therefore provocative. They spoke of then and now; they fitted our expectation of the past, but as we might envision the past were the author alive and writing in the present.

The mixed impression that this approach induced exemplifies a highly effective way in which a director can utilize an historical frame to produce a modern style. First, the frame set off the enacted events by defining the world in which they occurred. The young lovers were part of a small-town, in-bred society baking in the sun. Their impulsive affair contrasted with this environment. At the same time as the frame played bass to the treble of this action, it mediated between stage and audience by stressing what is familiar in the Veronese world. The director's art lay in his ability to suggest the familiar without distorting the integrity of the play. In this he was helped decidedly by the rage for Italy which took hold of post-war England and America.

With these observations in mind, we can now turn to the Shakespearian production that has recently excited the most widespread comment and interest: Peter Brook's *Midsummer Night's Dream*. Because of the production's novelty, the audience was surprised and at times blinded by the frame Brook chose. He presented the stage as a playing machine: a white box for a setting and acrobatics as behaviour. To the extent that much of the activity and devices spring from the circus, the frame can be considered decorative in part. But its dependence on circus associations was not absolute. Instead, the production embodied an outlook that Brook shares with other contemporary directors. Suspicious of conventional stage illusion and desirous of a concrete basis of theatrical reality, they begin with the actuality of actor as performer, not the performer as a weaver of fictional illusion, but the performer as prestidigitator. Thus, by combining features of several presentational modes, Brook effected a brilliant opacity, an unabashed playfulness that communicated vividly to the audience and induced an unrestrained sense of joy as long as the frame was in focus.

The frame also had a broader albeit negative dimension. In reviews of the play much was made of the fact that Brook's production was not the conventional one of dainty fairies and flitting Puck. By tricking expectation, Brook extended the aesthetic dimension of his frame. He violated the nineteenth-century image and thus appealed to an iconoclastic impulse in modern audiences. It is interesting, and perhaps significant, that people familiar with John Hancock's earlier treatment, which anticipated the attitude if not all the techniques of Brook, were not so thoroughly dazzled by this more recent production.

The largely decorative basis of the Brook version illustrates one of the current problems in staging Shakespeare. As we have seen, there are no traditional ways of producing Shakespeare today. There are only fashions. Consequently, every production is novel to some extent. This is to be expected and, up to a point, desired. Often, however, novelty becomes the most notable feature of a production. When this happens, it throws the play out of focus, for novelty is usually expressed through the frame chosen. Unless carefully bound within the parameters of the text, novelty encourages the audience to concentrate on the frame rather than the picture.

This misdirection of emphasis is particularly disturbing because it distracts the audience from the richness of Shakespeare's action. This too is evident in Brook's production. It is a work of delight and joy. But its high spirits are a product almost completely of the frame itself: of Oberon swinging in the air, of Puck scaling the balcony rail, of Hermia dangling puppetlike from a trapeze. Only rarely did the structure of the frame heighten the intrinsic action. One instance occurred when Hermia awoke to find herself alone in the forest. As she rushed about in search of Lysander, she became enmeshed in arboreal spirals of steel that vibrated as they were lowered over her. Seeing her caught in these toils created an overpowering sense of terror.

More usually, however, the substantive moments were independent of the frame. The mechanicals, in particular, were little affected by acrobatics, and the most poignant scene in the play was the simple one where the artisans first lament for translated Bottom and then leap for joy when he returns unexpectedly. Otherwise, the relations of Titania and Oberon, of Lysander and Hermia, and of Demetrius and Helena were conventionally realized. Except for an occasional bit of acrobatic business, often superbly performed, the lovers went through a sequence of farce pratfalls that were sometimes amusing and sometimes pedestrian, but seldom affecting. As a result, appreciable stretches of the play were routine and tedious, made even more so by their contrast to the exciting frame.

One of the more popular scenes concluded the first act. Titania awakens, falls in love with a Bottom sporting ass's ears, and calls her burly fairies to her. They hoist Bottom on their shoulders, one of the attendants thrusting his arm between Bottom's legs to simulate an erect and primed phallus. To the mocking strains of Mendelsohn's music and with streamers flying, Bottom is carried off. No question this was an uproarious exit made to thunderous applause. But the scene did not make sense. The ass may symbolize rampant sex, as Brook observes, but Shakespeare used the ass not so much for its sexual proclivities but for its deficiency of sense. Brook overlaid the text with the spectacle of Bottom's sexual prowess. While antithetical to the inherent action of the play, his interpretation might have been effective if he had pursued it. But he merely used the phallic image to heighten the act-ending. In the scene of Titania's dotage following the intermission, which presumably showed the aftermath of love, none of the activity developed any of the consequences of Bottom's paraded sexuality.

The virtues and limitations of the Brook production crystallize the current state of Shakespearian production. Not only does his production erase the memory of previous conventions, it also insists on the irrelevance of extra-theatrical or historical illusion. Between performer and spectator there is only the act of performing. From the pseudo-mythic tendencies of contemporary theatre Brook borrowed the motif of primitive sexuality for the Bottom-Titania meeting, but even this motif was subordinated to the act of performing itself, for what appears to interest Brook is not Bottom's potency so much as the triumphal march.

This emphasis upon performance as performance continues a trend in Shakespearian stage history. While all the major frames I have described have been employed concurrently, there has also been a shift of interest from earlier historical to the more decorative and abstract types. This rejection of history is, of course, part of a larger movement, not merely in the theatre but in men's minds, and especially in the minds of the young. Activism is substituted for adjustment, assault for persuasion. Theatrical gestures and inflections are shaped for maximum physical impact rather than associative or fictional allusion. As we can see from the Brook production, such an approach can be immensely exhilarating, although, as I believe, often at the cost of an inner coherence.

For theatrical art the a-historical or anti-historical approach is dangerous. Art cannot feed on itself, the theatre least of all. It cannot rely on training or novel rehearsal methods for its well-being. It needs to draw continuous imaginative nourishment from all sides and transmute that food into sharply defined actions-in-context. To some degree we are witnessing in today's theatre a partial attempt to create a supra-history that will embrace the entire range of human experience mythically. This attempt can be seen in the work of both the Open Theatre and the Polish Laboratory Theatre of Jerzy Grotowski. For example, Grotowski's *Akropolis* conflates classical and biblical experience within the frame of an abstracted concentration camp. What effect these efforts will have on Shakespearian production is too early to tell, but they may afford one means for giving the enduring personal interchange embedded in Shakespeare's text a meaningful physicalization.

What then is the responsibility – and the opportunity – for all of us? At this moment in stage history, the director has no alternative but to smell out the flowers of fancy. It is the scholar's and critic's task to appreciate the complexity of his efforts and the elusiveness of his goal.

The director sets players in motion within a defined space and time. It is not enough for him to see that the players speak clearly. Nor that the plot has coherence. Nor that he is conversant with Elizabethan ideas and habits. In addition, he has to discover a logical context for the players' motion, a context that will be not a manifestation of his cleverness but a pulsating world for the text. This context cannot be forced into existence: it must appear organically out of an attempt to understand our present place in the universe and reconcile that understanding with Shakespeare's imperatives of action. Only out of such a comprehensive insight can new frames emerge that will electrify Shakespeare's words anew. Indeed, this is a formidable process and, the more we understand it, the more we can participate in it whether as director, scholar, critic, or spectator.

NOTES

1 Muriel St Clare Byrne, 'Fifty Years of Shakespearian Production: 1898–1948' *Shakespeare Survey* 2 (1949) 15
2 Gareth Lloyd Evans, 'Interpretation or Experience? Shakespeare at Stratford' *Shakespeare Survey* 23 (1970) 131
3 John Russell Brown, 'The Study and Practice of Shakespeare Production' *Shakespeare Survey* 18 (1965) 67
4 Patrick Cruttwell, 'Shakespeare is not our Contemporary' *The Yale Review* 59 (Autumn 1969) 48
5 Robert Weimann, 'Shakespeare on the Modern Stage: Past Significance and Present Meaning' *Shakespeare Survey* 20 (1967) 115
6 Alfred Harbage, 'Shakespeare Without Words' *Proceedings of the British Academy* 55 (1969) 143
7 Peter Brook as quoted by Peter Ansorge, 'Director in Interview' *Plays and Players* (October 1970) 19
8 Weimann, 'Shakespeare on the Modern Stage' 117
9 Kenneth MacGowan, 'The Centre of the Stage' *Theatre Arts Magazine* 5 (April 1921) 92

Jill Levenson /
What the Silence Said: Still Points
in 'King Lear'

Only he who has attained to his own identity, can be silent, only when thinking has reached reality, will it come to a stop.[1]

At the end of Stravinsky's *Les Noces*, an extraordinary series of pauses punctuates the music. Creating and disappointing expectation almost simultaneously, the pauses compel the listener's attention, his energies, with at least as much force as the sounds. When the last vibration from the percussion blends completely with the stillness in which it began, we experience all the resonance of silence.

Silence in drama can create, disappoint, compel, and absorb as vigorously as the most eloquent musical pause. And this profound similarity exists because the dramatist and the composer share the power to create silence. The poet and the novelist must invoke or describe stillness; the painter and the sculptor can express it through space or light. But, for the makers of drama and music, silence itself furnishes means to express, invoke, even define other kinds of reality.

Despite this resemblance, our response to silence in the two modes differs as significantly as our general reactions to music and drama. We allow music to engage all of our faculties. We accept what is mysterious, otherworldly, non-rational, confusing, without questioning or analysis. In effect, we do not feel uncomfortable with those elements in music which are beyond rationalization. With drama, on the other hand, we immediately try to explain everything. An image from Pirandello's *Umorismo* describes the phenomenon: 'By means of logic the brain pumps feelings from the heart and extracts ideas. The feeling passes through the filter and leaves whatever it contains that is hot and cloudy; then it is refrigerated, purified, and i-de-a-lized.'[2] As Professor Harbage said recently of Shakespearian scholarship in particular, 'Sometimes we seem to be witnessing a game of critical scrabble, with the contestants each taking a handful of pieces from the plays and arranging them according to taste, with the one who achieves the most novel arrangement declared the winner of the game.'[3] In the terms of a contemporary philosopher, we are men of faith about music, men of reason about drama; Hebraists in one area, uninspired Hellenists in the other.[4]

Perhaps the drama of today, baffled by feeling and insistently cerebral, forces us to play intellectual games. But the older drama suffers through this rarefied response in production, in the classroom, in scholarship. And Shakespearian drama, which attracts large numbers of followers because of its rich blend of sentient thought, paradoxically suffers the greatest degree of dilution. As one result, we can no longer respond to the silences in Shakespeare's plays. We ignore or catalogue them, censure them as artistic blunders or commend them as artistic coups. But we do not listen to them.

In *King Lear* more than any other Shakespearian drama, silence gives form to the action, substance to the characters and themes. Appropriately, it plays a forceful rôle in the concentrated opening scene, where it combines with ritual to set the love-test parable in high relief from the rest of the play. Like music, drama begins in silence: 'Sound is an event: by its coming it breaks an original silence, and it ends in final silence.'[5] What Gisèle Brelet says about the originating stillness of music applies to plays as well: 'That silence into which music is born is not pure nothingness: in it dwell an attentiveness and an expectation.'[6] Unlike Shakespeare's other tragedies, *King Lear* prolongs the initial silence, the expectation, in the quiet conversation with which it opens. Anticipation grows until it is great enough to receive the protagonist. Then the sennet sounds. At the end of the scene, the jarring medley of court sounds fades into the subdued exchange between Goneril and Regan. This still moment prepares us for the 'final silence' of the scene, which in turn precedes the holocaust that begins with scene ii.

As the opening scene begins and ends in pronounced silence, so it develops or realizes itself. At its heart is Cordelia's stillness, which punctuates keenly the easy flow of words prescribed by ceremony. In music, the silence of punctuation has been called, 'the fullest and most important moment of musical becoming: the very moment when it is made real.'[7] Cordelia's speechlessness is such a moment in drama. Shakespeare created Cordelia's silence, for which no precedent exists in the fifty-odd versions of the Lear story.[8] Even in the folk-tale originals of the love-test, Cordelia's prototypes experience no difficulty expressing themselves, and answer their fathers with either a riddle or, less frequently, a straightforward declaration of filial devotion. Most often the youngest daughter responds simply that she loves her father like salt, and because he does not realize the value of salt, he angrily casts her out. After various adventures, the erring parent, forced to do without salt, learns its merit and that of his daughter. In the terms of folklore, the earliest Cordelias were Ingenious Heroines with didactic rôles who made clear the distinction between the real and apparent values of salt, and therefore between real and apparent values.[9]

When Geoffrey of Monmouth first linked the love-test story with the legend of King Lear and his daughters, he made the Ingenious Heroine more subtle and articulate than her predecessors, though no less didactic. This Cordelia gives her answer eagerly, 'desirous to make trial of ... [her father's] affection':

My father ... is there any daughter that can love her father more than duty requires? In my opinion, whoever pretends to it, must disguise her real sentiments under the veil of flattery. I have always loved you as a father, nor do I yet depart from my purposed duty; and if you insist to have something more extorted from me, hear now the greatness of my affection, which I always bear you, and take this for a short answer to all your questions; look how much you have, so much is your value, and so much do I love you.[10]

In the versions generally considered Shakespeare's immediate sources, Cordelia responds with varying degrees of wordiness, according to different motives. But she always answers at once. The ghost of Cordile in Higgins' *Mirror for Magistrates* speaks succinctly to expose her sisters' flattery: 'I will (said I) at once my love declare and tell ...'[11] Holinshed's Cordeilla is downright verbose:

Knowing the great love and fatherlie zeale that you have alwaies borne towards me (for the which I maie not answere you otherwise than I thinke, and as my conscience leadeth me) I protest unto you, that I have loved you ever, and will continuallie (while I live) love you as my naturall father. And if you would more understand of the love that I beare you, assertaine

your selfe, that so much as you have, so much you are worth, and so much
I love you, and no more.[12]

The Cordeill of *The Fairie Queene* with dignified simplicity 'said she
lov'd him as behoov'd ...'[13] Finally, Cordella in the anonymous Leir
play determines to edify her father by making plain her sisters' flattery
and stressing the integrity of good deeds. Like Shakespeare's Cordelia,
she speaks twice in asides, but they indicate the revulsion hypocrisy
makes her feel. (If Coleridge had known this version of the story, he
might have hesitated to burden Shakespeare's Cordelia with a reaction of disgust.) When Leir misunderstands her words, she tries to
help him interpret the riddle, disparages her sisters, and in the end,
irritates him so greatly that he cuts her off mid-sentence:

> CORDELLA Deare father –
> LEIR Peace, bastard Impe, no issue of King *Leir*,
> I will not heare thee speake one tittle more.[14]

Shakespeare's Cordelia differs strikingly from most of her pre-
cursors. Whereas many Ingenious Heroines intentionally play didactic
rôles during the love-test, she can barely answer Lear's question, and
Kent, the Fool, and Edgar assume the responsibilities of teaching in
the play. The prototypes generally prepare us for their responses; their
purposes in speaking are clear. But Cordelia reveals only her confusion and initially can say nothing.

What does her 'Nothing' express? If we find in it 'some little faulty
admixture of pride and sullenness,' or worse, a great and crucial
fault,[15] like Lear we deceive ourselves by distorting what we hear.
A remark by the composer John Cage about silence suggests what we
might find in Cordelia's: 'Keeping one's mind/on the emptiness,/
on the space/one can see anything can be in it, is, as/a matter of fact,
in it.'[16] Her stillness resonates like the silences of the Bible, fairy-tale
and folk ritual, analogous moments that need reflecting upon.

At once a narrative technique and complex symbol, silence in the
Bible points the inexpressible. S. Goitein's *Studies in Scripture*, an
excellent literary analysis of the Bible, explains one function of silence
in discussing the 'Binding of Isaac':

At the time of the binding itself no words were said – neither by father nor
son; for it is a very important principle in biblical narrative that when the
cry of crisis reaches the point no longer controlled by human speech ... the

writer passes over it in silence. In contrast to this, the action is pictured in
great detail, so that we may feel a shiver at Isaac's destiny ...[17]

Like most profound insights, this one states the obvious, that which
stands in our paths – unnoticed. Here is the familiar passage Goitein
cites:

When they arrived at the place God had pointed out to him, Abraham built
an altar there, and arranged the wood. Then he bound his son Isaac and put
him on the altar on top of the wood. Abraham stretched out his hand and
seized the knife to kill his son. (Gen 22:9–10)[18]

Deep silence characterizes not only the binding, but also the dialogue
with God (where we do not hear Abraham's answer) and the journey.
As Erich Auerbach interprets the story in *Mimesis*: 'the journey is like
a silent progress through the indeterminate and the contingent, a
holding of the breath, a process which has no present ...'[19] 'Everything remains unexpressed.'[20]

Still moments like these again and again heighten our experience
of the Old Testament. The dismissal from Eden happens swiftly in
dramatic images: 'He banished the man, and in front of the garden
of Eden he posted the cherubs, and the flame of a flashing sword, to
guard the way to the tree of life' (Gen 3:24).[21] During Noah's ordeal,
described by many concrete details, no one speaks a word. Although
Joseph's brothers discuss their treachery both before and after they
throw him into the well, narrative understatement accomplishes the
event itself: 'So, when Joseph reached his brothers, they pulled off his
coat, the coat with long sleeves that he was wearing, and catching
hold of him they threw him into the well, an empty well with no water
in it. They then sat down to eat' (Gen 37:23–5). Physical images of
destruction and force express the great anger of Moses, as a whale's
belly indicates the absurdity and extent of Jonah's plight. The week-
long silent reception of Job's calamity speaks for itself.

In the New Testament as well, profound events realize themselves
through silence. Clearly, the most intense stillnesses mark the drama
that culminates in the Passion. The Marys, Martha, and Salome, who
quietly serve Christ and witness his suffering, incarnate 'the moment
in and out of time.' But it is Christ himself whose silence resounds
most forcefully in each of the gospels. According to Matthew, Mark,
and John, Pilate marvels at it: 'Have you no reply at all? See how
many accusations they are bringing against you!' Luke describes the

episode with Herod as a clamour of words – lengthy interrogation, accusations, mockery – with Christ still and separate at the centre.

The impact of Christ's silence greatly impressed the writers of medieval passion plays, who prolonged the biblical moment – sometimes interminably. The scene of the silent response often occurs more than once in these dramas, accompanied generally by the noisy confusion of the frustrated judge(s). Christ answers neither Caiaphas nor Pilate nor Herod, despite coaxing, buffeting, and cursing which grows more and more scatological as the speaker's rage increases. In the Chester version, Caiaphas at first stands dumbfounded by the silence, and Herod threatens to expire for woe if Jesus does not speak, for he has decided that the accused is either 'dumbe and deafe as a doted doe, / or frentick,'[22] The Wakefield Master focusses on Caiaphas' reactions, a study in the perplexity of a stupid man. The priest condescends at first to persuade Christ with a Latin aphorism. This ploy failing, he resorts to one clean and one dirty curse; a rationalization that the accused is frightened; a petulant charge about loquaciousness in the past; a wheedling request to say something, 'Be it hole worde or brokyn'; a decision that Christ must be deaf or witless; and finally, a tantrum: 'So, I cry and I showte!'[23] The *Ludas Coventriae* interrogators turn to beatings when words produce no effect,[24] whereas those in the York Passion Play simply keep on talking. The York version, in fact, could rival any modern absurdist play as a rendering of verbal non-communication. The ultimate *reductio ad absurdum*, a scene that Bottom would have loved to act, shows Herod trying to reach Christ by shouting in strange tongues:

> ... uta! oy! oy! ...
> Say may thou not here me? oy! man, arte thou woode?[25]

One recognizes in these dramatic presentations of Christ's silence a revealing analogue for Cordelia's. In both, pauses in the midst of ceremony, hypocrisy, and wordiness force a confrontation with truths too large for the compass of language. Only the person who refrains from speaking recognizes, as Dante did, 'How scant is language, all too weak to frame my thoughts.' In each of the two situations, tragedy results from the failure of others to grasp this basic fact of life which the Bible continuously teaches implicitly through its narrative style and, of course, explicitly in its content.[26]

When Freud discussed Cordelia's rôle in his essay 'The Theme of the Three Caskets,' he pointed out that in fairy-tale and folklore too silence expresses 'thoughts beyond the reaches of our souls.' For him her quietness signifies death, and Lear's response to it conveys his unreadiness to accept his end.[27] But fairy-tale and folklore do not disclose thus categorically the meanings of stillness. Most frequently they imply that silence is an almost superhuman feat which can accomplish great deeds, break evil spells, and establish its custodian as a person of spiritual strength. The Grimm brothers relate two stories, cited by Freud, in which a maiden releases her brothers from a wicked enchantment which has turned them to swans or ravens by refraining to speak for several years:[28]

... there is but one [way to release them] in the whole world, and that is so hard that you will not save them by it, for you must be dumb for seven years, and may not speak or laugh, and if you speak one single word, and only an hour of the seven years is wanting, all is in vain, and your brothers will be killed by the one word.[29]

In a Transylvanian gypsy story which has many analogues, the hero saves a beautiful maid from an evil spirit by undergoing three hours of various torments without making a sound.[30] Through the sacrifice of her lovely voice, Hans Christian Andersen's Little Mermaid becomes a spirit of the air with a voice like ethereal music.[31] The dumbness of young Prince Ivan in an old Russian tale emblematizes his virtues. His parents, who misinterpret its significance, suffer a curse for their obtuseness.[32] Sweet Martha, in a variant of the Cinderella story, saves her own life and receives rich gifts by maintaining silence as she wards off death by frost.[33]

The special strength required to keep still on crucial occasions graces few fairy-tale protagonists. For every hero who achieves silence, another fails. The would-be deliverer of the legendary White Lady in the White Tower at Prague shouts in pain, prompted by three bayonet stabs in his breast.[34] In a Hessian story with a number of parallels, a forester finds it impossible to maintain the silence which could have saved a maiden bewitched into a swan.[35] An Irish variant of the Grimm swan tale describes the tragic fate of a sister who cannot remain quiet for crying;[36] and the wicked sisters of sweet Martha perish because they are 'rough of the tongue.'[37] Moreover, in many tales where an evil spell or threat forces the hero to suffer anguish and humiliation in silence, animals take over his speaking function or a revealing accident occurs which relieves and sometimes liberates the victim.[38] Ordinary mortals cannot bear too much silence.

Fairy-tale suggests a connection between silence and the super-human; folklore, with its emphasis on ritual silence, openly acknowl-edges the link. Perfect stillness, for example, confers special powers to see the realm of Faery.[39] Since noise disturbs the powerful, protec-tive spirits of the universe, any task that calls for supernatural assist-ance – from the sowing of flax to the performance of magic rites – must take place in wordless reverence. On the other hand, vehement uproar effectively dispossesses evil spirits.[40]

Like the Bible, then, fairy-tale and folklore reveal 'that language does have its frontiers ... which give proof of a transcendent presence in the fabric of the world.'[41] Additional evidence for this view about language and silence, already charted by other writers, occurs abun-dantly in classical mythology and both western and oriental philoso-phies.[42] In the context of this fruitful material, Cordelia's punctuating silence in the first scene and Lear's failure to understand it grow rich in implication.

When we first meet Lear, his bearing, his conduct, and the behav-iour of his court objectify order and control. The procession, the map of Britain already divided into three portions, the formal se-quences of address to his daughters, and to Burgundy and France, the rhetoric of his speeches, suggest that Lear governs a world well forti-fied against surprises. Ritual, it appears, has long captivated feeling and governed its expression. Consequently, Lear can demand public utterances of love from his children without making anyone but Cor-delia noticeably ill at ease. Even for such personal communications, forms exist which eliminate the possibility of awkward emotional out-bursts. Goneril and Regan accept these forms, indeed use them ex-pertly. Not the least bit startled by Lear's request, each answers him immediately in words that seem prescribed by custom for the occa-sion. They do not pause to reflect, to calculate; their expressions of love are automatic:

> LEAR Goneril,
> Our eldest-born, speak first.
> GONERIL Sir, I love you more than word can wield the matter ...
>
> (I.i.53–5)[43]

Terence Hawkes has pointed out play on the word *love* in their answers, meaning both estimate and hold in affection,[44] a subtlety which could reveal to a careful listener signs of treachery. But Lear is not a careful listener. He does not hear hypocrisy; he will not understand silence. At this moment in the play, he responds only to the denotative meanings of words.[45]

Cordelia's silence dramatically exposes Lear's perilous dependence upon the semblances of order. She cannot answer him because her unwieldy devotion resists the tether of language: 'I am sure my love's / More ponderous than my tongue' (1.i.77–8). Her reply is not automatic. And it is not wilful: 'I *cannot* heave / My heart into my mouth ...' (1.i.91–2). In Cordelia's silence, Lear confronts what I have called before a basic fact of life. That '... there are actions of the spirit rooted in silence. It is difficult to *speak* of these ...'[46] That 'the ineffable lies beyond the frontiers of the word,'[47] and human efforts to control experience often limit it, 'cutting the world down to size.'[48] But Lear does not comprehend these commonplaces. He behaves as if, in George Steiner's terms, the sum of human experience could be enclosed within the bounds of rational discourse, and 'all truth and realness ... [could] be housed inside the walls of language.'[49]

Lear's confusion and anger in confrontation with Cordelia's 'Nothing,' her silence, ring psychologically true. For the western mind has again and again shown itself fearful of voids and stillness, the indefinite and the immense. Melville's chapter on the terrifying whiteness of Moby Dick provides impressive testament to this familiar sensation: 'Is it that by its indefiniteness it shadows forth the heartless voids and immensities of the universe, and thus stabs us from behind with the thought of annihilation, when beholding the white depths of the milky way?'[50] The thoughts of a contemporary writer on silence effectively interpret Melville's: '... silence does not seem to be as assertive, as committal, as speech ... Perhaps the information given by not speaking has in it too much potentiality and possible surprise; it requires great confidence to endure it.'[51] Lear cannot endure it at this point; cannot even begin to understand that stillness can contain not only potential for evil but also potential for good,[52] not only signs of outrage but also hints of apocalypse.[53] Trepidation often causes us to forget that silence can affirm, however tentatively: 'Not one / sound fears the silence that extinguishes it. / But if you avoid it, that's a pity, because / it resembles life very closely & life and it / are essentially a cause for joy. People say, / sometimes, / timidly.'[54] In eastern philosophy we find the most optimistic appreciation of the void:

> Thirty spokes unite in one nave,
> And because of the part where nothing exists we have the use of
>   a carriage wheel.

> Clay is molded into vessels,
> And because of the space where nothing exists we are able to use them as vessels.
> Doors and windows are cut out in the walls of a house,
> And because they are empty spaces, we are able to use them.
> Therefore, on the one hand we have the benefit of existence, and on the other of non-existence.[55]

Lear, however, finds only negation and destructiveness in Cordelia's silence, which so obviously affirms her love as it nullifies the wordy vows of Goneril and Regan.

In the tragic events which result from Lear's misunderstanding, his own silences and ultimate comprehension of Cordelia's serve as important registers to his crescent perceptiveness. Cordelia's long absence, a kind of stillness, and her moments of speechlessness when she returns, mark the play with reminders of her constancy and the profound truths Lear could not grasp at the beginning. Unchanging in her inexpressible love for Lear, she can barely articulate her grief when late in the tragedy she learns how he has suffered:

> KENT Made she no verbal question?
> GENTLEMAN Faith, once or twice she heav'd the name of 'father'
> Pantingly forth, as if it press'd her heart;
> Cried 'Sisters! sisters! Shame of ladies! sisters!
> Kent! father! sisters! What? i' th' storm! i' th' night?
> Let pity not be believ'd!' (IV.iii.25–30)

Immediately before they are reunited, Cordelia, like an Old Testament figure, speaks not of her feelings, but of physical things and faith:

> CORDELIA Alack! 'tis he: why, he was met even now ...
> Crown'd with rank fumiter and furrow-weeds,
> With hardocks, hemlock, nettles, cuckoo-flowers,
> Darnel, and all the idle weeds that grow
> In our sustaining corn. (IV.iv.1–6)

> All bless'd secrets,
> All you unpublish'd virtues of the earth,
> Spring with my tears! (IV.iv.15–17)

And when they finally meet, her humble gestures and her tears make fluent her faltering words. At the end of the play she holds the stage in prolonged and profound silence. To Lear's joyful fantasy of their

future as God's spies, she responds simply by weeping, a muteness as
telling and complex as her first. The stillness of her death expresses
something new: 'The silence of the dead Cordelia is a final summary
of the presence of what Donne calls "absence, darkness, death; things
which are not," throughout the play, wherever a question is asked and
not answered, or a command is not obeyed.'[56]

While Cordelia remains constant, still, and comprehending, Lear,
dynamic and generally verbose, uncovers through his incredible pain
the values he had instinctively honoured but never understood. Until
his tragedy, there had always stood between Lear and wisdom what
Maynard Mack calls the imperative mood.[57] Other scholars have
noticed as well how Lear commands, pronounces, curses, invokes,
defies.[58] He does not argue, reflect, or reply to objections. He does
not doubt. The silence that precedes insight finds no lodging in him.
When intimations come that he has misjudged his daughters, and the
imperative mood shifts slightly toward the interrogative, there is no
one left in the kingdom he governed to answer his questions directly.
Because of his own blindness, he now lives in a world where 'the relation of meaning to verbal expression is in some way defective, oblique
or trumped-up.'[59] Goneril and Regan, as we have seen, adeptly distort
the meanings of words. Edmund creates his own definitions:

> EDMUND Our father's love is to the bastard Edmund
> As to th' legitimate. Fine word, 'legitimate'!
> Well, my legitimate, if this letter speed,
> And my invention thrive, Edmund the base
> Shall top th' legitimate – ...   (I.ii.17–21)

Kent must borrow other accents to serve Lear, and Edgar and the
Fool survive by riddling.

When ritual and linguistic forms disintegrate for Lear, he draws
upon his tremendous reserve of sensibility to face and defy the remaining vacuum. Silence distinguishes this process which mysteriously
transmutes anguish into cognition. In fact, silence is its only witness.
We experience Lear's pain and the resulting enlightenment, but the
moment of their conjunction is interior and private. Only after his
Knight remarks 'a great abatement of kindness' in Goneril's household, does Lear admit his own awareness of the slight, unmentioned
until now: 'Thou but rememb'rest me of mine own conception: I
have perceived a most faint neglect of late ...' (I.iv.63–4, 70–2). He
has also quietly perceived the Fool's unhappiness since Cordelia's
departure, and Goneril's ill humour: 'You are too much of late i' th'

frown' (I.iv.198). Though Lear's misjudgment of Cordelia tutors him in shame,[60] he mentions her rarely, elliptically, during her long absence from the stage: 'O most small fault, / How ugly didst thou in Cordelia show!' (I.iv.275–6); 'I did her wrong, –' (I.v.24). In Lear's relation with the Fool, as Granville-Barker astutely describes it, 'His silences are ... pregnant. He listens and finds cheer in the Fool's chatter and song, throws him an answer or so to keep it alive, snarls now and then like an old lion if a sting goes too deep. Yet his thoughts, we can tell, are away.'[61] While Kent relates the story of his disgrace, Lear says nothing. And when madness comes, when Lear sees most feelingly, speech wavers and sometimes goes out:

> I can scarce speak to thee; thou'lt not believe
> With how deprav'd a quality – O Regan!   (II.iv.137–8)

> I will have such revenges on you both
> That all the world shall – I will do such things,
> What they are, yet I know not, but they shall be
> The terrors of the earth.   (II.iv.281–4)

> No, I will be the pattern of all patience;
> I will say nothing.   (III.ii.37–8)

Before the mock trial on the heath, Lear stands still and amazed, and, in its wake, prepares for an instant of respite: 'Make no noise, make no noise; draw the curtains: so, so' (III.vi.85–6). Later the still distraught Lear meets Gloucester near Dover and counsels: 'Look with thine ears ... Hark, in thine ear ...' (IV.vi.152, 154). The words resonate, percipient, for Lear has learned to listen to silence, in silence.

Auerbach's penetrating study of biblical narrative illuminates the dramatic presentation of Lear's growing wisdom:

[Biblical style is] the externalization of only so much of the phenomena as is necessary for the purpose of the narrative, all else left in obscurity; the decisive points of the narrative alone are emphasized, what lies between is nonexistent ... thoughts and feeling remain unexpressed, are only suggested by the silence and the fragmentary speeches; the whole, permeated with the most unrelieved suspense and directed toward a single goal ... remains mysterious and 'fraught with background.'[62]

Lear's silences point his most intense experiences of pain and insight.

He may, like Job, describe his discoveries in concrete, physical terms, images which reveal how acutely he suffers and perceives on his very pulses, but the description inevitably follows the experience, which happened in silence.

At the tragedy's conclusion, Lear again confronts Cordelia silent. Understanding the implications of this stillness, he cries out against it, tries to evoke from it a different kind of message: 'What is 't thou say'st? Her voice was ever soft, / Gentle and low, an excellent thing in woman' (v.iii.272–3). His futile efforts make him impatient, abstracted, and, at the very moment when he shatters, omniscient. His last words direct us towards Cordelia, towards the lips that spoke so profoundly when they were still: 'an image which presents most of what can be said about the physical limitations to an aspiring mind.'[63] The tragedy of Lear, begun in prolonged stillness, muted at crucial points in its development, ends deep in silence. Ends with its most compelling motif, which expresses what its language can barely articulate:

> ... this world of fact we love
> Is unsubstantial stuff:
> All the rest is silence
> On the other side of the wall;
> And the silence ripeness,
> And the ripeness all.[64]

NOTES

1 Dieter Wellershoff, 'Failure of an Attempt at De-Mythologization: Samuel Beckett's Novels,' from *Der Gleichgültige: Versuche über Hemingway, Camus, Benn, und Beckett* (Cologne 1963), translated and reprinted in *Samuel Beckett* Martin Esslin, ed (Englewood Cliffs, New Jersey 1965) 107

2 Luigi Pirandello *Umorismo* (Rome 1960) 145–57, translated and reprinted in *Modern Drama* Anthony Caputi, ed (New York 1966) 476

3 Alfred Harbage, 'Shakespeare Without Words,' *Proceedings of the British Academy* 55 (1969) 131

4 William Barrett *Irrational Man: A Study in Existential Philosophy* (New York 1958) 77

5 Gisèle Brelet, 'Music and Silence' *La revue musicale* 22 (1946), reprinted in *Reflections on Art* Susanne K. Langer, ed (New York 1961) 103

6 Ibid 104

7 Ibid 113

8 My conclusions about Shakespeare's creation of Cordelia's silence are based primarily on material found in Wilfrid Perrett's definitive study, 'The

Story of King Lear from Geoffrey of Monmouth to Shakespeare' *Palaestra* 35 (1904).

9 Perrett, 'The Story of King Lear' 10–13

10 *Geoffrey of Monmouth's British History* in *Six Old English Chronicles* J.A. Giles, ed (London 1891) 115

11 *Parts Added to 'The Mirror for Magistrates': By John Higgins & Thomas Blenerhasset* Lily B. Campbell, ed (Cambridge 1946) 148

12 *Holinshed's Chronicle* Allardyce and Josephine Nicoll, eds (London and New York 1927) 226

13 Edmund Spenser *The Faerie Queene* introduction by J.W. Hales (London 1910) I, 290

14 *The History of King Leir, 1605* W.W. Greg, ed, Malone Society reprints (London 1907) B^r–B2^r

15 G.R. Elliott, 'The Initial Contrast in *Lear*,' *Journal of English and Germanic Philology* 58 (1959) 259

16 John Cage *Silence* (Cambridge, Mass. 1966) 176

17 S. Goitein *Iyyunim B'Mikra* (Tel Aviv 1957) 78. This passage and the book's title were translated for me from the Hebrew by Professor Monford Harris.

18 All biblical quotations come from the Jerusalem version.

19 Erich Auerbach *Mimesis* Willard Trask, trans (New York 1957) 7

20 Ibid 9

21 In *Paradise Lost* (XII.624–8), Milton introduces this silence into his description of the expulsion; Eve makes her final speech 'and *Adam* heard / Well pleas'd, but answer'd not; for now too nigh / Th' Archangel stood, and from the other Hill / To thir fixt Station, all in bright array / The Cherubim descended .. '

22 *The Chester Plays* Dr Matthews, ed, Early English Text Society edition (London 1916) II, 288

23 *The Wakefield Pageants in the Towneley Cycle* A.C. Cawley, ed (Manchester 1958) 81–2

24 *Ludus Coventriae or The Plaie called Corpus Christi* K.S. Block, ed, Early English Text Society edition (London 1922) 276, 286

25 *York Mystery Plays* L. Toulmin Smith, ed (New York 1885) 300

26 Passages that come to mind immediately are Psalms 4:4, 39:9, 65:2; Isaiah 53:7; Revelation 8:1.

27 Sigmund Freud, 'The Theme of the Three Caskets' *Imago* 2 (1913), translated and reprinted in *On Creativity and the Unconscious* Benjamin Nelson, ed (New York 1958) 65–75

28 *Grimm's Fairy Tales* Margaret Hunt, trans, James Stern, ed (New York 1944) nos IX and XLIX

29 Grimm Brothers, no IX, 62

30 Edwin Sidney Hartland *The Science of Fairy Tales* (London 1925) 246–7

31 *Hans Andersen's Fairy Tales* L.W. Kingsland, trans (London 1961) 84

32 'Prince Ivan, the Witch Baby and the Little Sister of the Sun' in *Old Peter's Russian Tales* Arthur Ransome, ed (London and Edinburgh 1916) 136–54

33 'Frost' in Ransome *Old Peter's Russian Tales* 54–69

34 Hartland *The Science of Fairy Tales* 245

35 Ibid 259

36 'The Unique Tale' in *The King of Ireland's Son* Padraic Colum, ed (New York 1916) 130–47

37 'Frost' 67

38 See, for example, Grimm Brothers, nos XXI and LXXXIX; 'The Girl Who Sought Her Nine Brothers' in *Tales from a Finnish Tupa* Aili Kolehmainen, trans, James Cloyd Bowman and Margery Bianco, eds (Chicago 1936) 116–25; 'Guleesh' in *Celtic Fairy Tales* Joseph Jacobs, ed (New York and London nd) 6–28.

39 Hartland *The Science of Fairy Tales* 64

40 Detailed references to the rôle of silence in folk ritual are most accessible through Stith Thompson, *Motif-Index of Folk-Literature*, 6 vols (rev. & enl., Bloomington, Indiana 1955–8) and J.G. Frazer *The Golden Bough* (3rd ed rev. & enl., London 1911–15).

41 George Steiner *Language and Silence* (New York 1967) 39

42 See, for example, E.E. Kellett, 'Dramatic Silences' *Contemporary Review* 132 (1927) 482–90; Steiner *Language and Silence*; Paul Goodman, 'On Not Speaking' *The New York Review of Books* (20 May 1971) 40–3

43 All references to the text of *King Lear* in this paper come from the Arden edition, Kenneth Muir, ed (London 1964).

44 Terence Hawkes, ' "Love" in *King Lear*' *Review of English Studies* n.s. 10 (1959), reprinted in *Shakespeare: 'King Lear'* Frank Kermode, ed (London 1969) 179–83

45 Cf Sigurd Burckhardt *Shakespearean Meanings* (Princeton 1968) 239

46 Steiner *Language and Silence* 12

47 Ibid

48 Goodman, 'On Not Speaking' 41

49 Steiner *Language and Silence* 13–14

50 Herman Melville *Moby Dick* Newton Arvin, introd (New York 1957) 192

51 Goodman 'On Not Speaking' 42

52 Barbara Everett, 'The New *King Lear*,' *Critical Quarterly* 2 (1960), reprinted in Kermode *Shakespeare: 'King Lear'* 199

53 Ihab Hassan *The Literature of Silence* (New York 1967) 214

54 Cage *Silence* 173

55 Quoted from Lao-tse by Barrett, *Irrational Man* 234

56 Everett, 'The New *King Lear*' 199

57 Maynard Mack *'King Lear' in Our Time* (London 1966) 89

58 See especially Paul A. Jorgensen *Lear's Self-Discovery* (Berkeley and Los Angeles 1967) 70 ff.

59 Winifred M.T. Nowottny, 'Some Aspects of the Style of *King Lear*,' *Shakespeare Survey* 13 (1960) 52

60 See Kent's speeches, IV.iii.39–48.

61 Harley Granville-Barker *Prefaces to Shakespeare* (Princeton 1946) I, 287. Granville-Barker makes many enlightening remarks about Lear and Cordelia's silences; so does Arnold Isenberg, 'Cordelia Absent' *Shakespeare Quarterly* 2 (1951) 185–94

62 Auerbach *Mimesis* 9

63 Everett, 'The New *King Lear*' 200

64 W.H. Auden, 'The Sea and the Mirror' in *For the Time Being* (London 1945) 8

Robert Weimann /
Shakespeare's Wordplay: Popular Origins and Theatrical Functions

If Shakespeare's verbal art and his stagecraft can be seen as interacting parts of a larger whole, then wordplay, like other figures of dramatic speech, may more closely be related to the tradition and the process of the Elizabethan theatre as a social institution. It is true, every new study of Shakespeare's wordplay will feel deeply indebted to the field-work of editors, such as John Dover Wilson, or to historians of Elizabethan English, such as Helge Kökeritz, or to such perceptive studies of the subject as M.M. Mahood's *Shakespeare's Wordplay* in which Shakespeare's puns are viewed in their structural context and meaning. Also there is the interesting connection between Shakespeare's wordplay and the tradition of Renaissance rhetoric, and certainly the critical habit of close reading and verbal exegesis has considerably increased our awareness of the presence and the import of Shakespeare's puns.

Still, to conceive of Shakespeare's plays as some kind of symbolic or dramatic poetry, or to relate dramatic speech to the practice and theory of Renaissance rhetoric, has imposed limitations upon an understanding not only of the origins and dramatic functions but also of the total meaning of Shakespeare's wordplay. If the forms and figures of his language must be seen as the work of 'a competent rhetorician' who had grasped, as T.W. Baldwin says, right from the beginning all 'the fundamentals of the current rhetorical system,'[1] this does not mean that Shakespeare's use of the arts of dramatic speech can all be traced to, or understood as part of, his reception of

Renaissance rhetoric and logic. Surely, the claim made by Sister Miriam Joseph now appears excessive and, in several respects, questionable: 'Rightly to appreciate Shakespeare's puns, one should regard them as examples of four highly esteemed figures of Renaissance rhetoric.'[2] Rather, let me suggest that the rhetorical approach to Shakespeare's wordplay, like the approach to his plays as symbols or poems, is based on, and has brought with it, a certain methodological perspective in the light of which the intimate links, in fact the interactions between Shakespeare's stagecraft and his verbal art, have largely been left unexplored. But the more we understand Shakespeare's work as that of a poet in the theatre, the more comprehensively the forms and figures of his language, including wordplay, can be seen, not merely as part of some poetic or symbolic structure, but functionally in the context of the theatre in which verbal art and social action have become indivisible.

To plead for a more comprehensive approach to wordplay in the drama is not to belittle Shakespeare's verbal artistry or to question the immense importance of his rhetorical training or to minimize its impact on his dramatic language, but it may be one way of drawing attention to the significance and the complexity of popular traditions of speech and acting in Shakespeare's medieval heritage. Even though Shakespeare's debt to the diction of common life has quite often been observed,[3] it seems characteristic of the direction of Shakespearian studies over the past thirty years that we do not have even an exploratory study of the native or popular sources of Shakespeare's wordplay. To say this is to argue not for an uncritical type of source study, but for an approach to origins as an element of structure – structure that is, not in the formalist sense of an autonomous aesthetic or linguistic whole, but as a moment in the social mode and theatrical function of dramatic speech. In this, social meaning and poetic structure become inseparable in their correlation to the theatrical process. It is within these correlations that I propose to discuss some (certainly not all) of the changing dramatic functions and meanings of wordplay, and in order to bring out some of their more neglected aspects I would like to map out some historical perspective of the tradition of wordplay in the pre-Elizabethan drama.

If, to begin with, we glance at some examples of wordplay in the medieval drama, we should not expect to find anything like the elaborate or subtle conceited wit of Lyly's or the infinite variety and ingenuity of Shakespeare's quibbles. But we do find a kind of punning, a jingling with rhyme, alliteration, and meaning in a context which – from one point of view – is remarkably superior to anything that we have in the sixteenth-century Senecan tradition or the humanist drama of the schools. It is the context of a living and largely communal kind of theatre in which dramatic speech and audience address, dialogue and aside, rôle and actor, constantly interact. The early forms of wordplay, as they reflect this very interaction, can profitably be studied in this wider context of dramaturgy. In fact, a theory of the meaning of wordplay can hardly be abstracted from this theatrical frame of reference which, in its broadest common denominator, is marked by the transition from ritual to representational drama, in the course of which a new imaginative and pictorial kind of awareness of human nature in society is born through the art of drama.

This, of course, is a vast generalization of a long process of growth, and in order to illustrate its beginnings, one would have to go back as far as *Mactacio Abel, Coliphizacio,* or the Croxton *Play of the Sacrament.* Here is that most astonishing type, sometimes called Garcio (as in Wakefield or Chester), who – much like Brewbarret in York, or the Croxton Colle, or Hawkyn in *Mary Magdalene* – invariably acts as cheeky boy and impertinent commentator. This figure is the first in pre-Shakespearian drama of whom it can be said that he has a strange and striking predilection 'to mistake the word.'

Take, for instance, Garcio as he echoes his master's proclamation of indemnity:

> CAYM I commaund you in the kyngis nayme,
> GARCIO And in my masteres, fals Cayme,
> CAYM That no man at thame fynd fawt ne blame,
> GARCIO Yey, cold rost is at my masters hame.
> CAYM Nowther with hym nor with his knafe,
> GARCIO What, I hope my master rafe.
> CAYM For thay ar trew, full many-fold.
> GARCIO My master suppys no coyle bot cold.
> CAYM The kyng wryt is you vntill.
> GARCIO Yit ete I neuer half my fill.
> CAYM The kyng will that thay be safe.
> GARCIO Yey, a draght of drynke fayne wold I hayfe.
> CAYM At thare awne will let tham wafe.
> GARCIO My stomak is redy to receyfe ... (419–31)[4]

This is an astonishing mixture of dramatic speech and extra-dramatic aside, which seems, throughout, to be inspired by some inverting pattern of interpolation which, though not amounting to any actual punning, is certainly conducive to playing with rhyme and meaning. When, for instance, Caym orders his boy to silence the audience and announce the proclamation of his indemnity ('Caym ... Bot thou must be my good boy, and cry oyes, oyes, oy!'), Garcio answers: 'Browes, browes, to thi boy' (415–17). Again, this is no more than a jingle, but it is based on a kind of verbal topsy-turvydom, which achieves its most grotesque forms of inversion in *Mary Magdalene*, where Hawkyn, cheeky boy and servant to a 'presbyter,' says a mocking nonsensical service, an obscene mixture of crazy Latin and pure alliterative nonsense. But he does so only after his master, that strange kind of a 'presbyter,' has asked him to ring the church bells, set up the altar, all in 'grett solemnyte.' But the boy seems to mistake his mission and asks back: 'whatt, master, woldyst þou have þi lemman to þi beddes syde?'[5]

Whatever the origins of the Garcio, Hawkyn, or Colle type, which is beyond all doubt related to Jack Finney,[6] that equally cheeky and hungry and rebellious servant in the Mumming plays, it is the dramaturgy of his position which seems significant. Like other figures of fun and foolery, he is very much at home on the *platea* and always close to the audience; he can – as the Wakefield Garcio does – open the scene of the play, greet the audience, and introduce himself with the customary direct address: 'All hayll, all hayll ... ffor here com I, a mery lad.'[7] There are obviously strong communal ties between the actor and the audience and it is out of the strength of these ties that Garcio can, from the *platea* position of his extra-dramatic asides, deliberately distort and invert the word. To characterize the complexity of his position in the play, one can say that it is a social, a spatial, as well as a verbal one, and that it is the interrelation among these aspects which establishes the context of mistaking and inverting the word. It is a highly flexible context in which the figure is (on the one hand) prepared to accept the subject of conversation in its virtual or literal meaning, while yet (on the other hand) he retains the obscene or irreverent freedom to be released from it.

This context is not primarily one of character: it is a dramaturgic one, and it is in the tradition of this dramaturgy that some (certainly not all) of Shakespeare's aggressive and obscene wordplay is rooted. But its basic requirements are there quite clearly, in the Wakefield cycle or the Croxton *Play of the Sacrament*. There Garcio and Hawkyn (just like the Tudor Vice or the Elizabethan clown) seem to perform on two levels: on the one hand they can perfectly integrate themselves into the representational mode of dramatic dialogue, thus associating themselves with an element of illusion around the *locus* of the moral or serious scene. On the other hand, they can easily dissociate themselves from the logic of verbal exchange, and perform outside the values and the illusion of such scenes, thus assuming a kind of *platea* position of public sport and social criticism from which their utterances are no longer perceived by their potential partners in dialogue. It is this extremely flexible position half-way between the post-ritual tradition of the actor's self-expression and his growing integration into the mimetic logic of dialogue which serves as an important matrix of wordplay in the more popular pre-Shakespearian drama.

In order to view this original impulse of native wordplay as part of a wider meaning, it seems important to observe the connections between the verbal expression of inversion and that more general element of topsy-turvydom, or nonsense, or madness which, in its more serious or grotesque forms, amounts to the turning upside down of accepted social norms and values. It is related to an 'unholy zest' which 'readily turns to a positive zest-for-unholiness' by which, as A.P. Rossiter suggested, some 'shadows of primitive paganism survived.'[8] But if this was so, and if there was indeed some lingering echo of a more primitive kind of ritual drama, the verbal forms of inversion are already transitional in the sense that on the one hand they have ceased to serve as part of a genuine ritual while on the other hand they have not yet been integrated into the representational mode of modern drama. Having lost their ancient ritual functions, they have not yet achieved the mimetic quality of modern dramatic dialogue. But these transitions and contradictions between self-expressive post-ritual release and mimetic representation furnish the very grounds on which the early forms of wordplay seem to thrive. Indeed these contradictions are incorporated or assimilated in the social, spatial, and verbal structures of the early forms of mistaking the word.

This, of course, is still a sweeping over-simplification which – even if it helps to approach the native origins of wordplay in terms of theatrical functions – says very little about the actual developments and uses of wordplay in pre-Shakespearian drama. In other words – and this is a question that must be faced – are there any points of contact between these early and elementary forms of mistaking the word and the infinite bounty of Shakespeare's highly sophisticated puns?

Although it should again be stressed that the popular tradition of
punning provides none of the more refined attractions of Shakespeare's 'fatal Cleopatra,' yet there are points of contact and, what
is more, Shakespeare seems to have been aware of them. When, in
The Two Gentlemen of Verona, Launce interprets his 'mastership'
as his 'master's ship,' Speed has the pregnant reply: 'Well, your old
vice still: mistake the word' (III.i.279).[9] This reference to the Vice
tradition, itself in the highly appropriate form of a pun, points to the
mainstream in which the tradition of mistaking the word was very
much alive in the late fifteenth and sixteenth centuries. This is not
the place to inquire into the traditional background of the Vice whose
dramatic vitality can definitely not be understood in terms of its
'homiletic function,' or even 'homiletic showmanship.'[10] This double-
faced figure of allegory and farce has a more complex background,
in which the non-allegorical element of 'folk-lore and pagan demonology' (as G.R. Owst calls it) has usually been underrated. At any
rate, it is as a medium of disorder and as a vehicle of the rejection of
the ruling social and Christian values that the Vice achieves the irreverent and obscene quality of his wordplay, just as it is its undoubted
links with the Folk-fool and Folly-figures of popular miming which
account for his immense theatrical vitality.[11] To illustrate this traditional element it must suffice here to refer to the continuity in the use
of such dramatic devices as the inverted proclamation which Garcio
and Colle had used as a medium of verbal topsy-turvydom. In the
moralities we have this same inversion of public statements, as in *All
for Money*, where a note in the text *expressis verbis* directs the actor
to extemporize his own version of topsy-turvydom – when it says:
'*Here the vyce shal turne the proclamation to some contrarie sence
at euery time all for money hath read it, and here foloweth the
proclamation ...*[12] The Vice, here as elsewhere, is eminently capable
of playing with words and gestures, and – as it appears – with the
tone of his voice; for the 'contrarie sence' which he is to produce
involves a choice of attitude so that the Vice in his wanton way asks
back (and perhaps harkens back to the cheeky boy tradition) and
says: 'Shall I in my mannes voyce or in my boyes voyce it declare?'
(1007)

This indicates more than verbal frolic: the actor momentarily dissociates himself from his own rôle, and the audience has before it not
the dramatic figure, but the real actor who shares or inspires its own
mood of release or, perhaps, negation. The Vice is extremely good
at having his 'contrarie sence'; in this he anticipates the Elizabethan
clown, for his capacity for impertinence is by no means confined to

the garbling of a proclamation, or to the exercise of his extemporal wit, for that matter. As early as in the undoubtedly popular *Mankind*, the figures of vice open the play with a prolonged series of irreverent verbal inversions of the standards of virtue. In the midst of his excessively latinized exhortations, Mercy, the orthodox representative of the word of the church, uses a biblical symbol of grace: '... The corn xall be sauyde, þe chaffe xall be brente.' Myscheffe, the major Vice, jumps to upset the homiletic metaphor by a cavalcade of punning and jingling 'contrary senses.' First he says, echoing the most widespread of all folk-play formulas:

> leue yowur chaffe, leue yowur corn, leue yowur dalyacyon!
> Yowur wytt ys lytyll, yowur hede ys mekyll, 3e are full of
> predycacyon.   (46–7)[13]

Not content with the nonsensical rejection of the homiletic metaphor, he proceeds to challenge Mercy and to drive him into the magic web of his own mad way of playing with words:

> But, ser, I prey [yow] þis questyon to claryfye:
> Dryff-draff, mysse-masche;
> Sume was corn, and sume was chaffe;
> My dame seyde my name was Raffe;
> On-schett yowur lokke, and take an halpenye.   (48–52)

And when Mercy, upon this renewed impertinency, politely remonstrates with the unwelcome Vice by asking him what he has come for, Myscheff takes his question literally and finally mistakes the word in the most thoroughgoing pagan fashion of an English country workman, when he answers, with seeming ingenuousness that he has come for work as a 'wyntur corn-threscher,' because he heard it was said 'the corn xuld be sauyde, and the chaffe xulde be feryde.' And from there he proceeds with an absolute farrago of commonsense and nonsense, which is worth quoting because the mistaking of the word is metaphorically expanded into a down-to-earth image of common misunderstanding:

> 'Corn seruit bredibus, chaffe horsibus, straw fyrybusque';
> Thys ys as moche to say to yowur leude wndyrstondynge,
> As þe corn xall serue to brede at þe nexte bakynge, ...
> The chaff, to horse xall be goode produce;
> When a man ys for-colde, þe straw may be brent,
> And so forth, &*cetera.*   (57–9; 61–3)

Whereupon Mercy (who obviously despairs of achieving any meaningful communication) says:

> A-voyde, goode broþer! 3e ben culpable
> To interrupte thus my talkynge delectable.
>
> ...
>
> Hye yow forthe on fote, brother, in Godis name!   (64f, 68)

But Myscheff now relinquishes his assumed rôle of a 'wyntur corn-threscher' and falls back into the extra-dramatic expression of his own true social function, and says: 'I say, ser, I am cumme hedyr to make yow game' (69). This is the kind of dramaturgy from which the early native wordplay receives its most sustained energy. Here it is possible to have a quibbling *reductio* of the symbolic content of metaphor, where a blunt kind of semantic pun goes hand in hand with alliterative or rhymed jingling, such as 'Dryff-draff,' 'mysse-masche,' 'sume was chaffe,' 'my name was Raffe,' etc.

But the important point is that this reflects a social and dramatic mode which anticipates the same function of verbal inversion that we have in some of Shakespeare's wordplay which can also serve as 'an outlet for scepticism about authority,' by undermining 'the social prestige' of such words as 'blood,' 'state,' 'great,' 'high,' and 'grace.'[14] Having lost any truly ritual quality, this early form of wordplay yet retains an element of the actor's sense of his social identity, which is not integrated into the representational function of dramatic allegory. While the allegorical figure of Virtue throughout submits to the disciplined imitation of verbal exchange, the Vice does not. On the contrary, his replies (if they may be so called) have a riddling quality of seeming irrelevance, which must (like Richard Tarlton's or even Shakespeare's porter's and grave-diggers') have invited the audience to assist in solving the riddling and quibbling allusions. Thus, the social act of verbal inversion can be said both to reflect and to provoke a certain dramaturgic position which must have been physically and morally close to a popular audience.

It is this social, spatial, and verbal release or distance from the representational forms of dialogue which Myscheff shares with the Colle and Garcio type as well as with several Elizabethan conventions of character. They all seem to take their cues from their partners in dialogue, but the way they reply is not in the nature of a reply at all; rather, it is like some of Hamlet's wilful retorts, impertinent in both the etymological and the modern sense of the term: 'impertinent' in the sense that it is not relevant to the logic or the subject of the discourse, and impertinent in the modern sense of 'cheeky' or 'saucy.' To oversimplify this point, one might say that the irrelevant aspect indicates the post-ritual tradition of the actor's festive release from representation; and that the cheeky aspect points to the degree in which this ritual tradition has been assimilated to the mimetic form and pressure of modern dialogue – dialogue, that is, as a dramatic image of the reality of human conversation in society. Here, as in the manner of Hamlet's or Lear's madness, we have 'matter and impertinency mix'd! Reason in madness!' (*King Lear* IV.vi.175 f).

The dramatist who uses 'impertinency,' be it in wordplay or in the convention of 'mad' speech, does so because he can exploit both the post-ritual and the mimetic dimensions of dialogue: he can still integrate the actor into the communal occasion of which the audience itself is a part, but he can already abstract the actor from this occasion and create the illusion of the dramatic image of human conversation. On the one hand the actor still has the traditional capacity for expressing himself (as an actor, not as a character) in his true social identity as the real agent of communal release; on the other hand, he has already, through the disciplined use of mimesis, transformed himself into a dramatic agent of the fictive presentation of reality. It is in the nature of pre-Elizabethan popular wordplay to draw on both dimensions simultaneously and in its verbal structure to crystallize, as it were, the process by which the post-ritual release is being incorporated into, and subjected to, the mimetic requirements of dramatic dialogue.

To view the social and dramatic mode of wordplay as an historical index to its theory and function helps us to see the obvious limitations of, and the slow and long process of growth and change in, the dramatic language of pre-Shakespearian drama. It does in no wise anticipate the complex spectrum of dramatic punning that Shakespeare was to use with so much virtuosity, even when a popular play like *Mankind* makes it abundantly clear that there was a changing and developing tradition of native speech and acting which did not need the art of rhetoric to be dramatically effective.

To suggest the nature of this change from a bird's-eye view, one can say that the ritual residuum of non-mimetic nonsense or irrelevancy becomes more and more integrated into the structure of dramatic dialogue. As the actor's social identity as the real agent of communal release dissolves, and as the communal 'game' (*Mankind* 69), 'sporte' (78), and 'revell' (82) recede, his punning is more firmly integrated into the mimesis of verbal exchange. But the social and dramatic modes of wordplay remain surprisingly traditional, at least up to the time when Phillip Stubbes launches his puritan attack on the 'blasphemie intollerable' of those 'doble dealing ambodexters' who (as he says) 'mix scurrilitie with diuinitie.'[15]

To illustrate this context, I can only refer in passing to plays such as Bale's *King Johan, King Darius, The Trial of Treasure,* and again *All for Money.* When, for instance, Sedycyon enters with an obscene remark, King Johan replies that this 'myrth in no wysse' can 'dyscontent' him, if only 'thow powder yt with wysdome and honeste.'[16] But Sedycyon, in his grotesque inversion of Christian values, not only mistakes the moralizing meaning of 'powder,' but makes a point of defending the principle of inversion behind the mistake:

> SEDYCYON I am no spycer, by the messe! ye may beleve me.
> KING JOHAN I speke of no spyce, but of cyvyle honeste.
> SEDYCYON Ye spake of powder, by the Holy Trynyte!
> KING JOHAN Not as thow takyst yt, of a grosse capacyte,
> But as Seynt Pawle meanyth unto the Collossyans playne:
> 'So seasyne yowr speche, that yt be withowt disdayne.'   (50–5)

Here is already more of an illusion of misunderstanding than in Myscheffe's provocative 'impertinency': the post-ritual quality of the actor's self-expression has been more firmly integrated in the art of dialogue. Still, the basic social mode and metaphorical process of punning are the same: here as there, an abstract or moralizing concept of grace or propriety is reduced to its metaphorical vehicle from the world of physical objects. The Vice ignores the abstract concept or tenor and jumps to perceive the ordinary and working day referent of the image, which is chaff and corn for Myscheff and 'spyce' for Sedycyon and which still has a certain Shakespearian parallel in Speed's preferring the physical vehicle of his 'master's ship' to the more abstract concept of 'mastership.' It is another instance of common misunderstanding in which the down-to-earth referent swallows up the symbolic or abstract content with, in the moralities, its biblical authority.

But it is not only the word of the church which can thus be mistaken: the words and standards of the ruling class can equally be reduced, as when in *All for Money* Sinne (the Vice) is being asked about the 'degree' from which he is descended:

> MONEY May I be so bolde to knowe of what kindred,
> Or else from what stocke you are proceeded.

SINNE The last stockes I was in was euen at Bamburie,
The be worme eaten which shewes them ancient to be:
If they were mine because they be so olde,
I would burne them in winter to keepe me from colde.
MONEY I meant of what degree you were descended.   (937–43)

Just as the chaff has, beyond its metaphorical reference to the Day
of Judgment, its use in feeding horses, so the worm-eaten wood of
Sinne's 'stockes' can keep a person from the cold. The Vice, it seems,
is impervious to the moral concepts of both aristocratic and Christian
living. Says a popular figure in *Fulgens and Lucrece*: 'Uertue, what
the deuyll is that?'[17] And Lust in *The Trial of Treasure*, again mistaking the world of ideas and the world of ideology, says: 'I pray thee,
tel me what meneth this word charity?'[18]

These examples must here suffice to suggest that there was a considerable tradition of popular wordplay from the mystery cycles to
the Tudor morality play; that this wordplay was not simply an
imaginative device or poetic convention but was firmly embedded
in the basic process and structure of the popular theatre; that it was
on this basis that it served as a highly significant medium of interaction between the mimetic form of dialogue and the communal
expression of festive release, between rôle and actor, drama and
audience; and that – finally – this unity of dramatic speech and public
acting must be considered as a most significant part indeed of Shakespeare's medieval heritage.

But to say that the tradition of popular punning is significant is
not to say that Shakespeare received it uncritically or that it provided
him with the only or even the most important source for the art of
quibbling. One would not wish to emphasize the importance of this
tradition at the expense of quite different sources, among which
Lyly's courtly comedies are certainly foremost. The point then that I
would like to make finally is not that Shakespeare adopted the wordplay in the Vice tradition but rather that he so adapted and developed
its theatrical and poetic context that he used it in many more functions, comic and tragic, than the traditional kind of 'impertinency'
ever allowed for. This must be stressed even when Shakespeare himself quite deliberately and directly associated the art of mistaking the
word with the Vice tradition. We remember Speed's remark in *The
Two Gentlemen* and we think of Richard of Gloucester's words:
'Thus, like the formal vice, Iniquity, I moralize two meanings in one

word.' (III.i.82f) But even when Shakespeare, as it were, quoted the
'formal vice' he did not simply incorporate the quotation but stylized
it with a new kind of effectiveness which is characteristic of the general
mode of his reception of the popular tradition. For Gloucester's reference to the 'formal vice' is – like Speed's – itself in the form of a
pun, and it is a vicious and highly sophisticated kind of 'contrarie
sence' in which Gloucester uses the verb 'moralize.' The sense of the
verb is sarcastically inverted, but this inversion works on two levels
and has a twofold function: first, it achieves a sarcastic irony which
is entirely in line with the new task of the mimetic creation of character as based on the illusion of a certain psychological coherence.
But second, behind the new psychology of this rôle there is still a
residuum of the actor's awareness of his own social function and
identity, so that the actor – in the quibbling use of the verb 'moralize'
– does not simply use a pun but seems to acknowledge its source by
referring to the origins, in the morality tradition, of such a technique
of confounding two meanings in one word. 'Moralize,' in this sense,
is a metaphorical statement about the literary history of the verbal
figure that the actor uses with a remarkable consciousness of its theatrical origins and functions.

Richard of Gloucester is, like Feste in *Twelfth Night*, a 'corrupter
of words,' and the vicious tradition of moralizing two meanings in
one word is very much alive in Shakespearian comedy as it is in
tragedy, where the convention of madness provides an effective frame
in which the device of the impertinent 'contrarie sence' still fulfills
important dramatic functions. When (to take only one example)
Claudius asks: 'How fares our cousin Hamlet?', the prince corrupts
the verb 'fare' by using it – in the Vice's fashion – in the material
sense of eating, not in its general or abstract meaning (of 'how do
you do') and replies:

> Excellent, i'faith; of the chameleon's dish.
> I eat the air, promise-cramm'd; you cannot feed capons so.
>
> (III.ii.91f)

Here as elsewhere Prince Hamlet applies the traditional strategy of
impertinency, which is perhaps most clearly observed by Guildenstern
when he protests to the impertinent Prince and says: 'Good my lord,
put your discourse into some frame, and start not so wildly from my
affair' (III.ii.299f). To start wildly from the affair of the dialogue
corrupts more than words: it corrupts, as it were, the dramatic illusion

of conversation. The result is not merely of a verbal nature: it affects the actor's relation to both the scene and the audience. For Hamlet at such moments releases himself from his own rôle of the Prince of Denmark: with the help of popular proverb and aside he momentarily dissociates himself from the illusion of the world of the court and revives a post-ritual capacity for reckless sport and social criticism. It is not surprising at all that Hamlet with some ninety quibbles has more puns than any other Shakespearian character.

There is a connection, I suggest, between the convention of madness and the tradition of topsy-turvydom with its verbal acts of inversion and release from dialogue. To be sure, madness is now become part of the method of characterization and composition: there is some truly functional method in this madness, for a new mimetic form of psychology and some compositional coherence are grafted upon the popular roots of a traditional topsy-turvydom. Hamlet is no Vice, and his genetic relations with the figures of mischief and release in the Morality are much more tenuous than in the case of Richard of Gloucester or even Shakespeare's clowns. For the Vice was, even for Gloucester, a 'formal vice'; for Feste, too, it was an object of quotation and recollection: 'I'll be with you again/In a trice,/Like to the old Vice,/Your need to sustain' (iv.ii.118–21), just as Speed said: 'Your old vice still' (iii.i.279). And these qualifications are, in Shakespeare, perhaps the most illuminating: the Vice was the *old* Vice, but *still* he could be used or referred to, and the words 'old' and 'still' indicate the dialectics of innovation and tradition, by which Shakespeare's wordplay actually thrived (among other things), upon the diminishing tensions of mimesis and ritual, matter and impertinency, the illusion of actuality in the presentation of dialogue and the abandonment of versimilitude.

NOTES

1 T.W. Baldwin *Shakspere's Small Latine and Lesse Greeke* (Urbana 1944) II, 680, 670
2 Sister Miriam Joseph *Shakespeare's Use of the Arts of Language* (New York 1947) 165
3 For instance, F.P. Wilson, 'Shakespeare and the Diction of Common Life' *Proceedings of the British Academy* 27 (London 1941)
4 Quotations from *The Towneley Plays* George England and A.W. Pollard, eds, Early English Text Society, ES 71 (London 1897)
5 Quotations from *The Non-Cycle Mystery Plays* Osborn Waterhouse, ed, Early English Text Society, ES 104 (London 1909)
6 On Jack Finney see my *Shakespeare und die Tradition des Volkstheaters:*

Soziologie-Dramaturgie-Gestaltung (Berlin 1967) 77f, 89ff. I have not seen Alan Brody's new study of *The English Mummers and their Plays* (London 1970). But Jack Finney's speech, while it has the same kind of impertinent direction, does not achieve the synthesis of self-expressive nonsensical aside and representational dialogue.

7 *Mactacio Abel* ll.1–2; cf *The Towneley Plays*

8 A.P. Rossiter *English Drama From Early Times to the Elizabethans* (London 1950) 73f

9 All quotations from William Shakespeare, *The Complete Works* Peter Alexander, ed (reprinted London 1962)

10 As Bernard Spivack (*Shakespeare and the Allegory of Evil* (New York 1958) claims with some emphasis. He refers to the authority of G.R. Owst (*Literature and Pulpit in Medieval England*, Cambridge 1933), but it should be noted that Owst, who does not consider the *dramaturgy* of the Vice, says about this dramatic figure (p.86): 'No doubt, it was not the Bible in the first instance, but some deeper and more ancient racial attachment to folk-lore and pagan demonology that gave rise to these spiritual abstractions, and endowed them with a history of their own.'

11 For evidence see the unpublished B Litt thesis of F.H. Mares, 'The Origin and Development of the Figure Called the "Vice" in Tudor Drama' (Lincoln College, Oxford, 1954), 49, 53f, which goes beyond the suggestions of scholars such R.J.E. Tiddy or Robert Withington, but tends to underrate the allegorical heritage of the Vice and the way it actually seems to thrive on the grotesque contradictions of Christian orthodoxy and pagan heresy. Cf F.H. Mares, 'The Origin of the Figure called "the Vice" in Tudor Drama' *Huntington Library Quarterly* 22 (1958) 11–29, and my comments in *Shakespeare und die Tradition des Volkstheaters* 487

12 Thomas Lupton *All for Money* Ernst Vogel, ed *Shakespeare-Jahrbuch* 40 (1904) ll.1008/9

13 All quotations are taken from *The Macro Plays* F.J. Furnivall and A.W. Pollard, eds, Early English Text Society, ES 91 (London 1904).

14 M.M. Mahood *Shakespeare's Wordplay* (London 1957) 31, 52

15 Phillip Stubbes *The Anatomy of Abuses* F.J. Furnivall, ed, 2 parts (London 1877–82) 141, 143

16 Quotations from *Specimens of the Pre-Shaksperean Drama* J.H. Manly, ed, 2 vols. (Boston/London 1897)

17 Henry Medwall *Fulgens and Lucres* F.S. Boas and A.W. Reed, eds, (Oxford 1926) II, 842f

18 *The Trial of Treasure* 68; cf *Quellen des weltlichen Dramas in England vor Shakespeare* Alois Brandl, ed (Strassburg 1898)

John C. Meagher /
Vanity, Lear's Feather, and the Pathology
of Editorial Annotation

There is a remark by C.J. Sisson that must strike a poignant echo in the heart of every right-thinking Shakespearian: 'Nowhere, in the whole range of Shakespeare's work, is the desire so acutely felt as in *King Lear* to be able to consult Shakespeare himself upon the words he had written and upon their significance in his mind.'[1] But when mere practicality tugs us out of such sweet reveries, where can we turn? The answer should be obvious. We should go to recent editions of the play and ponder the annotations, for there we can expect to find not only the past achievements of scholarly divination, winnowed by editorial judgment, but the editors' new contributions as well – the seasoned insights of scholars who have long held their sensitive ears to the Shakespearian ground, and can plausibly suggest the meanings of *Lear*'s movements upon it.

The answer should be obvious; but Shakespeare's editors have inherited bad habits in editorial annotation so persistently repeated and so thoroughly conventionalized from antiquity onwards that the obviousness has been obscured. What we should expect to find in editorial annotation is not what we get. What we do get is often far from the mark, both in accuracy and in relevance, but is protected by traditions so hoary and common that we have long since forgotten what we ought to expect, and quietly take eggs for money.

I will readily confess my admiration and gratitude for the work of many of the modern editors of Shakespeare and for that of their predecessors. But my present business is rather to concentrate on ways in which they have generally failed us, despite their labours and their learning. To that end, I would like to direct the reader's attention to two places in the text of *King Lear*. The two differ in character and in importance, but they are both points in the text at which we may appropriately be curious about 'the words Shakespeare wrote and their significance in his mind,' and their fates at the hands of the editors may be taken as representative examples of weaknesses and failures that are both important and typical in the traditional – and current – practice of editorial annotation. I shall eventually make some annotative suggestions about these two passages, but only as a tentative and illustrative appendix to an attempt at diagnosing editorial ills that seriously impede the development of our understanding of Shakespeare.

I VANITY THE PUPPET

When Kent intemperately assaults Oswald in ii.ii, his principal justifying reason is that 'you come with Letters against the King, and take Vanitie the puppets part, against the Royaltie of her Father' (1108–10).[2] The editors have not neglected us in the case of this odd reference to Goneril. Samuel Johnson glossed the phrase as 'Alluding to the old Moralities or allegorical plays, in which Vanity, Iniquity, and other vices were personified,' and his explanation is so evidently satisfying that virtually every subsequent editor has repeated some version of his comment. There have been advances in both the completeness and boldness of the note: the old Arden added that Vanity was 'a common character' in the moralities, and the more recent Arden adds that the moralities 'were often performed in puppet-shows'; Kittredge's *Sixteen Plays* pointed out that puppet-shows were popular and frequently produced moralities with allegorical characters, but the new revised Kittredge goes much further: 'Vanity was a stock figure in the older morality plays, and it survived in Elizabethan puppet shows.' So it goes with all editions I know, gathering such confidence through the years that the most recent *King Lear*, only a few days old at this writing, can gloss the phrase with a concise 'i.e. Goneril (here equated with a stock figure in puppet shows).'

Editors with more space at their disposal (e.g., Craig, Kittredge, Muir) sometimes amplify the note by citing other references to Lady Vanity in the works of Marlowe, Jonson, Munday. This is a useful kindness, but one may wonder why they decline to dedicate some of their extra space rather to more information about the puppet-show to which Shakespeare has apparently made Kent allude; or perhaps to the citation of one or two of the old moralities in which Lady Vanity figures so commonly. One usually must assume that they have their reasons, and pass on. On the other hand, if one is willing to take the trouble to investigate what is known about the repertories of puppet-shows, and to count the instances of Lady Vanity in the old moralities, one can even discover what those reasons are. Surprisingly – especially in view of the progressive confidence of the editors from Johnson on – the explanation is that there are apparently no examples to cite. Lady Vanity does not appear in the extant old moralities at all, only in the factitious morality played in *Sir Thomas More*. The development of Johnson's note represents not elaborated discovery but merely escalated guess.[3]

This particular note is, of course, a matter of relatively trivial importance. It is easy to forgive the editors' confusion of plausible conjecture with established fact on a point that does not deserve to occupy more than a small share of their attention and their labour. Still, to conserve an unsubstantiated note from earlier editions is a significant editorial fault, and to enlarge its unfounded claims is a greater one. And whether or not these faults have done any serious damage in this particular case (I shall later suggest that they may have obscured some potentially important hints about Shakespeare's understanding of Goneril), the case of Lady Vanity is further symptomatic of a still deeper weakness of traditional editorial annotation:

For suppose for a moment that the editors' disguised guesses are luckily right, and that Lady Vanity made frequent appearances in lost morality plays. How much closer would the note put us to understanding the significance of the phrase in *King Lear*, to consulting Shakespeare about his meaning? The advance, I suggest, would still be disappointingly small. The phrase would be rendered only generally intelligible; why Kent should be made to identify Goneril with any morality-play figure at all would still be anyone's guess, and we would be left entirely to our own resources to fathom why she should be aligned specifically with the puppet version of the character, or with Vanity rather than with a more obviously relevant vice (say, Hypocrisy, or Avarice; or even Ingratitude, if there be no particular point to having a morality-play antecedent).

No edition of *Lear* known to me gives direct attention to these more significant problems. Few provide material relevant to them, or even show signs that the editor has considered them, though nearly all simply repeat some version of Johnson's conjectural, misleading, and in any event unilluminating cross-reference to the moralities.

The history of Vanity the Puppet instances three common and ancient weaknesses in editorial practice. The first is uncritical traditionalism, by which an observation is accorded both an authority and a relevance to which it is not entitled, simply by virtue of its having been commonly made in previous editions; this is why the note on Lady Vanity in puppet moralities continues groundlessly to appear in editions of *King Lear*, even in those prepared by scholars with considerable knowledge of early Tudor drama. The second is undiscriminating assertiveness – the failure to differentiate, in the manner in which an editorial observation is presented, between what is founded on reliable evidence and what is at most plausible conjecture; this is why the note has not only deceived its general readers but even misled successive editors into presuming grounds for extending its claims. The third is interpretive centrifugality, the failure to distinguish between what is only somehow related to the text and what is genuinely relevant to its interpretation; this is why the fuller versions of the note can continue to be lavish with material that is only marginally preliminary to the illumination of Kent's epithet and yet fail almost altogether to attend to the problem of its meaning in *King Lear*.

Vanity the Puppet could have been passed by without notice from the editorial commentary, and hardly anyone would have minded. For that matter, hardly anyone would have *noticed*, to the extent that readers had been properly schooled in the polite understanding of another convention in editorial annotation – keeping problems at bay by not acknowledging them. Only the rarely virtuous editor admits in his notes that the text here or there seems oddly inconsistent or impenetrably obscure – unless, of course, it has become commonplace for editors thus to deal with this particular crux, repeating (usually with great impartiality and indifference) the helpless and desperate attempts of earlier editors to give sense by emendation where too little has been found by analysis. The standard response to a puzzling passage is rather to ignore it, and double the size of the subsequent note.

Not all instances of this disregard are real cases of dereliction of duty. Often – perhaps appallingly often – the reason for the editor's silence anent a knotty moment in the text is not that he is unable to solve it but that he is unable to see it. Readings of well-known texts become so thoroughly fixed that blind-spots endure easily; the meaning of the play settles in comfortably to the shape of the standard interpretative remarks made about it, seasoned with private insight. What runs apart from or counter to the interpretative main stream readily begins to look like a moment of inadvertent and unimportant carelessness. One can read a passage a dozen times without being arrested by an oddity which one learned to skip over the first time through, and ever after; one watches with keen relish everything that develops what one takes to be the main dramatic and thematic happenings, and may receive all else as little more than background noise. Even fairly important moments can be passed over, habitually bracketed out of significance in such a way that one need never confront the problem of their existence, or admit that they must be accounted for as items in a meaningful system. For instance:

II LEAR'S FEATHER

In the last moments of his weary life, King Lear, in a gesture of hope that Cordelia may not be dead after all, makes what is, under the circumstances, an entirely appropriate request:

> Lend me a Looking-glasse,
> If that her breath will mist or staine the stone,
> Why then she liues.

It was a standard test for the presence of faint life, and remains sufficiently well-known today that one need not suppose that it deserves an explanatory note, assuring us that Lear is being conventional rather than inventive on this point. But a few moments later, Lear makes a most surprising announcement: 'This feather stirs, she liues.'

Surprising? Let me count the ways. For one thing, we may fairly wonder what became of the request for a mirror. For another, we may wish to know where the feather came from. Going beyond both to a perspective that should include and reconcile them, we ought to ask why Shakespeare has Lear request a mirror if he intends to supply him eventually with a feather.

But the problem doesn't stop there. This isn't merely a question of logistics or of rival breath-detection techniques. It is, quite literally, a question of life and death – Cordelia's first, and therefore Lear's. It is potentially one of the most intense and important moments of the play. But reading or seeing the play for the fortieth time, we and the editors know heavily that Cordelia is irrevocably dead, and pity Lear's vain flash of hope. We probably discount entirely his news about the feather, knowing that it can't in fact be true that it stirs, regretfully certain that our state of anticipatory knowledge will soon settle over the stage entirely. In a way, we have already assumed its effective presence there. That is why we see nothing curious in the lack of response from other characters on stage: since we ourselves are entirely unable to believe Lear, we do not expect Edgar or Albany to do so.

Yet if we conjecture what that moment could have meant when *King Lear* was still new at the Globe, our habitual responses show up false as dicers' oaths. To begin with, Cordelia had always survived not only the battles but Lear himself. No member of Shakespeare's original audience who knew other versions of the Lear story would be likely to have a committedly pessimistic view of her chances for recovery here: quite the contrary.[4] Besides, Lear has clearly managed to survive Edmund's order of execution; why should anyone be sure that Cordelia won't recover when Lear's request for the mirror invites us to hope? Why should anyone doubt that her breath still moves when Lear announces that it is so? And, to go beyond these problems to the more inclusive perspective, why does Shakespeare permit Lear to announce Cordelia's survival if he really intends her to be, and to remain, dead – without even a last poignant Desdemonic swan-song?

These are not trivial difficulties. They are attached to a line which occupies such a strategic position in this play that one might well claim that nowhere, in the whole range of *King Lear*, is the desire so acutely felt as here to be able to consult Shakespeare himself upon the words he had written and upon their significance in his mind. Don't rush to the modern editions. They have nothing to say on this point. Either their editors are ignoring the problems of Lear's feather into pretended non-existence, or, their minds conditioned by repeated and virtually identical readings, they simply do not see that the line needs dealing with – that this is the sort of thing editorial annotation is for.[5]

III VANITY THE PUPPET

The text to which the annotating editor of a Shakespearian play addresses himself is not a set of *disjecta membra* but a script, whose words and phrases are correlatives of moments in a dramatic context. Failure to see them in terms of this context results in the overlooking or the falsification of problems. Detached from the drama, the import of the phrase 'This feather stirs' is obvious and untroublesome; but once it is apprehended in its native dramatic habitat, it becomes clear that the moment created by the phrase presents difficulties. Abstracted from the play, the phrase 'Vanity the puppet' still needs explaining; but the act of removing it from the dramatic context in which it was imbedded changes what it is we are trying to explain. At worst, this may totally obscure its functional effectiveness; but even at best, it falsifies the real character of the problem by ignoring some of the relations through which the epithet originally would have acquired and disclosed its meaning. The basic question to ask about this epithet is therefore not, as editors have traditionally supposed, 'What is the meaning of "vanity the puppet"?' but rather 'How can we account for Shakespeare's having Kent here call Goneril "vanity the puppet"?'

The difference between these two angles of approach is not always obvious. Indeed, once the right basic question is asked about this particular problem, the other question follows hard on its heels, for we obviously cannot explain why Shakespeare endowed Kent with the phrase until we have some idea what it means. But this is not to substitute the semantic question for the dramaturgical one, but only to recognize that it is probably on the semantic level that we shall find the main access to what remains unresolved in the complex that forms this dramaturgical problem. The straight explication of phrases will often be the means by which an annotating editor will resolve a difficulty in the dramaturgy of his text; but since this is not always the key to problems, it is perilous for an editor to neglect the discipline of the latter approach on the assumption that the former is an adequate substitute and short-cut. This path risks straying into centrifugal irrelevancies and missing the point. That, as I have already suggested, is precisely what has happened in the usual approach to this line, for the pursuit of morality puppet-shows has been unsuccessful not merely in discovering historical evidence but in helping us to understand why Kent would allude to them if there had been any. We must therefore try the tack that ought to have governed the enquiry in the first place: what are the historically and dramatically possible implications and values of the epithet in terms of which Kent's use of it becomes most intelligible?

The more theatrical sense of 'puppet' has proved a dead end, but there is an alternative route. The term was also generally used to designate a vain and 'dolled-up' woman – as in Swetnam's complaint that 'commonly women are the most part of the forenoone painting themselues and frizling their haires, and prying in their glasse ... like Poppets,' or Dent's 'Is it not a shame that women professing true religion, should make themselues such pictures, puppets and peacockes as they doe?'[6] If such should be the drift of Kent's intention, it is obvious that the two terms of the epithet would at least work neatly together, characterizing Goneril as the epitome of the vain woman, the personification of Vanity.

Vanity is not Goneril's most salient attribute and is certainly not the basis of Kent's attitude towards her; but then, Kent is not always directly on target, as the prodigal effulgence of his abuse of Oswald demonstrated a few lines earlier. It would certainly not be uncharacteristic of him to express his contempt and animus for Goneril through a reference to one of her less dramatically central imperfections. Still, if this is what Shakespeare wants him to do, we might fairly expect that the thrust and point of such an abrupt epithet would be better prepared than it appears to be in the earlier part of the play, and perhaps more effectively exploited than it appears to be in the subsequent part.

Because that expectation is fair, we may properly suppose that our understanding remains inadequate. It may be that the hypothetical interpretation of the epithet's general sense is wrong, or incomplete. But – especially in the absence of an interpretation that is manifestly more dramatically satisfying and historically tenable – we must also remember the possibility that the incompleteness lies rather in our understanding of the original *King Lear*.

Caveat lector henceforward, since a descent into the hypothetical bowels of original productions is always a risky undertaking. But it is a risk against which contemporary scholarship can indemnify us more extensively than might be suggested by customary editorial annotation, as timid in this regard as it is bold in projecting puppet moralities. And there can no longer be any doubt about whether the game is worth the candle: there is ample evidence that the design of Shakespeare's plays included important theatrical elements whose iceberg tips often barely break the surface of the surviving texts. Looked at in this way, even untroublesome passages may yield further insights into the meaning and organization of Shakespeare's plays; and when, as in this case, we reach an interpretative impasse at the surface of the text, we have hardly any choice. Suppose, then, that Kent's epithet is intended to identify Goneril as a personification of Vanity, as its most obvious defensible reading implies. How might this have resonated within the *King Lear* which Shakespeare conceived?

In the first place, such a special characterization would not be without point for the larger interests of the play. It would be functionally relevant to the play's treatment of Lear's relationship to his daughters if in casting off Cordelia with 'let pride ... marry her' (137) Lear were accepting in Goneril a more authentic embodiment of pride; and the vice of vanity is not without relevance to the character of Lear himself as he welcomes Vanity-the-puppet's fulsome flattery and gives her half his kingdom.[7]

Furthermore, other passages in the play suggest that Shakespeare may have conceived Goneril with particular reference to beauty and proud vanity as well as ingratitude. Her remark as Albany enters in iv.ii, 'I haue beene worth the whistle' (2300), has been generally (though not universally) understood as a comment on her own attractiveness. Lear curses her in ii.iv with 'Infect her Beauty, / You Fen-suck'd Fogges, drawne by the powrfull Sunne, / To fall, and blister' (1449–51: cf Q: '... and blast her pride'). And there is a further indication of the same characterization if Lear, when his last speech in that scene pleads in the singular, is addressing not Regan (the last previous speaker) but Goneril (to whose side Lear has perhaps just moved while saying 'Ile go with thee') :

> Thou art a Lady;
> If onely to go warme were gorgeous,
> Why Nature needs not what thou gorgeous wear'st,
> Which scarcely keepes thee warme (1567–70).

Such a special conception of Goneril would be at least a modest enrichment of the play. Not only would it individuate her interestingly: it would also enhance our sense of the logic of her egoism, and illuminate both her jealousy of Regan and her self-destructive vulnerability to Edmund's flattering attentions. Our recognition of this dimension in her character is perhaps adequately provided for by the bits of association just mentioned, driven home by Kent's decisive epithet. The original audiences, however, were not addressed by text alone: there were further resources available not only through easy and significant kinds of stage business[8] but also through costuming. For although Lady Vanity may have gone unemployed in the English morality plays, she enjoyed a certain career in emblematic art, and it was likely enough from such sources that the Lady Vanity of *Sir Thomas More* was partially or wholly derived. That play unfortunately does not specify the appearance of Vanity, but from her survival in a fairly large number of examples of sixteenth- and early seventeenth-century art, we can guess how cloth-painters and playwrights would conceive her. Lady Vanity is ordinarily presented

1 English woman with pendant mirror, from Wencelaus Hollar,
Ornatus Muliebris Anglicanus (London 1640)

2 Superbia, from the Seven Deadly Sins by Hieronymus Bosch (d 1516)

clothed in a particularly gorgeous or even gaudy gown, and her standard defining appurtenance is a mirror. She is the iconographical as well as the moral sister of Pride, and representations of the two are virtually interchangeable.[9]

I have already pointed out that there are grounds in Lear's last speech in ii.iv for supposing that Goneril was attired with Vanity's notable gorgeousness. I suggest that Kent's epithet, when looked at in the light of iconography, also may provide grounds for thinking that Shakespeare would have wished to provide her with a mirror as well. It would not have been difficult for him to arrange this through costuming. Small hand-mirrors, hung from the girdle on a ribbon, had been used in England since the generation before.[10] (see figure 1) If they were not an entirely accepted fashion by the early seventeenth century, so much the better for Shakespeare's purposes, for notice the impression that this fashion among Frenchwomen made on Fynes Moryson when he visited France a few years later: 'And they vse a strange badge of pride, to weare little looking glasses at their girdles.' Moryson's heraldic metaphor is significant.[11] The mirror was for him, even outside an artistic context, symbolic or emblematic of pride. Alternatively, given the evidence of both the thought and the iconography of the period, he might have called it an emblem of vanity.

If Shakespeare wished to characterize Goneril particularly with reference to Vanity (which seems to me highly plausible, on the evidence of the text) a costume mirror would probably have made her emblematic significance decisively available to his audience's understanding, particularly when given the guidance of Kent's epithet. Goneril could have made use of such a mirror for minor business on various occasions without exaggeration or distraction, quite enough to establish it as a specially defining emblem and justify Kent's epithet – for as the Fool remarks, 'there was neuer yet faire woman, but shee made mouthes in a glasse' (1686–7). In addition to the possibility that her 'I haue beene worth the whistle' was spoken while preening in the mirror, there are two other points in the play worth particular mention as instances in which Shakespeare may have made further capital of such a device. Since a mirror was a conventional emblem of prudence as well as of vanity (and was accordingly probably the pivotal motif in Vanity's attempt to pass as Wisdom in the *Sir Thomas More* 'Wit and Wisdom') it would give additional point to Albany's puzzled hesitation about the value of her policy if Goneril were consulting a mirror as Albany remarks 'How farre your

eies may pierce I cannot tell' (869). But even more striking are the
possibilities of its employment in iv.ii. Shortly after Goneril observes
that she has been worth the whistle, the outraged conscience of
Albany produces another line whose provocative oddity has been
neglected by editorial commentators: 'See thy selfe diuell' (2308).
The mood and general implication are intelligible enough, but why
'see'? Why the unimaginative coarseness of 'devil'? It is perhaps more
than mere coincidence that one of the standard variants in the
representation of Vanity in the art of the preceding century, especially
in northern Europe, was the placement of a supervising demon near
the figure of Lady Vanity as she gazes into her mirror, sometimes in
just such a way as to show us reflected in the glass the face not of the
lady but the devil. (see figures 2–4) Stephen Bateman provides an
English instance of this tradition in a woodcut complete with lady,
mirror, and devil, glossed with these verses: *'When daintie dames hath
whole delight: with proude attyre themselues to ray*: / Pirasmos
shineth in the sight: of glittering glasse such fooles to fray.'[12] (see
figure 5) If Shakespeare is not making allusive use of this iconographical motif in this instance, then I cannot give an adequately
justifying account of the precise form of Albany's 'see thyselfe diuell';
but if this is what he is doing, having Albany force upon Goneril and
upon us the ultimate secret of Vanity's own mirror, then it is not only
an intelligible line but a dramatically brilliant moment.

IV LEAR'S FEATHER

When Shakespeare decided to have Lear ask for a looking-glass, he
presumably intended either that the request should be honoured or
that there should be some point to its neglect. Given the respectful
manner in which the others treat Lear in the rest of the scene, it is not
likely that Shakespeare meant to suggest (as disregard for his commands suggests elsewhere in the play) that he is held in low esteem.
If the request is ignored, there must have been something about the
way it was made that disqualified it, perhaps as the plea of a man
whose wits are gone. I do not think that such a disqualification is built
into the lines themselves: their passion is strong, and their movement
from despair to hope is abrupt, but they hardly suggest insanity –
especially when we remember that Cordelia outlives Lear in earlier
versions of the story. If the request (or command) is ignored, it must
be that Lear's lines are meant to be accompanied by some stage
business that overrules them, or shows him clearly to be mad – e.g., if

3 Vanitas, from *Ritter von Turn* (Basel 1493)

the request were addressed specifically to the dead body of Goneril, brought on stage some twenty lines before. The gloomy responses of Kent, Edgar, and Albany, who are obviously not swayed by Lear's burst of hope, further suggest that his manner indicated madness. Whatever business accompanied Lear's next speech must then have been likewise clearly suggestive of madness, since no one appears to be in the least encouraged by Lear's claim to detect signs of life: perhaps it is not to her lips that he is holding the feather, or perhaps there is plainly no feather at all.

Still, one needs more. Why does Shakespeare have Lear ask for the glass in the first place if he is about to concentrate on feathers? Where does the feather come from if it is there, and what is going on if it isn't? At such a moment in such a play, it is not enough for lines to be intelligible: they ought to be functionally purposeful. Granted that one must be willing to forgive the playwright if he allows things to go slack even here – nevertheless, one cannot afford to be too easily satisfied, lest one mistake what is being offered. It is always methodologically appropriate to wonder whether, in the case of a disappointing or puzzling passage, more may be happening than meets the habitual eye. May the very existence of the remaining puzzles about Lear's feather become a point of entry into a rediscovery of Shakespeare's original design, necessarily obscured when we can rely only on the text, denied even a continuing stage tradition by Tate's literally deathless *Lear*?

It is at least possible, and worth the risk of precarious speculations. I would therefore like to propose one. Suppose that Shakespeare had Lear ask for a mirror for the purpose of supplying him with one. Suppose, that is, that Lear's first command is honoured, and that he is presented with a glass fetched quickly from offstage (as in *Richard II* iv.i) or even possibly from the body of Goneril. I think that what would plausibly follow is something like this: Lear holds the glass before the lips of Cordelia, studying it carefully for a sign of life. Then he brightens, turns to the surrounding lords (who, along with the audience, might well be suddenly galvanized into hope by the apparently positive result indicated by Lear's joy) – and then, crushing this last hope as abruptly as he had stimulated it, Lear speaks the line that proves that he had really seen nothing after all, shows him so mad as to be unable to distinguish which of the standard tests for breath he is actually employing: holding up the mirror, he tells us 'This feather stirs.' All's cheerless, dark, and deadly.[13]

I admit, of course, that these speculations are seriously weakened

4 Vanitas, by Daniel Hopfer (d 1536)

Of Pride.

When daintie dames hath whole delight : with proude attyre them selues to rayi
Pirasmos shineth in the sight : of glittering glasse such fooles to fray.

The signification.

THe woman signifieth pride : the glasse in her hand flattery or deceate : the deuill behinde her temptation : the
death head which she setteth her foote on, signifieth forget-
fulnes of the life to come, wherby commeth destruction.

H.iij.   Take

5 Vanity as Pride, woodcut by Stephen Bateman, from
A cristall glasse of christian reformation (London 1569)

by being so conjectural. I regret the absence of more definitive evidence, both inside and outside the text, for these or any other interpretations of Vanity the puppet and Lear's feather. But if my suggestions remain unconvincing, let the main point not be lost for all that. The primary issue is not my specific interpretative proposals but the general question of focus and technique. It behooves the interpreters of Shakespeare, and especially the editors, whose notes are importantly influential in forming attitudes concerning what questions ought to be asked of and about the text, to be far more scrupulous not only about the accuracy of their comments but about their interpretative relevance. What we want primarily to know, with maximum clarity and precision, is the detailed operation of Shakespeare's dramatic design. Whatever does not serve this end, or at least strive to be propaedeutic to it, should not masquerade as commentary.

It is commonplace to complain that despite the vast advances in bibliographical scholarship in this century, we have not yet managed to produce an adequately sound text of the canon of works in which we are most interested – and which especially motivated the bibliographical research in the first place. I wish to lodge a parallel complaint. Despite the great advances made during the same period toward understanding the fundamentally theatrical character of Shakespeare's dramatic works, we are still far from producing an edition that adequately reflects those achievements in its annotational illumination of the plays that most inspired them. A great deal of work remains to be done before such an edition can come about. But even at this stage, we are equipped to make substantial improvements; and as we move on from here we have good reason to suspect that important interpretative clues are hidden even in the most harmless and apparently trivial 'dead spots' in Shakespeare's dramatic composition, which may surrender their secrets if we will only learn to ask persistently the right, though often quite untraditional, questions.

NOTES

1 *Shakespeare's Tragic Justice* (London 1964) 78
2 This and subsequent quotations from the folio text of *Lear* are cited according to the lineation of Charlton Hinman's Norton Facsimile.
3 It is not impossible that the Lady Vanity who appears in the fragmentary 'Marriage of Wit and Wisdom' played in *Sir Thomas More* was inherited from some lost and unattested variant version of the source-play, *Lusty Juventus*. But the fact remains that the extant text of the latter play, whose lines are followed nearly *verbatim* by the More 'Wit and Wisdom,' lacks the character of Lady Vanity, whose place and speeches are occupied

rather by 'Abhominable Lyuyng.' The Vanity who appears in *Liberality and Prodigality* is masculine and representative of a different moral sphere (see note 9). I have found no other candidate in extant moralities or in allusions to lost ones. A list of known early puppet plays can be found in George Speaight, *The History of the English Puppet Theatre* (London 1955): neither there nor elsewhere have I found any evidence of a puppet Vanity.

4 The number of people already generally familiar with the Lear story was presumably large enough to be worth Shakespeare's notice, judging from the allusions to and versions of the Lear story that preceded Shakespeare's.

5 Critical commentaries on the play, it may be remarked, are not on the whole more successful than the annotating editors in making sense of this point, though a few writers have at least faced it. Predictably, they usually ignore it; and when they do not, they betray an outrageous untheatricality of imagination – e.g., one recent writer says that Lear 'seizes a stray feather, and applies it to her lips' (Paul N. Siegel *Shakespearean Tragedy and the Elizabethan Compromise* [New York 1957] 183). Granville-Barker at least had him pluck it from his costume; I find no writer since who understands the problem even as well as that.

6 J. Swetnam *The Araignment of Lewde, idle, froward, and vnconstant women: Or the vanitie of them* (London 1615) sig. E2^v; Arthur Dent *The Plaine Mans Path-way to Heauen* (London 1601) sig. D8^v

7 For this virtual identification of pride and vanity, see note 9.

8 Cf Spenser's Lucifera, 'And in her hand she held a mirrhour bright, / Wherein her face she often vewed fayne, / And in her selfe-lou'd semblance tooke delight,' and her courtiers, 'Some frounce their curled heare in courtly guise, / Some prancke their ruffes, and others trimly dight / Their gay attyre' (*Faerie Queene* I.iv.10, 14). It is clear that Shakespeare appreciated and used gestural business, not only for straight effects, as in Malvolio's repeated hand-kissing and Osric's courtly inability to keep his hat on, but also for clever side-play – as when Richard II inverts the meaning of his loyal followers' sobs in III.iii with 'Well, well, I see / I talke but idly, and you mock [Qq: laugh] at mee' (1758–9) and similarly twists the meaning of their pity as they wring their hands in IV.i: 'Though some of you, with *Pilate*, wash your hands, / Shewing an outward pittie' (2161–2).

9 That is, the species of pride and the species of vanity with which this paper is concerned were essentially identical. As the reader will undoubtedly have realized, 'vanity' was more commonly used in the sixteenth century to designate worthlessness, usually of a specious and ephemeral kind. This more generalized and less morally pointed concept is the one represented by the masculine Vanity in *Liberality and Prodigality* (where he is called 'Fortune's chief servant'), by the Vanità in Cesare Ripa's *Iconologia*, etc. A mirror was not standard equipment for this version of vanity. But the word 'puppet' in Kent's epithet clearly detaches Goneril from this Vanity and aligns her with the alternative tradition that concentrated especially on feminine self-admiration – a radically moral conception, whose nearest home base among the Deadly Sins was obviously Pride. Vain Woman thus readily became a favourite exemplar of Pride; she and her standard mirror can accordingly be found under the label Superbia as well as Vanitas –

hence, for instance, Spenser's Lucifera. See G.F. Hartlaub *Zauber des Spiegels* (München 1951) and Heinrich Schwarz, 'The Mirror in Art' *The Art Quarterly* 15 (1957) 97–118.

10 See, for instance, the portrait of Mary Ann Waltham reproduced in Herbert Norris *Costume and Fashion* (London 1938) III, 712; Jost Amman's Foemina nobilis Anglicana on sig. Y2 of *Gynoeceum, sive Theatrum Mulierum* (Frankfort 1586); Gheeraerts' portrait of Mary, Countess of Dorset, at Knole; the portrait of Elizabeth at Hampden House, attributed to Zuccaro; and the engravings from Wencelaus Hollar's *Ornatus Muliebris Anglicanus* (London 1640) reproduced in C.W. and P. Cunnington *Handbook of English Costume in the Seventeenth Century* (London 1966) 93 (my figure 1), 127.

11 *An Itinerary* (1617), sig. 3T4. A page later, we find Moryson discussing badges in their more literal and technically heraldic sense. His wonder at the French fashion may of course be feigned, an ironic dig at a practice that may not have been at all out of style in England: Amman and Hollar give some reason to suppose that, in fact, it was particularly typical of English women.

12 *A cristall glasse of christian reformation* (London 1569), sig. H3 (my figure 5). Among the European examples of this motif are Bosch's Superbia in Seven Deadly Sins (Prado, Madrid), my figure 2; and woodcuts in *Ritter von Turn* (Basel 1493) and by Daniel Hopfer, reproduced in Hartlaub *Zauber des Spiegels* figures 162–3 (my figures 3 and 4).

13 Since such a reading of Lear's final moments is rather against the grain of the standard more optimistic approach, it is perhaps worth reminding the reader that such a deliberately engineered shock to hope is not new to the play at this point. The procession of Cordelia's and Lear's army in v.ii climaxes a growing hope: its own pomp, the prayers of Edgar and Gloucester that the right may thrive, and the previous history of the Lear story (for the earlier versions had Lear restored to his throne through Cordelia's successful assisting invasion) lead us into the sounds of battle in a mood of controlled optimism sufficient to keep alive our hope for Lear's victory until it is abruptly gutted by Edgar's announcement that Lear and Cordelia have been vanquished and captured. That is, the experience structured there is a more large-scale version of what I suggest may be built into the incident of Lear's feather. One final point deserves mention: despite the way in which Lear's final lines are usually understood, it is not really self-evident that they are to be spoken in a tone of joy, particularly in the quarto version (where Lear's last utterances are 'O, o, o, o' and 'Breake hart, I prethe breake'); and we perhaps ought not to assume that Burbage was necessarily pointing to Cordelia's lips as he said 'Do you see this? Looke on her? Looke her lips, / Looke there, looke there.'

Roy Daniells /
An Address at a Banquet

O listen, listen, ladies gay
To this my merry roundelay.
O hearken, gents, and do not frown,
But gently set your glasses down.
Oh, bend on me your friendly glance,
And join in this most happy happenstance.

You are, for my delightful ditty,
Indebted to your own committee.
They hoped for him who had the gift
To launch the theme of Henry Fift,
But in default of Leslie Banks,
Haled up this groundling from the ranks.

For you, who sit up on the stage
Where Shakespeare's heroes nobly rage,
You favoured few, you band of brothers,
You seldom look at all us others
Who in the pit, below the scaffold,
By finer points are mostly baffled.
We cry and clap our horny hands
When your applause our own demands.

I bring, alas!no wreath of roses;
No learning my rude verse discloses;
But sprout no horns at me, like Moses,
Nor look down long Germanic noses.
Look up instead and see it there, –
My sweaty nightcap tumbling in the air!

As one whose poverty's derided,
By chance to some great feast invited,
Will hesitate, but feel he must,
Yet to the banquet brings his crust,
So now, brought safe inside the gate,
What you do not anticipate
I'll add, so please you, to the feast, –
My contribution, first and least.
Thus happily within the pale,
Here is my round unvarnished tale.

Take Holy Writ, by Shakespeare prized, –
The version King James authorized.
Then open it between your palms,
Turn over to the book of psalms,
Psalm forty-six, to be precise,
Then change the focus of your eyes
And count the words, with pencilled ticks,
Until you've numbered forty-six.
That word is SHAKE: take note, my friend,
Then start again, at t'other end.
Count upward in the same notation
(Omitting Selah, which is punctuation)
Until you reach, by careful count,
The forty-sixth word as you mount.
What word at this point should appear ?
You have three guesses! Yes, it's SPEAR.

When did this book come off the press?
That date, dear friends, you need not guess:
1611, you know it well,
A date that every child can tell.
And, as that year began, I'm told,
Shakespeare was forty-six years old.

Here is the plainest proof, that damns
All cyphers and all cryptograms.
To piece it out we need not go
To Sherlock Holmes or Edgar Allen Poe.
It is so palpable a hit
I won't ask, What d'you make of it?
Say what you will of scribes who've planned 'em,
Such marvels do not fall at random,
Nor come by stages incremental,
Nor yet by chance coincidental.
Here's proof, without debate or quibble,
Proof absolute that Shakespeare wrote the Bible!

Though you may think I but rehearse
A modicum of doggerel verse,
With your indulgence, it shall seem
A prologue to the swelling theme.
If come by chance or invitation,
Still bring with you Imagination.
Imagination, quick and warm,
This local scene shall quite transform,
His cherub wings borne here and there
By sightless couriers of the air.

Point Grey shall turn at his command
To distant seas, Illyrian sand,
Its winding shore that ocean breaches
Shall seem like bright Bohemian beaches.
This Simon Fraser, white and glyptic,
Like Athens loom, – Acropoliptic!
These colonnades by which you roam
Be pillared squares of ancient Rome,
And all Vancouver's wood and field and garden,
Arcadian lawns and forest glades of Arden.

O welcome here a thousand times,
Though in these worst and roughest rhymes.
And thanks to all and to each one
By whom this crowning deed is done.
O Jackson, Rowan, Leech, Marcotte,
Like Greasy Joan, they've stirred the pot.

O Lennam, Newman, Galloway,
Like Phyllis they have raked the hay.
Our gown of glory hope's true Gage,
To this high Strand our pilgrimage.
Here, blessed by Capel and McGavin,
We hail great Habenicht and Tony Lavin!
Though none may know exactly how,
Like Touchstone's maid, they've milked the cow.
And thanks, although she looks so young,
To fairy-godmother McClung.

From hour to hour, we'll ripe and ripe,
And pry into each archetype.
From morning, when the cocks do crow,
Till evening's watchdogs bark Bow-wow!
And, lest from hour to hour we rot,
Suppose the Bard has hither got.
Suppose him here, with eye seraphic,
Prepared to view some two hours' traffic
Of pastoral wit or tragic pogrom,
When gentle Ingram hands a programme
That shows in all its wealth unfurled
His service, like the antique world,
And stretches, like some cycle of Cathay,
Nine times the space that measures night and day!

What else can make us give our best,
What better serve as final test,
What add to zip and zoom true zest,
Than Shakespeare as imagined guest?
Suppose him here, he has good cause;
And act to merit his applause.
Whate'er you do, oh, do it still
Obedient to his grace's Will.

Speak not as in the agora,
For poppy and mandragora
Will give to sleep no more persuasion
Than will a long high-pitched oration.
From all indecencies abstain;
Nor show, like Egypt's Queen, your bluest vein.

And be not rough, like old King Odo,
But rather suaviter in modo.
Yet in the breeze don't feebly sway,
But be like Alfred, fortiter in re.
Don't tear an argument to tatters,
But give the gist, it's all that matters,
Nor jog along like horse with pack,
His footnotes pocking all the track,
Nor in a whirlwind saw the air.
Be buxom, blithe, and débonnaire.
As academics here we meet,
And custom makes our life most sweet.
Condense the journeyings of years,
The exploration full of fears
O'er spreading miles of desert sand,
Into an hour-glass close at hand
Whose grains shall turn to seeds, and fall,
Still whispering, Ripeness, that is all!

May music all your senses ravish;
Upon your stage may life be lavish,
Not bones of long canonization
But quick and fresh reincarnation.
For doubtless you recall by rote
This verse, which, by your leave, I'll quote:
'I dreamed that William Shakespeare's ghost
Tried for a civil service post.
The English paper for that year
Was on the subject of King Lear.
William, I am afraid, failed badly,
Because he had not read his Bradley.'

Some books upon our shelves confess
Much study is a weariness.
Good friends, for Shakespeare's sake forbear
To dig the dust enclosèd there.
Blest be the man that spares those tomes
And lets them rest in peace, like Forsytes' Soames.

Conjure the Shakespeare, strong and hale,
Age cannot wither, custom stale.
(For we believe them quite mistaken
Who say, Oh, he brought home the Bacon!)
Lay by each prejudice and grudge,
O gently hear and kindly judge,
As even now, without objection,
Your thoughts piece out my every imperfection.

Old men forget, but you'll recall
Each August, at impending Fall,
The days you passed at U.B.C., –
Like Proust, who dipped his cake in tea.
Old men forget, but you will not,
Your mind recurring to this spot,
Recalling deeds at Simon Fraser.
You'll stroke your beards, indeed you may, Sir!
Whose blacks and browns have turned to greys,
And murmur, Ah! those were the days!
When nine diurnal rounds we've spent,
Ceased words for lack of argument,
And left, without reproach or blame,
O Shakespeare studies will not be the same!
Their cloud-capped towers and gorgeous palaces
A wonderland so far surpassing Alice's.

With drums and trumpets, harps and tabours,
You'll reap the fruits of all your labours.
No soul inert, no spirit craven,
In Huntington shall seek a haven,
No student rough as General Custer
From Birmingham rub off the lustre,
Nor any come – to Hardison appalling –
And make him cry, The Folger's pole is falling!
Great Russell Street shall find its hub, –
Panizzi's dome, and not the Pub!

From east and west shall students rise,
All filled with joy and enterprise,
With none time-serving, none pedantic;
Some here, some t'other side th'Atlantic,

Prepared, once more – as good King Harry teaches –
To leap like you into – a pair of breeches!

Now thanks for all your courtesy;
Let your indulgence set me free,
As, like th'intruder come from Porlock,
I now retire, and pull my forelock.

Reports from Chairmen of Investigative Committees

J. R. BROWN

Investigative Committee on International Co-operation

During the week of the Congress this committee held three private meetings, and one open meeting at which its report was approved in general and its last recommendation approved by a unanimous vote of all present. There are four recommendations:

1/An International Shakespeare Association. In order to deal with the growing complexity of Shakespearian research and theatre activity, an international association with individual and corporate membership should be established as soon as possible.

2/Co-operative Tasks for an International Shakespeare Association. These should include: A/linking the work of the various Shakespeare associations, etc., and advising on the foundation and development of new associations; B/seeking affiliation with Unesco, the Modern Humanities Research Association, and other international organisations; C/establishing an information centre, covering research, publication, translation, and performance (reports of the investigative committees on Bibliography and Shakespeare and the Computer indicate the possible scope of this work); D/keeping and circulating a diary of future performances, conferences, graduate courses, and opportunities for other graduate work, educational experiments, etc; E/creating a centre for the noncommercial interchange of books and articles where scholarly needs arise, and for further dissemination of significant work through translation; F/advising on the initiation and planning of any further World Shakespeare Congress; G/aiding travel in the interests of Shakespeare scholarship and performances; H/co-ordinating and supporting requests for finance for internationally co-operative projects.

3/Further World Shakespeare Congresses. Plans for any subsequent World Shakespeare Congress should include: A/suitable location, organisation and finance; B/a representative national committee; C/the full support of one or preferably more universities; D/the support of at least one theatre company with an established Renaissance repertoire, and the availability of several theatre buildings; E/consultation with an international advisory committee, elected by an International Shakespeare Association if such an organisation has been founded.

4/Further Action. The World Shakespeare Congress has represented many different nationalities and interests, but it has no continuing organisation and no continuing finance. The Committee therefore asks the concluding Plenary Session of the Congress to pass a resolution that the report of this committee should be sent by a small ad hoc committee to the main national Shakespeare associations, trusts, and institutes specializing in Shakespeare, with a request that they should consider the needs of international co-operation, especially with regard to initiating an International Shakespeare Association.

HARRISON MESEROLE

Investigative Committee on Bibliography

In its deliberations previous to and during the meetings of the World Shakespeare Congress, the Investigative Committee on Bibliography limited its range of enquiry to the area of enumerative, classified bibliography, and within this area focussed on three inter-related questions: 1/What is the proper rôle of bibliography in Shakespeare studies? 2/What is the situation in Shakespeare bibliography today? 3/What plans should be made and programs undertaken in Shakespeare bibliography for the years ahead?

The principal raison d'être of any Shakespeare bibliography, whether it be a cumulative one covering sources published over a number of years (e.g., Ebisch and Schücking, *A Shakespeare Bibliography*, or Gordon Ross Smith, *Classified Shakespeare Bibliography*) or one published annually covering publications issued in the previous year (e.g., the bibliography in *Shakespeare Quarterly* or the Shakespeare section of the *MLA International Bibliography*) lies in its value as a work of reference. As such, it must be accurate in its recording of information. It must be sensibly organized, using carefully designed patterns of arrangement and classification. And data contained in it must be made quickly and fully accessible to scholars by means of additional apparatus such as tables of contents, author and subject indexes, and the like.

The situation today in Shakespeare bibliography does not present a sharply clear picture. Professor Takashi Sasayama, who took the lead in this phase of the Investigative Committee's work, demonstrates that seven or eight publications in the field appear annually and share specific portions of the over-all task of information control. These publications range from the bibliography in *Studies in Philology*, intended for the Renaissance specialist (but which has now ceased publication); through the bibliographies in the MHRA *Annual Bibliography of English Language and Literature* and in the *MLA International Bibliography*, intended for scholars in the field of English generally; to the compilations in the two Shakespeare *Jahrbuchs* (Heidelberg and Weimar), the reports of research and opportunities for research in the *Shakespearean Research Opportunities*, and the bibliography in *Shakespeare Quarterly* – all prepared for the specialist in Shakespeare.

All of these publications focus on what may be called 'Shakespeare Scholarship,' with considerably reduced attention to attendant fields of enquiry such as theatre repertoire, staging, directing, production techniques, theatre history, Shakespeare's historical and cultural milieux, etc.

All of these publications are useful. But let us face the facts squarely. First, published materials on Shakespeare continue to increase in number each year. Second, sources for publication in the field are similarly increasing both in number and in diversity. Third, considerable duplication of effort, and of published results, persists among the several publications in the field today, with resultant duplication of costs. Clearly, if we do not heed these facts – if the present situation in Shakespeare bibliography continues unaltered – we shall soon experience the inevitable result of the law of diminishing returns, in both an intellectual and an economic sense.

As a committee, therefore, we propose that efforts be made to enlist international co-operation in the establishment and operation of an international centre or clearing house for the compilation, organization, storage and dissemination of bibliographical records of published materials in the field of Shakespeare studies. Further: that modern electronic data-processing systems and equipment be employed wherever feasible in the operation of this centre.

As we view it, such a centre could be located in any one of the countries of the world in which the study of Shakespeare is energetically pursued. It should be staffed by an editor- or archivist-in-chief, his assistant editor, two or three clerical personnel, and a computer specialist. It should contain the usual equipment and furniture required for bibliographical work (files, shelves, typewriters, etc.) and a remote terminal to provide access to a computer for input of bibliographical records.

Into this centre should flow the bibliographical data gathered by specific teams of contributors from every country, and also data that interested Shakespearians from all over the world would be encouraged to submit. (This latter aspect of information gathering is of major importance if coverage of Shakespeare materials is to be significantly broad. Without the assistance of the individual scholar willing to send offprints, notices of books, pamphlets, and other materials, particularly when published in local journals or yearbooks of limited circulation, important items can easily be overlooked by even the most carefully constituted teams of 'official' contributors.) At the centre these data should be checked, edited, converted to machine useable form, and put into electronic storage according to a meticulously worked-out encoding (classification) system. At appropriate intervals – probably annually – selected portions of the total data file should be published in the usual way to respond to the needs of scholars belonging to the various Shakespeare associations supporting the centre, and at all times the entire data file should be made available for search by the individual scholar or group of scholars for special purposes.

Such a centre can be of significant value to Shakespeare study. In its operations it can serve both the many and the few, both the large association of Shakespearians and the individual student embarking upon a dissertation. It can answer the criticism frequently voiced about current Shakespeare bibliographies, a criticism that surfaced in the deliberations of the present committee, particularly in Professor F.W. Bateson's comments. Concerned specifically with the rôle of bibliography in Shakespeare studies, Mr Bateson granted the general usefulness of today's Shakespeare bibliographies but found them inadequate as reference sources for the solution of specific problems. The centre may answer another question often raised – again, raised in our committee discussions: whether a Shakespeare bibliography should be selective or comprehensive. With a properly constituted centre, we may almost have our cake and eat it too. There is very little practical limit to the number and kind of bibliographical records that can be put into electronic storage. And what we retrieve from a large data file can be as severely selective or as broadly comprehensive as may be wished by the individual searcher. Thus, we may annually draw on the total data base for a bibliography to serve the audience now addressed by the *SQ* listings, or for a more specialized list to assist in answering the question posed as an example by Professor Bateson: 'What is the exact age of Leontes at the beginning of *The Winter's Tale?*' And we may at the same time assure Professor Gordon Ross Smith, who in his work on the Investigative Committee argued strongly for a comprehensive bibliography – 'something that lists everything published that is relevant to Shakespeare' – that he may have that comprehensive compilation, or something very close to it.

The nature of the data base and of the encoding systems used in its preparation permits its annual input to be merged automatically into cumulated bibliographies, say at three- or five-year intervals, indexed automatically, and made suitable for inexpensive publication by photo-offset. These cumulations themselves can then be cumulated at longer intervals, producing the required successors to Ebisch and Schücking and Smith without the backbreaking labours of collation, cutting and pasting, and indexing that of necessity went into those admirable volumes. The entire data base can be easily corrected, duplicate entries resolved, articles in parts published over several years joined into a single entry, or the various individual volumes in a multi-volume series similarly joined. Reviews of a particular book can be coded to print out with the title of the book itself, while at the same time remaining separately retrievable under their author's names, or their subjects, or their publication dates.

The entire base can be searched to generate national bibliographies, either selective or comprehensive, and photographic negatives of these materials can then be supplied to a sponsoring association to permit printing and publication of that portion of the base.

Careful planning at the information-gathering stage of the bibliographical work could ensure the availability on request and for research purposes of photocopies of relevant work of especially limited distribution and accessibility, and of selected other materials to scholars in areas with limited library resources.

The system, moreover, is designed to accept abstracts of articles and books

to be stored as part of the over-all data file, either currently or retrospec-
tively. Using the same techniques employed by the MLA in their abstracts/
bibliography system, the rapid compilation of an annual collection of Shakespeare abstracts is thus as relatively automatic as the sorting and printing of
the bibliography itself.

The hard facts of economics aside for the moment, how well such a centre
can function is limited only by three considerations: first, the efficiency and
thoroughness of those who undertake to gather the bibliographical records
from published sources; second, the imagination and care exerted by the
editors who will process the data; third, the acuity we as bibliographers and
programers bring to the problems of classification, encoding, and manipulation of the data in the computer system. These are not, of course, simple
matters, however simply put. They will require exceptionally careful planning and implementation. But neither are they idealistic. The hardware (the
computers and other machinery) we need for this work now exists and has
in fact been put to use by other professional associations in the humanities
for just such a compilation of data proposed here for Shakespeare studies.
The software (the programs and designs for inputting and manipulating
data in the computer) similarly exists. Professor Bruce Nesbitt, whose work
on this committee was directed toward this problem, has actually designed
a program called BARD (Bibliographical Automated Retrieval Device) for
use in a computerized Shakespeare bibliography, and plans are now being
made to begin using this program with the *SQ* bibliography in 1972.

What is needed, then, to make such a centre a reality is, first, an international committee of scholars willing to give of their time and their expert
knowledge of Shakespeare to gather and submit the data to be recorded;
second, an editor and an editorial staff to handle these data and input them
into the system; third, a location for the centre; and fourth, and of primary
importance, the support of all Shakespeare scholars individually and of all
Shakespeare associations so that the funds needed to put the centre into
operation can be secured. In this connection, the Investigative Committee
on Bibliography strongly supports the movement to found an International
Shakespeare Association as discussed at the World Shakespeare Congress
Plenary Session. Such an international body would be the natural 'home'
for the centre we envisage. Such a body could take the lead in seeking international agreement on an acceptable format for entries submitted to and
stored in the bibliographical data base, and, most important, in arriving
at a set of indexing terms, similarly acceptable internationally, which will
provide the essential classification system for the data base.

It should be said, finally, that the centre we propose does not have to be
limited in its design or operations to the collection and storage of bibliographical data. Given sufficient staff, facilities, and funding, this centre
could store and make available to scholars machine-readable texts of Shake-
spear's plays; machine-produced concordances, indexes, glossaries, and other
similar aids; photo-reproductions of documents, manuscripts, typescripts,
and publications difficult of access; a library of translations; actual copies
of books, dissertations, and articles published in 'difficult' languages; records
of work-in-progress and of proposals for projects both by individual scholars
and teams of scholars. Nor does this brief list exhaust the possibilities. Our

principal concern at the outset, however, rests in the establishment of this centre primarily as a means of information control and dissemination.

None of this can be achieved without exceptionally careful and fore-sighted planning, dedicated effort, willing co-operation among individual scholars and associations without regard for national boundaries, and suffi-cient financing to establish the centre and get it into operation. Given these irreducible minimums, we shall still have to convince those of our colleagues who either distrust the electronic systems or question the value of a broadly based Shakespeare data file, that both the system and its products are genu-inely useful reference tools. Mr Bateson speaks for this group in filing a minority report of our Investigative Committee work which asks, in sum: Will the machine systems be able to supply a better Shakespeare bibliography than those produced to date by manual techniques? Will it be more than a mere 'allusion book'? Will it be more than mere listings of publications, however well classified and indexed?

Those of us on the Investigative Committee who have used a computer system for literary and linguistic bibliography are confident that the answer to all of these questions is yes. It is not, however, an automatic yes or an affirmation chorussed out of naïveté or mere enthusiasm. It is a conclusion supported by experience, many hours of work in design and programing, and recognition of the essential truth that whatever the system used in the preparation of future Shakespeare bibliographies, the usefulness of those bibliographies to Shakespeare studies will depend directly upon the acute-ness of mind and energetic labours of those charged with their compilation.

ELEMÉR HANKISS

Investigative Committee on New Research Methods

The members of the New Research Methods Committee do not feel them-selves qualified to make sweeping generalizations about the whole body of Shakespeare criticism but, in the course of a cursory survey of the field, they gathered the impression, and they would be glad if they were proved wrong, that Shakespeare criticism as a whole has been scarcely touched by the methodological revolution that has been sweeping through the social sci-ences, the humanities, and even some regions of literary criticism in the last twenty or thirty years. Shakespeare criticism, it seems to us, has hardly availed itself of the new methods and achievements of the most progressive and active social sciences, i.e., those of sociology, psychology (with the exception of the half-a-century-old Freudian and Jungian traditions), and has preserved its virginity against the attacks of the aggressive new methods, from among which let us mention here only contemporary semiotics, semantics, communication research, and the various so-called neo-struc-turalist and quantitative methods.

And, last but not least, Shakespeare criticism has not profited from one of the most promising new trends in the social sciences, i.e., from interdisci-plinary co-operation, in the frame of which several disciplines join forces and try to solve their problems together, adapting to their own needs one another's methods, controlling and complementing one another's results. However, participation in interdisciplinary co-operation will very likely become a categorical imperative if the conviction that has been gathering force now for some years and has been frequently alluded to at this Congress prevails among Shakespeare critics; the conviction, namely, that the essence of a literary work is not to be sought exclusively in the text itself, but much more in the interaction, in the dynamic or dialectical interaction between the author, the work of art, and the public.

Having assumed, a bit irreverently, that a minority of Shakespeare critics have not closely followed the methodological revolution alluded to above, the members of the Committee, in the full text of their report to the Congress, listed and described, without any pretension to completeness, some of those interdisciplinary methods, programs, hypotheses that, in their opinion, could be adopted and turned to profit by Shakespeare criticism. Here, pressed for space, all we can do is to mention some of these methods and programs and refer those who happen to be interested in them for further information to the full text of our Report, which will be published at a later date.

I CONTENT ANALYSIS This method consists, as it is well known, in selecting some, or some dozens of, concepts that are likely to play an important part in the work of art to be analyzed and then in tabulating all the occurrences of these concepts in the work of art, and, finally, in drawing conclusions as to the origin, the meaning, and the probable impact of the work upon its readers from the frequency and distribution of these categories in the text. Computer-made concordances are of considerable help to the content analyst, though, to our knowledge, the existing concordances have not yet got adequate retrieval programs for highly differentiated or complex semantic phenomena; they cannot, for instance, put out automatically the 'ironical' passages in *Hamlet* or words, phrases, and sentences that had, in Shakespeare's time, say, negative value-connotations, etc.

II CONTINGENCY ANALYSIS This recently developed variant of content analysis not only tabulates the occurrences of the selected categories: it first, segments the text into shorter units and, secondly, it registers the co-occurrences of the different categories within the same units. In this way, it is able to discover those motive clusters, category patterns, which, recurring throughout the play, become the radiating centres of the basic, and often latent, message of the play. The analysis of Shakespeare's imagery with this quantitative method would, as it has been already proved, qualify and probably sometimes even refute the results of traditional imagery analysis.

III MULTICHANNEL ANALYSIS In the terminology of communication theory, plays – Shakespeare's plays, for instance – can be defined as 'multichannel means of communication' as they transmit various kinds of information through several 'channels': through the hero's thoughts and emotions as expressed by his words, deeds, gestures; through the characters, i.e., through the 'field of force' or atmosphere that surrounds him; through the incidents of the plot; through the visual effects of the stage, etc. As it was shown by a recent experiment, tabulating these various kinds of impulses separately, and analyzing them first separately and then together, may shed new light on some important aspects of the play. One can, for instance, follow the fluctuation of impulse density throughout the play, a fluctuation that plays a major part in governing our dramatic or tragic experience; or one can register with considerable accuracy the spectators' constant alternation between sympathy for and antipathy to the heroes, which is another important factor in the creation of dramatic or tragic experience.

IV OSCILLATION ANALYSIS Some recent investigations have proved that a peculiar kind of 'oscillation' between positive and negative poles of value is one of the basic mechanisms not only of human mind but also of literary expression. The presence and importance of this continuous value-oscillation could be established in lyrical poems, from the simplest folksongs to highly sophisticated twentieth-century poems; in novels, in the description of the heroes, for instance, or in the closures, the concluding passages of the novels; in plays, in Shakespeare's *Hamlet* as well as in O'Neill's or Beckett's plays – and so on. The study of these oscillations may help us to describe, better than we have been able to do so far, the style of different authors and periods, to define literary genres, to distinguish literary works of real aesthetic value from cheap literature, etc.

V THE TECHNIQUE OF SOCIOMETRY The technique of sociometry, which is one of the most successful methods of social psychology, consists in putting some simple questions to the members of a group and in establishing the pattern of sympathies and antipathies within the group from the answers given to these questions. This method has been applied to the analysis of some famous tragedies; the heroes' deeds, gestures, and verbal utterances, all their explicit and implicit references to one another, were tabulated and, as a result, the continuously changing pattern of human relations within the plays could be traced. It turned out that the nature and direction of these changes are highly characteristic of the various plays and of the different periods in which the plays had been written. So much so that, by the help of this method, it seems to be possible to establish a typology of the various dramatic 'strategies' that have been used by playwrights.

VI THE TECHNIQUE OF THE SEMANTIC DIFFERENTIAL This technique, developed by Charles Osgood and his collaborators, consists in giving the subjects to be tested a set of bipolar adjectives and asking them to indicate, on a seven-step scale, the place of a given concept between each pair of adjectives: for instance, between pairs of adjectives like: good ... bad, strong ... weak, happy ... sad, true ... false, etc. The results of these ratings are then factor-analyzed, reduced to two or three dimensions only, to the dimensions of, let us say, Vitality, Morality, and Activity; and then, as a second step, every concept that has been rated can be automatically located in this two- or three-dimensional semantic space. Attempts have already been made to employ this method for the purpose of learning more about the impact of literary works on readers and spectators. People were asked to rate some famous literary heroes, Shakespearian heroes among them, against the Osgoodian scale and in this way it could be stated in which semantic or value-regions of the human mind these heroes abide. And since the pattern of the heroes' location in the semantic or value universe is characteristic of both the works of art analyzed and the subjects who did the ratings, this method seems to be well suited to throw some new light on how different people respond to different kinds of literary works.

Here we have to stop short, refer those interested in further methods and details to the full text of our Report, and to the Report of the Computer Committee, and come to practicalities, to our recommendations to the Congress. In general, we think that: 1/It is essential to publicize through all available channels the new possibilities opened to the study of literature by interdisciplinary methods and co-operation; 2/to begin with some opportunities that ought to be created to discuss the problems and possibilities of interdisciplinary investigation and to develop interdisciplinary research methods; 3/In launching some pilot projects, the first nuclei of interdisciplinary co-operation ought to be created.

In concrete, we suggest that: 1/It should be proposed to the editors of the *Shakespeare Quarterly* Annual Bibliography that they include in the Index the following, and similar, subject headings and cross references: *Methods of research:* Sociology, Psychology, Psychiatry, Mythology, Anthropology, History, History of ideas, Social history, Aesthetics, History of arts, Interdisciplinary analysis, Stylistics, Structuralism, Semiotics, Semantics, Morphology, Genology, Explication de texte, Quantitative analysis, Statistics, Communication theory, Information theory, Content analysis. 2/The same should be proposed to the editors of other important international bibliographies (PMLA, *Bulletin signalétique*, etc.) 3/Interdisciplinary research methods should be recommended to the attention of the editors of *Shakespeare Quarterly, Shakespeare Survey*, and other scholarly journals, and it should be suggested that they devote one or more issues to the problems of interdisciplinary investigations. 4/The attention of the organizers of the great international congresses (MLA, ICLA, FILLM, etc.) ought to be called to the importance of interdisciplinary co-operation, asking them to open separate sections to this field of research. 5/Interdisciplinary research methods ought to be brought to the notice of the heads of university departments urging them to start lectures, seminars, and summer institutes with interdisciplinary programs. 6/Recommendations should be sent to publishing houses to publish one or two highschool or university manuals introducing students to the methods, objectives, and results of interdisciplinary investigations. 7/The members of the Committee approve of, and support, the proposition of the Investigative Committee on International Co-operation, that a Shakespeare Information Centre be set up, pooling information from all over the world concerning research work in progesss and, from time to time, co-ordinating research programs launched in various countries. Interdisciplinary programs could also be promoted by this centre.

TOSHIKAZU OYAMA

Investigative Committee on Shakespeare Translation

It is often said that Shakespeare criticism is in trouble. If so, how could we expect Shakespeare translation to be out of trouble? Every translator of Shakespeare knows, if he is conscientious, that even the slightest turbulence in present-day Shakespeare criticism does not fail to have a direct impact on Shakespeare translation. Shakespeare criticism is also often criticized as reduction of Shakespeare. If so, what is Shakespeare translation to us and to Shakespeare? It is only our devotion to Shakespeare and our firm conviction that Shakespeare should be global, not the sole possession of those whose native tongue is English, that makes us explore the formidable task of translating Shakespeare. This is the starting-point of the committee and one of those rare points on which the four members could unanimously agree.

The committee prepared for the convention a printed report, *Shakespeare Translation*, in which each member gave an historical survey of Shakespeare translation in the country he represented and delineated briefly the present state of Shakespeare translation. The report shows that, even among the four members, there is a wide difference in their attitudes to Shakespeare translation, their methods, and their perspective of possible international cooperation in the field of Shakespeare translation. The divergence is especially noteworthy between the statements by the European delegates and those of the Asian, as may be naturally inferred from the wide difference of the nature of the language and cultural background. Germany would be accredited with the oldest history in Shakespeare translation, having her own problem, however, which is that German translation has tended to become stereotyped, as the result of the cumulative efforts. French translations, from the nature of the language, cannot avoid the tendency to become longer than the original. India has also a fairly long history of Shakespeare translation. However, the peoples of India are still in great need of standard translations in various dialects. Japan has no less serious problems. In the case of the Japanese translation, perhaps we might even say that 'translation' is not the right word for the kind of work involved and the result thereof, the reason being that, because of the nature of the language, there is such a wide range of choice for the equivalent and the parallel to the original and the entire business is left to the free choice of the translator.

The scope of discussion was wide and the remarks made were divergent, because of differences in the nature of the language and the cultural and historical background of each delegate of the committee. (The page numbers refer to the printed report.)

The delegate from India, Dr Chakravorty, contends: 'In every non-English-speaking country an Authorized Version of Shakespeare in translation should be established as early as possible. The Translation Committee of the Congress should be associated with it and should ratify each translated text' (11–12). The Authorized Version must be of such competence that every translator, whether scholarly, professional, or amateur may depend upon it. For that purpose Dr Chakravorty proposes that 'a board of translators' should be established as was in the case of King James' Bible. He stipulates that the authorship of the translation for which each translator is responsible should strictly be unspecified (13–14). As to the style of the translation, he would like to follow the example set by the Loeb Classics editions of Greek text and advises that the Authorized Version of Shakespeare in translation should entirely be in prose. Dr Chakravorty earnestly hopes that an early application should be made to Unesco and other organizations for the realization of the project. Dr Chakravorty also emphasizes the importance of the translation of standard Shakespeare criticism.

Dr Gabler, the German delegate, warned at the outset of the committee session that, in a discussion on translation on an international level, stern distinction should be made between Shakespeare translation and criticism of Shakespeare translation and held strongly that the discussion should be focussed on the principles of Shakespeare translation, not on the actual problems involved in the translation, thus rendering it possible to evolve the criteria by which each translation could be easily evaluated. It is mainly this viewpoint that guided Dr Gabler in his historical survey of German translation. He summarizes: 'On the whole ... one of the most widespread features of German Shakespeare translations in the course of the past 200 years has been continuous "poeticizing" which blurs and obliterates many of the distinctions of style and the language of situation and character in Shakespeare' (39). He admits that, although there has been disenchantment with the Schlegel-Tieck translation, a monument of German romantic literature, and much has been done by many other scholars, the translation of Shakespeare into German has reached a point of crisis. Dr Gabler, therefore, welcomes the recent project of the Deutsche Shakespeare Gesellschaft in Bochum to establish new prose translations of Shakespeare's plays with twentieth-century critical insight and scholarship. He firmly believes that such exact prose versions could convey to a German reader more fully than any done in German blank verse the complexity and density of Shakespeare's dramatic and verbal art. As a help to the full understanding of Shakespeare's wide range of verbal art, Dr Gabler advocates 'a comparative reading' of the various versions in German translation and concludes that 'the obvious vehicle ... in this case be a study edition based for each play on one existing translation, and liberally annotated from others wherever these bear out a different aspect of the original' (41).

The delegate from Japan, Professor Toshiko Oyama, begins her brief survey of Shakespeare translation in Japan by pointing out that Japan's access to Shakespeare's plays was rather late as compared with that of other countries, especially in Europe. With the opening of the new era, Shakespeare was gradually introduced along with the desire to absorb western civilization. The first was an adaptation of *Hamlet* (1875) which appeared in one of the leading journals of the period and which was followed by many adaptations and translations. Among all the translators of Shakespeare, Shōyō Tsubouchi had a unique reputation. Shōyō, who was himself a Kabuki writer, translated Shakespeare mainly in Kabuki style, with the rhythm of Japanese ballad drama of 7–5 metre, using the conventional Japanese poetic images. Although at present his translations are outmoded, they have had an immense influence upon his successors in the field. In Japan, every translator of Shakespeare must face the problem of language, because Japanese belongs to an entirely different language family from the European languages. Too much consciousness of the difference sometimes makes a Japanese translator feel that it is impossible to render Shakespeare into Japanese. The fact remains, however, that there are a great many Shakespeare lovers in Japan and most of them enjoy Shakespeare through translations. Japanese translations of Shakespeare may roughly be divided into three groups: 1/modern, easily understood, colloquial Japanese prose translation, some of them very free and bold adaptations and many stage versions today belong to this group; 2/literal, word-for-word translation, faithful to the original; although translations of this kind are helpful to the students of Shakespeare, they often mar the naturalness of the Japanese expressions and could hardly be presented on the stage; 3/eclectic versions: translation based upon sound knowledge of the differences of the languages and the verse systems; translation faithful to the original, keeping the Shakespearian images and metaphors as much as possible, but rendering Shakespearian blank verse into Japanese 5–7–5 verse form with its tremendous varieties and irregularities. Mrs Oyama concludes that 'translations of this group have a great variety in themselves, but they have one point in common – and that is an effort to reproduce Shakespeare faithfully' (51).

Faithfulness to the original is also the point emphasized by Professor Spriet of the University of Bordeaux. He claims that theatrical adaptations should be excluded from the discussion of Shakespeare translation. There are many excellent theatrical adaptations, he admits, but adaptations are, after all, adaptations, not translations. They tend to be no more Shakespeare's plays in French than the adaptors' own creative writing. Professor Spriet puts it decisively: 'The "sine qua non" condition of a satisfactory translation is a certain measure of faithfulness to the original' (59). However, he also emphasizes that faithfulness is not the exclusive criterion of translation. Scholarly renditions which have no other qualities than their faithfulness to the original cannot be recommended either. An acceptable translation is 'a compromise between diverse and possibly contradictory demands.' Professor Spriet describes his basic attitude: 'It [an acceptable translation] must be faithful, yet definitely French both in morphology and syntax. It must be precise, yet free enough to devise equivalents when literality does not make sense or is an excuse for unimaginative clumsiness. Translation is the art of finding the equivalent which does not betray the original and conforms to the laws of the language into which it is translated' (59). Translation is an organism, the complexity of which could only be rendered by the happy unification of the rare gift of imaginative creativity and sound knowledge of Shakespeare scholarship. This leads to his belief that 'there is not *one* good translation of a given play but several renditions which are diversely acceptable ones, according to the expectations of the reader or spectator' (61). Professor Spriet evaluates the attempts of the contemporary French poets who are experimenting in new poetic structures in French to make it more flexible, less restricted by coherence and logical clarity. He agrees with Bonnefoy, a contemporary French poet, who recommends word-for-word translation, thus preserving the complexity and density of Shakespeare's lines. Professor Spriet predicts with Bonnefoy that the time has come for a new translation of Shakespeare in France.

Considering the nature of the problem it was clear from the beginning of discussion that the committee could not expect any definite conclusion. However, it became clear that there were several points where all the discussants could meet and cultivate common ground:

1/Word-for-word prose translation is the most appropriate style for the new Shakespeare translation. Although the basic attitudes are not the same, all the members agreed that the most commendable form of a new version is the exact prose translation. Mrs Oyama's attitude in this respect is slightly complex. From the nature of the Japanese language and its style, she wants to translate Shakespeare's rhythm into the native rhythm pattern of the old Japanese ballad drama. However, her basic principle is to render Shakespearian images and metaphors in their entirety. It is obvious that her destination is word-for-word translation. This unexpected convergence of the opinions of all the members of the committee seems to be of special interest and importance, since it seems to be clearly indicating the direction toward which every new version of Shakespeare translation, of every nation, of every language, is aligned.

2/Shakespeare translation should be explored as a new territory of comparative literature.

3/It may be possible to contribute to new interpretations of Shakespeare through translation.

4/From these points of discussion, it became clear that there will be a much wider range of possibilities for international co-operation in the field of Shakespeare translation than has hitherto been supposed.

5/It has been decided by the committee to continue the publication of a review of Shakespeare translation. The title is to be *Shakespeare Translation in Progress*, thus making the small pamphlet prepared by the committee for the 1971 Congress the first issue of the series. Global contributions are invited to the annual publication.

6/At the end of the session, the discussion became heated on Shakespearian stage versions. However, for any conclusive words we must wait for another session, in another Congress.

MIHAIL BOGDAN

The Variorum Glossary Investigative Committee

Although as a poet and dramatist Shakespeare has been an intensively cultivated field of research, his vocabulary and use of words have not yet been fully explored. And, if in the vast field of Shakespearian scholarship there is reason for discontent, many of the inadequacies derive from a misunderstanding of the words Shakespeare uses and particularly of the ways in which he uses them. For it is common knowledge that much of Shakespeare's genius stems from his manipulation of words, the manner in which he takes existing words and gives them new turns of meaning.

The Variorum Glossary Investigative Committee, therefore, believes that the basic problem of Shakespeare studies is the vocabulary. A complete control of Shakespeare's text, and this is what all Shakespeare scholars are striving after, can be achieved only after the accurate meanings have been established. The basic problem is, then, the Shakespeare lexicon, the meanings of words in isolation and in their various linguistic, social, and dramatic contexts.

So far as we know, there is no definitive dictionary of early modern English, nor any definitive dictionary of Shakespeare. And there is no last word on the text or on the canon of Shakespeare. Although Shakespeare is available to various interpretations, depending on the angle of vision, the basic meaning of the words used by him in his plays and poems can be fairly accurately determined; alternative meanings can also be determined, leading to the overtones that give Shakespeare's language its richness and variety. But the words and their meanings are basic, and it is only by them and through them that we can come to an understanding of Shakespeare's works.

The need for a Shakespeare glossary was felt before a hundred years had elapsed from the poet's death. In 1710 (see Louis Marder, 'Shakespeare Glossaries – 1710–1948' SNL [Dec 1970]) Charles Gildon made up a 175-word glossary which was followed in 1768 by Richard Warner's 19-page glossary. The British Museum records a substantial number of manuscript copies now lost.

Through the centuries the approaches to the Shakespeare lexicon have been different. Although the prime concern was the establishing of the exact meaning, lexicographers have not infrequently directed their efforts in other less dramatically relevant channels, e.g., emphasizing Celtic or Gaelic origins (Charles Mackay), or dealing in particular with Germanic words in contrast to the native elements (Eilert Ekwall), or giving Lowland Scots definitions (John Phin). Most glossaries are anxious to deal with obscurities, archaisms, obsolete and crux words (Thomas Hanmer, Edward Capell, James O. Halliwell, Alexander Dyce, etc), while others have in mind the foreign student of English (Nicholaus Delius, Leon Kellner).

The two works which attain to the highest degree of completeness and linguistic accuracy are Alexander Schmidt's *Shakespeare Lexicon* and C.T. Onions' *Shakespeare Glossary*, both of which deserve special attention, while the findings of NED should also be seriously taken into consideration. Schmidt's work, a complete dictionary in itself, carefully examines the meaning and use of every word found in the *Globe* edition of Shakespeare's works, giving an almost full concordance of citations for each entry. Onions supplements and improves on Schmidt in his *Glossary* based on Craig's *Oxford Shakespeare*. And yet Onions' work suffers from certain limitations. Some of these stem from the limitations of his primary source, the NED. Onions omits the phrase and context, and his treatment of technical and specialized terms is inadequate. Not all technical terms hold equal dramatic importance in Shakespeare's text. It appears that Shakespeare's use of terms from law, medicine, music, and botany is of a general sort. But his sea and naval terms call for a closer examination. They run through his work in varying degrees and are used with a precision and aptness which call for special consideration, their frequent overtones acquiring dramatic significance.

Alexander Schmidt's classical *Shakespeare Lexicon* (Berlin 1874) reprinted and enlarged in later editions, is no longer adequate for modern requirements. Almost a century has passed since its publication. Leon Kellner's *Shakespeare Wörterbuch* (Leipzig 1922) is meritorious though too concise and elementary a glossary, being written for a broader public: it can no longer serve modern scientific purposes. The recent Shakespeare concordances by Marvin Spevack (*A Complete and Systematic Concordance to the Works of Shakespeare* volumes I and II [Hildesheim 1968]) and T.H. Howard-Hill (*Oxford Shakespeare Concordances* [Oxford University Press 1969] in separate volumes for the various plays) supply no more than useful and labour-saving raw materials for our undertaking. They are the products of computer machinery which now have to be filled with brain and life, and must be evaluated. The rest of the books and articles that exist in the field of Shakespeare lexicons and glossaries may be designated only as more or less valuable preliminary work.

Present lexicons and glossaries do not represent the latest scholarship in Elizabethan language and culture. Some indication of the size of such scholarship may be deduced from quick reference to the recently published articles on such words as 'prenzie' (MM III.i. 93), 'ducdame' (AYLI II.v. 60), 'pajock' (Ham III.ii. 295), 'pertaunt' (LLL v.ii. 67) in literary and philological journals from *Notes and Queries* to the *Modern Language Review* and the *Shakespeare Quarterly*, as well as journals in other disciplines, notably linguistics and speech.

Moreover, present lexicons antedate research into Elizabethan connotations and word-play – studies such as those by Mahood, Partridge, and Elton. Examples are the different levels of meaning for words like 'tombe' (RJ II.iii. 9; *All's Well* II.iii. 147; MAN v.iii. 9), 'traitor' (TC IV.ii. 38–9), and 'naughty' (MM II.i. 77–8; TC IV.ii. 38).

Also needed is recognition of current socio-linguistic research into languages, laying bare the extraordinary complexity of social implications in speech in any language community. Should linguists not begin to reconstruct, however crudely, something of the same sort for the English of Shakespeare's time? Only a vast mass of lexicographical data from the period would enable us to do so.

The future Shakespeare lexicon should, therefore, consider *all* the dispersed research work on Elizabethan word-material of the last half-century, and also give cultural, historical, ideological, and etymological information.

If present lexicons are not satisfactory, does not the NED provide adequate supplementation? The NED has indeed served the needs of English literary and linguistic scholarship for almost a century, and it still remains an indispensable means of reference for English scholars throughout the world. But its usefulness is limited for scholars working in the Elizabethan period. Dissatisfaction with the NED as a dictionary of Elizabethan English has existed since the 1930s (see W.S. Mackie, 'Shakespeare's English: and how far it can be investigated with the help of the "New English Dictionary"' *Modern Language Review* 21 (1936) 1–10; Hilda Hulme, 'Shakespeare and the Oxford English Dictionary' *Review of English Studies* ns 6 (1955) 128ff; and Louis Marder, 'The Future of Shakespearian Scholarship' *Shakespeare Newsletter* [April 1964] and 'Shakespeare Glossaries – 1710–1948' *Shakespeare Newsletter* [1970], 22–3). A wider range of Elizabethan meanings, more quotations illustrating usages, more exact dating of the usages are needed. The NED is also based on printed sources, and Onions has cut his work off from much earlier manuscript material, which is an indispensable primary source. His starting point was too late. This has led to inadequacy in recognizing and in defining many technical and specialized terms in Shakespeare, and, as a result, interpretation has suffered. One example among many is the veiled answer of Enobarbus to Antony, 'I'll strike and cry "Take all." ' He does not mean that he will set upon the enemy but that he will surrender. This is doubly unfortunate because the use of sea and naval terms (sometimes in a subtle way) is characteristic of Enobarbus. There are many examples of such omissions and of error.

Since there is this general agreement that we need some kind of a new

Shakespeare dictionary, the next question is, 'What kind of dictionary?' There are really three possibilities – ruling out a supplement to Schmidt as not adequate to our needs: 1/a revival of the project for a dictionary of Early Modern English, or, on a more limited scale, a dictionary of Tudor and early Stuart English; 2/a variorum Shakespeare glossary somewhat along the lines suggested by Professor Marder; and, 3/since 1 and 2 could not be available for some time and require intricate organization, a shorter, more immediately available Reader's Glossary, concentrating primarily on the likely-to-be misunderstood ambiguous words in Shakespeare – a glossary sensitive to the latest scholarship on Elizabethan language and useful for the foreign as well as the native reader.

The magnitude of such a task as the Dictionary of Early Modern English is self-evident. Such magnitude accounts for the erratic history of that project – dormant from 1939 to 1965, when it was revived by Professor Fries shortly before his death in 1967. In 1968 it received new life with grants from the American Council of Learned Societies and the Rackham School of Graduate Studies to Professors Richard W. Bailey, Jay L. Robinson, and James M. Downer. However, the project appears quiescent at this time. A similar project at the University of Leeds has been discontinued.

It could be one of the functions of a committee such as ours, at the proposed Shakespeare Centre, to inquire more thoroughly into the fate of these and similar projects, co-ordinating its activities with these projects, if alive, and, if not, perhaps helping to revivify them or even to interest new sponsors should they be needed.

If the Dictionary of Early Modern English is not forthcoming, a more modest goal for the World Shakespeare Congress, and one sooner realized, would be a New Shakespeare Glossary. It might even serve as a first stage for the DEME. The proposed Shakespeare Centre might well define the task, suggest some guidelines, and initiate interest in the project to attract competent editors and adequate sponsorship.

Professor Marder's description might serve as a starting point for such guidelines: 'a Variorum Glossary of all the words, names, and places in Shakespeare compiled in a historical, interpretative, illustrative, literary, and lexical manner.' It 'could contain every word (and proper name) with every form separately listed, part of speech, pronunciation (and its variation in scansion), etymology, denotative definition, connotative meanings, usage, label (i.e., obsolete, law, medicine, etc, dialect, phrases, explication, variorum notes, source, NED first usage, frequency of occurrence in Shakespeare (in Q, bad Q, Folios), last use if obsolete, use by contemporaries, and cross references. Sufficient citations should be included for clarification.'

The committee would stress the importance of identifying idioms, puns, allusions, proverbs, sayings. Works such as Tilley's dictionary of Elizabethan proverbs should be utilized. Elizabethan connotations for mythological characters and place names should also be included.

The lexicon should make extensive use of manuscript materials such as the Bagot letters at the Folger Library, for non-standard words and phrases as well as colloquial meanings.

Shakespeare's knowledge and use of technical terms of whatever kind should be re-examined for such a glossary, because much interesting work has been done by professional men on various aspects of these. Law terms have an added importance since the publication of *Shakespeare's Legal and Political Background* by G.W. Keeton in 1967. Alexander Falconer has made important contributions in elucidating naval and sea terms.

There is a need for the editors of such a glossary to set up a rather more sophisticated 'socio-linguistic' range to identify the social and regional provenance of terms in relation to technical ranges, social patterns, argot, cant, scholasticism, forms of address and reference. (Have we really, for instance, got to the bottom of the thou/you implications in Shakespearian England, or the implications of names and titles in address forms?)

The lexicon needs an extensive 'sweep' through the period sources, printed and manuscript, and, in consequence, a much greater range of citations to 'fix' and define words and their collocations within the limited period.

The dictionary should be currently informed on textual controversies, but such controversies should be recognized only to a limited extent, i.e., as far as it is evident and convincing. There should be a selected variorum listing with variant definitions as far as these are relevant. It is unnecessary to give all the variants.

Definitions should be expressed in language that is up-to-date and appropriate. Great care should be bestowed on hitting the actual meaning and possible connotations of the words at Shakespeare's time. The words should be shown in the context of Shakespearian lines.

Such a lexicon is a project to which this committee can only call the attention of Shakespearians in the hope of interesting qualified scholars and adequate sponsorship.

Within the scope of this committee, however, could be the more immediate Reader's Glossary. The presence on the committee of members from a variety of non-English speaking countries would be of special advantage in orienting such a glossary to the needs of the student whose native language is not English. Such a glossary, while more complete than the usual footnotes in a critical edition of Shakespeare or an appended glossary, would nevertheless be selective of words, terms, and names whose meaning is not immediately understood, or with overtones specially significant to the play. While this committee is now formally ended, its members may wish – on their own initiative – to undertake such a project.

Marvin Spevack, using the *Shorter Oxford English Dictionary* tapes of Thomas Finkenstaedt, has begun work on a computerized Shakespeare lexicon of a more limited scope than the Variorum Glossary. However, it will be oriented primarily towards grammatical aspects. Its interest will be primarily for the scholar, while the shorter glossary projected by this committee would be a reader's glossary.

Other tasks are needed, which should be called to the attention of Shakespearian scholars. One is a comparison of selective lexical translations into various European languages – especially the manner in which ambiguities (like the sullied/solid of *Hamlet*) have been handled by different translators. Some kind of pattern for interlinguistic studies of this kind might be suggested by the proposed Shakespeare Centre.

Also needed are: 1/a comprehensive review of research to date on Elizabethan language; 2/an annotated bibliography of materials such as manuscript glossaries useful to the student of Elizabethan words; 3/an annotated bibliography of all significant books and articles on Elizabethan word meanings, grammar, pronunciation, idioms, and similar topics; 4/an essay on needs in future research in this field; 5/the taping of selected concordances to writers contemporary with Shakespeare, to such works as the Book of Common Prayer, and to selected sources for colloquialisms and dialect, like the Bagot letters. Some scholar should undertake to seek out already existing tapes of Elizabethan books, if any (for example, a taping of a concordance to the Geneva or Bishops' Bible). Other scholars could make new tapes of useful concordances to other Elizabethan books (Lyly, Greene, etc.).

Obviously one of the essential tasks is as much co-ordination as possible of all present and future efforts at compiling Shakespeare glossaries. The needs of Shakespearians are best served by avoiding as much duplication of effort as is possible.

Obviously, too, our task as a committee of this Congress is best accomplished by a co-ordination of our labours with those of other committees of this Congress: sensitivity to the latest trends in textual study in Shakespeare is basic to a true lexicon of Shakespeare's works. Research in Shakespearian language can be facilitated by acquaintance with new research methods. Certainly the use to which the computer can be put, as well as the delegation of certain tasks to computer experts, is important to the compilation of a glossary. Much of the labour will have to be international. The proposed Shakespeare Centre can facilitate this by helping to locate sponsors. And, the new lexicons may provide future translators with the understanding of the language they will translate. A project such as the glossary will then depend heavily on communication with other groups. Such communication the proposed International Federation of Shakespearians and future Congresses can best provide.

It is to be hoped that there are scholars willing to address themselves to these tasks.

SALLY YEATES SEDELOW

Investigative Committee for
Shakespearian Studies and the Computer

The Investigative Committee on Shakespearian Studies and the Computer has considered a number of areas for which computer assistance seems promising. Specifically, Marvin Spevack of the University of Munster has written a report on 'Concordances: Old and New'; T.H. Howard-Hill, of the University of Wales at Swansea, on 'A Common Shakespeare Text File for Computer-Aided Research: A Proposal'; Barron Brainerd, of the University of Toronto, on 'The Computer in Statistical Studies of William Shakespeare'; Dolores Marie Burton, of Boston University, on 'Research-in-Idleness or PUCK among the Bibliographers: Reflections on a Fully Automated Shakespeare Bibliography'; R.L. Widmann, of the University of Pennsylvania, on 'Text Collating and Editing'; Fred MacFadden, of Coppin State College (Maryland), on 'Opportunities for Teaching and Researching

Shakespeare with the Computer'; and Sally Yeates Sedelow, of the University of Kansas, on 'The Use of the Computer for Stylistic Studies of Shakespeare.' Professors Spevack and Howard-Hill are well-known for their Shakespearian concordances, which were produced by the computer. Professor Brainerd, a mathematician, has just published a book entitled *Introduction to the Mathematics of Language Study*. Professor Burton is a very active bibliographer and her annotated bibliography of 'Studies of Shakespeare's Language and Style' will appear soon in *Shakespearean Research Opportunities*. Professor Widmann is working on *A Midsummer Night's Dream* for the New Variorum Shakespeare, Professor MacFadden is former Chairman of the Humanities Division at Coppin State College and is thus concerned with a variety of applications of computer-based studies of language and literature, and Professor Sedelow, the author of this summary, for a number of years has been concerned with developing theory and methods for the use of the computer for stylistic studies of literature. (Acknowledgements must also be made for assistance in preparing for the World Shakespeare Congress to C. Carroll Hollis, in his role as chairman of the English Department at the University of North Carolina at Chapel Hill. And special thanks are due to Mr Jack Cobb, who served as my graduate assistant for research related to the Congress.) Thus, the range of experience and research emphases represented by the Committee is considerable and we have undertaken a fairly comprehensive investigation of uses and possible uses of the computer for Shakespearian scholarship and teaching.

The members of this Committee are, first of all, in agreement as to the general desirability of the use of the computer in Shakespearian studies. Professor Sedelow urges that the computer be regarded as, in effect, a 'research assistant' and Professor Brainerd points to the greatly expanded accuracy and working speed made possible by the computer. Thus, as a research assistant, the computer can be used for tedious, dehumanizing 'tasks' and can be counted upon to do these tasks reliably and quickly. Professor Spevack notes that the computer 'can provide us, simply and quickly, with what we have never had before – completeness ... Completeness is an attitude toward scholars and machines. It is in itself a form of analysis. Broadly and imaginatively conceived, it can be enormously sophisticated: solid and many-sided, refined and flexible. It can enable as many users as possible to proceed from text to concordance, or from concordance to text, in ways hitherto impossible within the scope of a single work.'

Professor Spevack's comments on completeness lead into a second generalization upon which this Committee is in agreement – that is, that the computer opens up an enormous range of new possibilities for Shakespearian research and teaching. Professor MacFadden's report takes a very broad look at possible computer-aided studies of Shakespeare. Some of his suggestions will seem odd to Shakespearian scholars although perhaps not, as Professor MacFadden implies, to all computer scientists. Other suggestions, such as patterns of foreign word borrowings in Shakespeare or rhyme-scheme preferences, will seem more congenial to the Shakespearian scholar. Among Professor MacFadden's categories are graphic arts communications, musicology, speech, and so on. With reference just to concordances, Professor Spevack notes that, once a concordance is available on magnetic tape, it 'provides a basis for projects which can be derived from the concordance as well as a bridge for projects of both a more restricted and less restricted nature. Among those to be derived directly from a complete and therefore most flexible concordance are numerous subconcordances and specialized indexes, as well as studies ranging from, say, the style of a certain period or genre to the vocabulary of the social strata in Shakespeare. Of a broader nature are those projects which add new information or techniques to the investigation of literary and linguistic aspects of Shakespeare, other writers, and even early modern English.' Professor Spevack's comments indicate that even from a relatively restricted project, such as a concordance, may be derived many other useful computer-aided studies.

Given these two general principles – that it is desirable to use the computer both for certain tasks which were traditionally accomplished without computer assistance; and that the computer does indeed make possible a new range of investigations – certain requirements for translating those principles into action were apparent to almost all members of our Committee. The first such requirement is discussed in greatest detail in Howard-Hill's report, which notes that 'texts of Shakespeare in both modern and old spelling should become generally available for scholarly study.' Howard-Hill points out that 'already there are many potentially worthwhile research projects which are being hindered because computer-readable versions of Shakespearian texts are not available, or are uneconomical to prepare. Good work which could be done is being put aside, or being carried out without the aid of the computer because it is still too difficult, time-consuming, and expensive for all but the most determined scholar to work with the computer ... The establishment of a generally accessible computer-readable Shakespearian text is the first, necessary, step towards the most useful computer study of Shakespeare.' A corollary to the need for Shakespearian text or texts in computer-accessible form is the requirement, also recognized by most members of the Committee, for computer programs to process the texts.

Recognition of the needs for putting a version or versions of the Shakespearian canon into computer-accessible form and for making available computer programs to deal with the text, prompted a number of Committee members to urge that a centre be established for computer-based Shakespearian studies.

During working sessions at the World Congress, the Committee developed recommendations for centres, or nodes within networks, ranging from a very minimal custodianship of the Shakespearian corpus, in computer-accessible form, to a rather extensive provision of computer services. In the Committee's view, the most viable long-range possibility would be one or more networks, either wholly or partially dedicated to Shakespearian studies.

Another desideratum generally recognized by Committee members is maintaining the integrity of the text. First of all, material should not be cut from a text, or a given edition of a text, before the text is put into computer-accessible form. Secondly, if material (e.g., syntactic categories) is *added* to the text, Sedelow urges that the criteria used in such 'pre-editing' should be explained clearly and explicitly, so that anyone wishing to replicate a given procedure would have a precise understanding of its underlying assumptions. Brainerd argues that, in general, there should be precisely stated standards with reference to the definitions and procedures used in any research project (e.g., the definition of *word* when word counts are undertaken).

Since several of the reports concentrate upon special topics, the essence of their content has not been conveyed in the summary above. Therefore, brief commentary on these reports follows.

In his discussion of statistical studies, Professor Brainerd asks, 'In what areas can this greatly expanded accuracy and speed of counting (as supplied by the computer) be best applied?' He goes on to answer, 'Disputed authorship studies come to mind first; however, studies of the chronology of works within a given author (Yardi 1945), studies of the evolution of the style in a genre through time and across national boundaries, and studies of variations of style from one genre to another are also obvious possibilities. What these applications have in common is that they are rooted in the idea of comparison of texts. Numerical results about a single text are for the most part uninteresting and only become useful when such results are obtained for other texts and comparisons made. In order to weigh the value of the evidence obtained from such comparisons, it is usually necessary to resort to statistical methods.'

To indicate just how statistics might be used, Professor Brainerd concentrates upon the question of disputed authorship and provides a fine statistical tutorial as he explores solutions to that question.

In her 'Reflections on a Fully Automated Shakespeare Bibliography' Dolores Burton urges the scholar to 'imagine ... that research is conducted before a computer terminal, an arrangement consisting of a telephone, a typewriter keyboard, and a display unit resembling a color (green only) television set and that one can summon the genie in the tube to accomplish ninety percent of this work. A long-distance phone call establishes communication with the Shakespeare data bank, and typing a few words produces a bibliography program named PUCK. What's needed is a list of all that has been written on the syntax of Shakespeare since 1955. Unfortunately, there are many Athenians in the woods and, if a particular one is wanted, he must be described exactly. The user may therefore be asked first to name the dates of his inquiry (1955–1970), the languages he wishes to read (English), and the type of document he requires (books and journal articles). The computer begins immediately to sort the items in the bibliography thus saving time for the more detailed search that will follow. The next step, the crucial retrieval operation, consists of matching the words of the user's request with the information stored in the machine. Instructions to the computer should be sufficiently broad to elicit all the items required and narrow enough to block irrelevant material.' Professor Burton stresses in her report the importance of the subject index for an automated bibliography and she suggests a number of approaches which might be considered for the production of such a subject index. She further points out that a computer-based bibliography 'will be a more flexible document in the computer than it was on the printed page. Annual issues will no longer be discrete with entries fixed irrevocably in a given form and order. Items can be moved in the machine so that, for example, reviews appearing in 1953,

1954, and 1955 for a book originally cited in 1951 will now be listed immediately under the book. Discussions which continue over a number of years (Richard Flatter on the Hecate scene in *Macbeth*) could be grouped together and the fact that a particular entry has provoked such discussion can be noted with the original entry. Articles or books overlooked in a given year and added subsequently need no longer appear out of chronological order but can be placed by the machine under the appropriate date of publication.'

Professor Widmann is using the computer 'to find all types of variants in a number of editions of *A Midsummer Night's Dream*. The editions, which have been keypunched and put onto magnetic tape, range from the six seventeenth-century editions through many of the 18th century editions and do include some 19th and 20th century editions. As of this writing, 25 editions have been keypunched and are ready for searching for the variants, including accidental, semi-substantive, and substantive variants, even though only the substantive and the important semi-substantive variants will be recorded in the section of Historical collation in the New Variorum *MND*.' Professor Widmann notes that 'Sample runs of 45 lines of 6 editions were done in the Spring of 1969 and sample runs using a very refined FORMAT program were done in the Spring of 1970. Both sets of sample runs convinced us, textual collation via computer was possible, desirable, and successful.'

Professor Sedelow suggests that the computer be used extensively for stylistic studies and offers to make her own programs available to a centre/network for computer-based Shakespearian studies. In her report, she exemplifies the use of a series of programs called VIA, which are used for *thematic* analysis, by talking about their use with reference to a particular theme, 'love,' in *Hamlet*. She also urges that Shakespearian scholars make their expertise available for basic studies on the nature of language and literature. A number of the studies proposed by Professor MacFadden in his report and by Professor Marder in the article cited from the *Shakespeare Newsletter* could not now be carried out by computer because they are beyond our current state of knowledge about language. She asks, therefore, that Shakespearian scholars consider the utility for them of a centre or network for computer-based studies of *language* and that they then think out the connections that might exist between a Shakespearian centre and such a more broadly focussed centre.

In conclusion, the Investigative Committee on the Computer in Shakespearian Studies is optimistic about the prospective contributions of computer technology to the future of Shakespearian scholarship and it urges, 1 / that the computer be used for many tasks which have in the past unnecessarily burdened the scholar and hampered his creativity; 2 / that the computer be used to open up new prospects for Shakespearian research and scholarship; 3 / that the possibility of a centre or network to facilitate computer-based Shakespearian studies be seriously explored, and that the exploration include a possible national and international computer-based language analysis network as context for such a Shakespearian studies centre.

Members of the Congress

Asterisks indicate members who did not attend the Congress.

Robert P. Adams *University of Washington*
Geoffrey Aggeler *University of Utah*
Peter Aichinger *Collège militaire royal, Québec*
Michael J.B. Allen *University of California, Los Angeles*
Gary T. Anderberg *College of Notre Dame, California*
Alexander Anikst *Institute of the History of the Arts, Moscow,* USSR*
LeRoy E. Annis *University of Puget Sound, Washington*
Warren B. Austin *Stephen F. Austin State University, Texas*
Luella Balfour *Kelowna, British Columbia*
Francine Ballard *Macomb County Community College, Michigan*
Michael Ballin *Waterloo Lutheran University, Ontario*
Eileen Ban *New York*
Jerry Bangham *London, Ohio*
C.L. Barber *University of California, Santa Cruz*
Laird H. Barber *University of Minnesota*
Jonas A. Barish *University of California, Berkeley*
J. Leeds Barroll *University of South Carolina*
David B. Barron *Skokie, Illinois*
F.W. Bateson *Oxford University*
Michael Bawtree *Stratford Shakespearian Festival*
Andrianne Baytop *Douglass College, New Jersey*
Martha Beck *Muskingum College, Ohio*

George J. Becker *Western Washington State College*
Bernard Beckerman *Columbia University*
Allen Bell *Selkirk College, British Columbia*
Mary Bell *University of Lancaster, England*
Robert M. Bender *University of Missouri*
Robert Bennett *University of Delaware*
Gerald Eades Bentley *Princeton University*
Mrs G.E. Bentley *Princeton, New Jersey*
Herbert Berry *University of Saskatchewan*
Sister Mary Louise Beutner *Santa Clara University, California*
David Bevington *University of Chicago*
Abraham Bezanker *San Jose State College, California*
P.C. Birkinshaw *University of Cape Town, South Africa*
Albert G. Black *California State College, Long Beach*
Sheila Blanchard *Northern Illinois University*
Max Bluestone *University of Massachusetts, Boston*
Mihail Bogdan *University of Cluj, Romania*
Jeannine Bohlmeyer *Bethel College, Minnesota*
Fredson Bowers *University of Virginia*
Norman P. Boyer *California State College at Los Angeles*
Muriel C. Bradbrook *Girton College, Cambridge University*
Barron Brainerd *University of Toronto*
Janya Brant *Theatre West, Hollywood, California*
Norman A. Brittin *Auburn University, Alabama*
Nigel Brockmann *Keele University, England*
George L. Brodersen *University of Manitoba*
Nicholas Brooke *University of East Anglia, England*
Elizabeth Broughton *North Vancouver Community Arts Council*
Allen E. Brown *Virginia Commonwealth University*
John Russell Brown *University of Birmingham, England*
Fred Broyles *Spokane Community College, Washington*
Geoffrey Bullough *Edinburgh, Scotland*
Dolores M. Burton *Boston University, Massachusetts*
Robert Butman *Haverford College–Bryn Mawr College, Pennsylvania*
Anna Cail *Vernon, British Columbia*
Andrew S. Cairncross *Texas Technical University*
Charles Scott Campbell *Red Deer College, Alberta*
Stephen C. Campbell *University of Moncton, New Brunswick*
Elisabeth Case *Cambridge University Press*
Jagannath Chakravorty *Jadavpur University, Calcutta*
Beatrice Chapin *Kelowna, British Columbia*
Earl John Clark *Northeastern Illinois State College*
James Clark *San Jose State College, California*
Mort Clark *Westchester Community College, New York*
Thomas Clayton *University of Minnesota, Minneapolis*
Wolfgang Clemen *University of Munich*
Ruby Cohn *California Institute of the Arts*
John Coldewey *University of Colorado*
Joan Coldwell *University of Victoria, British Columbia*

J. Scott Colley *Vanderbilt University, Tennessee*
Lowell W. Coolidge *College of Wooster, Ohio*
Betty K. Cooper *Canadian Broadcasting Corporation*
David Copelin *University of California, Davis*
Derek F. Crawley *Queen's University, Ontario*
Dolora Cunningham *San Francisco State College*
Irene Dash *Queensborough Community College, New York*
Catherine Day *Kelowna, British Columbia*
William H. Desmonde *Croton-on-Hudson, New York*
Herbert B. Dewey *State University of New York*
John Doebler *Arizona State University*
Florence Donaldson *Vancouver, British Columbia*
Marjorie Donker *Western Washington State College*
Joyce Doolittle *University of Calgary*
T.S. Dorsch *University of Durham, England*
Eugene Dow *Pierce College, California*
Esther M. Doyle *Juniata College, Pennsylvania*
Thomas A. Duff *Seton Hall University, New Jersey*
Catherine M. Dunn *San Fernando Valley State College, California*
Robert P. Dunn *Loma Linda University, California*
Umberto Eco *University of Bologna*
S.P.J. Ellis *Chung Chi College, Hong Kong*
Robert Ellison *Playhouse Theatre Company, Vancouver*
W.R. Elton *City University of New York*
Mladen Engelsfeld *Zagreb University, Yugoslavia*
Robert Escarpit *Université de Bordeaux*
Leonore Ewert *University of Victoria, British Columbia*
M.D. Faber *University of Victoria, British Columbia*
Alex F. Falconer *University of St Andrews, Scotland*
Doris V. Falk *Douglass College, Rutgers University, New Jersey*
Dean B. Farnsworth *Brigham Young University, Utah*
Lawrence Fast *Vancouver City College*
Alberta Feynman *Skidmore College, New York*
Robert E. Fitch *Pacific School of Religion, Berkeley, California*
Fred Flahiff *University of Toronto*
Robert Fleissner *Central State University, Ohio*
R.A. Foakes *University of Kent, Canterbury*
Brendan E. Foley *Vancouver City College*
Marion Folsom *Rollins College, Florida*
Charles R. Forker *Indiana University*
Frances M. Frazer *University of Prince Edward Island*
Arthur H. Frietzsche *California State Polytechnic College*
Minako Fukui *Otemae Women's College, Japan*
Hans W. Gabler *University of Munich*
W.R. Gair *University of New Brunswick*
David Galloway *University of New Brunswick*
C.O. Gardner *University of Natal*
Chester A. Garrison *Oregon State University*
Bruce Geisinger *San Jose State College, California*

Miriam Gilbert *University of Iowa*
Sister Cyrille Gill *Rosary College, River Forest, Illinois*
Christopher Givan *University of California, Santa Barbara*
Shirley Goldberg *Southwestern Oregon Community College*
Mel Goldstein *University of Hartford, Connecticut*
Walter Gordon *Loyola University of Los Angeles, California*
Robert M. Gorrell *University of Nevada*
Wilson B. Gragg *State University College, Buffalo, New York*
Elliott Grant *Festival Editions of Canada, Limited*
John H. Gray *University of Santa Clara, California*
Robert D. Greenberg *Boston University, Massachusetts*
Alexander Grinstein *Wayne State University School of Medicine, Michigan*
Michel Grivelet *University of Dijon*
John C. Guilds *University of South Carolina*
Ann Haaker *California State College, Fullerton*
Rudolph E. Habenicht *Simon Fraser University*
Werner Habicht *University of Bonn*
Charles Haines *Carleton University, Ontario*
Jay L. Halio *University of Delaware*
Eleanor Hambley *Macomb County Community College, Michigan*
Elemér Hankiss *University of Szeged, Hungary*
Robert Hapgood *University of New Hampshire*
Alfred Harbage *Harvard University*
E.F. Harden *Simon Fraser University*
O.B. Hardison jr *Folger Shakespeare Library*
Susan Hardy *University of Toronto*
Carl Hare *University of Victoria*
Hymen H. Hart *University of Illinois at Chicago Circle*
Joan Hartwig *Florida State University*
Chris Hassel *Vanderbilt University, Tennessee*
Anne Louise Hastings *Ohio Northern University*
Tanju Hayashi *Kinki University, Japan*
Ann Hayward *West Chester, Pennsylvania*
Wayne Hayward *West Chester State College, Pennsylvania*
Charles Haywood *Queens College of the City University of New York*
Hugh Louis Hennedy *St Francis College, Maine*
Ray S. Hewitt *Oregon State University*
G.R. Hibbard *University of Waterloo, Ontario*
Richard Hillier *University of Wyoming*
Charlton Hinman *University of Kansas*
Myra Hinman *University of Kansas*
Akiko Hirai *Tokyo, Japan*
Audrey Hlady *North Vancouver, British Columbia*
H.J. Hocking *Kelowna, British Columbia*
C. Walter Hodges *Bishopstone, England*
F. David Hoeniger *University of Toronto*
Charles K. Hofling *David P. Wohl Memorial Mental Health Institute, Missouri*
Norman Holland *State University of New York*

Carolyn Holt *York University, Ontario*
E.A.J. Honigmann *University of Newcastle-upon-Tyne*
Bruce D. Hood *Stanislaus State College, California*
Lynn K. Horobetz *University of San Diego, California*
Richard Hosley *University of Arizona*
T.H. Howard-Hill *University of Wales, Swansea*
Clara Howe *Central State University, Ohio*
Thomas D. Howe *Central State University, Ohio*
Cyrus Hoy *University of Rochester, New York*
G.K. Hunter *University of Warwick, England*
Mrs Donald F. Hyde *The Shakespeare Association of America*
R.W. Ingram *University of British Columbia*
Takeshi Ishihara *Rissho Women's University, Japan*
Berners W. Jackson *McMaster University, Ontario*
J. Jacquot *Centre national de la recherche scientifique, Paris*
Roman Jakobson *Harvard University**
Jerry D. James *University of California, Santa Cruz*
Frederick S. Janzow *Concordia Teachers College, Illinois*
Ejner Jensen *University of Michigan*
Lowell Johnson *St Olaf College, Minnesota*
George B. Johnston *Virginia Polytechnic Institute and State University*
Ian C. Johnston *College of New Caledonia, British Columbia*
Dorothy Jones *University of Northern Colorado*
Eldred D. Jones *Fourah Bay College, University of Sierra Leone*
Gordon P. Jones *Memorial University of Newfoundland*
M.T. Jones-Davies *University of Paris, Sorbonne*
Joel H. Kaplan *University of British Columbia*
Yoshiko Kawachi *Kyoritsu Women's University, Japan*
Marjory Kellett *Vancouver, British Columbia*
William Kemp *Mary Washington College of the University of Virginia*
Nico Kiasashvili *Tbilisi State University, USSR*
Jae-Nam Kim *Dongguk University, Korea*
Thomas J. King *City College of New York*
Tetsuo Kishi *Kyoto University, Japan*
H.D.F. Kitto *University of Bristol, England*
William N. Knight *Wesleyan University, Connecticut*
Yukiko Kotani, *Tokyo, Japan*
Jan Kott *State University of New York, Stony Brook*
Grigori Kozintsev *State Cinema Institute of USSR*
Jerome Kramer *University of Ottawa*
Julia Kristeva *Centre national de la recherche scientifique, Paris**
Takeshi Kurahashi *Waseda University, Japan*
Jean E. LaFreniere *Macomb County Community College, Michigan*
Jean Lalonde Lind, *Washington*
Elizabeth Lambert *Simon Fraser University*
Mrs Harold Lamoureux *Shakespeare Society, Kelowna, British Columbia*
William Lang *University of Arizona*
J.A. Lavin *University of British Columbia*
John Lawlor *University of Keele, England*

Robert G. Lawrence *University of Victoria, British Columbia*
Cleo Leavitt *Seattle, Washington*
Louis LeCocq *University of Lyon*
Clifford Leech *University of Toronto*
Martin Lehnert *Humboldt University, Berlin*
Gordon Lell *Concordia College, Minnesota*
Trevor Lennam *University of Calgary, Alberta*
Jill Levenson *University of Toronto*
J.W. Lever *Malta*
John S. Levin *Douglas College, British Columbia*
Lionel Levy *The Players Company, San Bernardino, California*
Peter Loeffler *University of British Columbia*
Barry L. Logan *Fresno State Colleg, California*
John H. Long *Greensboro College, North Carolina*
Robert Lordi *University of Notre Dame, Indiana*
John Thomas Lucas *Dawson College, Montreal*
F.R. MacFadden *Coppin State College, Maryland*
John A. MacPherson *St Francis Xavier University, Nova Scotia*
Reta Anderson Madsen *Webster College, St Louis, Missouri*
Dimitri Malavetas *National Theatre of Greece*
David A. Male *Sittingbourne College of Education, England*
Michael Manheim *University of Toledo, Ohio*
Sister Frances M. Manning *University of Dallas, Texas*
Paul J. Marcotte *University of Ottawa*
Louis Marder *University of Illinois, Chicago*
Wilfred Martens *Pacific College, Fresno, California*
Michael Mason *Royal Military College of Canada, Ontario*
Gino J. Matteo *St Michael's College, University of Toronto*
Kathleen Matthews *Altadona, California*
Alethea S. Mattingly *University of Arizona*
Temple Maynard *Simon Fraser University*
Marcia McClung *The Canada Council*
Robert McDonnell *Western Washington State College*
J.W. McFarlane *University of East Anglia, England*
D.F. McKenzie *Victoria University of Wellington, New Zealand*
Marshall McLuhan *University of Toronto**
James G. McManaway *The Shakespeare Quarterly*
Trevor McNeely *Brandon University, Manitoba*
Waldo McNeir *University of Oregon*
John Meagher *St Michael's College, University of Toronto*
Dieter Mehl *University of Bonn*
Giorgio Melchiori *University of Rome*
Ronald M. Meldrum *Washington State University*
Leonard R. Mendelsohn *Sir George Williams University, Quebec*
Jack Mercer *Selkirk College, British Columbia*
Barbara Heliodora Carneiro de Mendonça *Escola de Teatro, Rio de Janeiro, Brazil*
The Rev. W. Moelwyn Merchant *University of Exeter, England*
Grazia Merler *Simon Fraser University*

George J. Merrill *Lakehead University, Ontario*
Harrison T. Meserole *Pennsylvania State University*
Marjorie Miller *Augustana College, Illinois*
Peter Milward *Sophia University, Japan*
Marco Mincoff *Sofia University, Bulgaria**
Victor E. Mitchell *University of Calgary, Alberta*
Aita Mitsuhata *Tokaigakuen Girls' Junior College, Japan*
Sumiko Mizoguchi *Tokyo University*
Paul-Emile Morin *Manatee Junior College, Florida*
Arthur Motyer *Mount Allison University, New Brunswick*
Przemyslaw Mroczkowski *Jagellonion University of Cracow, Poland*
Kenneth Muir *Liverpool University*
Garry Murphy *Southern Illinois University*
Sydney Musgrove *University of Auckland, New Zealand*
Ryoichi Nakagawa *Ohtsuma Women's University, Japan*
Fumio Nakajima *The Shakespeare Society of Japan*
Masako Nakamichi *Tokyo, Japan*
Keiko Nakano *Okayama University, Japan*
Shigehisa Narita *Kyoritsu Women's College, Japan*
Norman Nathan *Florida Atlantic University*
Bruce Nesbitt *Simon Fraser University*
Verna Ness *Oregon College of Education*
Jeanne T. Newlin *Harvard University*
Gerald Newman *Simon Fraser University*
Alexander Nikoljukin *Institute of World Literature of the Academy of Sciences, Moscow, USSR**
Jack Nimitz *Los Angeles Valley College, California*
Tadashi Nishijima *Aoyama Gakuin Women's Junior College, Japan*
Robert L. Oakman *University of South Carolina*
Mrs Pat O'Byrne *University of Calgary, Alberta*
Patrick O'Donnell *Princeton University*
Akira Ogawa *Tokyo, Japan*
Hiroko Oki *Beppu University, Japan*
H.J. Oliver *University of New South Wales, Australia*
Tucker Orbison *Bucknell University, Pennsylvania*
Alan Osler *York University, Ontario*
Yorio Otaka *Nagoya, Japan*
Toshikazu Oyama *Seijo University, Japan*
Toshiko Oyama *Tsuda College, Japan*
Jiro Ozu *Tokyo University, Japan*
Paul Palven *Fordham University, New York*
Anne Paolucci *St John's University, New York*
John Frederick Parker *Vancouver City College*
Brian Parker *Graduate Centre of the Study of Drama, University of Toronto*
Noel Parker-Jervis *University of Alberta*
A.C. Partridge *University of Witwatersrand, South Africa*
Peter Pauls *University of Winnipeg, Manitoba*
Michael Payne *Bucknell University, Pennsylvania*
Josephine A. Pearce *Bradley University, Illinois*

Robert Pepper *San Jose State College, California*
Thomas A. Perry *East Texas State University*
Phillip Persky *San Jose, California*
James W. Peters *Douglas College, British Columbia*
Douglas Peterson *California State College, Hayward*
Anthony Petti *University of Calgary, Alberta*
Allene Stuart Phy *George Peabody College, Kentucky*
Rebecca Pitts *Indiana University, Purdue University*
Roger Porter *Reed College, Oregon*
Joseph G. Price *Pennsylvania State University*
Charles T. Prouty *Yale University*
William Prouty *University of New Brunswick*
Elizabeth J. Proven *Douglas College, British Columbia*
Norman Rabkin *University of California, Berkeley*
Frederick L. Radford *University of Alberta*
Lloyd E. Raskin *Macomb County Community College, Michigan*
Sister Miriam Joseph Rauh *Saint Mary's College, Indiana*
John Reibetanz *University of Toronto*
Julia Reibetanz *University of Toronto*
Stephen Reid *San Fernando Valley State College, California*
Paul Reigstad *Pacific Lutheran University, Washington*
Harvey L. Resnik *National Institute of Mental Health, Washington*, DC
Brian H. Roberts *Victoria, British Columbia*
E.A.K. Roberts *Malaspina College, British Columbia*
Jeanne A. Roberts *American University, Washington, D.C.*
Marvin Rosenberg *University of California, Berkeley*
Lawrence Rosinger *Henry Ford Community College, Michigan*
Donald F. Rowan *University of New Brunswick*
Norma Rowen *University of Victoria, British Columbia*
Donald Rubin *York University, Ontario*
Harriet Rucker *Seattle, Washington*
John Rupp *Clatsop Community College, Oregon*
Fielding Russell *Georgia Southern College*
Horst Ruthrof *Rhodes University, South Africa*
Roman Samarin *Institute of World Literature of the Academy of Sciences, Moscow*, USSR*
Wilbur Sanders *University of Cambridge*
Lyuba Sarieva *Sofia University, Bulgaria*
Noshir Sarkari *Vancouver, British Columbia*
Takashi Sasayama *Osaka City University, Japan*
Naomi Saslaw *Ashland College, Ohio*
Barbara Schafer *University of Keele, England*
Ernest Schanzer *University of Munich*
Robert M. Schuler *University of Victoria, British Columbia*
Murray Schwartz *State University of New York, Buffalo*
David Scott *Memorial University, Newfoundland*
Florence Scott *Toronto, Ontario*
Alice Lyle Scoufos *California State College, Fullerton*
Thomas A. Sebeok *University of Indiana**

Sally Yeates Sedelow *University of Kansas*
Daniel Seltzer *Princeton University*
Yukio Seto *Tochigi Prefectural Senior High School, Japan*
G.B. Shand *York University, Ontario*
Catherine M. Shaw *University of California, Riverside*
John Shaw *Hiram College, Ohio*
Esther Shephard *San Jose State College, California*
Sosuke Shibasaki *Tokyo, Japan*
Paul N. Siegel *Long Island University, New York*
Blanche Mowat Simpson *Kelowna, British Columbia*
Kristian Smidt *University of Oslo, Norway*
Gordon Ross Smith *Temple University, Pennsylvania*
Marion B. Smith *Brock University, Ontario*
Mary E. Smith *University of New Brunswick, St John*
Susan Snyder *Swarthmore College, Pennsylvania*
Christopher Spencer *University of North Carolina, Greensboro*
John Spencer *University of Leeds, England**
T.J.B. Spencer *University of Birmingham, England*
Marvin Spevack *University of Munster*
Pierre Spriet *University of Bordeaux*
Louis C. Stagg *Memphis State University, Tennessee*
Rudolph Stamm *University of Basle, Switzerland*
William Stewart *University of Tampa, Florida*
Katherine Stockholder *University of British Columbia*
Zdeněk Stříbrný *Charles University, Prague**
Martin E. Tabnik *New York University*
Yasunari Takahashi *University of Tokyo*
Keizan Taniguchi *Ryukoku University, Japan*
R. Thad Taylor *Shakespeare Society of America*
Stephen J. Teller *Kansas State College*
Hilda L. Thomas *University of British Columbia*
Sister Mary Thomas CSJ *St Thomas Seminary College, Washington*
William B. Thorne *Queen's University, Ontario*
Helen Topham *University of Hawaii*
Josip Torbarina *Zagreb University, Yugoslavia**
Frances M. Treadgold *Shakespeare Society, Kelowna, British Columbia*
Jane Tryon *University of Toronto*
Frederick Turner *University of California, Santa Barbara*
Moria Turner *Los Angeles City College*
Ralph L. Tweedale *Southfield, Michigan*
Lila Tyng *Gladstone, New Jersey*
Brian Tyson *University of Lethbridge, Alberta*
Reiko Usui *Seijo University, Japan*
Takeshi Usui *Seijo University, Japan*
Raymond Utterback *Georgia State University*
Eric Vaughan *Kansas State College*
Paul Vehvilainen *Portland State University, Oregon*
John Velz *University of Texas*
John M. Wagner *California State College, Fullerton*

RoseMary Wagoner *Seattle, Washington*
Eugene M. Waith *Yale University*
T.R. Waldo *University of Florida*
Charles E. Walton *Kansas State Teachers College*
Erdmann Waniek *University of Oregon*
Mrs Erdmann Waniek *University of Oregon*
John Wasson *Washington State University*
Aleksandra Wawrzyszko *Simon Fraser University*
Herbert Weil *University of Connecticut*
Robert Weimann *Humboldt University, Berlin*
Philip Weller *Eastern Washington State College*
Sister Maria A. Werner csc *Saint Mary's College, Indiana*
Alfred W. Wheeler *Quarto Company of Honolulu*
Glynne Wickham *University of Bristol*
Ruth Widmann *University of Pennsylvania*
Lillian Wilds *California State Polytechnic College*
David Wilson *Simon Fraser University*
Donald L. Wing *Macomb County Community College, Michigan*
Irving Wolfe *University of Montreal*
Hyung-Kyu Woo *Shakespeare Society of Korea*
James O. Wood *San Jose State College, California*
Mrs John Woodworth *Kelowna, British Columbia*
Celeste T. Wright *University of California, Davis*
Maurice Yacowar *Brock University, Ontario*
Suk-ke Yoh *The Shakespeare Society of Korea*
Alan Young *Acadia University, Nova Scotia*
Karen Youngberg *Augustana College, Illinois*
Anthony Yu *University of Chicago*
In-Sob Zong *Hankuk University, Korea*

This book

was designed by

ANTJE LINGNER

under the direction of

ALLAN FLEMING

and was printed by

University of

Toronto

Press